Practice-Based Research

Practice-Based Research shows mental-health practitioners how to establish viable and productive research programs in routine clinical settings. Chapters written by experts in practice-based research use real-world examples to help clinicians work through some of the most common barriers to research output in these settings, including lack of access to institutional review boards, lack of organizational support, and limited access to financial resources. Specialized chapters also provide information on research methods and step-by-step suggestions tailored to a variety of practice settings. This is an essential volume for clinicians interested in establishing successful, long-lasting, practice-based research programs.

R. Trent Codd, III, EdS, is the president and founder of the Cognitive-Behavioral Therapy Center of Western North Carolina, P.A., where he provides clinical services and conducts practice-based research.

Practice-Based Research

A Guide for Clinicians

Edited by
R. Trent Codd, III

NEW YORK AND LONDON

First published 2018
by Routledge
711 Third Avenue, New York, NY 10017

and by Routledge
2 Park Square, Milton Park, Abingdon, Oxon, OX14 4RN

Routledge is an imprint of the Taylor & Francis Group, an informa business

© 2018 R. Trent Codd, III

The right of R. Trent Codd, III to be identified as the author of the editorial material, and of the authors for their individual chapters, has been asserted in accordance with sections 77 and 78 of the Copyright, Designs and Patents Act 1988.

All rights reserved. The purchase of this copyright material confers the right on the purchasing institution to photocopy pages which bear the photocopy icon and copyright line at the bottom of the page. No other part of this publication may be reproduced, stored in a retrieval system, or transmitted in any form or by any means, electronic, mechanical, photocopying, recording or otherwise, without prior permission in writing from the publisher.

Trademark notice: Product or corporate names may be trademarks or registered trademarks, and are used only for identification and explanation without intent to infringe.

Library of Congress Cataloging-in-Publication Data
Names: Codd, R. Trent, III, editor.
Title: Practice-based research : a guide for clinicians / [edited by] R. Trent Codd, III.
Description: New York, NY : Routledge, 2018. | Includes bibliographical references.
Identifiers: LCCN 2017055883 (print) | LCCN 2017056816 (ebook) | ISBN 9781315524610 (eBook) | ISBN 9781138690974 (hardback) | ISBN 9781138690981 (pbk.) | ISBN 9781315524610 (ebk)
Subjects: | MESH: Behavioral Research | Private Practice
Classification: LCC R850 (ebook) | LCC R850 (print) | NLM WM 20 | DDC 610.72—dc23LC record available at https://lccn.loc.gov/2017055883

ISBN: 978-1-138-69097-4 (hbk)
ISBN: 978-1-138-69098-1 (pbk)
ISBN: 978-1-315-52461-0 (ebk)

Typeset in Minion
by Florence Production Ltd, Stoodleigh, Devon, UK

Contents

Author Biographies vii
Foreword xiii
Acknowledgments xv

Part I: Introduction to Practice-Based Research 1

1 **Introduction to Practice-Based Research** 3
   R. Trent Codd, III

2 **Practice Research Networks: Where Science and Practice Meet** 8
   Soo Jeong Youn, Louis G. Castonguay, Henry Xiao

Part II: Research Methods in Practice-Based Research 23

3 **Research Methods in Practice Settings** 25
   Scott H. Waltman

4 **Single-Case Research Designs in Clinical Practice Settings** 44
   R. Trent Codd, III

5 **Practice-Based Research: A Pragmatic Approach** 61
   Guy Bruce

Part III: Practice-Based Research in Private Practice — 79

6 A Step-By-Step Guide for Creating an Independent Institutional Review Board (IRB) for Private Practitioners — 81
Travis L. Osborne

7 Using Social Enterprise Concepts to Create a Sustainable Culture to Fund Research in a Fee-For-Service Setting — 108
Jenna T. LeJeune and Jason B. Luoma

8 Research in Private Practice Settings — 130
Travis L. Osborne

9 Simultaneous Practice and Research: A Model for Conducting Research in Private Practice — 153
Jacqueline B. Persons

10 Practice-Based Scholarship — 170
Amy Wenzel

Part IV: Practice-Based Research in Other Clinical Setting — 191

11 Implementation Science at the End-Point: A New Approach for Researchers in Primary Care — 193
Jodi Polaha and Ivy Click

12 Research in Partial Hospital Settings — 212
Marie Forgeard, Courtney Beard, Norik Kirakosian, and Thröstur Björgvinsson

Part V: Conclusion and Future Directions — 241

13 Future Directions for Practice-Based Research — 243
Shannon Wiltsey Stirman

Appendix: Research Consultant Directory — 250

Index — 253

Author Biographies

Courtney Beard, PhD, is a clinical psychologist with expertise in anxiety disorders, cognitive biases, cognitive behavior therapy, and treatment outcome research. She is assistant director of the clinical research program at McLean Hospital's Behavioral Health Partial (BHP) Hospital Program and assistant professor of psychology at Harvard Medical School. Dr. Beard's research aims to delineate cognitive mechanisms underlying psychiatric disorders, develop treatments to target these mechanisms, and implement these treatments in real world settings. Dr. Beard has a small private practice focused on delivering exposure therapy for anxiety disorders.

Thröstur Björgvinsson, PhD, ABPP, is an associate professor of psychology at the Department of Psychiatry, Harvard Medical School; the director of the Behavioral Health Partial Hospital Program at McLean Hospital, and co-director of psychology training at McLean Hospital/Harvard Medical School. He is also the founder and director of the Houston OCD Program, a specialized residential OCD program in Houston, Texas, and a co-founder and co-director of the OCD & Anxiety Program of Southern California. He has a national and international reputation as a clinical innovator, particularly in the implementation of cognitive behavior therapy (CBT) for the treatment of severe anxiety and obsessive compulsive disorders. His research interests focus on treatment outcomes, seeking to establish the effectiveness of CBT for a wide range of psychiatric disorders within a partial hospital program. He has published over 70 scholarly articles and given over 300 presentations and workshops, nationally and internationally, on evidence-based treatments for anxiety disorders and depression.

Author Biographies

Guy Bruce, EdD, BCBA-D, Since earning his EdD in educational psychology from the Behavior Analysis in Human Resources program at West Virginia University, Dr. Bruce has taught behavior analysis in both undergraduate and graduate programs and worked as consultant to for-profit and not-for-profit organizations. He has supervised students completing their intensive practicum training for BCBA certification. He is the author of *Instructional Design Made Easy*, a workbook for designing more efficient learning programs and PARSE™, a data-based process that can be used by schools to help their students achieve desired learning outcomes. His goal is to help individuals and organizations achieve desired results through the use of positive methods to improve their performance. His current projects include delivering Effective Supervisor Workshops, ProgressCharter®, a mobile application to evaluate student progress, analyze the causes of inadequate progress, and recommend the necessary changes in staff resources, training, and management, and HealthVisor, a mobile application to improve user health.

Louis G. Castonguay, PhD, completed his doctorate in clinical psychology at S.U.N.Y. Stony Brook, a clinical internship at U.C. Berkeley, and a Post-doctorate at Stanford University. He is currently a professor at the Department of Psychology at Penn State University. With more than 190 publications (including nine co-edited books), his scholarly work and research focus on different aspects of the process of change and training, especially within the context of psychotherapy integration. He is also involved in the investigation of the efficacy of new integrative treatments for generalized anxiety disorder and depression, and the development of Practice Research Networks aimed at facilitating the collaboration between clinicians and researchers. He has received several awards, including the Early Career Contribution Award from the Society of Psychotherapy Research, and the David Shakow Award from the Division of Clinical Psychology of the American Psychological Association (APA). He has also received four recognitions from the APA Division of Psychotherapy: the Jack D. Krasner Memorial Award, the Distinguished Contributions to Teaching and Mentoring, the Distinguished Research Publications Award, and the Distinguished Psychologist Award for his life time contributions to the field of psychotherapy. He also served as president of the North American Society for Psychotherapy Research, as well as the International Society for Psychotherapy Research.

Ivy Click, EdD, is an assistant professor in the Department of Family Medicine at East Tennessee State University and an academic associate at Arizona State University. Additionally, she serves as research director for the Appalachian Research Network (AppNET), a practice-based research network of primary care clinics in East Tennessee and Southwest Virginia. Her research interests are broad and include rural health disparities, medical school practice outcomes, program evaluation, women's health, LGBTQ health, substance abuse and misuse, and interprofessional education. She has received funding from the Tennessee Department of Health to study the Neonatal Abstinence

Syndrome (NAS) problem in the state. She has a passion for research and enjoys mentoring fellow faculty, residents, and students in research methods and statistics.

R. Trent Codd, III, EdS, is president of the Cognitive-Behavioral Therapy Center of Western North Carolina, P.A., located in Asheville, NC. He's a board certified behavior analyst and fellow of the Academy of Cognitive Therapy. He's a full-time clinician who specializes in evidence-based practice with extensive training in several empirically-supported therapies including Beckian Cognitive Therapy, and Clinical Behavior Analytic approaches such as Goldiamond's Constructional/Non-linear Functional Analytic Approach, Acceptance and Commitment Therapy, Functional Analytic Psychotherapy, and Radically Open Dialectical Behavior Therapy. His clinical interests are particularly focused on disorders of overcontrol and OC-spectrum disorders. His research interests parallel his clinical interests with additional interest in evidence-based instructional methods. He is co-author of *Teaching and Supervising Cognitive Behavioral Therapy*.

Marie Forgeard, PhD, is a clinical psychologist specializing in the study of creativity, openness to experience, mood disorders, treatment outcomes, and well-being. Her research has examined these topics in a variety of samples, including professional/aspiring artists and scientists, individuals experiencing highly stressful life events, and individuals suffering from psychopathology.

Norik Kirakosian is a student in the Psychology department at Northeastern University, and a research assistant at McLean Hospital's Behavioral Health Partial (BHP) Hospital Program. Norik's research interests broadly center around the study of LGBTQ mental health.

Jenna LeJeune, PhD, is co-founder of and director of Clinical Services at Portland Psychotherapy Clinic, Research and Training Center in Portland, Oregon. In her clinical practice, Jenna specializes in using Acceptance and Commitment Therapy (ACT) with adults struggling with various relationship difficulties, including problems with intimacy and sexuality, trauma-related relationship challenges, and also struggles people may have in their relationship with their own bodies. Her research focuses on developing compassion-focused interventions for those struggling with chronic shame and self-criticism within a contextual behavioral science framework. Jenna is also a peer-reviewed ACT trainer and provides ACT trainings for professional around the world.

Jason Luoma, PhD, is director of Portland Psychotherapy Clinic, Research, and Training Center, a research and training clinic based on a social enterprise model that uses business revenue to fund substantial and ongoing research activities. As a researcher, Dr. Luoma studies shame, self-criticism, stigma, and the interpersonal effects of emotion, and published the first randomized trial of an intervention focused on helping people with shame in the *Journal of Consulting and Clinical Psychology*. He is also an internationally recognized trainer in Acceptance and Commitment Therapy, former chair of the ACT training committee, and a past president of the Association for Contextual Behavioral Science. His work on shame and compassion can be read at www.actwithcompassion.com.

Travis L. Osborne, PhD, ABPP, is the co-director of The Anxiety Center and director of training at the Evidence Based Treatment Centers of Seattle (EBTCS), a specialty outpatient practice. He is also a clinical instructor with the Department of Psychology at the University of Washington and is board certified in Behavioral and Cognitive Psychology by the American Board of Professional Psychology (ABPP). Dr. Osborne specializes in the treatment of anxiety disorders, obsessive-compulsive and related disorders, and trauma and related disorders, with a particular emphasis on exposure therapy for anxiety-related problems. Additionally, he is a clinical supervisor for post-doctoral fellows and doctoral students in clinical psychology and has provided numerous presentations and trainings for clinicians on exposure therapy and evidence-based treatments for anxiety disorders. Over the last decade, Dr. Osborne has become increasingly interested in practice-based research and currently oversees the research program at EBTCS. He is a co-founder of the Behavioral Health Research Collective (BHRC), a non-profit organization whose mission is to host an Institutional Review Board (IRB) that provides ethical review and oversight of research projects conducted by mental health professionals in practice settings. He has served as chair of this IRB since 2011. Dr. Osborne is also a member of the Translating Science to Practice committee of the Society for a Science of Clinical Psychology (SSCP).

Jacqueline B. Persons, PhD, is director of the Oakland Cognitive Behavior Therapy Center, a group private practice in Oakland, CA, where she maintains a practice providing CBT to adults with mood and anxiety disorders and consultation to clinicians seeking to build their clinical and research skills. She is also clinical professor, Department of Psychology at UC-Berkeley. Dr. Persons is past president of the Association for Behavioral and Cognitive Therapies and of the Society for a Science of Clinical Psychology. She is the author of two well-regarded books and many articles and chapters on case formulation in cognitive behavior therapy, she provides training workshops to students and clinicians around the world, and she conducts research that focuses on psychological mechanisms underpinning symptoms of psychopathology, and the process and outcome of naturalistic case formulation-driven cognitive-behavior therapy. She received her PhD in clinical psychology from the University of Pennsylvania in 1979.

Jodi Polaha, PhD, is a licensed psychologist and associate professor in the Department of Family Medicine at East Tennessee State University. She earned her doctorate from Auburn University in 1998 and has spent her entire career as a "pracademic" doing clinical work, program development, training, consulting, and research in primary care behavioral health. Her research focuses on implementation science as a strategy for engaging systems change within primary care, particularly around implementing interprofessional collaborative practice models and the translation of empirically-supported behavioral health interventions to this setting.

Scott Waltman, PsyD, ABPP, is a clinician, trainer, and practice-based researcher. His interests include evidence-based psychotherapy practice, training, and implementation in systems that provide care to underserved populations. Dr. Waltman has published practice-based research in several reputable journals and has presented his findings at national and international conferences. He is certified as a qualified cognitive therapist and trainer/consultant by the Academy of Cognitive Therapy. He also is board certified in Behavioral and Cognitive Psychology from the American Board of Professional Psychology. He graduated from Pacific University in Oregon where his training focused on Cognitive-Behavioral Therapy (CBT) and Acceptance and Commitment Therapy (ACT) for anxiety, addiction, relational problems, and personality disorders. Dr. Waltman has experience working with severe and persistent mental illness in inpatient settings, and completed his APA-Accredited predoctoral internship at the Colorado Mental Health Institute in Pueblo, Colorado; there he worked on the Advanced Cognitive Behavioral Unit where he received intensive training in CBT and Dialectical Behavior Therapy (DBT). He also completed an APA-Accredited Postdoctoral Fellowship at Harbor-UCLA Medical Center. There he treated patients in the community mental health center's CBT clinic. Dr. Waltman was also the clinical coordinator and lead trainer for the Los Angeles Department of Mental Health CBT Dissemination Project. More recently, Dr. Waltman, worked as a CBT trainer for one of Dr. Aaron Beck's CBT implementation teams in the Philadelphia public mental health system. Currently, he works as a clinical psychologist for the Department of Defense where he is a frontline clinician and co-investigator on a randomized clinical trial of CBT for insomnia delivered via telebehavioral health. Clinically, Dr. Waltman strives to flexibly and compassionately apply cognitive and behavioral interventions to help people overcome the barriers in their lives, to facilitate building meaningful lives that are guided by passion and values. In addition to working with adults, Dr. Waltman has experience working with adolescents with severe emotional, behavioral, and legal problems. Dr. Waltman is also a dual-diagnosis counselor who is certified as a Master Addiction Counselor (MAC) by the NADAAC.

Amy Wenzel, PhD, ABPP, is owner of Wenzel Consulting, LLC, clinical assistant professor of psychology in psychiatry at the University of Pennsylvania School of Medicine, adjunct faculty at the Beck Institute for Cognitive Behavior Therapy, trainer-consultant with the Academy of Cognitive Therapy, and affiliate at the Postpartum Stress Center. She is author or editor of 21 books and has authored over 100 peer-reviewed journal articles and book chapters. Her research has been funded by the National Institute of Mental Health, the American Foundation for Suicide Prevention, and the National Alliance for Research on Schizophrenia and Depression (now Brain and Behavior

Research Foundation). She is on the scientific advisory board of the American Foundation for Suicide Prevention and has held several leadership positions within the Association for Behavioral and Cognitive Therapies. She has been featured in many psychotherapy video demonstrations for the American Psychological Association, and provides training and supervision in cognitive behavioral therapy around the globe.

Henry Xiao, MS, is completing his doctorate in clinical psychology at the Pennsylvania State University under Louis G. Castonguay, PhD. His research focuses on psychotherapy process and outcome, with a focus on therapist effects, delivery of psychotherapeutic services, and treatment attendance and dropout. He is an active member of the Society for Psychotherapy Research.

Soo Jeong Youn, PhD, completed her doctorate in clinical psychology at the Pennsylvania State University, and an APA accredited clinical internship at Massachusetts Mental Health Center, Division of Public Psychiatry, Beth Israel Deaconess Medical Center, Department of Psychiatry, Harvard Medical School. She is currently completing a post-doctorate fellowship at Community Psychiatry, Program for Research in Implementation and Dissemination of Evidence-based Treatments at Massachusetts General Hospital. Her research interests include bridging the gap between research and practice by conducting practice oriented research (POR). She has extensive experience in the development of Practice Research Networks, with the goal of facilitating the collaboration between clinicians and researchers in conducting psychotherapy research studies that synergistically address clinical and scientific goals. Her research interests also focus on psychotherapy process and outcome, including therapist effects, measurement based care, and psychotherapy implementation, dissemination, and training.

Foreword

A major sea change is underway in the mental health field generally, and clinical psychology in particular. We are entering the "era of dissemination and implementation", which will compel us to reverse the traditional relationship that has existed between academically based treatment development/testing and practice based implementation. Previously, field based clinicians received their marching orders from the academic scientists who developed and tested new treatment approaches. Although this approach to treatment development and testing has resulted in significantly stronger psychotherapeutic approaches across the diagnostic spectrum, the science to practice pipeline is notoriously slow. It takes on average 15 years for a new treatment idea to make it from academia into the real world practice setting. For example, the cognitive model of depression was first described in 1962, but the first published efficacy study of cognitive therapy did not appear in print until 1989. In a rapidly changing healthcare environment, this type of slow, laborious approach to treatment development will simply not give practicing clinicians the leverage needed to flexibly adapt their psychotherapeutic practices to changing system- and client-level realities.

Not withstanding the time it takes to move an idea through the science to practice pipeline, it appears we have reached the limits of what the academically based model of treatment development has to offer in a more general sense. Treatments that work in tightly controlled academic studies, using highly trained research therapists working with clients selected for having a narrowly defined mental health problem, do not generalize well into the world of clinical practice. These "empirically supported treatments" are often too long, complex and expensive to be feasible in the real world practice setting. In addition, treatment refusal rates are high, therapy drop out rates hover around 50%, and there is a well documented "voltage drop" of around 10% in clinical response rates once an empirically supported treatment is disseminated into the field. The overall effectiveness rate of empirically supported treatments hovers around 50% among the clients that complete them in real world settings. But this result hides a much more sobering truth: If treatment refusal, dropout, non-response and relapse rates are added together, the overall effectiveness of most empirically supported treatments drops to well below 30%. This is the world in which the practicing clinician lives.

The much discussed "scientist-practitioner gap" can be better understood from this perspective. Academic clinical scientists are absolutely sure their treatment works just fine because their treatments do work in the test tube environment of a randomized clinical efficacy trial. Mental health clinicians are sure these treatments don't work nearly as well as advertised in clinical practice, because they actually don't work nearly as well, once all of the messy, uncontrolled client level, economic level, insurance level and practice level variables come into play. There is no hero, nor is there a goat, in this sharp division between contexts. Indeed, it is unlikely to go away as long as the existing science to practice pipeline remains intact.

The "new normal" in the era of dissemination and implementation will be to place the onus of responsibility for treatment development and testing on the clinical practice sector, what is termed "community based treatment development" and "practice based research". Fortunately, there are practice-based researchers (i.e., clinicians who are both delivering clinical services and evaluating their impact) who have been plying their trade for years, and have much knowledge, experience and wisdom to share with the rest of us newbies. This book presents the reader with an opportunity to investigate the world of practice-based research, and to marvel at the intellectual integrity, depth of knowledge, and ingenuity of this diverse group of experts. The topics covered range from the theoretical, to the methodological, to the economic, to the highly practical issues associated with conducting practice-based research.

Once we shed our conditioned resistance response to anything that resembles "research" in the traditional sense, we can open up to the excitement of uncovering treatment innovations in daily clinical practice, and then testing them out using simple, effective evaluation methods. The future well being of psychotherapy depends on the willingness and ability of individual or networks of mental health clinicians to design and test novel treatment approaches, such that they can be disseminated within the larger practitioner community. Let's get started with that grand mission!

Kirk D. Strosahl, PhD

Acknowledgments

I am particularly grateful for the encouragement and support of my family during the completion of this project. Thank you Ginger, Isabella, and Caroline.

I wish to acknowledge my close professional colleagues who've played various roles in my professional development through the years. Thank you Dennis Tirch, Laura Silberstein-Tirch, Scott Temple, Donna Sudak, Joe Layng, Michelle Drapkin-Clarke, Kelly Wilson, Steven C. Hayes, Mike Twohig, Douglas Woods, Bill Barley, Mavis Tsai, Bob Kohlenberg, Tom Lynch, Erica Smith, Sophie Rushbrook, Roelie Hempel, Gareth Holman, Donna Sudak, Leslie Sokol, and Marci Fox.

My colleagues at the Cognitive-Behavioral Therapy Center of Western North Carolina also deserve recognition: Rick Baker, Lisa Neff, Signi Goldman, John Ludgate, Jessica Smith, Erin Shadle, Haley Elder, Heidi Germano, Amy Johnson, Earlene Reese, and Mara Leary. Thank you for your support and for being wonderful to work with.

Last, but certainly not least, to the contributors to this volume: thank you for your hard work and for your meaningful contributions.

PART I

Introduction to Practice-Based Research

CHAPTER 1

Introduction to Practice-Based Research

R. Trent Codd, III

Introduction

Robert Boyle, James Joule, and Albert Einstein were remarkable scientists. Boyle's work had a substantial impact on several areas of science and he is often regarded as the first modern chemist. He is probably most famous for what is now known as "Boyle's law," which expresses the inverse relationship between the pressure and volume of a gas at a constant temperature (West, 1999). Joule, a physicist and mathematician, for whom the unit of energy we describe as a "joule" is named, made a series of important scientific discoveries including those that laid the foundation for the first law of thermodynamics. Einstein, a theoretical physicist, developed the theory of relativity. The respective productivity of these scientists is a readily apparent commonality among them. However, they have something else in common that is less well-known: all three produced much of their scientific findings while in non-academic jobs. Boyle worked in a lab that he established in his sister's home, where he also resided, and where he produced roughly one book each year (Principe, n.d.). Joule conducted experimental work while working as a businessman running a brewery. Einstein produced his paradigm-shifting work in physics while he was employed in the Swiss Patent Office.

The important work that Boyle, Joule and Einstein accomplished outside of an academic setting is germane to research activity in mental health practice settings. Many barriers to practice-based research are discussed in this book, but one barrier, because it is psychological and therefore more camouflaged than the others, is important to bring into the open early on. This barrier involves the false idea that clinical research primarily or exclusively occurs, or should only occur, within the confines of academic settings. It is a formidable obstacle. This notion, however, does not comport with the history of science as Boyle, Joule, and Einstein (among others) demonstrate, and to endorse this idea is to place an unnecessary boundary around clinical mental health research. The constraining effects of this barrier are observable in several ways. First, after graduation clinical settings may be chosen for employment when the individual lacks interest in research activity. This choice is frequently derived from the belief that research activity does not occur in such settings, thus aligning their interests (or lack thereof) with their work setting. In contrast, a graduate with a keen interest in research would likely pursue an academic career based on the same belief about the locus of research activity. Thus, clinical settings select persons, on average, with minimal research interests. Also, because it is not seen as important, graduate training tends not to provide instruction in research methods most relevant to the practice setting, thus failing to develop an appropriate repertoire for conducting research in these settings among their graduates. Programs also fail to deliver instruction in navigating the unique barriers to research activity present in those settings, which further reduces the probability that those with adequate repertoires will be successful in establishing a program of research. Finally, inadequately prepared clinicians contribute to negative downstream effects at the organizational level. Clinical organizations typically do not have contingencies in place that support research activity and this is likely a result of would-be-clinician researchers who are ineffective at advocating for such organizational support and who, as they climb the organizational ladder, either do not appreciate the importance of research among their subordinates or do not know how to arrange effective supporting contingencies.

Advantages of Practice-Based Research

Practice-based research, in simple terms, refers to research conducted within natural practice settings (Nutting & Strange, 1998). Despite many calls for increased research activity of this kind among mental health professionals (e.g., DeFife et al., 2015), research productivity among the professions has remained staggeringly low, with the modal publication rate among clinical psychologists, for example, being a depressing zero (Davis et al., 2013; Eke, Holttum, & Hayward, 2012; Lundervold & Belwodd, 2000).

This is unfortunate because practice-based research offers several advantages to the field. First, it provides a mechanism for increasing the representation of diverse populations and less frequently occurring clinical presentations in empirical work. Designs that do not require large sample sizes are available (e.g., Single Case Experimental Designs), thus allowing clinicians, who make contact with these patients as part of routine practice, to ask and answer important empirical questions. Second, because efficacy and effectiveness can be evaluated simultaneously, rather than through the typical so-called efficacy-effectiveness pipeline, it frequently results in more rapid translation of research to clinical practice. Third, since it occurs in the practice setting it is more representative of the complexities found in clinical practice. This advantage escapes the often-encountered difficulties with translating research findings discovered in tightly controlled settings to the natural practice environment. A fourth advantage relates to long-standing difficulties with the dissemination of empirically supported treatments (ESTs). Substantial evidence suggests many patients with indications for an EST, many of which have been available for a long time, are not receiving them (e.g., see Lilienfeld et al., 2013; Shafran et al., 2009). The reasons for dissemination difficulties are multifactorial, but likely to be attenuated through an increased frequency of empirical investigation in "real world" contexts where the complexities of those environments must be considered from the beginning. Such investigations may reduce practitioner resistance to the adoption of treatment practices based on these empirical findings because they may be less likely to be seen as irrelevant to their patient and practice population.

Plan of the Book: Addressing one Key Barrier at a Time

The impoverished research rate among mental health practitioners is not surprising given the plethora of barriers to practice-based research activity. One barrier has already been mentioned: the notion that research activity is or should be confined to the academic setting. To dispel this notion, several chapters in this book highlight the ongoing vibrant research programs of their authors, collectively representing several different practice settings. A related psychological barrier is the inability to see what's possible in the practice setting. Toward this end, Soo Jeong Youn, Louis G. Castonguay, and Henry Xiao present a chapter on practice research networks in their aptly titled chapter *Practice research networks: Where science and practice meet*, and Amy Wenzel in *Practice Based Scholarship* emphasizes several not-so-apparent ways a private practitioner can be involved with empirical research and contribute to the field.

Another barrier relates to a clinician/would-be researcher's research repertoire, which is absent or inadequate to the practice setting. Indeed, several researchers have identified poor research methods training as a barrier to practice-based research activity (e.g., Baker, McFall, & Shoham, 2009; Davis et al., 2013; Lundervold & Belwodd, 2000). In addition, research methods emphasized in the graduate training of most mental health professionals center around group designs, especially randomized controlled trials, which are more challenging to execute in practice settings relative to other research methods (Codd, 2017). These barriers are directly addressed in the chapters *Research Methods in Practice Settings* by Scott Waltman, *Single-case experimental designs* by Trent Codd, and *Practice-Based Research: A Pragmatic Approach* by Guy Bruce. Additional considerations for research methods are addressed in various chapters regarding practice-setting.

Lack of access to an Institutional Review Board (IRB) is another barrier to practice-based research activity. IRB review and monitoring of research projects are important ethical components of research. IRB involvement is also required by many journals and conferences for publication and presentation respectively. Travis Osborne addresses this difficulty, along with possible solutions, in two chapters. In the first, *Research in private practice settings*, he discusses several barriers encountered in these settings including the problem of IRB access, and in the second, *A step-by-step guide for creating an independent Institutional Review Board (IRB) for private practitioners*, he offers a chapter whose only focus is a detailed description of a solution to this hurdle.

Unsurprisingly, financial considerations represent another set of obstacles. While this is addressed in many of the setting-specific chapters, Jenna LeJeune and

Jason Luoma provide us with a fresh and innovative solution in *Using Social Enterprise Concepts to Create a Sustainable Culture to Fund Research in a Fee-For-Service Setting*.

There are many different practice settings, each with their own unique considerations and barriers. Three chapters located in the second and third parts of this book, each focus on a different practice setting. Jacqueline Persons complements Travis Osborne's chapter with her focus on private practice considerations in *Simultaneous Practice and Research: A Model for Conducting Research in Private Practice*. This is followed by Jodi Polaha and Ivy Click's *Implementation Science at the End-Point: A New Approach for Researchers in Primary Care* as well as in *Research in Partial Hospital Settings* by Marie Foregeard, Courtney Beard, Norik Kirakosian, and Throstur Bjorgvinsson. These chapters also address organizational factors, another common impediment to the initiation and maintenance of a practice-based research program.

Finally, Shannon Wiltsey Stirman in *Future Directions for Practice-Based Research*, pulls everything together and offers an elaborated discussion of two important areas: 1) academic partnerships for implementation research and 2) the use of technology in the facilitation of practice-based research endeavors.

Because space is limited and the barriers are numerous, the research methods and barriers to practice based research (PBR) addressed in this book are not comprehensive (e.g., clinician attitudes toward research are not addressed in the present volume). However, careful consideration resulted in the identification of the most fundamental factors impeding PBR and the authors in this volume address these items thoroughly. The sincere hope is that the strategies and solutions described in this volume result in the initiation or expansion of vibrant practice-based research programs.

References

Baker, T. B., McFall, R. M., & Shoham, V. (2009). Current status and future prospects of clinical psychology: Toward a scientifically principled approach to mental and behavioral health care. *Psychological Science in the Public Interest*, 9, 67–103.

Codd, III, R. T. (2017). Protecting the Scientific Lexical Canon. *The Behavior Therapist*, 40(5), 185–191.

Davis, S., Gervin, D., White, G., Williams, A., Taylor, A., & McGriff, E. (2013). Bridging the gap between research, evaluation, and evidence-based practice. *Journal of Social Work Education*, 49(1), 16–29.

DeFife, J., Drill, R., Beinashowitz, J., Ballantyne, L., Plant, D., Smith-Hansen, L., Teran, V., Werner-Larsen, L., Westerling, III, T., Yang, Y., Davila, M., & Nakash, O. (2015). Practice-based psychotherapy research in a public health setting: Obstacles and Opportunities. *Journal of Psychotherapy Integration*, 25(4), 299–312.

Eke, G., Holttum, S., & Hayward, M. (2012). Testing a model of research intention among U.K. clinical psychologists: A logistic regression analysis. *Journal of Clinical Psychology*, 68(3), 263–278.

Lilienfeld, S. O., Ritschel, L. A., Lynn, S. J., Cautin, R. L., & Latzman, R. D. (2013). Why many clinical psychologists are resistant to evidence-based practice: Root causes and constructive remedies. *Clinical Psychology Review*, 33, 883–900.

Lundervold, D. A. & Belwood, M. F. (2000). The best kept secret in counseling: Single-case (N = 1) experimental designs. *Journal of Counseling & Development, 78*, 92–102.

Nutting, P. A. & Strange, K. C. (1998). Practice-based research. In R. B. Taylor (Ed.) *Family Medicine: Principles and practice* (5th ed.). New York: Springer.

Principe, L. M. (n.d.). Robert Boyle. In *Encyclopaedia Britannica Online.* Retrieved from www.britannica.com/biography/Robert-Boyle

Shafran, R., Clark, D. M., Fairburn, C. G., Arntz, A., Barlow, D. H., Ehlers, A., Freeston, M., Garety, P. A., Hollon, S. D., Ost, L. G., Salkovskis, P. M., Williams, J. M. G., & Wilson, G. T. (2009). Minding the gap: Improving the dissemination of CBT. *Behaviour Research and Therapy, 47*, 902–909.

West, J. B. (1999). The original presentation of Boyle's law. *Journal of applied physiology, 87*(4), 1543–1545.

CHAPTER 2

Practice Research Networks: Where Science and Practice Meet

Soo Jeong Youn, Louis G. Castonguay, Henry Xiao

Being a private practitioner is a demanding task, requiring providers to juggle various responsibilities and roles just to accomplish the day-to-day responsibilities of providing clinical care to their patients. In addition, they are faced with the challenge of increasingly having to demonstrate adherence to evidence-based practice and accountability from insurance companies. However, the divide between research and clinical practice is well documented, and many psychotherapists do not resort to empirical findings to aid their clinical practice (Castonguay, Youn, Xiao, Muran, & Barber, 2015), as many clinicians view it difficult to apply the results to their individual clients (Boswell, Kraus, Miller, & Lambert, 2015; Castonguay, Locke, & Hayes, 2011).

Various reasons have been proposed to understand this difficulty in implementing research findings into routine clinical work. For example, the generalizability of findings from traditional randomized controlled trials (RCTs) has been perceived as being limited in clinical relevance (Castonguay, Barkham, Lutz & McAleavey, 2013). Additionally, others have argued that research does not focus on concerns that are applicable to routine clinical care and clients seen in these settings (e.g., Beutler, Williams, Wakefield, & Entwistle, 1995). Different evidence based practice efforts have tried to address this science-practice gap through validation and dissemination of specific treatments or emphasizing common mechanisms of change across modalities. For example, effectiveness studies have been conducted in order to assess whether treatments shown to be effective in RCTs can be implemented and adopted in routine clinical care (e.g., Tai et al., 2010). Others have focused on empirically based principles of change (Castonguay & Beutler, 2005) and common mechanisms across orientations, such as the therapeutic alliance (Norcross, 2011).

An alternative proposed to this top-down approach, or "empirical imperialism" (Castonguay, 2011), is practice-oriented research (POR). In POR, clinicians are active participants in all aspects of research, including the design, implementation and dissemination of research protocols and findings, which allows them not only to contribute to the advancement of scientific knowledge but to also be involved in setting up the agenda of future research (Zarin, Pincus, West, & McIntyre, 1997). This bottom-up approach encourages and fosters a sense of joint ownership, mutual collaborations, and respect between researchers and clinicians in conducting psychotherapy research that is clinically relevant and scientifically rigorous (Castonguay, et al., 2013). This approach, built on complementary expertise and experiences, is characterized by studies that are conducted as part of clinical routine, fostering the participation of clinicians in different aspects of the decision, design, implementation, and dissemination of research, and allowing for the use of data collected in day-to-day practice. Therefore, POR studies are intrinsically relevant to clinicians' concerns and can optimally "confound" research and practice: in other words, when the design and implementation of research activities are simultaneously and intrinsically serving both scientific and clinical purposes (Castonguay, 2011).

The goals for this chapter are to present 1) different types of infrastructures that can be built to conduct research in clinical practice, 2) types of clinically actionable studies that have been conducted within these infrastructures, and 3) discuss the benefits, obstacles, and strategies to deal with these, that clinicians are likely to experience when conducting research studies in their clinical practice.

What are Practice Research Networks?

Practice research networks (PRNs) are infrastructures in which researchers and clinicians collaborate to conduct research. As stated by Parry, Castonguay, Borkovec, and Wolfe (2010), PRNs

> have been alternately defined as a "group of practicing clinicians that co-operates to collect data and conduct research study" (Zarin et al., 1997), and "... large numbers of practicing clinicians and clinical scientists brought together in collaborative research on clinically meaningful questions in the naturalistic setting for the sake of external validity and employing rigorous scientific methodology for the sake of internal validity."
>
> (Borkovec, 2002, p. 313)

Researchers and clinicians may collaborate on any and all aspects of research, from the inception of clinically relevant ideas, study design, implementation, and dissemination of results. PRNs allow for the consideration and respect for the needs and resources of both clinicians and researchers in order to balance internal validity as well as feasibility when designing the protocols to be implemented. By having practitioners be an active voice in setting the research agenda (Zarin et al., 1997), the types of infrastructures developed as well as the studies conducted within these partnerships reflect a plurality in the psychotherapy phenomena explored.

PRNs were first established in the 1950s in healthcare to address research needs in particular domains, such as nursing, or locations, such as primary care in rural areas. Behavioral or psychological health PRNs emerged in the 1990s, and since then, several infrastructures have been developed to conduct psychotherapy research. As described in Castonguay, Barkham, Lutz, and McAleavey (2013), despite the variability in these infrastructures, they can be grouped into three broad categories based on the focus of the PRN: professional organizations, specific disorders, and common clinical settings.

Categories of PRNs

Professional Organization PRNs

Professional organization PRNs are primarily sponsored by professional organizations. The research conducted within these PRNs include samples that are often nationally representative, with large numbers of collaborators, and the studies usually cover a wide range of topics, with a tendency to focus on better understanding practices in routine care, although some have also looked at outcomes of care.

Professional organization PRNs have included national organizations of all sizes and foci, such as the American Psychiatric Association, American Association for Marriage and Family Therapy, American Counseling Association, Association for Cognitive Analytic Therapy, American Psychological Association, Art Therapy Practice, and the National Association of Social Workers.

They have also included locally based organizations. An example of a geographically based professional organization PRN is the Pennsylvania Psychological Association PRN (PPA-PRN), which was founded to conduct psychotherapy research in outpatient clinics in Pennsylvania. Since the inception of this PRN, researchers and clinicians have been fully involved in all aspects of the research studies conducted within this infrastructure, including in the development of goals, study design, implementation of the studies within their regular practices, and dissemination of the results.

Disorder-specific PRNs

Disorder-specific PRNs are collaborations developed to focus on specific clinical problems such as substance abuse, disruptive behavioral problems in children, child maltreatment, eating disorders, and autism. Within these foci, these PRNs have conducted studies exploring a variety of topics and study design complexity, reflecting the various interests of the clinicians and researchers involved in each PRN as well as the differing resources available to them.

For example, the Practice and Research: Advancing Collaboration is a PRN designed to explore therapeutic processes and outcome in the treatment of disruptive behavioral problems (DBP) in children (Garland, Hurlburt, & Hawley, 2006). This infrastructure included the collaboration between 80 providers from six different clinics with researchers in developing, implementing, and analyzing a research study exploring the use and outcome of evidence-based practice for DBP.

The Healthy Families America Research Practice Network (Galano & Schellenbach, 2007) focuses on the prevention of child maltreatment. Researchers and clinicians jointly created a common standardized database, as well as conducted a large multisite study that involved the implementation of evidence-based interventions.

Alternatively, instead of establishing long-term collaborative relationships, PRNs have also served as avenues through which researchers can recruit clinicians to collaborate in studies targeting specific disorders. For example, randomly selected clinician members of the American Psychological Association or American Psychiatric Association were contacted by Westen, Shedler, Durrett, Glass, & Martens, (2003), who requested data from these practitioners for their national study looking at psychopathology in adolescents. The BRIDGE ("Bond-Regulate-Interact-Develop-Guide-Engage") Collaborative is another instance of such collaboration. With a specific target population in mind, Stahmer, Brookman-Frazee, Lee, Searcy, & Reed (2011) established this cooperative effort between researchers, clinicians, as well as parents, and funding agencies to implement evidence-based interventions in community settings for infants and toddlers at risk of developing autism spectrum disorders.

PRNs Based on Common Settings

The third category of PRNs are rooted in specific clinical settings. For example, the Center for Collegiate Mental Health (CCMH) is based in college counseling centers, and it was developed to enhance the college mental health services through the collaboration of counseling center clinicians, researchers, university and college administrators, and industry leaders (Castonguay, Locke & Hayes, 2011). This PRN includes more than 400 counseling centers who collect standardized outcome data as part of their routine clinical practice using a multidimensional outcome measure that was specifically designed to address the mental health concerns of college students seeking counseling.

Another example of a common setting PRN is the Pennsylvania State University Psychological Clinic (Castonguay, Pincus, & McAleavey, 2015). Primarily a training clinic for PhD students in clinical psychology, it operates as a PRN by having standardized the diagnostic assessment procedures, built a research committee (which is comprised of faculty, staff members, students, and clinicians in the community) for the purpose of reviewing research proposals, established an agreement with the Institutional Review Board to streamline the research review process, as well as included core assessment measures as part of clinical routine that can also be used for research, training, and clinical purposes.

Types of Clinically Actionable and Scientifically Rigorous Studies Conducted

Assessment of Change Using Standardized Outcome Monitoring

A variety of POR studies have already been conducted in these different naturalistic settings and have addressed several topics of clinical utility and relevance. An increasing focus has been the ongoing assessment of change using standardized outcome monitoring. Also known as the patient-focused approach, it involves the careful assessment and tracking of clients' progress over the course of treatment using standardized outcome measures, and providing clinically relevant feedback to therapists that can be actionable in their practice (e.g., Adelman, Castonguay, Kraus, & Zack, 2015; Boswell, Kraus, Miller, & Lambert, 2015; McAleavey, Lockard, Castonguay, Hayes, & Locke, 2015). It should be highlighted that this type of research is not meant to replace clinical judgment: instead, it aims to provide clinicians with tools that can be used to augment clinical decision making with results that are available instantaneously and directly applicable to day-to-day practice.

To date, at least ten different measures/systems have been developed to track mental health change in routine care, and each has its own strengths and limitations (Drapeau, 2012). Regardless of the specific system, the most common use of outcome monitoring has been to track symptomatology change. By asking clients to complete an outcome measure pre- and post-treatment, clinicians can have access to data from the client regarding their functioning, which can supplement their clinical judgment as to the helpfulness of treatment and when to conclude therapy. Outcome monitoring can provide additional, more frequent information about the client's progress when administered at shorter intervals, such as after each session or every other session. This increased frequency can aid clinicians' treatment planning and implementation, as providers would have data immediately applicable to the client's functioning before their session, which can be used to guide session content. Furthermore, outcome monitoring can serve as a powerful tool for clients since by being asked to reflect on their own functioning, they would have information regarding their own improvement—which in turn can further improve the therapeutic alliance, as well as adherence to and belief in treatment (Youn, Kraus, & Castonguay, 2012).

Various outcome monitoring systems also include an "off-track" feedback alert that signals clinicians when clients are not responding to treatment as expected. This early deterioration detection may aid treatment (Lambert, 2010): if clinicians are alerted to the fact that their client's progress is slower than expected when compared to other clients who share similar demographic information and initial severity status, providers can then use this information to supplement their treatment decisions, discuss it with the client, and/or seek supervision and consultation. In addition, some of these feedback systems have been shown to accurately predict other clinically meaningful variables, such as potential treatment failure, risk of hospitalization, or drop-out (Boswell et al., 2015; Xiao, Castonguay, et al., 2017). For different reasons, it is difficult to accurately predict clients who will deteriorate or are at risk for experiencing negative outcomes during treatment (Lambert, 2010). Thus, these kinds of clinical tools can augment clinical judgment and decision making related to the type of care to provide for clients who may be at risk for premature termination or harm during therapy.

The clinical applicability to standardized outcome measures is not limited to tracking symptomatology change, but can also serve a diverse range of other clinical functions. For example, clients may be reluctant to verbally express or discuss difficulties they are experiencing with their psychotherapists for various reasons, such as embarrassment, ambivalence about distress they're experiencing, or even unawareness. Thus, in these kinds of situations, outcome measures can become an alternative communication outlet through which clients express distress with their clinicians (Youn, Castonguay et al., 2015; Youn, Kraus & Castonguay, 2012). Clients have also used ongoing assessments to keep track of their own progress, which can in turn be discussed with their providers as it relates to their treatment goals and the use of different clinical interventions, such as development of new understanding of self. For example, a client described feeling positive about the improvement as measured by a standardized outcome measure, relating this progress to newly found strengths within themselves, and increased sense of agency in their development (Youn, Castonguay et al., 2015).

Client and Therapist Characteristics

Understanding client characteristics have also been the focus of study in POR. Studies have looked at clients' sociodemographic factors, treatment history, diagnostic variables, pretreatment severity, family functioning and attachment styles as they relate to treatment process and outcome, including drop out (Adelman et al., 2015; Castonguay et al., 2015; Holmqvist et al., 2015; McAleavey et al., 2015; Szapocznik et al, 2015; West et al., 2015; Xiao, Castonguay, et al., 2017).

Similarly, therapist and treatment setting characteristics have also been explored in POR. For example, therapists' personal style, hours per week of direct care provided, and therapist effects (Holmqvist et al., 2015; Fernández-Álvarez et al., 2015; West et al., 2015; Youn, Xiao, et al., 2015) have been the focus of some studies conducted within PRNs. In addition, practice settings and their characteristics, such as the referral process, utilization and provision of different types of clinical services (e.g., psychotherapy and/or pharmacological treatment), payment source and management of care (Fernández-Álvarez et al., 2015; McAleavey et al., 2015; West et al., 2015) have been investigated, as well as how some of these variables interact with each other. Some authors, for instance, have looked at how client and therapist's congruence and differences in their perception of the client's difficulties and diagnostic presentation impact treatment, while others have investigated treatment utilization rates and treatment provided across client's race and ethnicity (Hayes et al., 2011; Holmqvist et al., 2015; West et al., 2015).

Process Studies

Diverse POR programs have also focused on conducting psychotherapy process studies. Topics have included the use and adherence of empirically supported interventions and treatments, evidence based practice in routine clinical care, relationship between training, therapist and intervention use, the therapeutic alliance, helpful and hindering events in psychotherapy, and principles of change in naturalistic settings (Adelman et al., 2015; Boswell, Castonguay & Wasserman, 2010; Castonguay, Pincus & McAleavey, 2015; Castonguay, Youn, McAleavey et al., 2015; Fernández-Álvarez et al., 2015; Garland & Brookman-Frazee, 2015; Holmqvist et al., 2015; Koerner & Castonguay, 2015; Strauss et al., 2015; Szapocznik et al., 2015; West et al., 2015). POR studies have also evaluated various assessment measures, including DSM-5 diagnostic criteria in routine clinical practice (McAleavey et al., 2015; West et al., 2015), as well as supervision of evidence-based interventions (Garland & Brookman-Frazee, 2015).

Effectiveness of Psychotherapy

Last but not least, the effectiveness of various types of psychotherapy treatments and interventions has been assessed in differing settings, such as psychological services or in private practice (Holmqvist et al., 2015; Koerner & Castonguay, 2015), as well as for a wide range of clinical problems (Adelman et al., 2015; Fernández-Álvarez et al., 2015; Holmqvist et al., 2015; Szapocznik, et al., 2015). The rich diversity of naturalistic settings has facilitated the use of different research methodologies in conducting POR, including RCTs and single-case experimental designs, and studies have looked at the impact of specific training programs for various process variables, such as fostering alliance skills, behavioral activation techniques, and two-chair techniques associated with emotion focused therapy (Koerner & Castonguay, 2015). Lastly, POR studies have also explored the comparative effectiveness of routine clinical care to RCT trials (McAleavey et al., 2017).

Benefits, Obstacles, and Recommendations

Challenges Establishing PRNs and Conducting POR

Despite the clinical focus of POR and clinical-research partnerships, a number of obstacles and challenges have been identified when conducting this kind of research initiatives (Castonguay et al., 2013). First, one of the biggest difficulties encountered in the implementation of POR is the perception that it is irrelevant or even hindering of clinical work. This concern is especially present when implementing outcome monitoring systems. For example, if clinicians perceive outcome monitoring as either impeding the establishing of a therapeutic relationship, potentially generating negative reactions from clients such as increasing client resistance, or resulting in negative evaluation of services, and even potentially decreasing referrals or income, then the likelihood of adopting this kind of system or conducting research in clinical practice decreases substantially (e.g., Boswell et al., 2015; Fernández Álvarez et al., 2015; Holmqvist et al., 2015; Strauss et al., 2015). It has even been argued that any research activity can have the potential effect of competing for the clinician's attention away from exclusively focusing on clinical issues. Thus, participating providers may find it difficult to ascertain the immediate applicability of the research data, and to ask them to instead focus on the long-term value of it may be a challenge (Fernández-Álvarez et al., 2015).

Another challenge observed includes the fear that the data collected, such as outcome data, may reveal negative findings, or that the results may be used to negatively evaluate a clinician or treatment center's performance, or impact referrals or income opportunities (Adelman et al., 2015; Boswell et al., 2015; Strauss et al., 2015). Not knowing who will have access to outcome data, or how this data may be used can also be experienced as a threat to each provider's sense of autonomy, and agency (Boswell et al., 2015). It is thus understandable that clinicians have questioned whether specific outcome results can accurately reflect their work as assessed through their clients' change, as well as the appropriateness of interpreting outcome data without considering the context in which it is collected and/or other sources of information, such as the complexity and/or severity of a client's difficulties (McAleavey et al., 2015; Strauss et al., 2015).

Clinicians' anxiety and apprehension is not just towards outcome monitoring. First, clinicians and clients have both raised concerns about breaches in confidentiality, which can also be a frequent barrier in conducting practice-oriented research in naturalistic settings (Boswell et al., 2015; Koerner & Castonguay, 2015). Introducing changes into clinical routine as part of new research initiatives can also increase anxiety. For example, if research protocols include videotaped observation of sessions as a way to monitor therapy adherence, or adoption of a new treatment manual into treatment as usual, these changes can raise anxiety among providers (Szapocznik et al., 2015). For less experienced clinicians, having to ask clients to participate in research can lead to feelings of impostor syndrome, as they may feel as though they are adding burden to their clients by asking them to complete research questionnaires while not feeling like they are providing them with optimal clinical care (Castonguay et al., 2015).

In addition to obstacles related to relevance, immediate clinical value, and clinician and client anxiety, challenges related to feasibility of protocols in naturalistic settings have to be addressed when implementing POR. Despite initial excitement or interest, research projects that include too many tasks or intense supervision have been difficult to sustain and adopt as part of routine clinical practice after the completion of the study (Koerner & Castonguay, 2015; Szapocznik et al., 2015). Furthermore, pragmatic obstacles, such as availability of time, staff, and resources can hinder the implementation of the research procedures, especially if there are incompatibilities between research and clinical tasks.

Perhaps the least surprising problem faced by any partnership is communication and collaboration difficulties. These kinds of challenges can threaten the sense of shared ownership that is the backbone of all POR and PRNs (Castonguay et al., 2015). In order to facilitate a genuine sense of partnership, first and foremost, it is recommended that researchers be continuously vigilant of potential pitfalls of empirical imperialism. These can take the form of subtle manifestations, such as impromptu or innocuous conversations about study design without having practitioners or their input present. Alternatively, they can also be the explicit dismissal or exploitation of practitioners, as when the researcher designs all aspects of a research protocol, discusses its implementation with a clinic director in order to take advantage of the clinic's setting and clients, and then practitioners and clients are asked to complete the research tasks, which may not necessarily align with their own values (Koerner & Castonguay, 2015).

Even when a partnership is continuously striving for a true collaborative spirit, communication problems are to be expected. POR by definition includes the teamwork of different stakeholders, who may not only use variant language to communicate similar and discrepant perspectives, but also have to respond to different demands, expectations, and goals (Garland & Brookman-Frazee, 2015). Thus, it is unavoidable that conflictual needs will arise, and even orchestrating the exchange of information to fulfill these can be a challenge on its own (McAleavey et al., 2015).

So Why do it? Benefits of PRNs and POR

Despite the numerous challenges, clinicians have reported benefits in being part of PRNs and conducting POR. To begin with, research shows that researcher-clinician partnerships have already had a positive impact on psychotherapy in clinical routine, increased client retention in treatment, as well as including feedback on client progress through outcome monitoring has been shown to significantly reduce deterioration (Adelman et al., 2015; Lambert 2010; Szapocznik et al., 2015). Extending traditional RCT research that compares treatment modalities, POR studies have focused on process variables, such as exploring individual therapists' differing areas of expertise in fostering client change (e.g., Kraus et al., 2016; Youn, Xiao et al., 2015). This data has the potential to provide feedback about a practitioner's unique strengths and limitations which would benefit clients, facilitate training opportunities and referrals. Additionally, others have found that data collected as part of clinical routine, including session notes and assessment measures, can help triage difficulties in treatment process and provide guidance for potential clinical changes, such as adjusting frequency of sessions, or adding couples or family therapy (Fernández-Álvarez et al., 2015). The implementation of different research protocols can also lead to immediately actionable clinical information. For example, clients' feedback post-session about helpful and hindering events in session has allowed clinicians to be more attuned to their clinical needs while also collecting research data (Castonguay, Boswell, et al., 2010). Training studies provide therapists, both experienced and trainees, an opportunity to learn and implement new evidence based treatment interventions (Koerner & Castonguay, 2015), especially if these training protocols were developed with clinician input, and thus address problems that are clinically applicable to their clients. PRN collaborations can also at times have had an unintended process benefit of leading to changes in practice: West et al. (2015) found that being part of PRN studies fostered changes in clinicians' practice and also in their participation in using and disseminating research findings and procedures.

Professional development is another area that has been reported to benefit from PRN partnerships. At its foundation, PRNs naturally allow for establishing and growing both local as well as national connections with others who share similar interests and views of psychotherapy, research and practice, and thus have been described as fostering reciprocal learning, with researchers gaining "greater respect for the immediate and often risky clinical challenges therapists faced" and clinicians having "greater appreciation for the rigor of the research process and the ultimate aim of improving care" (Garland & Brookman-Frazee, 2015, p. 9). Furthermore, some therapists have found it professionally validating to investigate phenomena that occur in their day-to-day routine (Koerner & Castonguay, 2015), and clients have reported experiencing a feeling of pride in their contribution to projects that increase our understanding of psychotherapy (Castonguay, Nelson et al., 2010).

The benefits of PRNs and POR are not limited to individual practitioners or clients. Organizations and clinical settings have reported making gains in terms of recognition, quality of care, and overall climate and satisfaction. For example, administrators, stakeholders and clinic directors have used outcome monitoring data to show evidence for their clinic's effectiveness, and to advocate for additional funding and resources. This type of data can also help clinicians to understand the clients' clinical presentations and refine the services and treatments provided to attend to these needs (Adelman et al., 2015; Youn, Castonguay et al., 2015).

It is not a stretch to also argue that PRNs and POR have positively impacted and contributed to the health care system overall. Data collected within PRNs has provided information about current mental health needs and trends (Xiao, Carney, et al., 2017), client characteristics that may help predict increased inpatient hospitalization use (Boswell et al., 2015) as well as areas of continued understanding and improvement, such as resource allocation for specific populations (West et al., 2015). Furthermore, since POR is necessarily guided in part by practitioners' interests, it has fostered and facilitated the important knowledge related to under-investigated treatments, service effects, long term impact, and cost-benefits of therapy (Castonguay, Youn, Xiao et al., 2015).

How to: Recommendations and Strategies for Establishing PRNs and Conducting POR

In order to address the obstacles listed above and foster PRN partnerships, several recommendations and strategies have been suggested. First and most importantly, POR studies will be more likely to elicit therapists' engagement and collaboration if they are directly applicable and related to clinical practice. However, in order to maintain the practitioners' commitment, experiences from various PRNs have shown that being "clinically relevant" and interesting are not enough; the studies have to also simultaneously help clinicians with their clinical work (Castonguay, Youn et al., 2015). One way to make the research helpful is to integrate it into already established clinical tasks. For example, using the research data in supervision has been shown to increase therapists' motivation to collect it (Fernandez-Alvarez et al., 2015). In addition, when research protocols confound research and practice they are most helpful to clinicians as they are able to provide guidance about interventions immediately (Koerner & Castonguay, 2015).

In other words, research and practice are truly syntonic, and therefore most helpful when practitioners performing a task are unable to answer whether they are gathering clinical information or completing a research activity, and thus, are performing both at the same time (Castonguay, 2011). Furthermore, POR is most likely to be successfully implemented and continued to be used post-study completion when the research procedures do not introduce major changes to the already established clinical practice (Castonguay et al., 2013). It is not surprising to state that most clinicians will find it difficult to put aside their way of practicing and adopt a new theoretical orientation or treatment modality as part of a research protocol. Thus, it is instead recommended that POR studies include tasks that are additive to current clinical repertoire, such as obtaining feedback on helpful interventions from clients (Castonguay, Youn, McAleavey et al., 2015), and training on specific new interventions for specific problems (Adelman et al., 2015), as well as flexible in their implementation of the activities to be sensitive to existing clinical reality and availability of resources (McAleavey et al., 2015).

Second, to address fear of negative impact and confidentiality issues, transparency is a necessary component in these researcher-clinician partnerships. This can take the form of a full written format disclosure regarding issues of confidentiality (Boswell et al., 2015), and/or explicit verbal reassurance that clinicians' outcome data will not be used to negatively impact their practice, reimbursement, or clinical judgment (Strauss et al., 2015). In terms of apprehension as to whether the research is helpful to their clients, using data has been shown to help decreasing such fear (Castonguay, Youn et al., 2015). When the results of data collected within one's given practice is used to show one's effectiveness, it can be a very validating experience for clinicians, regardless of whether they are in training or experienced, and can sometimes even facilitate a corrective experience around use of POR (Youn, Kraus, & Castonguay, 2012). Furthermore, having practitioners share their experiences being involved in PRN partnerships and/or using POR data with each other is an effective way to disseminate the enthusiasm and benefits of these collaborations as these recounts are not perceived as biased (Castonguay, Youn et al., 2015). Continued conversation and feedback between researchers and clinicians, even after the implementation of a research protocol, will continue to enhance these partnerships.

Third strategy: communication, communication, communication; strong and frequent communication cannot be emphasized enough in establishing and maintaining PRNs. As mentioned above, difficulties and differing options will most likely emerge in these kinds of partnerships as diversity of thoughts and perspectives is encouraged as they are viewed to strengthen these collaborations. Thus, regular meetings to allow for discussions, understanding, validation and strategizing ways to incorporate the concerns and needs of the various stakeholders will help address the challenges and obstacles in constructive ways (Castonguay, Youn et al., 2015).

Time and resources are also constant challenges in PRNs. A strategy to address these is the "routinization" of a protocol, where the various research tasks are carefully planned out and embedded within clinical routine so that clinicians and/or clients participating in the studies do not have to think about or try to remember what activity needs to be completed, and instead can automatize their responsibilities. Technology has been frequently employed to routinize these tasks, such as through email and/or phone consultations, and it is also recommended that, if possible, a pilot test of the protocol be tested in their clinical routine before study launch (Koerner & Castonguay, 2015).

Conclusion

As argued by Castonguay, Youn et al. (2015), PRN collaborations represent ambitious goals by "fostering rapprochements of minds, integrating research and clinical work, and improving our understanding and practice of the mental health field" (p. 182). Ideally these kinds of partnerships can provide mutually beneficial and symbiotic relationships between clinicians, researchers, and the various collaborators and stakeholders, and potentially seamlessly integrate and even bridge the gap between research and practice. By presenting the types of PRN relationships available and possible, the types of research studies conducted in them, as well as the benefits, obstacles and strategies to address these, it is our hope that if clinicians are interested in engaging in and contributing their expertise to research initiatives, PRNs and POR is an avenue they will consider.

References

Adelman, R. W., Castonguay, L. G., Kraus, D. R., & Zack, S. (2015). Conducting research and collaborating with researchers: The experience of clinicians in a residential treatment center. *Psychotherapy Research*, 25(1), 108–120.

Beutler, L. E., Williams, R. E., Wakefield, P. J., & Entwistle, S. R. (1995). Bridging scientist and practitioner perspectives in clinical psychology. *American Psychologist*, 50, 984–994.

Borkovec, T. D. (2002). Training clinic research and the possibility of a national training clinics practice research network. *The Behavior Therapist*, 25, 98–103.

Boswell, J. F., Castonguay, L. G., & Wasserman, R. H. (2010). Effects of psychotherapy training and intervention use on session outcome. *Journal of Consulting and Clinical Psychology*, 78, 717–723.

Boswell, J. F., Kraus, D. R., Miller, S. D., & Lambert, M. J. (2015). Implementing routine outcome monitoring in clinical practice: Benefits, challenges, and solutions. *Psychotherapy Research*, 25(1), 6–19. (Erratum published, 2015, Psychotherapy Research, 25, p. iii).

Castonguay, L. G. (2011). Psychotherapy, psychopathology, research and practice: Pathways of connections and integration. *Psychotherapy Research*, 21, 125–140.

Castonguay, L.G., Barkham, M., Lutz, W., & McAleavey, A. A. (2013). Practice-oriented research: Approaches and application. In M. J. Lambert (Eds.) *Bergin and Garfield's Handbook of psychotherapy and behavior change* (6th ed.). New York: John Wiley & Sons.

Castonguay, L. G. & Beutler, L. E. (Eds.) (2005). *Principles of therapeutic change that work*. New York: Oxford University Press.

Castonguay, L. G., Boswell, J. F., Zack, S., Baker, S., Boutselis, M., Chiswick, N., . . . Holtforth, M. G. (2010). Helpful and hindering events in psychotherapy: A practice research network study. *Psychotherapy: Theory, Research, Practice, and Training*, 47, 327–344.

Castonguay, L. G., Locke, B. D., & Hayes, J. A. (2011). The Center for Collegiate Mental Health: An example of a practice-research network in university counseling centers. *Journal of College Student Psychotherapy, 25*, 105–119.

Castonguay, L. G., Nelson, D., Boutselis, M., Chiswick, N., Darner, D., Hemmelstein, N., ... Borkovec, T. (2010). Clinicians and/or researchers? A qualitative analysis of therapists' experiences in a practice research network. *Psychotherapy: Theory, Research, Practice, and Training, 47*, 345–354.

Castonguay, L. G., Pincus, A. L., & McAleavey, A. A. (2015). Practice research network in a psychology training clinic: Building an infrastructure to foster early attachment to the scientific-practitioner model. *Psychotherapy Research, 25*(1), 52–66.

Castonguay, L. G., Youn, S., McAleavey, A. A., Boswell, J. F., Janis, R., Xiao, H., Boutselis, M., Braver, M., Chiswick, N., Hemmelstein, N., Jackson, J., Lytle, R., Morford, M., Scott, H., Spayd, C., & O'Leary Wiley, M. (2015, June). The use of empirically supported techniques: Did I do what I thought I would do and/or what I thought I did? Paper presented as part of a panel at the 2015 Society for Psychotherapy Research (SPR), 46th International meeting, Philadelphia, PA.

Castonguay, L. G., Youn, S., Xiao, H., Muran, J. C., & Barber, J. P. (2015). Building clinicians-researchers partnerships: Lessons from diverse natural settings and practice-oriented initiatives. *Psychotherapy Research, 25*(1), 166–184.

Drapeau, M. (2012). The value of tracking in psychotherapy. *Integrating Science & Practice, 2*, 2–6.

Fernández-Álvarez, H., Gómez, B., & García, F. (2015). Bridging the gap between research and practice in a clinical and training network: Aigle's program. *Psychotherapy Research, 25*(1), 84–94.

Galano, J. & Schellenbach, C. J. (2007). Healthy Families America Research Practice Network: A unique partnership to integrate prevention sciences and practice. *Journal of Prevention and Integration in the Community, 34*, 39–66.

Garland, A. F. & Brookman-Frazee, L. (2015). Therapists and researchers: Advancing collaboration. *Psychotherapy Research, 25*(1), 95–107.

Garland, A. F., Hurlburt, M. S., & Hawley, K. M. (2006). Examining psychotherapy processes in a services research context. *Clinical Psychology: Science and Practice, 13*, 30–46.

Hayes, J. A., Youn, S., Castonguay, L. G., Locke, B. D., McAleavey, A. A., & Nordberg, S. (2011). Rates and predictors of counseling center use among college students of color. *Journal of College Counseling, 14*(2), 105–116.

Holmqvist, R., Philips, B., & Barkham, M. (2015). Developing practice-based evidence: Benefits, challenges, and tensions. *Psychotherapy Research, 25*(1), 20–31.

Koerner, K. & Castonguay, L. G. (2015). Practice-oriented research: What it takes to do collaborative research in private practice. *Psychotherapy Research, 25*(1), 67–83.

Kraus, D. R., Bentley, J. H., Alexander, P. C., Boswell, J. F., Constantino, M. J., Baxter, E. E., & Castonguay, L. G. (2016). Predicting therapist effectiveness from their own practice-based evidence. *Journal of Consulting and Clinical Psychology, 84*(6), 473–483. Available from: http://psycnet.apa.org/doi/10.1037/ccp0000083 http://dx.doi.org/10.1037/ccp0000083

Lambert, M. J. (2010). Prevention of treatment failure: The use of measuring, monitoring, *and feedback in clinical practice.* Washington DC: American Psychological Association Press.

McAleavey, A. A., Lockard, A. J., Castonguay, L. G., Hayes, J. A., & Locke, B. D. (2015). Building a practice research network: Obstacles faced and lessons learned at the Center for Collegiate Mental Health. *Psychotherapy Research, 25*(1), 134–151.

McAleavey, A. A., Youn, S., Xiao, H., Castonguay, L. G., Hayes, J. A., & Locke, B. D. (2017). Effectiveness of routine psychotherapy: Method matters. *Psychotherapy Research.* Advanced online publication. https://doi.org/10.1080/10503307.2017.1395921

Norcross, J. C. (2011). *Psychotherapeutic relationship that work* (2nd ed.). New York: Oxford University Press.

Parry, G., Castonguay, L. G., Borkovec, T. D., & Wolfe, A. W. (2010). Practice research networks and psychological services research in the UK and USA. In M. Barkham, G. E Hardy, & J Mellor-Clark (Eds.) *Developing and delivering practice-based evidence: A guide for the psychological therapies.* New York: John Wiley.

Stahmer, A. C., Brookman-Frazee, L., Lee, E., Searcy, K., & Reed, S. (2011). Parent and multidisciplinary provider perspectives on earliest intervention for children at risk for autism spectrum disorders. *Infants and Young Children, 24,* 344–363.

Strauss, B., Lutz, W., Steffanowski, A., Wittmann, W., Böhnke, J. R., Rubel, J., . . . Kirchmann, H. (2015). Benefits and challenges in practice-oriented psychotherapy research in Germany: The TK and the QS-PSY-BAY projects of quality assurance in outpatient psychotherapy. *Psychotherapy Research, 25*(1), 32–51.

Szapocznik, J., Muir, J. A., Duff, J. H., Schwartz, S. J., & Brown, C. H. (2015). Brief strategic family therapy: Implementing evidence-based models in community settings. *Psychotherapy research, 25*(1), 121–133.

Tai, B., Straus, M. M., Liu, D., Sparenborg, S., Jackson, R., & McCarty, D. (2010). The first decade of the National Drug Abuse Treatment Clinical Trials Network: Bridging the gap between research and practice to improve drug abuse treatment. *Journal of Substance Abuse Treatment, 38*(1), S4-S13.

West, J. C., Moscicki, E. K., Duffy, F. F., Wilk, J. E., Countis, L., Narrow, W. E., & Regier, D. A. (2015). APIRE practice research network: Accomplishments, challenges, and lessons learned. *Psychotherapy Research, 25*(1), 152–165.

Westen, D., Shedler, J., Durrett, C., Glass, S., & Martens, A. (2003). Personality diagnoses in adolescence: DSM-IV axis II diagnoses and an empirically derived alternative. *American Journal of Psychiatry, 160,* 952–966.

Xiao, H., Carney, D. M., Youn, S., Janis, R. A., Castonguay, L. G., Hayes, J. A., & Locke, B. D. (2017). Are we in crisis? National mental health and utilization trends in counseling centers. *Psychological Services, 14*(4), 407–415.

Xiao, H., Castonguay, L. G., Janis, R. B., Youn, S., Hayes, J. A., & Locke, B. D. (2017). Therapist effects on dropout from a college counseling center practice research network. *Journal of Counseling Psychology, 64*(4), 424–431.

Youn, S., Castonguay, L. G., Xiao, H., Janis, R., Mcaleavey, A. A., Lockard, A. J., . . . Hayes, J. A. (2015). The Counseling Center Assessment of Psychological Symptoms (CCAPS): Merging Clinical Practice, Training, and Research. *Psychotherapy, 52*(4), 432–441.

Youn, S., Kraus, D. R., & Castonguay, L. G. (2012). The treatment outcome package: Facilitating practice and clinically relevant research. *Psychotherapy, 49*(2), 115–122.

Youn, S., Xiao, H., Janis, R., Castonguay, L. G., Hayes, J. A., & Locke, B. (2015, June). Therapist effects in naturalistic settings. Paper presented as part of a panel at the 2015 Society for Psychotherapy Research (SPR), 46th International meeting, Philadelphia, PA.

Zarin, D. A., Pincus, H. A., West, J. C., & McIntyre, J. S. (1997). Practice-based research in psychiatry. *American Journal of Psychiatry, 154,* 1199–1208.

PART II

Research Methods in Practice-Based Research

CHAPTER 3

Research Methods in Practice Settings

Scott H. Waltman

This chapter will focus on describing practical research methods in practice settings. Practice-based research (PBR) is ideally suited for investigating real-world practice (Codd, 2016) including: (1) identifying and clarifying barriers and problems in routine clinical practice, (2) testing program and treatment improvement initiatives, and (3) evaluating process, adherence, competence, and clinical effectiveness of evidence-based psychotherapies when delivered in real-world clinical settings (Westfall, Mold, & Fagnan, 2007). Practice-based or naturalistic research can be conducted with or without the collaboration of academic researchers, with corresponding pros and cons. This chapter is written for the semi-reluctant practice-based researchers who are working without the aid of academic researchers, and is intended to be received as a how-to guide.

The prospect of conducting research in a practice-based setting can be both exciting and overwhelming. Learning to do something new and taking risks requires a lot of vulnerability (Brown, 2012) and a willingness to tolerate uncertainty (Hayes & Smith, 2005). This chapter won't explicitly incorporate self-practice, but it is recommended that practitioners seek to apply the same level of patience, compassion, and encouragement to themselves as they would to the individuals with whom they work!

Practice-based research (PBR), though challenging, can lead to improvements in clinical care, time efficiency, and staff well-being. Consider the following examples of PBR. In a community mental health clinic, they sought to decrease the problem of no-shows to intake appointments (Williston, Block-Lerner, Wolanin, & Gardner, 2014). First they looked at the extant literature to see what other people had found to be effective solutions, and found that reminder calls and letters were useful strategies. The practice-based researchers decided to try sending out orientation and reminder letters to prospective clients who had scheduled intake appointments. As these particular practice-based researchers had a special interest in Acceptance and Commitment Therapy (Hayes & Smith, 2005), they opted to include in their research conditions an acceptance-based letter that discussed the costs of experiential avoidance and benefits of acceptance. In that PBR study, 99 prospective clients were randomized to receive no orientation letter, a general orientation letter, or an enhanced orientation letter. This resulted in a reduction in the intake appointment no-show rates in the enhanced orientation letter condition (67 percent show rate with the enhanced letter as compared to 52 percent in the no letter condition); however, the reduction was not found to be statistically significant—not due to chance. The practice-based researchers acknowledged that in order to detect a small effect size they would have needed to have a sample size of 785 clients (Williston et al., 2014). Was this study a success? Years later the supervisor from that study reports still using the letter in his practice setting, so the site was happy with the outcome. Issues related to sample size, power analysis, and statistical significance will be discussed below.

Another example of a common PBR method is outcome tracking. In a clinic staffed by psychology graduate students, the supervisors wanted to be informed about the clinical outcomes in their clinic to better inform supervision and training needs (Waltman, Rex, & Williams, 2011). The first step was determining what information was desired and how to track it. The researchers created an outcome tracking sheet that contained informed related to diagnosis, demographics, course of treatment, scores from outcome tracking measures, and clinician judgment of the successfulness of treatment. However, when the practice-based researchers went to analyze the data, an unanticipated barrier they encountered was that the type of data they collected did not lend itself well to the intended statistical procedures. A majority of the collected data was nominal as opposed to interval or ratio and thus the practice-based researchers had to rely on the less preferred and less precise nonparametric statistics (Waltman et al., 2011). In both of the presented examples, meaningful lines of inquiry were performed and some limitations were observed related to study methodology.

Common Barriers to PBR

Common limitations related to PBR include low internal validity, low generalizeability (external validity), low publishability, and low fundability (Cahill, Barkham, & Stiles, 2010). Internal validity refers to the degree of experimental control and the quality of the study such that error is minimized and confidence can be placed in the conclusions of the study (Campbell & Stanley, 1966). External validity refers to the degree to which the results of the study can be generalized, or applied, to people and situations outside the research setting (Campbell & Stanley, 1966).

Threats to Internal Validity

Selection and Bias

This speaks to how participants are assigned to the different research conditions. For example, consider the PBR study above with the orientation letters. The practice-based researchers randomized clients to be in one of the three study conditions. If they had rather let clients choose to receive a letter, or which type of letter to receive, this would have introduced an additional potential confounding variable (i.e., another possible explanation for their results), as perhaps different dispositional factors associated with various preferences are associated with the outcome being studied. This is why academic researchers seek to include randomization in their studies (Pannucci & Wilkins, 2010). Randomization may not be practical, or desired, in a practice-based setting (Cahill et al., 2010), which is a limitation to internal validity.

One strategy that researchers use when randomization is not possible is called matching. This involves identifying participant attributes and variables that are hypothesized to have an impact on the outcome variables and matching severity ratings of participants to ensure an even distribution across research conditions. This strategy is also often impractical in naturalistic or practice-based settings. A viable strategy in PBR is to measure these hypothesized variables at baseline so that possible differences across conditions can be detected and, if necessary, statistical methods of controlling for those differences can be attempted.

Drop-out

Wierzbicki and Pekarik (1993) estimated the average rate for premature termination in outpatient psychotherapy to be 46.86 percent. Clients drop out of therapy, employees change jobs, and participants drop out of studies. This is a threat to a study's internal validity when there are reasons to think that this dropout is not due to chance.

For example, there are some indications in the literature that younger clinicians may be more at risk for burnout syndrome (Garcia et al., 2015); however, as Maslach, Schaufeli, and Leiter (2001) point out, findings like these should be interpreted with caution as there may be a survival bias. It might be that early career employees experience burnout and subsequently leave their jobs. Thus, a cross-sectional look at burnout would give the perception that the more experienced (and correspondingly probably older) employees have lower levels of burnout; however, these findings might just be related to the possibility that the more burnt-out people have already changed their jobs earlier in their career. Therefore, it is important to assess for possible between-group differences with participants who drop out and participants who complete the research protocol.

History

Context is important, and the idea behind the history bias is that research does not occur in a vacuum. It is important to account for external events having a possible impact on your outcome variables. To illustrate this point, consider some PBR that investigated the clinical effects of a new mindfulness-based treatment protocol with adolescents who had presenting problems related to externalizing behaviors, a historical bias occurred when the course of the treatment overlapped with the school year ending (Waltman, Hetrick, & Tasker, 2012). This resulted in nonrandom client dropout and changes to the daily environment and psychosocial stressors of the youth, making it more difficult to attribute clinical outcomes solely to the intervention (Waltman et al., 2012).

Maturation

Threats related to maturation refer to normative development as a confounding variable. For example, if you are working in a practice-based school setting and you are measuring change over time, it will be important to try to account for changes in maturity, cognitive abilities, and physical abilities that could also be accounted for by the aging process. The simplest way to account for this is to have a comparison or control group.

Expectancy, Observer, and Rater Bias

In pharmaceutical trials, double-blind studies are considered to be the gold-standard. This means that both the patient and provider are unaware of the treatment condition (e.g., new medication versus placebo). These types of studies are thought to be the most scientifically rigorous. It is unlikely that medication trials would take place as a part of PBR, but these ideas are still relevant. For instance, well-controlled studies have demonstrated that competency ratings completed by non-blind raters (e.g., supervisors) are consistently more generous than the ratings provided by blind-raters (Dennhag, Gibbons, Barber, Gallop, & Crits-Christoph, 2012). So, if you are studying the outcomes of a training program and your outcome variable is a performance-based rating, using non-blinded raters is a threat to the internal validity of your PBR (see Creed et al., 2016). In cases where judgment is required to assess an outcome variable, it is recommended that steps (e.g., assigning codes or pseudo-names to participants) are made to blind the rater to participant identity and research condition.

Regression to the Mean

In general, more extreme scores tend to be less extreme over time. Consider the example of designing a practice-based investigation to improve a clinician's no-show rate. Getting an accurate baseline assessment of the no-show rate can be tricky, as there is likely to be random variation week to week; therefore, a single slice in time may not accurately reflect the overall picture (Jones, & Spiegelhalter, 2009). There are complicated statistical strategies that can be used to account for regression to the mean. A more practical strategy is to measure baseline, post, and follow-up at multiple time points. For example, if you wanted to look at a clinician's no-show rate, to get an accurate estimate it would be helpful to look at more than a single week to estimate the rate. The average of several weeks in a row would be more reliable than a single week, and the average of several months in a row would be even more reliable.

Reliability of Measures

The selecting of optimal measures for a study can be an arduous task that involves scouring the literature and the Mental Measurements Yearbook (Spies, Carlson, & Geisinger, 2010) for measures that are psychometrically sound. That endeavor is not practical for PBR. Beidas and colleagues (2015) conducted an exhaustive review and put together a list of 29 adult and 20 youth measures that are free, brief, and validated for use in low-resource mental health settings (see Beidas et al., 2015 for list of measures and where to obtain them). An example of a high-quality free-to-use measure is the Patient Health Questionnaire-9 (PHQ-9; Kroenke, Spitzer, & Williams, 2001), a tool that can be used to screen for depression and has enough sensitivity to be used for monitoring the progress of treatment over time.

In some cases, you might be investigating something that has not been extensively studied, and high-quality, free-to-use measures may not have been developed, or perhaps the existing measures do not seem relevant to your study. In these cases, you might find yourself developing your own measure; it can be helpful to base your measure on an already existing measure. The important thing to keep in mind is that the way the questions are structured will affect what you are able to do with the data. Statistically speaking there are four different types of scales that data can fall into: nominal, ordinal, interval, and ratio. In general, ratio is preferred as you can do the most with it; nominal and ordinal data tend to be limited to less-preferred nonparametric statistics and frequency data. This is why academic researchers are always using likert scales. This involves using a continuum to rate the variable of interest (e.g., rating quality or satisfaction on a 0 to 6 scale; 0—not at all, 1—slightly, 2—moderately, 3—very, 4—extremely or on a 0 to 6 scale; 0—totally unacceptable, 1—unacceptable, 2—slightly unacceptable, 3—neutral, 4—slightly acceptable, 5—acceptable, 6—totally acceptable).

Threats to External Validity

It is commonly held that internal and external validity are diametrically opposed; that is to say as internal validity increases, external validity decreases. This assumption can be misleading as poor internal validity does not necessarily indicate good external validity; rather, it is important to note that certain elements associated with high internal validity (e.g., the use of randomization to treatment condition or excluding individuals with comorbid diagnoses) do not reflect routine practice in community settings. Therefore, achieving both high internal and external validity is formidable, and practice-based researchers would do well to seek to minimize error and foster adequate internal validity.

External validity refers to how well the findings and conclusions from the study can be generalized or applied to other settings. Intuitively, research conducted in practice-based settings would apply well to other practice-based settings; however, patient and situation/research design factors often hinder the ability to generalize findings from one PBR setting to another. In PBR, factors relating to client background/history, demographics, and treatment recruitment procedures often have larger impacts on external validity due to small sample sizes.

Sampling Bias

This speaks to how participants are recruited for your PBR. For example, imagine you are interested in studying the effectiveness of a mindfulness-based group therapy and you hang fliers in your clinic asking interested parties if they would like to participate. While allowing clients to decide what type of treatment they would like to receive is good clinical care, this creates a self-selection bias that limits the generalizeability of your potential findings to individuals who have similar demographics and histories, openness to mindfulness-based interventions, and the personality characteristics associated with self-selecting to treatment. If your goal as a practice-based researcher is to conduct and publish research that will have a large impact on the field in general, then collaborating with an academic or career researcher is recommended. On the other hand, if your goal is to improve local practice, then external validity is less of a concern, as instead of accounting for how your sample and procedures reflect the general public or a larger body of individuals, you need only account for how well your sample reflects the individuals with whom you work.

Cahill and colleagues (2010) conducted a systematic evaluation of PBR studies and developed a framework to measure the quality of PBR. They focused on the reporting of the study, external validity, internal reliability, and selection bias. How well the study is designed from the outset has a large bearing on what you are able to find and the meaning you are able to make from your findings. In other words, problems with the study design can increase the amount of error or noise in your data, and improving the PBR study design, can decrease error and lead to a better ability to detect meaningful findings (Cahill et al., 2010).

Practice-Based Research Methods

Research is typically framed as an application of the scientific method (Crawford & Stucki, 1990): (1) define a question; (2) gather information and resources; (3) form an explanatory hypothesis; (4) test the hypothesis by performing an experiment and collecting data in a reproducible manner; (5) analyze the data; (6) interpret the data and draw conclusions that serve as a starting point for new hypothesis; (7) publish results; and (8) retest. This framework is expanded below to address some of the common stuck points and pitfalls to conducting research in a practice-based setting. The other chapters in this volume will also be important resources on the topic.

While PBR can seem like an overwhelming amount of work, like most things, it is a lot of little tasks to be done. The following 11 steps will help you conduct research in your practice-based setting. Remember, the trick is to practice self-compassion and encouragement, focus on doing one thing at a time, and schedule time to work on the project.

Step 1. Have a question.
Step 2. Consult the literature/subject matter experts.
Step 3. Define the research question.
Step 4. Design the study.
Step 5. Seek consultation feedback.
Step 6. Pilot/proof of concept.
Step 7. Evaluate and refine.
Step 8. Conduct study to scale.
Step 9. Clean data and analyze results.
Step 10. Interpret results in light of extant literature.
Step 11. Disseminate your findings.

Step 1. Have a Question

The first and probably most important step is to find a topic or line of inquiry that you are extremely passionate about. There is a *huge* valley in between the excitement of starting a project and finishing it (Bonezzi, Brendl, & Angelis, 2011), and the middle part is where stuff sort of falls off. In general, when completing a difficult task like PBR, motivation tends to be highest at the beginning when you are excited by the potential outcome and near the end when you get closer to finishing it (Bonezzi et al., 2011). It is crucial to pick something that you really care about to decrease the likelihood of your project fading away during the crucial middle parts. A useful strategy to enhance motivation and increase reinforcement is to set regular weekly or bi-weekly goals and monitor your progress towards these goals (Harkin et al., 2016).

The typical scope of PBR lends itself well to increasing motivation to complete a task. As practice-based researchers are typically clinicians or supervisors of clinicians, questions relating to improving client care and improving local practice are often motivating topics. The trick is to start small. Consider the earlier example with the letters designed to decrease no-show rates. Those researchers could have picked any number of components of the situation to study; they could have looked at: (1) descriptive factors relating to the no-shows (e.g., which types of clients are not showing up, which days and times is this a greater problem, are certain clinicians or front desk staff experiencing higher or lower rates than the average); (2) surveying the clients who did not show up to find out what barriers they encountered; (3) surveying the clients who did attend their intakes to learn more about what helped them make it in; (4) they could look at interventions to reduce the rate; or (5) a host of other options. These researchers took the pragmatic stance of asking, "What have other folks done?" and "What low-cost interventions can be done to reduce the no-show rate?" Focusing the topic to a question makes the project much more manageable.

Step 2. Consult the Literature/Subject Matter Experts

Full disclosure—depending on the topic this can be a time consuming task, and not all practice-based researchers hold this to be necessary. Dodd and Epstein

(2012) assert that, as reviewing the literature can be intimidating, practice-based researchers may choose to skip this step. There are definite pros and cons to this strategy. The obvious pro is that there will be less reading to do and this might save time and effort. The drawbacks fall into two categories: not being able to draw from the existing literature, and increased difficulties publishing your findings. Consulting the existing literature and knowledge base allows you to learn about what other people have found and to use that to inform your PBR. Advances in science tend to be incremental and, therefore, replicating academic research in your practice-based setting or extending someone else's findings are ideal prospects. Remember the letters' study? The authors had the intention of identifying and testing practical interventions to address the intake no-show problem. Consulting with the literature allowed them to identify a practical strategy to test out that had a high likelihood of producing the desired results—possibly saving copious amounts of time and heartache.

Briefly, it is important to note that skipping the literature review may make it more difficult to publish your results as a peer-reviewed article. A common problem with PBR is that it is already hard to publish (Cahill et al., 2010), which has resulted in low publication rates (Codd, 2016). As stated above, scientific innovation tends to be incremental, and peer-reviewers and journal editors will want you to connect any possible findings to the existing research by discussing the empirical support for the inquiry and how the findings relate back to the extant literature. If you hope to publish your results, then the literature review will be an important step, if you are sure this is not a priority then you may choose to not spend a lot of time on this step.

Traditionally, conducting literature reviews was a lengthy process that involved going to a university library and using a card catalog to identify articles and books to look up by hand. However, a number of recent advances have made this process much easier. An obvious barrier to the literature review process is not having access to an academic library or scholarly journals. So-called "paywalls" can make conducting a literature review a costly process. Some clinicians choose to teach a course at a local college or university so that they can have access to the academic library, while others seek out academic collaborators so that other team members on the project can be in charge of searching the literature; these may not be a practical or ideal solution for everyone. Another option is to use technological advances such as Google Scholar and RSS feeds (see Dubuque, 2011) to help track targets topics and identify desired articles. Purchasing a handful of targeted articles will be much cheaper than subscribing to a few journals. Some publishers are even starting to allow digital rentals of journal articles, and of course many textbooks can be accessed through your local library's interlibrary loan program.

A newer resource is the online community found at ResearchGate (*www.researchgate.net/*; see Thelwall & Kousha, 2015). ResearchGate is a social media site for researchers. It allows researchers from all over the world a forum to promote their published work, bank unpublished work, ask questions, and get support. Many also use it as a resource to circumvent "paywalls" by requesting courtesy digital copies of a desired article directly from the author.

If you don't know where to start, what to use, or where to look, ResearchGate is a great resource for you. There is a place to ask general questions and researchers who have conducted research on the topic can help point you in the right direction. Emphasizing function over form, the goal of a literature review is see what other folks have done to inform your line of inquiry. Best practice would involve a formal literature search and review; however, practice-based researchers who choose to skip that step may benefit from seeking consultation from other researchers via social networking sites like ResearchGate.

Step 3. Define the Research Question

This is a key step in the research process. Here is where you state exactly what you are interested in learning. For example, with the letters' study described earlier, they were broadly interested in reducing intake no-shows, but the research questions were much more specific than this; for example, "Will clients who receive an orientation letter have a higher show-rate than clients who do not receive a letter?" Defining the research question will make it a lot easier to design your study.

There are types of research questions that lend themselves well to PBR; namely descriptive, needs assessment, simple outcomes, association, between group differences, and prediction. A *Descriptive study* is one where you are seeking to understand things as they are. A research question in a descriptive study would look like, "What is our current rate of intake no-shows?" A descriptive study is a good first step in understanding a phenomenon. A *Needs Assessment* is an investigation into what is and what is desired. Research questions in a needs assessment may include, "What is the level of training for local mental health providers in a Cognitive Processing Therapy?" "What level of training would be commensurate with best-practices?" and "What will it take to get our clinicians trained to that level?" A research question in a *Simple Outcomes* study would inquire about current clinical, training, or administrative outcomes; for example, "What percentage of our clients demonstrates the expected response to treatment?" A research question in a study of *Association* looks at the relationship between factors; "What is the relation between symptom severity and premature termination?" Research questions relating to the studying of *Between Group Differences* are well exemplified in the letters' study example above. Studies of *Prediction* require more sophisticated research designs than association/correlational studies, but they still can be done in PBR settings; example questions would include, "Does a higher level of symptom severity at intake predict subsequent treatment dropout?" or "Do client satisfaction ratings from the first three sessions of treatment predict treatment response?" Conversely, there are types of research questions that do not lend themselves to well to PBR, namely studies of causation that are better studied in a highly controlled setting.

Step 4. Design the Study

The way the study is designed can impact both the ability to carry out the study (DeFife et al., 2015) and the ability to make meaningful inferences from the PBR (Cahill et al., 2010). Practical research designs for the aforementioned types of studies (i.e., descriptive, needs assessment, simple outcomes, association, between group differences, and prediction) will be elaborated below.

Types of Variables

Before discussing research design, it will be important review the types of variables.

Dependent Variable

The dependent variable is the variable of interest. In the example above, the dependent variable is the intake no-show rate. It is called the dependent variable because, in your study, it is hypothesized that it will be influenced, affected, or determined by the other variables.

Independent Variable

The independent variable is something that should be constant and it is hypothesized to have a relationship/effect on the dependent variable. In the example above, the independent variable would be whether the client received a letter and which type of letter they received.

Confounding Variable

The confounding, or extraneous variable, speaks to the host of other factors that could influence the dependent variable (outcome). Confounding variables can mediate or moderate the effects of the independent variable; for example, in the intake no-show study, possible confounds could be access to a reliable mailing address and client literacy, both of which could have had some bearing on the impact of the independent variable. Confounding variables could also be third variables that could have separate relationships with the dependent variable; for example, length of waiting period and appointment day and time might have an impact on the intake no-show rate. It is important that researchers try to anticipate and measure possible confounding factors so that they can try to use statistical methods to control/account for third variables.

Descriptive

When conducting a simple PBR study of descriptive, the distinction between types of variables is less important. You simply need to decide: what it is you want to know more about, how you want to measure/assess that, and what point(s) in time you want to measure/assess those variables.

Needs Assessment

A needs assessment is a type of program evaluation intended to help identify what specifically an agency/program needs. The first step in conducting a needs assessment is to determine what exactly you want to learn about your agency/program. Then you want to look at what existing sources of data already exist (e.g., are measures already included in intake packets or is there a course of treatment or length of treatment tracking program being used by the billing department). After seeing what data you already have, you'll want to gather new types of data to suit your needs; this may include surveys, open-response questions, likert questionnaires, tracking systems, etc.

Once you've gathered all your data, you'll want to analyze it. Preferred data analytic strategies will depend on what your goal was. For example, if your goal was to conduct a needs assessment to assess whether client treatment needs were met by current treatment options, you would want to look at frequency data for types of presenting problems, literature regarding preferred methods for treating those types of problems, and availability of those treatments in your setting. After you've analyzed your data, the final step is to do something with it to meet the needs you've identified.

Simple Outcomes

Assessing simple, clinical, administrative, or training outcomes can be done in a relatively straightforward manner. The main thing to be measured is your outcome variable (the dependent variable). Depending on your interests this could be symptom severity, turnover, competency attainment, etc. To increase the quality of your PBR it will help to measure and track other variables that might also have an impact on your outcome variable; this could include basic demographics or other factors thought to have a possible impact on what you are investigating.

A key step in measuring simple outcomes is deciding what time points you want to have measurements from; a minimum would be pre and post (before and after), and a better model includes the addition of mid-point and follow-up assessments. If you are tracking clinical outcomes then finding an outcome tracking measure that can be administered every session (see Beidas et al., 2015) will allow for a more nuanced look at treatment response.

Association

Cross-sectional studies look at the association or correlation between variables of interest. These types of studies include: identifying which potential association you are interested in studying, hypothesizing which variables you think might be correlated, measuring those variables, and correlating those values. The goal of PBR is typically to improve local practice; correspondingly, it will be important to identify potential correlations that are relevant to local practice. Asking yourself why you would care about a potential correlation or what that correlation would mean for local clinical practice can help determine the importance of the PBR.

Between Group Differences

Studies of between group differences build on the concept of simple outcomes. The outcome variable (dependent variable) will still be a clinical, administrative, or training outcome (e.g., symptom severity); however, the study design becomes more complex as you are looking at multiple levels for the independent variable of treatment condition or client group.

The key decision in these types of studies is how the different participants get routed to the different treatment conditions. Randomization, though a preferred method in the literature, is often thought to be unrealistic in practice-based settings (Cahill et al., 2010). In non-randomized between group trials, it is important to measure potential confounding variables at baseline so that individual differences and characteristics can be compared and contrasted to assess how similar the two treatment groups are.

Prediction

Studies of prediction/regression are more complicated than the other types described above, but they can still be done in practice-based settings. In a study of prediction, the predictors are the independent variables and the outcome variable (dependent variable) is what you are trying to predict. Predictors need to be measured at an earlier time point than the outcome so that a temporal relationship can be established. To help inform potential timelines, it can be helpful to first start with simple outcome tracking to see what happens session to session. If you can see where changes in the outcome variable are occurring you can look at those time points (and right before those time points) to help uncover important information about the predictors (e.g., ideal time points to measure). A note about prediction: It is really hard to predict things that have a low rate of occurrence, and predicting events that occur frequently may not be necessary—ideally, practice-based researchers seek to predict things that happen at a moderate frequency.

Other Considerations for Designing Your Study

Research Ethics

Another chapter in this volume will address the important ethical considerations such as respect for persons, beneficence, and justice (see Sales & Folkman, 2000). Key components to consider include: informed consent, opting out, multiple roles, benefits of participating, confidentiality, and privacy.

Tau vs. Tau + Innovation

If you are conducting research within the context of a clinical milieu (e.g., an inpatient or residential treatment facility), it is important to account for the context in which the clinical innovations you are testing occur. Typically, in these scenarios you are testing the additive benefits of the new intervention as opposed to treatment as usual (TAU). In these cases, it will be important to have a control or comparison TAU group so that you can compare the benefits of the standard treatment with the benefits of the standard treatment plus your innovation.

Instrument Selection

As described above, generally speaking there are four types of data (i.e., nominal, ordinal, interval, and ratio). You want to make sure that the manner in which you are gathering your data will allow you to employee your planned statistics. Gathering your data on continuous scales (e.g., likert scale, percentiles, symptom inventory scores, and frequency counts) will typically allow you the most options in what you can do. Continuous data can always be coded into categories (e.g., a continuous range of ages could be coded as 18 to 24, 25 to 34, etc) at a later time.

Time

There are a number of approaches to time in conducting a research study: archival, retrospective, cross-sectional, and prospective. Archival studies are those in which researchers use data captured for routine purposes and analyze it for research purposes. Advantages to this approach are that it takes advantage of already existing data and can be easier to get exempted from Institutional Review Boards. Disadvantages to archival data research are that the data is often poorly organized, missing, and not in formats that lend themselves well to sophisticated statistical analyses. Retrospective studies involve surveying people now about what happened to them in the past, and a major limitation to retrospective studies is that they rely on the unreliable memory and recall of participants. Cross-sectional studies involve analysis of data collected from a single point in time; this type of research design lends itself well to correlational studies. Prospective studies are the most difficult to do, but are considered to be the most desirable. This involves gathering data at multiple time points across a period of time.

Effect Sizes and Recruitment Targets

While a test of statistical significance is informative about whether actual between-group differences are observed, the effect size is informative to the magnitude (or meaningfulness) of that difference. The smaller the effect size, the more participants you need to be able to detect the finding. The number of participants you have will affect what types of analyses you can do, and the more complicated your study design the more participants you will need. In order to figure out how many participants you will ideally need, there are free calculators, such as *G*Power 3* (*www.gpower.hhu.de/en.html*; Faul, Erdfelder, Lang, & Buchner, 2007), that you can download. Notably, this type of analysis is rarely done in practice-based settings as it is typically the case that practice-based researchers make due with whatever number of participants they are able to identify.

Feasibility of RCTs in PBR

According to Dodd and Epstein (2012), randomized controlled trials (RCTs) are impractical and perhaps inconsistent with the idea of PBR. They assert that non-randomized (i.e., quasi-experimental) research design is the "gold-standard" of the PBR realm. As stated above, randomization to treatment and rigid adherence to treatment protocols may not be practical or desirable in practice-based settings.

Creating a Data Analysis Plan

Planning analysis you will do makes it easier to ensure you are collecting the right type of data. This part will only serve as a brief overview of basic statistics. For a more comprehensive review see one of several excellent resources; for example, Urdan's (2001) *Statistics in Plain English* is a great resource for the non-statistician. Notably, a number of statistical assumptions (e.g., linearity, normality, homoscedasticity) underlie these analyses and it is recommended that you consult with a more thorough statistical guide when conducting your analyses. Additionally, in this day and age there is a wealth of free statistical tutorials on YouTube (*www.youtube.com/*) that you may choose to peruse in your decision-making process.

Correlations

The simple correlation is straightforward and simple to do. This is a statistical analysis that examines the strength of the relation between two variables. When your plan is to conduct a correlation, the main thing to consider is the type of data that you use. While there are ways of correlating nominal and ordinal data it can be complicated for someone who is newer to statistical analyses. It is generally recommended to use variables that are on a continuous scale (e.g., a likert scale or total score from symptom inventory) when using these analyses.

Group Mean Differences

The t-tests and Analysis of Variance (ANOVA) can be used to measure the difference in group means (averages) on the outcome variable (dependent variable). You want the grouping variable to be categorical (e.g., letter or no letter) and then you want the outcome variable to be continuous. The t-test can be used when there are two groups (one independent variable with two levels) and the ANOVA is used when there are more than two levels on the independent variable. There are iterations of the ANOVA that are more complicated that involve multiple independent variables (Factorial ANOVA), multiple dependent variables (MANOVA), and means of controlling for covariates (ANCOVA); in general, it is recommended to first get some experience with the more basic analyses.

Regression

Regression equations are conceptually similar to a correlation in that they look at the relationship between independent and dependent variables, but the main aim of regression is prediction. Regression analysis is based on the general linear model, which will remind you of your high school algebra class. The basic idea is that you want to know how well the independent variable(s) predict the dependent variable. Simple linear regression will involve all continuous data. There are forms of regression (e.g., logistical regression) that can be used to predict a categorical variable (e.g., dropout or recovery).

Chi-Square

The chi-square (X^2) is one of the most popular nonparametric statistics—this is something you can use with categorical data. The chi-square analysis looks at goodness-of-fit between what would be expected and what is actually observed. You can also use this strategy to gauge differences in various demographic factors when using non-random assignment to see if the variation in demographic or other factors is more than would be expected.

Qualitative Research

As PBR is inductive in nature, qualitative research methods can be an ideal fit for the practice-based researcher. Within the realms of academic research, qualitative research has historically been viewed as a less-than methodology when compared to quantitative research; however, disciplines such as nursing and social work have maintained strong traditions in qualitative research. Learning to be a proficient qualitative researcher is a difficult and lengthy process and conducting qualitative research often demands much more time and attention than quantitative methods. There exists host of different methods and schools of thought within the field of qualitative research. Thematic Analysis is often suggested a good starting method to learn (see Braun & Clark, 2006 for a comprehensive description of how to conduct Thematic Analysis). Braun and Clark (2006) describe the phases of Thematic Analysis as being: (1) familiarizing yourself with the data, (2) generating initial codes, (3) searching for themes, (4) reviewing the themes, (5) defining and naming the themes, and (6) producing the report.

Step 5. Seek Consultation Feedback

Once you've defined the research question and determined how you will go about answering that question, be sure to take a moment to reflect on all the hard work you've done and why this matters to you. If this is something that really matters to you, it can be helpful to take on the mindset that anything that is worth doing, is worth doing right. This is why it is useful to see out consultation and feedback on your design. On the other hand, it's important to take all feedback and advice with a grain of salt—keeping in mind that you've likely spent more time looking into this and thinking into it than the advice giver. It is useful to talk with both clinical staff and other researchers to get their take. Clinical folks often have very useful observational/anecdotal accounts that are rich with great ideas and research folks can help make suggestions to improve the research design or suggest possible confounds you might not have anticipated. ResearchGate has an 'ask a question' feature that researchers from around the world use to ask questions about the research they are designing/conducting.

Step 6. Pilot/Proof of Concept

This next step requires some patience. The idea is to pilot your study on a small scale before conducting it on a large scale. If you have ever watched the popular television series *MythBusters* you will notice that they always conduct their study on a small scale first so they can prove the concept and refine their methodology. Piloting the study allows you to check the logistics of the design, see if any unanticipated events or factors are observed, and get a rough look at the possible effects you will observe with your study. It is risky to skip this step; for example, one study found that many participants didn't realize that items for the questionnaire were printed on both sides of the page and, consequently, much data was lost (Waltman et al., 2011)—something that could have easily been avoided had there been a pilot trial.

Step 7. Evaluate and Refine

There are a few questions to ask yourself when evaluating the pilot study. Did everything go as planned? Why or why not? Did anyone have any confusion with any of your forms? Does the data as you are gathering it lend itself to your data analysis plan? What happened that was unexpected? Contemplating questions similar to these can help to refine your research design.

Step 8. Conduct Study to Scale

After piloting and refining your study design, it is finally time to conduct your study to scale! Depending on your plan, this can be a relatively lengthy or brief process. The goal is to have everything planned out and troubleshooted before this step so that now you can simply focus on implementing the plan. However, almost nothing ever goes exactly as planned. The trick is to stay grounded and make the best of whatever happens. All learning is valuable. Document any deviations from the study design as they will be important to address in the interpretation and dissemination of your findings.

Step 9. Clean Data and Analyze Results

After you've finished collecting data, the next step is to create a database, clean your data, and analyze your results. Using a software program like Excel, SPSS, or

RedCap is recommended when creating a database. It is also important to note that manner in which the data is entered into the database matters. The preferred method is double entry (Barchard & Pace, 2011) where two separate people enter the same data to ensure it is accurately entered. Simply having another person visually verify the data entry can lead to dramatic increases in error rates, with one study finding a 2,958 percent increase in errors with visual verification as opposed to double entry (see Barchard & Pace, 2011). Errors matter because they create noise in the data which can make it harder to detect the effect you are studying.

Another common practice that is risky is entering the data directly into the database. It is really easy to accidentally overwrite/delete data. A preferred method is to use software like Microsoft Access, Google Forms, RedCap, Qualtrics, or even SurveyMonkey for your data entry; all of these methods will create a database with your entries. The hardest part of data analysis is creating a good database; once that is complete, using statistical analysis software like SPSS, SAS, or Stata is relatively straightforward depending on how familiar you are with the software package. Consulting with manuals, online tutorials, and statistical experts is generally recommended when learning or using an analysis that is new to you.

Step 10. Interpret Results in Light of Extant Literature

The question to ask yourself is: what are the implications of your findings? Have you extended or clarified previous findings? Have you failed to replicate someone else's findings? What was your specific research question? How do your findings answer that question? How do your findings relate to the literature that you reviewed?

Step 11. Disseminate your Findings

Traditionally, PBR has been difficult get published (Cahill et al., 2010) owing to poor internal and external validity—this makes it hard to have confidence in the conclusions of the study and producing difficulty generalizing those findings to other settings. There are two strategies to overcome these barrier: (1) as much as possible control for threats to internal and external validity with the study design; and (2) choose venues most similar to your population or setting to disseminate your findings. Poster presentations at conferences are a great venue for the practice-based researcher seeking to gain experience disseminating findings. Publishing research papers can be an exciting/excruciating process. Researchers are encouraged to be wary of predatory open-access/pay-to-publish journals. Asking the ResearchGate community about the reputation of a journal is prudent.

In Closing

Conducting research in a practice-based setting can be both challenging and rewarding, with the added bonus of potentially improving local practice. At first glance, this practice may seem daunting, but it is actually a lot of small, doable steps. The trick is to use self-practice, self-compassion, and self-reinforcement to help yourself stay engaged with the process.

References

Barchard, K. A. & Pace, L. A. (2011). Preventing human error: The impact of data entry methods on data accuracy and statistical results. *Computers in Human Behavior, 27*(5), 1834–1839.

Beidas, R. S., Stewart, R. E., Walsh, L., Lucas, S., Downey, M. M., Jackson, K., . . . Mandell, D. S. (2015). Free, brief, and validated: Standardized instruments for low-resource mental health settings. *Cognitive and Behavioral Practice, 22*(1), 5–19.

Bonezzi, A., Brendl, C. M., & Angelis, M. D. (2011). Stuck in the middle: The psychophysics of goal pursuit. *Psychological Science, 22*(5), 607–612.

Braun, V. & Clarke, V. (2006). Using thematic analysis in psychology. *Qualitative Research in Psychology, 3*(2), 77–101.

Brown, B. (2012). *Daring greatly: How the courage to be vulnerable transforms the way we live, love, parent, and lead.* New York: Gotham Books.

Cahill, J., Barkham, M., & Stiles, W. B. (2010). Systematic review of practice-based research on psychological therapies in routine clinic settings. *British Journal of Clinical Psychology, 49*(4), 421–453.

Campbell, D. T. & Stanley, J. C. (1966). *Experimental and quasi-experimental designs for research.* Chicago, IL: Rand McNally.

Codd, III, T. R. (2016). How to develop a robust practice-based research repertoire. *The Behavior Therapist, 39*(4), 118–120.

Crawford, S. & Stucki, L. (1990). Peer review and the changing research record. *Journal of the American Society for Information Science, 41*, 223–228.

Creed, T. A., German, R., Frankel, S., Green, K., Jager-Hyman, S., Pontoski, K., . . . Beck, A. T. (2016). Implementation of transdiagnostic Cognitive Therapy in Community Behavioral Health: The Beck Community Initiative. *Journal of Consulting and Clinical Psychology, 84*(12), 1116–1126.

Defife, J., Drill, R., Beinashowitz, J., Ballantyne, L., Plant, D., Smith-Hansen, L., . . . Nakash, O. (2015). Practice-based psychotherapy research in a public health setting: Obstacles and opportunities. *Journal of Psychotherapy Integration, 25*(4), 299–312.

Dennhag, I., Gibbons, M. B. C., Barber, J. P., Gallop, R., & Crits-Christoph, P. (2012). Do supervisors and independent judges agree on evaluations of therapists' adherence and competence? *Psychotherapy Research, 22*(6), 720–730.

Dodd, S. & Epstein, I. (2012). *Practice-based research in social work: A guide for reluctant researchers.* London: Routledge.

Dubuque, E. M. (2011). Automating academic literature searches with RSS feeds and Google Reader™. *Behavior Analysis in Practice, 4*(1), 63–69.

Faul, F., Erdfelder, E., Lang, A., & Buchner, A. (2007). G*Power 3: A flexible statistical power analysis program for the social, behavioral, and biomedical sciences. *Behavior Research Methods, 39*(2), 175–191.

Garcia, H. A., McGeary, C. A., Finley, E. P., Ketchum, N. S., McGeary, D. D., & Peterson, A. L. (2015). Evidence-based treatments for PTSD and VHA provider burnout: The impact of Cognitive Processing and Prolonged Exposure Therapies. *Traumatology, 21*(1), 7–13.

Harkin, B., Webb, T. L., Chang, B. P., Prestwich, A., Conner, M., Kellar, I., ... Sheeran, P. (2016). Does monitoring goal progress promote goal attainment? A meta-analysis of the experimental evidence. *Psychological Bulletin, 142*(2), 198–229.

Hayes, S. C. & Smith, S. X. (2005). *Get out of your mind & into your life: The new acceptance & commitment therapy.* Oakland, CA: New Harbinger Publications.

Jones, H. E. & Spiegelhalter, D. J. (2009). Accounting for regression-to-the-mean in tests for recent changes in institutional performance: Analysis and power. *Statistics in Medicine, 28*(12), 1645–1667.

Kroenke, K. S., Spitzer, R. L., & Williams, J. B. (2001). The PHQ-9: Validity of a brief depression severity measure. *Journal of General Internal Medicine, 16*, 606–613.

Maslach, C., Schaufeli, W. B., & Leiter, M. P. (2001). Job burnout. *Annual Review of Psychology, 52*, 397–422.

Pannucci, C. J. & Wilkins, E. G. (2010). Identifying and avoiding bias in research. *Plastic and Reconstructive Surgery, 126*(2), 619–625.

Sales, B. D. & Folkman, S. (2000). *Ethics in research with human participants.* Washington, D.C.: American Psychological Association.

Spies, R. A., Carlson, J. F., & Geisinger, K. F. (2010). *The eighteenth mental measurements yearbook.* Lincoln, NE: Buros Institute of Mental Measurements.

Thelwall, M. & Kousha, K. (2015). ResearchGate: Disseminating, communicating, and measuring scholarship? *Journal of the Association for Information Science and Technology, 66*, 876–889.

Urdan, T. C. (2001). *Statistics in plain English.* Mahwah, NJ: Lawrence Erlbaum Association.

Waltman, S. H., Hetrick, H., & Tasker, T. (2012). Designing, implementing, and evaluating a group therapy for underserved populations. *Residential Treatment for Children & Youth, 29*(4), 305–323.

Waltman, S. H., Rex, K. H., & Williams, A. (2011). Naturalistic examination of a training clinic: Is there a relationship between therapist perception and client self-report of treatment outcome? *Graduate Student Journal of Psychology, 13*, 17–24.

Westfall, J. M., Mold, J., & Fagnan, L. (2007). Practice-based research — "Blue Highways" on the NIH roadmap. *JAMA, 297*(4), 403–406.

Wierzbicki, M. & Pekarik, G. (1993). A meta-analysis of psychotherapy dropout. *Professional Psychology: Research and Practice, 24*(2), 190–195.

Williston, M. A., Block-Lerner, J., Wolanin, A., & Gardner, F. (2014). Brief acceptance based intervention for increasing intake attendance at a community mental health center. *Psychological Services, 11*(3), 324–332.

CHAPTER 4

Single-Case Research Designs in Clinical Practice Settings

R. Trent Codd, III

Introduction

Scientific activity in the mental health professions can be categorized into two distinct approaches: one involving a focus on the discovery of individual behavioral processes and one involving actuarial science (Branch & Pennypacker, 2013). For the most part, research methods and, consequently, research activity in the mental health professions have emphasized actuarial pursuits while simultaneously de-emphasizing the empirical examination of the individual.

The dominance of actuarial methods is problematic for several reasons. First, the subject matter of the clinical mental health professions involves individuals, not groups, because clinicians work with individual clients. Thus, group-based research methods produce data that are generally unhelpful in a clinical context. For example, actuarial data might reveal risk factors for suicidal behavior—organized at the group level—such as by demographic or clinical characteristics, however, most persons with membership in these high-risk groups will not die by suicide. A common clinical task is to ascertain whether an individual client will engage in suicidal behavior, and this type of group-level data does not adequately assist in such determinations.

This is not to suggest that data produced by group designs are of no use to mental health professionals; indeed, they are beneficial when asking certain types of questions including those involving the large-scale delivery of a psychological intervention. They can answer important questions including how much better is a particular intervention compared to some other condition, for how many individuals is an intervention superior, and what characteristics predict certain outcomes?

These kinds of questions, however, are not most pertinent in routine clinical practice where a clinician must determine which clinical interventions will be most useful for a unique individual. Because of the clinician's primary task, it is this author's contention that group-based methods are of secondary interest to mental health professionals, while research methods appropriate to the study of an individual participant have the most relevance. It is a shame that many authors of research methods texts place group methods, most notably randomized trials, at the top of the hierarchy of research designs while generally placing individual-focused designs, such as single-case research designs, at the bottom (e.g., Balshem et al., 2011; Schulz, Altman & Moher, 2010).

This author contends that single-case research designs (SCRDs) are underused by most mental health professionals (though my contention is not unique, e.g., see Branch & Pennypacker, 2013) and thus, the focus of this chapter is to introduce the value of SCRDs for practice-based research. A comprehensive exposition on SCRDs is not pursued in this chapter, as it would exceed the intended purpose and has already been accomplished (see Resources for Further Reading below for key writing in this area). Rather, the purpose of this chapter is to inspire practice-based researchers to make greater use of SCRDs, especially with traditional psychotherapy clients. The chapter goals are accomplished by highlighting the weaknesses of group designs for our subject matter, which are often underappreciated, conveying the advantages of SCRDs for practice-based research, and dispelling myths about SCRDs. In addition, key SCRD characteristics and design types are introduced along with a brief review of relevant work published in the psychotherapy literature. The provision of example studies with psychotherapy clients is important because many published SCRD studies, and indeed many SCRD texts, describe investigations with clinical populations that differ from typical psychotherapy clients (i.e., the common practice of using examples of developmentally disabled populations). This unbalanced presentation of examples makes it difficult for researchers new to SCRDs to envision their application to psychotherapy clients.

Why Single-Case Research Designs?

Group designs, which have come to dominate research activity in the mental health professions, pose several problems for practitioners and the clients they serve. As noted previously the types of questions which may be pursued with these designs, along with their answers, have value in particular circumstances. However, the dominance of group designs obstructs the broader use of other designs which, in turn, thwarts the effective examination of other types of research questions. The general group-based approach involves drawing a sample from a population of interest and in turn making inferences about where that population's mean might be. When a practicing clinician consumes this type of research they must make an additional inference from the reported group data to unique individuals (i.e., their clients). Unfortunately, it is not possible to make such an inference based on this type of data. Yet making determinations about an individual's care is the most crucial task confronting clinicians.

Group designs, especially randomized trials, contain the additional disadvantages of being expensive, time consuming, and requiring large numbers of participants. These disadvantages present challenges to full-time researchers in academic settings where a greater infrastructure for negotiating these obstacles exists; the problem is compounded for the practice-based researcher where little such infrastructure is present.

SCRDs are advantageous to the mental health practitioner/researcher and circumvent many of the difficulties noted with group designs. For example, they require fewer participants and, thus, recruitment efforts are less burdensome. Also, there is no requirement to form a control group, which, if required, would entail withholding or delaying treatment for some participants. Further still, these designs are readily implemented in routine practice settings and are frequently used to drive individualized client treatment as a matter of standard evidence-based practice. One benefit of their compatibility with routine practice settings is less burden for clients who agree to research participation because SCRDs frequently do not fundamentally change a client's usual care experience. This reduced burden should also increase recruitment.

There are many other advantages to SCRDs. First, they are more cost effective relative to group designs. The need for fewer participants, which has already been mentioned, translates into an additional advantage of requiring less research staff (e.g., less personnel needed to consent participants). It also confers the advantage of affording empirical examination of clinical presentations with low prevalence because there may be insufficient numbers of participants to fulfill the requirements of group designs. Second, SCRDs are applicable to a wide range of research questions. Third, data interpretation does not require extensive training in statistical analysis as visual analyses are most frequently used. The final, and perhaps most important, advantage of SCRDs is that they are constructed to evaluate the types of research questions most pertinent to clinicians (discussed in more detail below).

SCRDs also have many advantages in terms of routine clinical care, especially for the evidence-based practitioner. However, these advantages and applications are not the focus of this chapter (interested readers are referred to Hayes, 1981 & Hayes, Barlow, & Nelson-Gray, 1999). Instead this chapter's focus is on the value of SCRDs in the production of generalizable outcomes for the purposes of contributing to the research literature.

Single-Case Research Design Myths

To fully appreciate the value of SCRDs, several long-standing myths regarding these designs must first be discussed. The three most prominent myths are dispelled below. These myths are that SCRDs are synonymous with case studies, that they are low in generalizability, and that they are weak with respect to controlling for threats to internal validity.

Myth One: SCRDs are the Same Thing as Case Studies

A case study is a research method that typically involves a detailed narrative description of an individual case without the manipulation of any variables. Because they are purely descriptive and do not manipulate variables in a systematic way, they are unable to specify associative or cause-effect relationships. That is, case studies cannot demonstrate experimental control. They are frequently confused with SCRDs because of their focus on individual participants, however, case studies and SCRDs differ substantially with respect to methodological power, as SCRDs can document cause-effect relationships between important variables. SCRDs retain the phrase "single-case" in their name because they examine participants one at a time. The manner in which this is accomplished differs by SCRD type and is detailed later in the chapter.

Myth Two: SCRDs are Low in Generalizability

One consequence of the domination of group designs in mental health research has been the gradual restriction of the term "generalization" of research data to solely mean generalizing at an actuarial level. This linguistic constraint has led to several unfortunate consequences. New researchers are socialized to the concept as the only type and/or the only important type of generalization in mental health research. Because generality is an important quality of research data, researchers– neophyte and experienced alike—pursue research questions with designs they believe capable of producing data of this kind (i.e., group designs). Because SCRDs are increasingly perceived is incapable of producing generalizable data, they are not frequently pursued. Unfortunately, this perspective also appears to be held by many institutional review boards (IRBs) in the United States. Survey research reveals many IRBs do not consider these designs to meet the definition of human subjects research, with several such IRBs implementing policies formalizing their positions that SCRD studies do not constitute research and therefore do not require IRB review (Cen et al., 2016). However, there are many types of generality and actuarial generalization is, in this author's view, the least important to the practicing clinician.

SCRDs efficiently produce generality at the individual participant level, the most important type of generality to the applied practitioner. Many mental health researchers suggest that SCRDs should be limited to restricted circumstances (Nock, Janis & Wedig, 2007), such as a building block to a larger group design approach, but this author contends that the reverse should be implemented (see Codd, 2017 for a discussion of this point). To understand the power of SCRDs to produce data high in individual participant validity, some of the designs key features must first be discussed (see below).

Myth Three: SCRDs Don't Adequately Control for Threats to Internal Validity

Most SCRDs are experimental designs. Thus, they must adequately address external validity concerns (described previously) as well as threats to internal validity. To illustrate the power of SCRDs, the manner in which they protect against threats to internal validity are now discussed.

Overall, internal validity threats are addressed through the logical features of each design and replication of effects. The power of replication can most readily be seen with an examination of the ABA design. This design involves alternating between baseline (A) and intervention phases (B) and replication is observed across phases. For example, assuming that an effect is present, once a stable pattern of data is observed during the baseline phase, one would see a clear change in the data pattern once the intervention was implemented, and then once again see a change in the pattern back to what was observed during the baseline condition when the intervention is withdrawn. Thus, with a single participant, at least two replications of the effect would be observed. It's customary for studies making use of ABA designs to include at least three participants so, assuming this minimum, one would observe six replications of the effect, two for each participant. There is one additional method by which replication is demonstrated in these designs. Multiple measurements are taken during each phase with each instance of measurement also being an attempt at replication. There is no theoretical limit to the number of phases a researcher might pursue (e.g., ABABAB) with each additional phase demonstrating additional replications of the effect. Moving in the opposite direction with fewer phases, such as that found in the A-B design, however, does not include sufficient opportunity for repetition of effects to adequately rule out other causal variables that might be impacting the dependent variable (DV) beyond the independent variable (IV). The multiple baseline design demonstrates replication across the various behaviors (or processes), settings or participants considered in the experiment, while the alternating treatments designs demonstrates replication through the exchanging of interventions.

Specific SCRD Internal Validity Threats

Specific threats to internal validity and how they are controlled for in SCRDs are (Kratochwill et al., 2010):

1) Ambiguous temporal precedence. This threat concerns the sequence of cause and effect. Temporal precedence is demonstrated through systematic manipulation of the IV within SCRDs. The ABA design also most clearly demonstrates how this is accomplished. In this design, the IV is not manipulated until the B phase and then not manipulated again (i.e., withdrawn) until the second A phase. Everything else is held constant across all phases. Of course, the more phase repetitions present in an experiment the clearer the temporal sequence of cause and effect is.
2) Selection. Systematic differences in participant characteristics threaten internal validity if such differences play a role in an observed effect. This threat is attenuated by using the participant as their own control and by exposing the participant to all experimental phases.
3) History. This threat to internal validity is realized when events coincide with the intervention and thus could be the cause of any observed effects. The primary method by which the SCRD researcher protects against this threat is through replication because more replications of the effect reduce the likelihood that events are occurring at the same time as IV manipulations.

4) Maturation. Natural changes occur that can result in changes in the DV. To protect against this internal validity threat, the design must tease out the effects of natural transformations relative to the intervention being evaluated. This is accomplished through multiple demonstrations of the effect at several different time points. Best practice requires at least three of each (i.e., demonstrations & time points) to be confident that this threat has been sufficiently addressed.
5) Statistical regression. This threat occurs when extreme scores are revealed during initial measurement and subsequently change to less extreme scores (i.e., regression to the mean) during subsequent measurement periods. The change in scores, then, is not due to the intervention, but rather this well-known statistical phenomenon. SCRDs control for this threat, like many other internal validity threats, through its core feature of repeated measurement because this technique affords close examination of characteristics of the data under the varying conditions.
6) Attrition. Participant dropout is significant when one is concerned about threats to internal validity. This is addressed by including at least five measurement periods within a phase and at least three phase repetitions (Kratochwill, 2010).
7) Testing. This threat to internal validity occurs when the cause of observed effects is participant exposure to a test during measurement periods. The primary strategy for addressing this concern is repeated assessment of the DV because it enables the researcher to diagnose the presence of a testing validity threat.
8) Instrumentation. When features of a measure change in some way, these changes can produce effects that can be confounded with the evaluated intervention. Several methods are used to protect against this threat. One of the primary methods involves the use of consistent assessment methods with multiple persons measuring the DV with high degrees of interobserver reliability.
9) Interactive effects. This threat refers to the interaction of two or more internal validity threats. The primary method of protection is the implementation of features that protect against the singly described internal threats to validity (However, the interested reader is referred to Kratochwill, 2010 for further discussion and relevant recommended reading).

Single-Case Research Designs: Key features

Single-case research designs are referred to by various terms, including: single-subject design, n-of-1 trials, time series designs and case studies (incorrectly labeled as such, as noted previously). This non-comprehensive listing of terms, save for "case study," are largely synonymous and generally include the features detailed below.

One Participant is Examined at a Time

It is customary to include more than one participant in a SCRD study, but regardless of the SCRD type or the number of total participants, each participant is observed one at a time. Importantly, each participant serves as their own basis of comparison and, therefore, as their own control. This contrasts with the need in group designs to construct a control group that is roughly equal to a treatment group across many important characteristics.

Visual Analysis of Data is Emphasized

Proponents of group designs stress quantitative analyses of data. In contrast, SCRD researchers de-emphasize statistical procedures, instead preferring visual data analysis based on graphical data displays. The reliance on visual analysis to the exclusion of statistical methods has been the basis of some criticism of these designs and continues to be the subject of debate (the finer points of this debate exceed the scope of this chapter, but the interested reader is referred to Kratochwill and Levin (2014), especially Chapter 3 in that volume). The SCRD researcher believes that if quantitative procedures are necessary to discriminate an effect, then the effect is not robust as any strong effect would be captured by visual inspection of the data. Importantly, empirical examination indicates that researchers can be trained to visually analyze data with reliability and validity (Wolfe & Slocum, 2015).

Variables are Continuously Measured

An individual participant in an SCRD is observed continuously, while relevant variables are measured, rather than at discrete time points. This is notable because discontinuous measurement procedures are less sensitive to changes in critical variables.

Replication is Emphasized

Group designs can only replicate an effect once per experiment. This process can become unwieldy considering the length of time required to complete group experiments. SCRDs, in contrast, can demonstrate many replications of a treatment effect within and across individuals in a single experiment. The ability to replicate is more than just an advantage of these designs, it's a core feature of the design logic: if one can hold everything constant while simultaneously making changes in a single variable, many different times, one can be confident that they are demonstrating a powerful effect.

Stable Baseline

In most circumstances, the SCRD researcher takes baseline data and does not proceed to independent variable manipulation until stability in the baseline is observed. The recording of stable baseline data provides the basis for comparison. In clinical practice, this can present some ethical challenges as one would not withhold treatment from a suffering client while awaiting stability in their baseline data. However, several methods exist for circumventing this difficulty. For example, one might ask a psychotherapy client to begin data collection in advance of an initial appointment (e.g., measures can be emailed/mailed to the client along with intake paperwork) or between an intake appointment and the first treatment session, commonly one week apart. If the client is unable to make it in for various reasons (e.g., illness or a scheduling conflict) the baseline data collection period is naturally extended. Another strategy is for the most pressing issue to be addressed clinically while measurement can be initiated for other clinical concerns. When awaiting a stable baseline is ethically contraindicated, the PBR researcher should exercise flexibility and look for opportunities such as these to take baseline data.

Single-Case Research Design types

Many types of SCRDs exist and the selection of design should be determined by the research objective. A comprehensive review of these designs is beyond the scope of this chapter, but the reader is encouraged to pursue the recommended reading listed below, located under "Resources for further reading." The emphasis in this chapter is on three types of SCRDs that are particularly amenable to practice-based psychotherapy research. The present emphasis on a subset of SCRDs is not meant to suggest that other SCRD types lack relevance to psychotherapy research. Rather, space limitations necessitate a more focused discussion on fewer designs. As each design is introduced, a few studies exemplifying the execution of that design are provided. The reader is encouraged to retrieve and review these studies in detail for further study and mastery of the material.

A-B Designs

The A-B design is the simplest to execute in the practice environment, however, its simplicity comes at a cost with the design's inability to demonstrate experimental control. Nonetheless, it produces meaningful data. This design involves two phases: baseline (A) and treatment (B). The baseline phase involves continuous measurement of the dependent variable which endures until the data achieve stability. Once a stable pattern emerges in the data, the treatment phase is initiated, which involves the implementation of the treatment while maintaining the measurement procedures. The difference in the data pattern between the A and B phases, if any, hint at a possible relationship between the independent and dependent variables. It is not possible to rule out the impact of variables other than the treatment in any observed changes in the dependent variable, because this would require at least one additional phase involving a return to baseline conditions, known as an ABA design. The return to baseline involves the removal of the treatment and, as such, involves a type of replication. If the treatment is responsible for changes in the dependent variable then one should see clear changes in the data as the treatment is imposed and removed. However, there are many circumstances where a return to baseline is not possible. The most notable reason involves ethical constraints such as circumstances where removal of an intervention might result in a return in self-injurious behavior. Another example involves the use of treatment interventions whose effects cannot be removed. For example, consider a successful cognitive restructuring procedure resulting in substantial belief change. Withholding further use of this procedure is unlikely to result in the participant's belief reverting back to baseline levels of believability. In circumstances such as these, the A-B design is a worthy alternative.

Codd, Twohig, Crosby and Enno (2011) used an A-B design with three consecutive referrals seeking treatment for anxiety disorders in a private practice setting. They evaluated Acceptance and Commitment Therapy (ACT) as a unified treatment protocol for these three clients who presented with panic disorder with agoraphobia, comorbid social phobia and generalized anxiety disorder, and posttraumatic stress disorder. In addition, they did not use in-session exposure therapy because that was an already well-established treatment procedure for anxiety disorders, and their interest was in examining ACT-specific processes and this exclusion was necessary to remove potential confounding effects. All three clients responded favorably to the treatment at post-treatment with gains maintained at follow-up. This study is notable because it 1) was conducted in the natural setting with "real" clients, 2) was one of the first to demonstrate the transdiagnostic nature of ACT in that the same ACT protocol was effective with different anxiety disorder presentations and 3) because it showed that ACT works without the use of in-session exposure.

Alternating Treatments Design

Alternating treatments designs, also called multielement designs, have much to offer the practice-based psychotherapy researcher. These designs involve alternating between two or more interventions and then comparing them against each other. The alterations are generally made over a short time horizon with the order presented randomly. For example, the treatments might be alternated across days with different sessions occurring on the same day or within different segments of the same session. The random presentation is important because it controls for sequence effects. Other potential confounding variables, such as the individual(s) delivering the interventions, should similarly be held constant or randomly involved to minimize the influence of these variables in the observed data pattern. These designs are particularly useful at answering questions such as "which intervention or combinations of interventions will be most effective with this client?"

Alternating treatments designs (ATDs) provide a few advantages to the practice-based researcher, especially around difficulties with baseline data. First, they do not require a phase where stable baseline data, or any baseline data, must be taken prior to the evaluation of interventions (although baseline data is still advantageous if it is possible to obtain as this data can also be compared to each intervention condition). In a clinical context, this means that treatment can be initiated more quickly. Rapid onset of treatment initiation is often necessary in an applied setting because it is not ethical to prolong a client's suffering and because it is not always practical to defer active treatment for the time frames required for the establishment of a stable baseline. A second advantage is that it does not require the withdrawal of an active treatment. The removal of an effective treatment may not be ethical in many circumstances such as those involving self-injurious behavior. Third, some baseline data never become stable, impeding the implementation of other SCRDs. An ATD, however, does not require stable data, allowing the researcher confronted with this difficulty to make use of this design.

Although ATDs have many advantages they also have some limitations, the most notable of which is their susceptibility to multiple treatment interference. This occurs when the effects from two treatments are confounded. The remedy to this limitation is to include a final phase which only includes the most effective treatment because this allows for the examination of that treatment delivered in isolation. Another limitation is that there's a ceiling on the possible number of treatment comparisons before interpretation becomes unwieldly. Some published ATD studies have included up to five comparisons, but three is ideal with four recommended as the upper limit (Cooper, Heron & Heward, 2007).

Shingleton et al. (2016) used an alternating treatments design to evaluate the impact of adjunctive motivational text messages in the treatment of 12 persons with eating disorders characterized by high dietary restriction and restraint. Their primary outcomes of interest were level of kilocalorie intake and dietary restraint, neither of which were impacted by their eight-week protocol. However, they did determine that their intervention was acceptable among their sample and that it did positively impact aspects of participant motivation.

Maitland and Gaynor (2016) compared Functional Analytic Psychotherapy (FAP) against supportive psychotherapy to evaluate several hypotheses derived from FAP's theorized mechanisms of action. Thirteen participants who self-reported difficulties with interpersonal relating, received six to ten weekly psychotherapy sessions (all were offered ten sessions). Each session was randomized to FAP or supportive listening (SL), with the following restrictions applied: the first session was SL, the last FAP, and no more than two consecutive sessions of the same treatment could occur. Sessions were coded for adherence to the prescribed condition. They evaluated their data with visual inspection and quantitative methods and found they were consistent with their FAP-generated hypotheses.

Multiple-baseline Design

There are several types of multiple-baseline designs. These include multiple-baseline across behaviors, clients, and settings. Multiple-baseline across behavior designs evaluate the same client, but evaluate the impact of interventions across different non-correlated clinically relevant behaviors. Typically, overt behaviors are examined, but one could also examine different psychological processes. The multiple-baseline across clients involves a focus on the same intervention but across similar clients (e.g., those with a particular disorder). Finally, multiple-baseline across settings involve the evaluation of an intervention to an individual client, but in different environments.

The general process begins by initiating measurement of the dependent variable for all participants concurrently and continuing this measurement throughout the study period. Baseline measurement continues until the data are stable for the first participant (or behavior/setting), at which point the intervention is delivered to them while holding everything else constant for all other participants (or behaviors/settings). This continues until stability is achieved for the first participant (or behavior/setting) under the intervention condition at which point the intervention is then applied to the next participant (or behavior/setting). This continues across all remaining participants (or behaviors/settings). This design is particularly useful when behavior is irreversible or when it would be unethical to reverse it.

Tolin et al. (2009) implemented a multiple baseline to assess the utility of daily cognitive-behavioral therapy for school refusal behavior. Four adolescent participants were included in the study and a 15-session flexible protocol implemented. The flexible nature of the protocol allowed individualization with respect to the function of each participant's school refusal behavior. The primary outcome of interest was daily school attendance, but they also measured functional impairment and global impressions of improvement using standardized assessments at pre- and post-treatment as well as at three-year follow-up. The baseline periods were achieved because of the natural variability in therapist availability and scheduling. All four participants showed improvement in the primary outcome of interest—school attendance—during the treatment phase relative to baseline during the short-term. The improvement for three of the four participants was significant whereas one participant only realized moderate improvement. Unfortunately, the long-term results were not as impressive. While three out of four participants showed meaningful improvement in school attendance at follow-up, none sustained 100 percent attendance. One participant was lost to follow-up and the remaining three participants had all pursued alternative education options (e.g., night school, GED). This study is worthy of examination because it shows the implementation of multiple baseline without purposely withholding treatment while waiting for a stable baseline; they took advantage of natural clinical environmental factors (e.g., scheduling factors) while data was being collected for this purpose. In addition, they were able to implement a flexible protocol allowing for individualization of treatment for each participant.

Recognizing the important role of shame in contributing to, as well as maintaining PTSD, Au et al. (2017) investigated a compassion-based therapy targeted at shame in traumatized individuals. They used a randomized, non-concurrent multiple-baseline across participants to evaluate a six-week intervention in ten adults and found nine of the ten participants realized decreases in PTSD symptom severity and eight of the ten participants demonstrated meaningful reductions in shame.

Eilers and Hayes (2015) conducted two experiments, the first of which used a non-concurrent multiple baseline across participants,[1] to evaluate cognitive defusion and exposure in the reduction of problem behavior in three participants with autism spectrum disorder. They found a reduction in problem behavior for all three participants as a result of their intervention, which was maintained at three-month follow-up. They conducted a second follow-up experiment using an alternating treatments design. In this follow-up study, they compared defusion and exposure to a control exercise and exposure condition with four ASD participants. They found that cognitive defusion exercises can enhance the effects of exposure in the examined context.

Kanter et al. (2006) used an A/A+B design. This is a type of A-B design in which the B phase is made up of two components: the intervention present during the A phase and the one introduced during the B phase. This a useful study to examine because they overcame the frequent ethical concern of waiting on a stable baseline in clinical practice. They negotiated this concern by delivering an empirically-supported treatment during the baseline phase that did not overlap with their targets of interest. More specifically, they were interested in evaluating functional analytic psychotherapy (FAP) for major depressive disorder, which primarily targets interpersonal repertoire deficits. Thus, they delivered cognitive behavioral therapy, a best practice, during the baseline phase.

In a follow-up study Landes et al., (2013) also used an A/A+B design to further isolate and evaluate the theorized active components of FAP. In particular, they were interested in disentangling the effects of individual components including the therapeutic relationship. That is, they evaluated the impact of general therapeutic relationship-building skills, which are part of FAP and other psychotherapies, and whether they could be enhanced by the addition of specific FAP mechanisms. During the A phase they only included relationship-building interventions and did not add FAP-specific mechanisms to these interventions until the B phase. This controlled for the effects of the therapeutic relationship.

Basic Procedural Steps in SCRD Implementation

Step One: Start With the Dependent Variable (DV) of Interest

It is important that the selection of SCRD occurs after the dependent variables are determined (Horner & Odom, 2014). Many clinicians make the error of first selecting a SCRD and then working to make everything fit their design. But each design is a different tool designed for a different job. Selecting a DV as a first step should inform one of the ideal design to pursue.

Ideally, dependent variables should be assessed via the use of behavioral measures rather than paper-pencil measures that are based on classical test theory, because the latter are further removed from behavior. However, one can make use of such measures in SCRDs. Many clinician-researchers make use of process measures such as the acceptance and action questionnaire-II (Bond et al., 2011) and the automatic thoughts questionnaire (Hollon & Kendall, 1980).

Dependent variables selected for measurement should ideally be frequent in occurrence, should generally be able to achieve a stable pattern without intervention and should be formulated in such a way that a high degree of interrater reliability is afforded.

Step 2: Determine Design Type and Begin Continuous Measurement

Continuous measurement of the dependent variable should be initiated at the beginning of the study and not cease until its completion. Generally, the initial focus is to solely observe the data until they achieve stability. The minimally accepted number of data points necessary to establish a pattern is three, but ideally five or more are collected (Kratochwill, 2010). Alternating treatments designs are an exception because they do not require that a stable baseline be established.

Step 3: Continue Implementation of the Logic Dictated by the Selected Design Type

The logic of the design selected dictates the next step. For example, if implementing an ABA design the IV is varied after a stable baseline is established. This is sustained until the data reorganize, with stability, in the new condition. Once consistent responding is observed the IV is withdrawn. Continuous measurement of the DV is maintained across all phases of the experiment.

Step 4: Graph and Analyze your Data

Graphing and analyzing data begins concurrently with the onset of DV measurement procedures because this material informs the researcher in the systematic manipulation of the IV. However, once the study is complete a final analysis is rendered on the entire visually-displayed data set.

Developing Competence in SCRDs

Several steps are recommended for developing competence in the use of these designs. These steps are:

1) Consume comprehensive foundational SCRD texts and articles. Recommendations in this regard are provided below under "Resources for further reading."
2) Read as many published articles that make use of SCRDs with your populations of interest as possible. Journals that routinely publish SCRD studies are listed in the resource section below. Conduct a literature search to reveal other pertinent articles.
3) Seek research consultation and begin designing experiments. A list of research consultants is available in the appendix.
4) Read Codd (2016) for behavioral strategies pertaining to research repertoire development.

Conclusion

Single-case research designs (SCRDs) have much to offer the practice-based researcher, yet their use is not optimized. Several factors are responsible for their underuse including the heavy emphasis on actuarial methods within the mental health professions and widespread inadequate understanding of their experimental power, especially in relation to randomized trials. In this chapter, the relative strengths and weaknesses of group- and individual-focused designs were discussed and the value of SCRDs for practice-based research emphasized. Then basic SCRD features and design types were introduced. Finally, a basic path for acquiring competence in SCRDs was offered.

Note

1. This variant of the multiple baseline design is used when simultaneous observations of multiple participants is not practical. See Watson and Workman (1981).

Resources for Further Reading

Issues Pertaining to Generality

Branch, M. N. & Pennypacker, H. S. (2013). Generality and generalization of research findings. In G. J. Madden (Ed.) *APA Handbook of Behavior Analysis, Vol. 1*, Washington DC: APA Publications, pp. 151–175.

Codd, III, R. T. (2017). Protecting the Scientific Lexical Canon. *the Behavior Therapist*, 40(5), 185–191.

Wasserstein, R. L. & Lazar, N. A. (2016). The ASA's statement on p-values: Context, process, and purpose, *The American Statistician*, 70(2), 129–133.

Single-Case Research Designs

Kazdin, A. E. (2011). *Single-case research designs: Methods for clinical and applied settings.* Oxford University Press.

Smith, P. L. & Little, D. R. (2018). Small is beautiful: In defense of the small-N design. *Psychonomic Bulletin & Review*, 1–19.

For Acquiring SCRD Competence

Codd, III, R. T. (2016). How to develop a robust practice-based research repertoire. *the Behavior Therapist*, 39(4), 118–120.

On the Limitations of Between-Groups Studies

Abraham, N. S., Byrne, C. J., Young, J. M., & Solomon, M. J. (2010). Meta-analysis of well-designed nonrandomized comparative studies of surgical procedures is as good as randomized controlled trials. *Journal of Clinical Epidemiology*, 63, 238–245.

Concato, J., Shah, N. & Horwitz, R. I. (2013). Randomized controlled trials, observational studies, and the hierarchy of research designs. *New England Journal of Medicine, 342*, 1887–1892.

Goodman, C. (2009). *Comparative effectiveness research and personalized medicine: From contradiction to synergy.* The Lewin Group Center for Comparative Effectiveness Research.

Grove, A. (2011). Rethinking clinical trials. *Science, 333*, 1679.

Guyatt, G. H., Haynes, R. B., Jaeschke, R. Z., Cook, D. J., Green, L., Naylor, C., Wilson, M. C., & Richardson, W. S. (2000). Users' guide to the medical literature: XXV. Evidence-based medicine: Principles for applying the users' guides to patient care. *Journal of the American Medical Association, 284*(10), 1290–1296.

Guyatt, G., Sackett. D., Adachi, J., Roberts, R., Chong, J., Rosenbloom, D., & Keller, J. (1988). A clinician's guide for conducting randomized trials in individual patients. *Canadian Medical Association Journal, 139*, 497–503.

Janosky, J. E. (2005). Use of the single subject design for practice based primary care research. *Postgraduate Medical Journal, 81*, 549–551.

Keenan, M. & Dillenburger, K. (2011). When all you have is a hammer ... RCTs and hegemony in science. *Research in Autism Spectrum Disorders, 5*, 1–13.

Larson, E. B. (1990). N-of-1 clinical trials: A technique for improving medical therapeutics. *Western Journal of Medicine, 152*, 52–56.

Morgan, D. L. & Morgan, R. K. (2001). Single-participant research design: Bringing science to managed care. *American Psychologist, 56*, 119–127.

Potts, M., Prata, N., Walsh, J., & Grossman, A. (2006). Parachute approach to evidence based medicine. *British Medical Journal, 333*, 701–703.

Powers, S. C., Piazza-Waggoner, C., Jones, J. S., Ferguson, K. S., Daines, C., & Acton, J. D. (2006). Examining clinical trial results with single-subject analysis: An example involving behavioral and nutrition treatment for young children with cystic fibrosis. *Journal of Pediatric Psychology, 31*, 574–581.

Reichow, B., Volkmar, F. R., & Cicchetti, D. B. (2008). Development of the evaluative methods for evaluating and determining evidence-based practices in autism. *Journal of Autism and Developmental Disorders, 38*, 1311–1319.

Schork, N. J. (2015). Time for one-person trials. *Nature, 520*, 609–611.

Scuffham, P. A., Nikles, J., Mitchell, G. K., Yelland, M. J., Vine, N., Poulos, C., ... & Glasziou, P. (2010). Using N-of-1 trials to improve patient management and save costs. *Journal of General Internal Medicine, 25*(9), 906–913.

Journals that Routinely Publish SCRDs

This is not a comprehensive listing, but represent the primary outlets.

Behavior Modification
Behaviour Research and Therapy
Behavior Therapy
Behavioural and Cognitive Psychotherapy
Clinical Case Studies
Cognitive and Behavioral Practice
Journal of Contextual Behavioral Science
Journal of Applied Behavior Analysis
Journal of Behavioral Therapy and Experimental Psychiatry

References

Au, T. M., Sauer-Zavala, S., King, M. W., Petrocchi, N., Barlow, D. H., & Litz, B. T. (2017). Compassion-based therapy for trauma-related shame and posttraumatic stress: Initial evaluation using a multiple baseline design. *Behavior Therapy*, 48(2), 207–221.

Balshem, H., Helfand, M., Schünemann, H. J., Oxman, A. D., Kunz, R., Brozek, J., . . . & Guyatt, G. H. (2011). GRADE guidelines: 3. Rating the quality of evidence. *Journal of clinical epidemiology*, 64(4), 401–406.

Bond, F. W., Hayes, S. C., Baer, R. A., Carpenter, K. M., Guenole, N., Orcutt, H. K., . . . & Zettle, R. D. (2011). Preliminary psychometric properties of the Acceptance and Action Questionnaire–II: A revised measure of psychological inflexibility and experiential avoidance. *Behavior Therapy*, 42(4), 676–688.

Branch, M. N. & Pennypacker, H. S. (2013). Generality and generalization of research findings. In G. J. Madden (Ed.) *APA Handbook of Behavior Analysis, Vol. 1*, Washington DC: APA Publications, pp. 151–175.

Cen, R., Hussain, A., Pak, K. J., Mitchell, G., Nikles, J., Gaudreau, S., . . . & Breault, J. L. (2016). Do N-of-1 Trials Need IRB Review? *Journal of Empirical Research on Human Research Ethics*, 11(3), 250–255.

Codd, III, R. T. (2017). Protecting the Scientific Lexical Canon. *the Behavior Therapist*, 40(5), 185–191.

Codd, III, R. T. (2016). How to develop a robust practice-based research repertoire. *The Behavior Therapist*, 39(4), 118–120.

Codd, R. T., Twohig, M. P., Crosby, J. M., & Enno, A. (2011). Treatment of three anxiety disorder cases with acceptance and commitment therapy in a private practice. *Journal of Cognitive Psychotherapy*, 25(3), 203–217.

Cooper, J. O., Heron, T. E., & Heward, W. L. (2007). *Applied behavior analysis* (2nd ed.). Upper Saddle River, NJ: Pearson Education.

Eilers, H. J. & Hayes, S. C. (2015). Exposure and response prevention therapy with cognitive defusion exercises to reduce repetitive and restrictive behaviors displayed by children with autism spectrum disorder. *Research in Autism Spectrum Disorders*, 19, 18–31.

Hayes, S. C. (1981). Single-case experimental design and empirical clinical practice. *Journal of Consulting and Clinical Psychology*, 49, 193–211.

Hayes, S. C., Barlow, D. H., & Nelson-Gray, R. O. (1999). *The scientist-practitioner: Research and accountability in the age of managed care* (2nd ed.). Needham Heights, MA: Allyn & Bacon.

Hollon, S. D. & Kendall, P. C. (1980). Cognitive self-statements in depression: Development of an automatic thoughts questionnaire. *Cognitive therapy and research*, 4(4), 383–395.

Horner, R. H. & Odom, S. L. (2014). Constructing single-case research designs: Logic and options. In Kratochwill, T. R., & Levin, J. R. (Eds.) *Single-case intervention research: Methodological and statistical advances* (pp. 27–51). Washington, DC: American Psychological Association.

Kanter, J. W., Landes, S. J., Busch, A. M., Rusch, L. C., Brown, K. R., Baruch, D. E., & Holman, G. I. (2006). The effect of contingent reinforcement on target variables in outpatient psychotherapy for depression: A successful and unsuccessful case using functional analytic psychotherapy. *Journal of Applied Behavior Analysis*, 39(4), 463–467.

Kratochwill, T. R., Hitchcock, J., Horner, R. H., Levin, J. R., Odom, S. L., Rindskopf, D. M., & Shadish, W. R. (2010). Single-case designs technical documentation. Retrieved from: http://ies.ed.gov/ncee/wwc/pdf/wwc_scd.pdf

Kratochwill, T. R. & Levin, J. R. (2014). *Single-case intervention research: Methodological and statistical advances*. Washington, DC: American Psychological Association.

Landes, S. J., Kanter, J. W., Weeks, C. E., & Busch, A. M. (2013). The impact of the active components of functional analytic psychotherapy on idiographic target behaviors. *Journal of Contextual Behavioral Science, 2*(1), 49–57.

Maitland, D. W. & Gaynor, S. T. (2016). Functional analytic psychotherapy compared with supportive listening: An alternating treatments design examining distinctiveness, session evaluations, and interpersonal functioning. *Behavior Analysis: Research and Practice, 16*(2), 52.

Nock, M. K., Janis, I. B., & Wedig, M. M. (2007). Research designs. In Nezu, A. M. & Nezu, C. M. (Eds.) *Evidence-based outcome research: A practical guide to conducting randomized controlled trials for psychosocial interventions* (pp. 201–218). New York: Oxford University Press.

Schulz, K. F., Altman, D. G., & Moher, D. (2010). CONSORT 2010 statement: Updated guidelines for reporting parallel group randomised trials. *BMC medicine, 8*(1), 18–26.

Shingleton, R. M., Pratt, E. M., Gorman, B., Barlow, D. H., Palfai, T. P., & Thompson-Brenner, H. (2016). Motivational text message intervention for eating disorders: A single-case alternating treatment design using ecological momentary assessment. *Behavior Therapy, 47*(3), 325–338.

Tolin, D. F., Whiting, S., Maltby, N., Diefenbach, G. J., Lothstein, M. A., Catalano, A., & Gray, K. (2009). Intensive (daily) behavior therapy for school refusal: A multiple baseline case series. *Cognitive and Behavioral Practice, 16*(3), 332–344.

Watson, P. J. & Workman, E. A. (1981). The non-concurrent multiple baseline across-individuals design: An extension of the traditional multiple baseline design. *Journal of Behavior Therapy and Experimental Psychiatry, 12*(3), 257–259.

CHAPTER 5

Practice-Based Research: A Pragmatic Approach

Guy Bruce

When an editor asked Skinner to describe his activities as a research psychologist, Skinner read through his old notes, records, and publications. He made an interesting discovery. His research method was very different from the scientific method that statisticians recommended for doing research. He had failed to state a hypothesis, construct a theory, or design an experiment to test the falsity of his hypothesis about the cause of behavior change. He had not compared the averaged performance of two groups of subjects, each subject randomly assigned to a treatment or a control group. He had not done the calculations necessary to evaluate the probability that a difference between the averaged measures of the behavior of the two groups was statistically significant! Instead of apologizing for his noncompliance, he asserted the following, "But it is a mistake to identify scientific practice with the formalized constructions of statistics and scientific method" (Skinner, 1972, p. 101). Instead of the expected treatise on scientific method, he offered "A Case History in Scientific Method." The editor was not pleased (Skinner, 1984).

A Different Way to do Research

Skinner's case history illustrates a different way to do scientific research. In Skinner's own words, "So far as I can see, I began simply by looking for lawful processes in the behavior of the intact organism" (p 104). What did he mean by "lawful processes?" Catania (1998) defines "processes" in this way,

> We study the relation between environmental events and the organism's behavior by manipulating the environment and observing how this affects what the organism does. We operate on the organism's environment, or in other words, we perform experimental operations. In the analysis of behavior, operations are what the experimenter does and processes are the changes in behavior that result.

(pp. 13–14)

What Skinner did was manipulate his subject's environment and observe the changes in his subject's behavior. In order to discover "lawful processes," he first needed continuous, accurate and sensitive measures of behavior change, his dependent variable of interest. He built several devices. They measured both the change in the number of responses and the amount of time in which those responses occurred, from a decrease in the number of times that a rat ran back into a tunnel and the time it stayed in the tunnel before venturing out again to changes in the rate of lever presses. Skinner ultimately settled on response rate as his measure of behavior because it proved to be the most sensitive measure of behavior change. Skinner was interested in behavior change as his *dependent variable*. Behavior change is a dependent variable because changes in behavior depend on changes in one or more of the environmental events that the researcher manipulates, which are called *independent variables*. Skinner's search for orderly changes in behavior was based on an assumption that every basic or applied scientific researcher shares. Changes in an organism's behavior are dependent on changes in the environment of that organism. Behavior is orderly.

But how did Skinner decide which environmental events to manipulate and what types of changes in behavior to measure? Since he had no hypotheses to prove about rat behavior, he was "free" to study any type of relationship between environmental changes and behavior change which might be interesting to him. His first experiment tested the effects of repeated click sounds on the number and duration of a rat's retreats back into the tunnel. He discovered his first orderly relationship. "Repeated clicks had less and less of an effect" (p. 104). Then he found something more interesting to study, the postural reflexes of young rats. Losing interest in the behavior of young rats because "it can't be usefully extrapolated to everyday life" (p. 106), he returned to the study of the effect of clicks on the starts and stops of adult rats as they ran down a runway that he had constructed. Since he had no hypothesis to prove, he was able to follow his first principle, "When you run into something interesting, drop everything else and study it" (p. 104). Skinner continued to modify his apparatus, eventually eliminating the runway and adding a feeder that the rat could operate by pressing a lever. The feeder allowed him to measure changes in the rates of the rat's lever presses. Then the feeder broke down, more than once. When the feeder stopped working the rat's lever presses no longer produced food. Skinner noticed a change in the rat's behavior each time the feeder quit working. The response rate decreased. So, he began systematically disconnecting and then reconnecting the feeder, illustrating the procedure that we now call "replication." Replication is making repeated changes in an independent variable, such as whether lever presses will or will not produce food and observing changes in a subject's behavior. Replication allowed Skinner to discover a functional relationship between changes in a rat's behavior and a change in the rat's environment. Response rates increased when lever presses produced food, and decreased when they did not, each time Skinner repeated the experimental test.

What allowed Skinner to discover the behavior change process that we now call "reinforcement," a process that subsequent researchers have been able to reproduce with all types of behaviors and subjects, from cockroaches to humans (Dixon, M., Daar, J., Gunnarsson, K. and Shayter, A., 2016; Holland, J. G., 1958)? First, he was unfettered by a theory or hypothesized cause of behavior change. Thus he was free to discover orderly changes in behavior. Instead of making guesses about how changes in an individual's behavior were related to environmental changes and then designing experiments that would disprove his guesses, the "*hypothetical-deductive method*," he was free to search for those relationships using the "*inductive method*." Instead of the usual top-down method of research, which required that the researcher commit to a theory or explanation of behavior before observing actual relationships between changes in environment and changes in behavior, Skinner tried a bottom-up method, allowing himself to discover orderly relationships by recording sensitive measures of behavior change, repeatedly changing only one independent variable at a time, and observing the behavior changes that occurred each time he made a change in the subject's environment. He built a theory of behavior change from his accumulation of carefully observed relationships between behavior and environment change. Secondly, he collected accurate and sensitive measures of behavior change, his dependent variable, which allowed him to see those changes when they occurred. And finally, he "had the clue from Pavlov: control your conditions and you will see order" (ibid).

Beginning with his very first experiment Skinner was very careful to control his conditions. For example, he designed a "silent release box, operated by compressed air and designed to eliminate disturbances when introducing a rat into the apparatus" (ibid). Then he "built a soundproofed box containing a specially structured space" (ibid). By eliminating extraneous noises, he was able to see the effects of the changes he was manipulating on the rat's behavior more clearly. Eventually, he added a feeder that the rat could operate by pressing a lever. By "control your conditions" Pavlov meant that a researcher should only make one change in the environment at time, changing one independent variable, such as whether food follows or does not follow lever presses, while holding constant all other environmental changes, such as extraneous noise, and measuring the behavior change that occurs each time he changes that one condition. Our term for Pavlov's advice, "Control your conditions and you will see order" is *experimental control*. It is the method that allowed Skinner and those who followed him to discover orderly changes in behavior that were related to orderly changes in the environment.

Another difference in Skinner's approach was to study the relationship between changes in an independent variable, such as whether food followed or did not follow lever presses, and changes in the response rates of an *individual* subject. Other psychology researchers studied how changes in independent variables were related to changes in the average behavior of a group of subjects. For example, they might study the relationship between changes in an independent variable, such as whether lever presses produced or did not produce food, and the average response rate of a group of rats. As Figure 5.1's hypothetical data illustrates, changes in the average response rate of a group of individuals may not equal the change in any individual's response rate! For some individuals, there may be an increase in response rates, while for others there may be no change or even a decrease in response rates (Cooper, Heron & Heward, 2007). The product of such

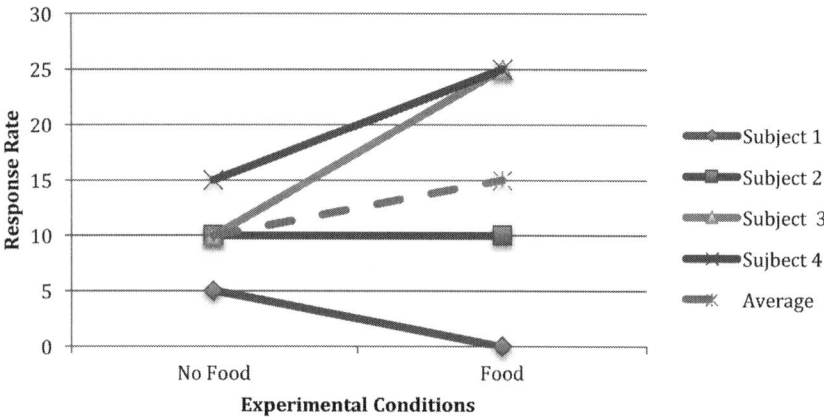

Figure 5.1 Change in the average response rate of a group of rats may not equal the change in response rate of any individual in the group.

research is explanations and procedures that are not very effective in changing the behavior of the individual subject. As Skinner stated:

> When you have the responsibility of making absolutely sure that a given organism will engage in a given sort of behavior at a given time, you quickly grow impatient with theories of learning ... No one goes to the circus to see the average dog jump through the average hoop significantly oftener than untrained dogs raised under the same circumstances ...
>
> (p. 114)

Skinner's "Case History in Scientific Method" illustrated his pragmatic approach. The Encyclopaedia Britannica (accessed August 23, 2017) defines "pragmatism" as a "school of philosophy, dominant in the United States in the first quarter of the 20th century, based on the principle that the usefulness, workability, and practicality of ideas, policies, and proposals are the criteria of their merit." As Skinner (1972; 1945) wrote in another seminal paper, "The Operational Analysis of Psychological Terms":

> The ultimate criterion for the goodness of a concept is not whether two people are brought into agreement but whether the scientist who uses the concept can operate successfully upon his material-all by himself if need be. What matters to Robinson Crusoe is not whether he is agreeing with himself but whether he is getting anywhere with his control over nature.
>
> (p. 383)

Skinner's scientific methods were those that allowed him to make progress towards his goal of getting somewhere with his control over behavior. They included an experimental approach to the study of orderly relationships between changes in behavior and changes in the environment; changing only one environmental variable at a time while holding all others constant; recording sensitive measures of changes in the response rates of the individual subject; repeatedly changing an independent variable and observing the result for the same subject and then other subjects; and inductively discovering explanations that allow for more accurate prediction and more effective control of behavior. Skinner's approach proved to be highly productive. Not only has it produced useful explanations of behavior, but it has led to the design of effective procedures for changing behavior that have improved outcomes for a variety of clients, such as special and regular education students with learning difficulties, employees with poor productivity or at high risk of injury, patients with health problems due to unhealthy eating and activity choices, and the organizations that serve these clients.

The pragmatic approach that Skinner described in his "A Case History," can also be used to improve the products of practice-based research. While basic research focuses on the discovery of explanations that allow for more accurate prediction and effective control of behavior, practice-based research focuses on the discovery of procedures that can improve outcomes for clients. Another word for "pragmatism" is "sensitivity." As Skinner wrote:

> The organism whose behavior is most extensively modified and most completely controlled in research of the sort I have described is the experimenter himself. The point was well made by the cartoonist in the Columbia Jester. The caption read: 'Boy have I got this guy conditioned. Every time I press the bar he drops down a piece of food.' The subjects we study reinforce us more effectively than we reinforce them.
>
> (pp. 122–123)

An effective practitioner is highly sensitive to the effects of his interventions on the behavior change of his clients. He or she collects accurate, frequent, and sensitive measures of client behavior change, and when those measures show that the client is not making adequate progress, he or she changes the intervention. A pragmatic approach to practice-based research can discover the combination of independent variables that will ensure that each client will make efficient behavior change to achieve his or her life goals.

A Case Study in Practice-Based Research

One possible goal of practice-based research is to discover procedures for increasing the efficiency of behavior change. For example, the goal of my dissertation research project (Bruce, 1991), was to identify the relationship between the timing of instructions with respect to practice opportunities, my independent variable, and the efficiency of behavior change, a measure of student progress, my dependent variable. Would students make more efficient progress if instructions were available during each practice opportunity than if they were available immediately following each practice opportunity? An accurate description of that relationship could be used to discover more efficient teaching and training procedures. More efficient teaching and training procedures could allow students and trainees to learn more in less time, thus reducing the time cost of their education and training. Improved efficiency could also allow students who start out behind their peers, lacking the prerequisite skills to learn language and social skills, as well as reading, writing, and math, to catch up without the need to increase the amount of time that they work with teachers or study independently. More efficient teaching procedures could also reduce the monetary costs of education, since less teacher interaction time would be required for students to make adequate progress.

Components of Pragmatic Practice-Based Research

Useful research, whether basic or practice-based, has the same pragmatic components, as I shall illustrate in my case study.

1. *An Inductive Approach* focuses on discovering functional relationships between behavior change and environment change, not proving one's hypotheses to be false. Don't let your hypotheses about the variables that are related to behavior change get in the way of discovering useful explanations. It is perfectly natural for researchers to have opinions about how an environmental variable, such as how the timing of instructions, might affect the efficiency of behavior change. However, it is more useful to ask a question about such a relationship, such as, "What is the relationship between the timing of instructions with respect to practice and the efficiency of behavior change?" There are two benefits to asking a question. A question is not a hypothesis that needs to be defended. Once the researcher states a hypothesis he or she now has something to prove. There is a natural tendency to design and interpret his or her experiment in ways that support his or her hypothesis. On the other hand, a question is not a guess to be proven. It is an answer to be discovered. And whatever the answer, as long as the experiment is designed so that the answer is useful, the researcher will be successful.

The most useful practice-based research questions come from two sources, the researcher's experience as a practitioner and the research literature (Sidman, 1960). As a behavior analyst with experience attempting to teach many different types of students, such as individuals with learning difficulties, staff who worked with those individuals, undergraduates failing their freshman calculus and chemistry classes, and those struggling to pass a course on the applications of behavior analysis and teaching, I became curious about the relationship between the timing of instructions and student progress. By the timing of instructions I mean whether instructions on how to perform a task are presented at the same time as an opportunity to practice, or following that practice opportunity. Would the timing of instructions affect the efficiency of student progress?

The answer to a useful practice-based research question will eventually lead to the discovery of a useful procedure for helping clients, either because the researcher is able to observe a practically significant relationship between his independent variable, such as the timing of instructions, and his dependent variable, the efficiency of student progress, or because he discovers that there is no useful relationship between those variables. If the answer is either no useful relationship or unclear, the pragmatic researcher has two options: 1) design a new experiment that will provide a clear answer or 2) ask a different question and design an experiment to answer that new question. As the conversation between Skinner's rats illustrated, an effective researcher allows his or her behavior to be shaped by his or her subjects. A pragmatic researcher is sensitive to the effects of his independent variables on his subjects' behavior.

2. *Behavior change of the individual* is the pragmatic researcher's dependent variable because the goal of pragmatic research is to discover procedures useful in helping each individual—"No one goes to the circus to see an average dog jump through an average hoop" (Skinner, 1972, p. 114). Of course, there is no such thing as an average dog, or for that matter, the average client. Instead different individuals seek help from behavior analytic practitioners. Each individual has a unique genetic and environmental history. For that reason, a relationship between the average progress of a group individuals and the timing of instructions may not represent the relationship between the timing of instructions and the actual progress of any individual in the group. Several years ago, I attended a behavior analysis conference in which the speaker displayed two graphs side by side. On the left side of the screen, she displayed a slope representing the average behavior change of a group of subjects. On the right side of the screen, she displayed the slopes of each subject's behavior change. None of the individual's slopes looked like the average slope!

I designed my experiment so that I could observe the effect of the timing of instructions on the behavior change of each of my subjects. Each subject's behavior change was studied under two experimental conditions. In one condition instructions were provided at the same time as the practice opportunity. In the other, instructions were provided immediately following each practice opportunity.

3. *Sensitive measures of behavior change* are needed to discover useful relationships between behavior change (the dependent variable) and environmental change (the independent variable). A measure of behavior change that includes both the number of times that a behavior occurs and time it takes to occur will always be more sensitive to change than a measure of either count or time alone. It was the change in the rate of lever presses (the number of lever presses per minute) that Skinner observed when he repeatedly disconnected and reconnected the feeder that delivered food pellets following each lever press. This was the first clear demonstration of the relationship between behavior change and the consequences of behavior that we now call "reinforcement." However, Skinner's measure of behavior change had a third dimension. He also recorded the time required to produce the change in response rate. *Celeration* is the term for the change in response rate per unit of calendar time which was first coined by Ogden Lindsley, a student of Skinner's who was an early pioneer in the behavior analytic study of

68 Guy Bruce

human operant behavior (Pennypacker, H. S., Gutierrez, Jr., & Lindsley, O. R, 2003). However, Skinner's measure of behavior change was a special type of celeration, the change in response rate per the amount of time during which his rat interacted with the feeder. To distinguish this measure from celeration, the change in rate per calendar time, I coined the term, *celeration efficiency*. *Celeration Efficiency* is the change in the rate of behavior (count per time) per the amount of time that the subject interacts with the independent variable or behavior change procedure that the practitioner implements. To illustrate how celeration efficiency can be measured in applied research, let's return to my case study.

To obtain accurate measures of celeration efficiency, I programmed an Apple® personal computer to record each of my two subject's rates of selecting sequences of three Zaph Dingbat comparison stimuli from a set of ten different Zaph Dingbat characters displayed across the bottom of the screen, when a sequence of three different Zaph Dingbat sample characters from a set of ten were presented at the top of the screen. (See Figure 5.2.) The sample characters were not only different from each other, but also from the comparison set. Each of the ten comparison stimuli had been assigned as the correct comparison for one of the ten sample stimuli after a baseline test in which the subjects were asked to pick the comparison that went with the sample. The assigned comparisons were always characters that the subject never selected during the baseline test, thus ensuring a baseline rate of zero selections per minute. *Baseline* is a term for measures of behavior recorded prior to changes in an independent variable or implementation of a behavior change procedure. Instead of rates of lever presses, the computer

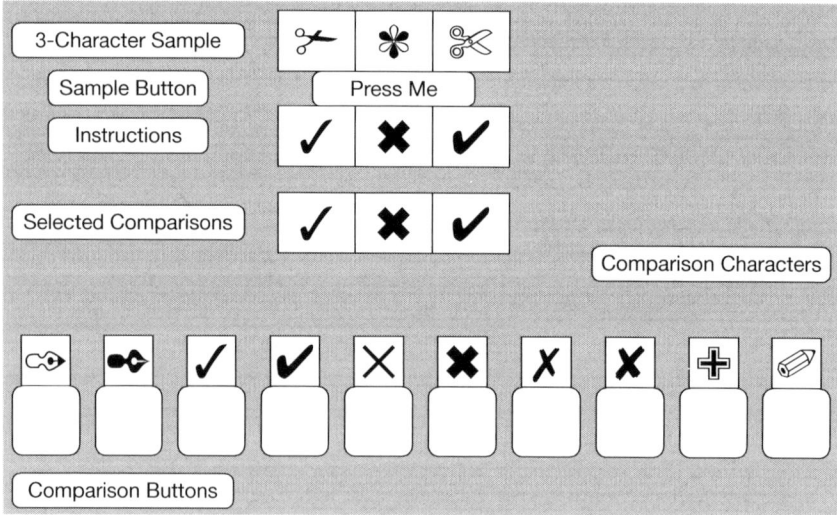

Figure 5.2 Screen used to teach arbitrary matching conditional discriminations. The Assigned Comparisons, which appear just below the 3-Character Sample, are the instructions for selecting the identical comparisons from the bottom of the screen.

recorded the rate of comparison selections when samples were presented, a type of behavior called a *conditional discrimination.*

I selected conditional discriminations as my behavior of interest because clients often have difficulty learning them, yet they form the building blocks of useful repertoires. A somewhat famous example of the importance of conditional discriminations in everyday life is illustrated in the movie, "Rain Man." The main character, a young man with autism, is crossing the street when the "Walk" sign changes to "Don't Walk." He stops in the middle of the street even though a car is rapidly approaching (Levinson, 1988). A safe crossing depends on appropriate responding to the sign as well as the approaching traffic, an example of a conditional discrimination.

The computer was programmed to record and calculate the number of experimenter-assigned comparison stimuli selected by the subject per second when the computer presented the assigned sample stimuli without instructions, and to the record the cumulative number of minutes of the subject's interaction with the program during baseline and in each of the two experimental conditions (instructions presented during or following practice opportunities). I was then able to graph the change in each subject's rate of conditional discriminations (number per second) per the cumulative time in minutes that he or she interacted with each experimental condition, a measure of the celeration efficiency in each condition. (See Figures 5.3–5.6.) The computer program allowed me to automate the recording of my behavior change measures, thus ensuring their accuracy, in the same way that Skinner automated his recording of his subject's response rates and changes in response rates per minute of interaction with the lever.

4. *Experimental Control*—Skinner followed Pavlov's advice, "Control your conditions and you will see order" and that proved to be very useful advice. In order to control conditions the experimenter must change only one independent variable at a time. Or put another way, he or she must hold all other variables constant that might be related to behavior change of interest, while systematically manipulating (a fancy word for changing) one independent variable at a time. Skinner connected the feeder so that lever pressing produced food, then he disconnected the feeder so that lever pressing did not. He was careful to make no other changes in his subject's environment when testing the effect of connecting and disconnecting the feeder, so that he could clearly see whether there was an orderly relationship between rates of lever pressing and whether lever pressing produced or did not produce food (Skinner, 1972).

It's not easy to control one's conditions, but the discovery of orderly relationships between behavior and environmental change is worth it. The experimenter's first step is to list all the environmental variables that might be related to behavior change, and then design an experiment in which as many of these as possible are held constant, while changing only one variable at a time. For example, I identified the following variables as ones that could affect behavior change in my case study, a) the subject's baseline rates of conditional discriminations prior to interacting with the experimental conditions, b) differences between the samples and comparisons presented in each experimental condition, c) the effectiveness of the instructions in reliably evoking the selection of the comparison assigned to each sample, d) the procedure for fading the presentation of the instructions in each experimental condition, e) the type of consequence provided for selecting the assigned comparison, f) the timing of the consequence delivery, g) the procedure for awarding incentives, h) the duration of each subject's interaction with each experimental condition, i) the order in which the experimental conditions were presented during each session, and j) the procedural integrity with which my independent variable was manipulated and all other variables were held constant. My goal was to hold each of these variables constant, so that I could see more clearly any relationship between my independent variable, the presentation of instructions during or following each practice opportunity, and my dependent variable, the celeration efficiency of each subject's conditional discrimination performance.

a) *Baseline Rates.* To ensure that each subject's baseline rates of conditional discriminations were equal for the two experimental conditions, I recorded stable measures of each subject's comparison selections when I presented each of the samples with the instruction, "select the comparison that goes with the sample." Once I had obtained stable measures of the subject's initial selections, I assigned comparisons that the subject never selected when each sample was presented. I then recorded baseline measures for conditional discriminations in which 3-sample sequences were presented and the subject was asked to select a three-comparison sequence. This ensured that each subject's baseline selections were at zero per second for each set of conditional discriminations.

b) *Differences Between Sample and Comparison Sets.* To control for potential differences in the effects of different sample and comparison sets on celeration efficiencies, if one set of ten samples and ten comparisons was assigned to the condition in which instructions were available during the practice opportunity for one subject, that same set was assigned to the condition in which instructions were available following a practice opportunity for the other subject. This is a technique called "*counterbalancing.*" Presenting the same sample and comparison set across two different experimental conditions allowed the experimenter to see whether differences in sample and comparison sets are related to different celeration efficiencies.

c) *Differences in the effectiveness of instructions.* The instructions were the assigned comparisons for each of the sample characters. To test their effectiveness in evoking the selection of identical comparisons, I presented a sequence of three comparisons from a set of ten at the middle of the screen and requested that the subject click on the comparisons in the set of ten at the bottom of the screen which looked like ones in the middle of the screen. During this instruction-testing condition, the assigned samples were not presented. You might think that testing of what is sometimes called "identity matching" would be unnecessary, since my two subjects were college students. However, testing revealed the one subject did not consistently select two of the ten assigned comparisons, when the identical comparisons were presented at the middle of the screen. At this point the experimenter can either replace these instructions with other instructions that will reliably evoke correct selections, e.g., replace the two comparison stimuli with others that reliably evoke selecting the matching comparison, or provide training to ensure that all the comparison stimuli reliably evoke selecting the identical comparison. I chose the second option, using a stimulus-control shaping procedure (Schilmoeller, G. L., Schilmoeller, K. J., Etzel, B. C., and LeBlanc, J. M., 1979). The two characters were drawings of two cubes, one with a shadow extending to the right and the other with a shadow extending to the left. The shaping procedure exaggerated each of the shadows, allowing the subject to consistently select the comparison cube that was identical to each sample cube, then gradually decreased the length of the shadows until the subject was consistently selecting the cube that was identical to the sample cube.

d) *Fading Procedure.* The procedure for fading the instructions needed to be the same whether the instructions were presented during or following a practice opportunity. There are a number of different types of fading procedures. For this study, I provided a progressive time-delay procedure, in which the instruction, the comparison stimulus identical to the assigned comparison stimulus, was presented in the middle of screen just below the assigned sample character, with zero delay on the first time the assigned sample was presented, and if the subject selected the assigned comparison character from the bottom of the screen, on the next presentation of the same sample, the computer would add one second of delay to the presentation of the instruction stimulus. Each time the subject selected the correct comparison stimulus, one second was added to the delay between the next presentation of that same sample and the presentation of the instruction. Each time a subject selected an incorrect comparison stimulus, one second would be subtracted from the delay between the next presentation of that same sample and instruction. This procedure was the same whether the instruction was presented during or following each practice opportunity.

e) *Type of consequences presented.* In both experimental conditions, the same consequences were presented. The computer made a beep sound following each selection of the assigned comparison.

f) *Consequence timing.* In both experimental conditions, the computer *immediately* beeped following selection of each assigned comparison.

g) *The incentive procedure.* Immediately following each two-minute interaction with either experimental condition, the computer displayed a screen with the total amount of money earned for selections of the assigned comparisons during the previous two minutes, with each correct selection equal to one penny. The higher the subject's rate of correct selections the more money he or she earned during the two minutes. Subjects were paid in cash at the end of each daily session.

h) *Subject Interaction Time.* The computer kept the subject's interaction time with each experimental condition constant at two minutes per session, for the same number of sessions in each condition.

i) *Sequence of Experimental Conditions.* The two experimental conditions, instructions presented during or following each practice opportunity, were alternated every two minutes, with the condition presented first randomly selected at the beginning of each daily session.

j) *Procedural Integrity.* To ensure procedural integrity in both the experimental manipulation of the timing of instructions and the experimental control of the other variables, I programmed the computer to alternate the presentation of experimental conditions, to manipulate the timing and fading of instructions in each experimental condition, deliver consequences, and hold constant other variables that might affect behavior change, following Skinner's example of using automation to ensure procedural integrity. To paraphrase Pavlov's advice, automate the control of your conditions, and you will see order.

5. *Both within-subject and across-subject replications* are necessary to demonstrate relationships between measures of behavior change and environmental change. Skinner repeatedly connected and disconnected the feeder for the same rat, repeating his experiment so that he could observe whether the changes in his independent variable, whether lever presses produced or did not produce food, were reliably related to the changes in the rat's rate of lever pressing. He then replicated his experiment with a second rat and observed the same relationship. And there have been many additional replications since his first experiment, with different rats, then pigeons, monkeys (Skinner, 1972), humans (Holland, 1958), and, yes, even cockroaches (Dixon et al., 2016). Each replication across subjects that demonstrates the same orderly relationship strengthens the scientist's belief in the generality of the observed relationship. Each within-subject replication that demonstrates the same orderly relationship strengthens the scientist's belief that such a relationship exists (Sidman, 1960).

I replicated my experiment both within and across my two subjects, observing the same orderly relationship with each replication. (See Figures 5.3–5.6.) Providing instructions during practice opportunities produced higher celeration efficiencies than providing them following practice opportunities. I know what you are thinking. "You only replicated with two subjects. Suppose they are the only two who demonstrate this relationship?" Your question is the next one that the inductive researcher should ask. Will the relationship be observed with additional subjects? The only way to answer that question is to replicate the experiment with additional subjects. And of course, the pragmatic researcher and practitioner must be prepared for replication results that do not show the same orderly relationship. He or she must be prepared to do another experiment to discover the conditions in which the relationship occurs. That is the inductive approach to research. Hold one's explanations and theories lightly. Be ready to change them with new experiments reveal different relationships, building principles and theories of behavior change from the ground up.

Practice-Based Research: Pragmatic Approach 73

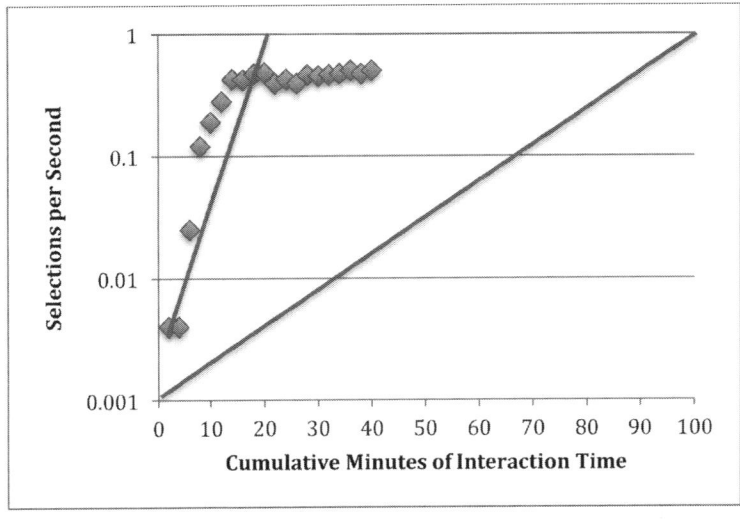

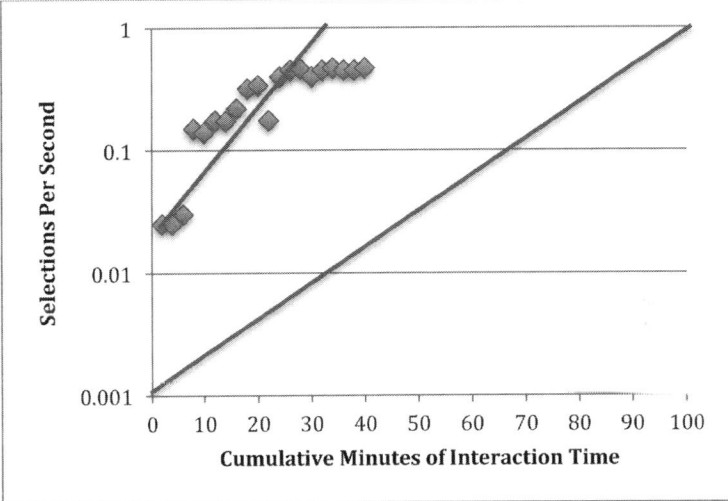

Figure 5.3 Compare the slopes of subject B's celeration efficiencies when instructions are available during (top graph) and following practice opportunities (bottom graph).

6. *Use standard charts to discover practically significant, not just statistically significant differences* in measures of behavior change, which are consistently related to changes in independent variables. Practically significant means changes in behavior of the individual subject large enough to be useful to the practitioner, client and stakeholders. To discover practically significant behavior-change procedures, the researcher must replicate his or her experiment both within and across subjects and observe practically useful changes in the behavior of each subject. Skinner's

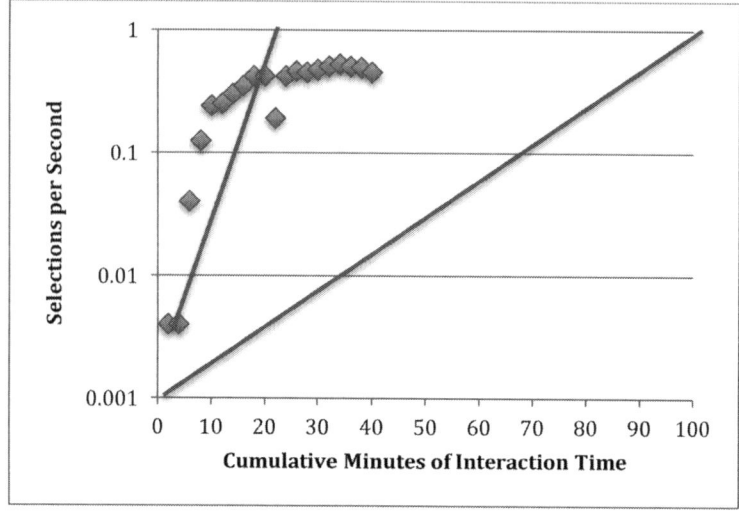

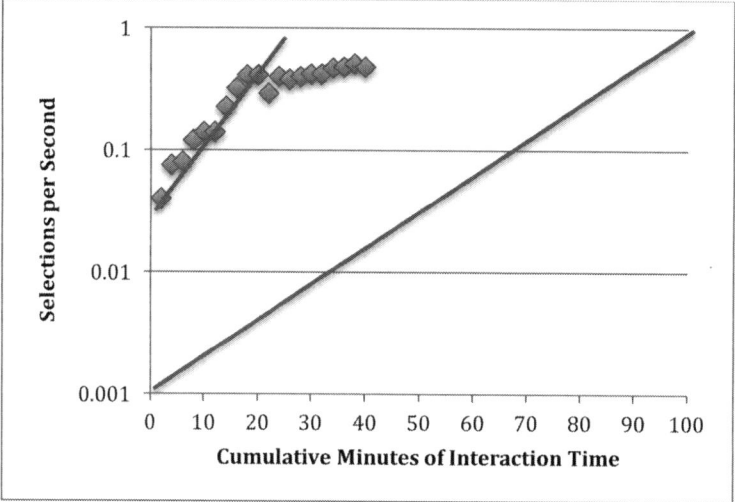

Figure 5.4 Compare the slopes of subject B's celeration efficiencies when instructions are available during (top graph) and following practice opportunities (bottom graph). This is an example of within-subject replication.

case study illustrated the use of standard graphic displays to reveal practically significant changes in response rates that occurred each time he connected and disconnected the feeder. The display showed different response rates as different slopes and was standard in that the same slope always had the same value, making it easier to evaluate the amount of change in response rates.

My practice-based research on the effects of independent variables, such as the timing of instructions on "celeration efficiency," has also relied on standard charts

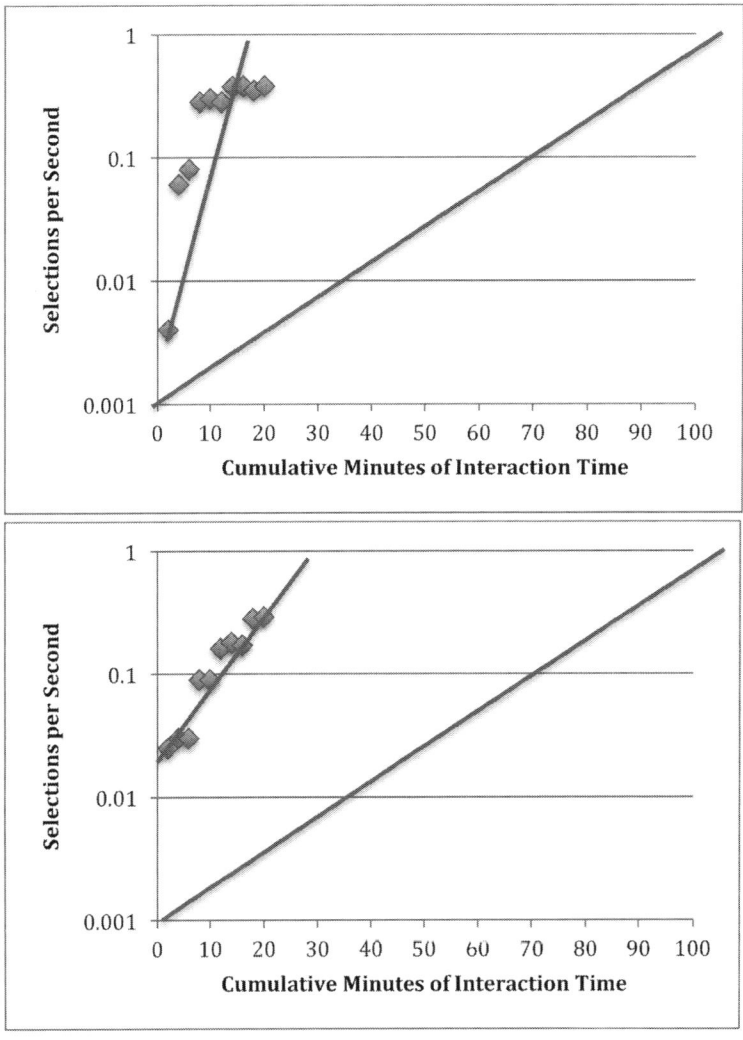

Figure 5.5 Compare the slopes of subject R's celeration efficiencies when instructions are available during (top graph) and following practice opportunities (bottom graph). This is an example of between subject replication.

to evaluate the practical significance of differences in each subject's celeration efficiencies related to changes in the values of independent variable manipulated by the researcher. Just as different response rates can be seen as different slopes in Skinner's standard charts, different celeration efficiencies are seen as different slopes in the standard celeration efficiency chart. These standard celeration efficiency charts are a variation of the standard celeration charts first developed by Pennypacker, Gutierrez, and Lindsley (2003). The celeration efficiency charts

76 Guy Bruce

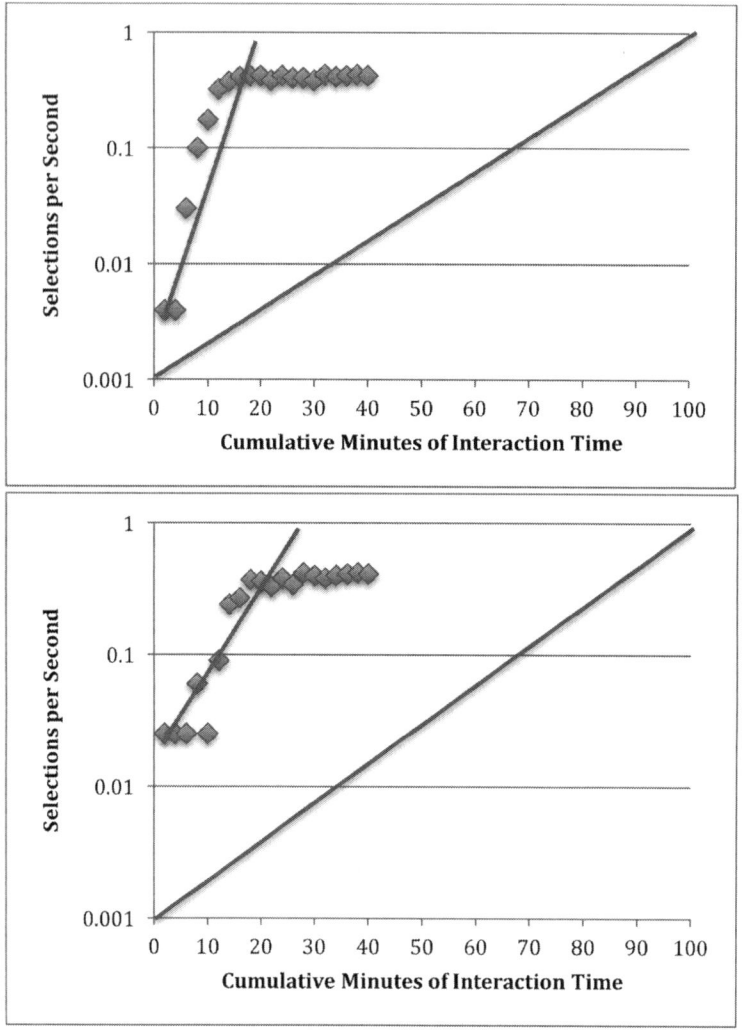

Figure 5.6 Compare the slopes of subject R's celeration efficiencies when instructions are available during (top graph) and following practice opportunities (bottom graph). This is an example of within-subject replication.

have a three-cycle log vertical axis with the lowest cycle set to accommodate the lowest observed response rates, a horizontal axis with an equal-interval scale from 0 to 100, 200, 1000, etc., and a standard aspect ratio between the vertical and horizontal axes (2:3), so that the same slope always has the same value. Response rates are plotted along the vertical axis by the subject's cumulative interaction time in minutes along the horizontal axis. (See Figures 5.3–5.6.)

Summary: A Pragmatic Approach to Practice-Based Research

Applied Behavior Analysis has produced many effective procedures to help clients with behavior deficits and excesses, improving clinical and educational outcomes, staff safety and productivity, organizational performance, and self-management. The pragmatic approach may be reduced to only three steps: 1) collect frequent, accurate sensitive measures of individual behavior change; 2) repeatedly change one environmental variable at a time to discover orderly relationships between behavior and environmental change; 3) If you don't see orderly relationships, try changing a different variable until you discover variables and procedures that produce practically significant differences in the behavior of the individual client. Skinner's discovery of the relationship we now call "reinforcement" has allowed practitioners to design and implement effective behavior change procedures to improve the performance of many different types of clients, from young children with autism to employees operating nuclear reactors. My discovery of the relationship between the timing of instructions and celeration efficiency may allow practitioners to improve the efficiency of student and staff behavior change through the design and implementation of teaching procedures that make instructions available during, instead of following, practice opportunities.

References

Bruce, G. S. (1991). *The Effects of Priming During or Following Responding on the Celeration of Codic Verbal Relations*. Dissertation submitted in partial fulfillment of the EdD, West Virginia University.

Catania, A. C. (1998). *Learning*. (4th ed.). Upper Saddle River, NJ: Simon and Schuster.

Cooper, J. O., Heron, T. E., & Heward, W. L. (2007). *Applied Behavior Analysis* (2nd ed.). Upper Saddle River, NJ: Pearson Education.

Dixon, M., Daar, J., Gunnarsson, K., & Shayter, A. (2016). Stimulus preference and reinforcement effects of the Madagascar hissing cockroach (*Gromphordahina portentosa*): A case of reverse translational research. *Psychological Record*, 66, 41–51.

Encyclopaedia Britannica. Accessed August 23, 2017. Available from: www.britannica.com/topic/pragmatism-philosophy

Holland, J. G. (1958). Human vigilance. *Science*, *128*(335), 61–67.

Levinson, B. (1988). *Rain Man*. United Artists.

Pennypacker, H. S., Gutierrez, Jr., & Lindsley, O. R. (2003). *Handbook of the Standard Celeration Chart*. Cambridge Center for Behavioral Studies: Boston, MA.

Schilmoeller, G. L., Schilmoeller, K. J., Etzel, B. C., & LeBlanc, J. M. (1979). Conditional discriminations after errorless and trial-and-error training. *Journal of the Experimental Analysis of Behavior*, 31, 405–420.

Sidman, M. (1960). *Tactics of Scientific Research*. New York: Basic Books.

Skinner, B. F. (1984). *A Matter of Consequences*. Washington Square: New York University Press.

Skinner, B. F. (1972). A Case History in Scientific Method. In *Cumulative Record: A Selection of Papers* (3rd ed.), (pp. 101–124). New York: Appleton-Century Crofts.

Skinner, B. F. (1972; 1945). The Operational Analysis Of Psychological Terms. In *Cumulative Record: A Selection of Papers* (3rd ed.), (pp. 370–384). New York: Appleton-Century-Crofts.

Additional Readings

Branch, M. N. & Pennypacker, H. S. (2013). Generality and Generalization of Research Findings (Chapter 7) *The APA Handbook of Behavior Analysis: Vol. 1 Methods and Principles*. In G. J. Madden (Editor-in-chief).

Johnston, J. M. & Pennypacker, H. S. (2009). *Strategies and Tactics of Behavioral Research*, (3rd ed.). New York: Routledge.

Vargas, J. (2004). Contingencies Over B.F. Skinner's Discovery of Contingencies. *European Journal of Behavior Analysis*, 5(2), 137–142.

PART III

Practice-Based Research in Private Practice

CHAPTER **6**

A Step-By-Step Guide for Creating an Independent Institutional Review Board (IRB) for Private Practitioners

Travis L. Osborne

Although review by an Institutional Review Board (IRB) is not required for all research studies (typically it is only required for federally-funded research), ethical oversight of research protocols by IRBs is the standard in the United States and lack of IRB approval can limit the ability of those conducting research to disseminate their findings. More specifically, some peer reviewed journals will not publish articles on research that has not undergone IRB review and some professional associations may have the same requirement for presentations of research data at conferences. Aside from opening up access to disseminating research findings, IRB review offers an important and well-validated system of checks and balances for the ethical conduct of research and protection of human subjects and can also potentially provide an added layer of liability protection to those conducting research. In short, there are numerous reasons why IRB review of research is desirable, even when not necessary from a regulatory or legal standpoint.

Lack of access to IRB review can be a significant obstacle for practitioners who want to conduct practice-based research (see Osborne & Luoma, in press, for a more complete discussion of this topic). Many IRBs are attached to academic or research institutions and often cannot be utilized by individuals outside these organizations. Additionally, private IRBs are often too cost prohibitive for practice-based researchers given that much of this research is not grant-funded and thus, funds may not be readily available to pay for the often-high fees charged by these organizations. The benefits of IRB access to practice-based researchers are clear, but solutions to the problem of lack of IRB access are somewhat limited and variable in their efficacy (Osborne and Luoma, in press).

The purpose of this chapter is to provide a step-by-step guide to creating an independent IRB. The model described here is based on the successful development and implementation of an IRB by a group of mental health professionals who conduct practice-based research. The hope is that this model can serve as a roadmap to others who are interested in creating similar mechanisms to support this type of valuable research. Whenever possible, practical advice and actionable steps are provided that pertain to the many facets of starting and running an IRB. Although complex and challenging, the process of developing an IRB is feasible for those with research training and experience and who are willing to put in the time and work necessary to learn about the structure and functions of IRBs. The potential benefits of developing more of these mechanisms for practice-based researchers have important implications for helping to address the pronounced science-practice gap that exists in the mental health field (see Kazdin, 2008).

Creating the Behavioral Health Research Collective (BHRC)

Nearly a decade ago, a group of mental health providers from across the United States, all working in clinical practice or consultation settings, began discussing the possibility of forming an IRB to address the obstacles they had experienced when trying to access IRB review for their research projects. All members of the group shared a common value of contributing to the scientific literature in their respective areas of expertise, despite having chosen not to work in more traditional research-focused settings. Over the course of these discussions, individuals from seven organizations[1] decided to form the Behavioral Health Research Collective (BHRC) IRB. This IRB specializes in the ethical review of practice-based, behavioral health research protocols and has been registered with the Office for Human Research Protections (OHRP), part of the U. S. Department of Health and Human Services (HHS), since 2011.

The steps described here for forming an IRB to support practice-based research are drawn primarily from the experiences of the individuals who developed and operate the BHRC IRB, including the author, who serves at the Chair of the IRB. Specific examples of how the various steps described were implemented by this IRB are provided when relevant to help illustrate the concepts and tasks being discussed. It is important to note that the structure and operations of this IRB have been shaped by the aims of the organization and thus, other models could certainly be developed for IRBs with different aims. Our hope is to provide one example of a viable, fully functioning IRB that exists outside an academic context in order to provide both inspiration and a "how to" manual for those as passionate about this issue as we are.

A Step-By-Step Guide to Forming an IRB

Mission, Values, and Goals

Before beginning the work of creating an IRB, it can be important to first identify and clarify the IRB's intended mission, values, and goals. In addition to helping ensure that all individuals involved in forming the IRB share a similar vision and set of expectations for what will be created, taking sufficient time to carefully consider the *purpose* of what is being created is essential for guiding the many decisions that will need to be made along the way.

The primary mission of any IRB necessarily involves the ethical oversight of research in order to help ensure the safety of research participants. Thus, a commitment to the ethical conduct of research is paramount. A fully functional IRB must be able to provide the kind of scrutiny of research protocols and corresponding guidance to researchers that is needed to maintain adherence to ethical standards and regulations. Although a primary emphasis on ethical oversight is necessary, this commitment alone is not sufficient for clarifying all of the IRB's values and objectives. Other important questions to consider and discuss during this stage of the process include:

- What is the purpose of forming the IRB?
- What problem(s) will the formation of the IRB seek to address or solve?
- What types of research will the IRB review?
- Who will staff the IRB (i.e., administrative staff, Chair, IRB members)?
- How will the IRB be funded?
- Will IRB members be paid or volunteer their time?
- How much work will the IRB realistically be able to manage?
- Are the individuals involved willing to commit the considerable time and energy required to learning about IRB regulations and functions?
- What are the expectations regarding the IRB's longevity? Will this be a short-term or long-term endeavor?

Proceeding to the steps that are described later in this chapter is not recommended until these and other pertinent questions have been fully examined. As will become evident, many of the decisions that will need to be made when establishing the IRB will hinge on the answers to these questions. Failure to take adequate time to fully flush out the IRB's scope and priorities on the front-end will lead to numerous challenges later.

Early in the formation of the BHRC IRB, the group's members drafted the following statement of purpose based on discussions about the function and scope of the IRB:

> Behavioral Health Research Collective (BHRC) is a non-profit organization that was founded by a group of mental health professionals who are in clinical practice and who conduct research outside of a university or other institutional setting. The purpose of BHRC is to host an Institutional Review Board (IRB) that provides a low-cost mechanism for its members to submit research protocols for ethical review. A core feature of BHRC's mission is to help promote the ethical practice of research in "real-world" settings.

This statement directly outlines several of the IRB's values and objectives, which had direct implications for key aspects of the IRB's structure and operations. For instance, the inclusion of only mental health professionals in the formation of the group influenced decisions about the types of research that would be reviewed, namely behavioral health/mental health research. The decision to focus on practice-based research further narrowed the scope of the protocols the IRB was willing to review. Additionally, an explicit goal of offering a low-cost mechanism for ethical review had a direct bearing on the financial structure of the IRB, including such issues as the cost of application fees (fees were set very low to cover minimum operating costs), and whether IRB members would be paid for their time (it was decided that IRB members would not be paid and would volunteer their time as a form of professional service). The decision to not pay IRB members had further implications for how much work the IRB could handle; decisions were made about limiting the number of organizations who could submit applications to the IRB and the frequency of IRB meetings in order not to overburden the voluntary workforce. The goal of promoting practice-based research also led to the group committing to not only review these types of research protocols, but also to efforts to facilitate the development of other IRBs to do similar work via conference presentations and publications on this topic. Clearly, each of these issues would have been more difficult to navigate were it not for a clear set of principles and goals to guide this process.

Selecting Colleagues to Help Form the IRB

Not surprisingly, the formation of an IRB from the ground up involves a substantial amount of work and time. Moreover, because the central purpose of an IRB is to provide ethical oversight of research and to protect human subjects, identifying at least a few individuals who have strong training and experience in conducting research is essential. Although including individuals who have previously worked with an IRB is ideal, most clinicians likely do not have this background. Given that, the following types of experiences are likely to be an asset for individuals involved in creating the IRB:

- Prior training in research methods
- Prior training in research ethics
- Prior training in ethical decision making, even if not specific to research
- Regular consumption of research, including reading peer reviewed articles and/or attending professional conferences that include presentations of research data
- Current or prior experience working on research studies or in a research environment
- Current or prior experience with designing and running a research study (including thesis and dissertation projects)
- Involvement in the dissemination of research findings (i.e., presenting research data at conferences, writing papers for scientific publication)
- Serving as a journal editor and/or conducting peer reviews of manuscripts for scientific journals

After a group of individuals has been identified to form the IRB, decisions need to be made about how tasks will be divided up and assigned. As the BHRC IRB was being developed, the primary individuals from each organization who were involved in creating the IRB each agreed to put in a number of hours of work on various tasks (i.e., researching the standard operating procedures (SOPs) of existing IRBs, consulting with various IRB and other related professionals, reviewing drafts of SOPs and IRB forms). Additionally, the decision was made to hire an administrative coordinator early in the process to assist with creating IRB forms and other administrative responsibilities. One of the individuals involved also enlisted the help of a postdoctoral fellow to provide the bulk of the work involved in drafting the IRB's SOPs. Practicum students, interns, graduate students who have an interest in research and/or IRB development, and practice/agency staff could also be additional sources of help when completing the various tasks required to form an IRB.

Establishing the Business Structure of the IRB

Several important decisions will need to be made about the business structure of the IRB, including which organization will host the IRB, what the financial structure of the IRB will look like, and whether the IRB will obtain liability insurance. The specific decisions related to these issues are likely to vary widely across settings based on the context and needs of those involved in forming the IRB.

Deciding what organization will host the IRB should occur fairly early in the process, as this decision will dictate many other choices. The federal guidelines that pertain to IRBs do not include specific regulations about what kinds of organizations can host an IRB. Some practice settings may be large enough that a single organization could itself host the IRB (this would be akin to IRBs that are run by universities or hospitals, which typically only serve employees of those institutions). In the case of the BHRC IRB, all of the organizations involved were relatively small and from the beginning the nature of the project was envisioned as a kind of "co-op." Thus, a decision was made that none of the individual organizations would host the IRB and instead, a separate non-profit organization would be created to host the IRB. The board members of this non-profit organization were made up of individuals from those organizations involved in forming the IRB. This business structure had the advantage of not placing the liability of running the IRB on any single entity disproportionately. It also allowed for the possibility of flexible membership over time; if organizations decided to leave the IRB, they could do so and be replaced by other organizations without having to change which organization hosted the IRB. At the same time, the decision to create a separate organization to host the IRB also created a bit more work, as this involved having to complete all of the steps required to start a new non-profit corporation (e.g., file articles of incorporation with the state, get a federal tax ID number, set up a bank account, etc.). However, this additional work was deemed worthwhile by those involved as the business structure suited the needs of the participating organizations.

After the decision has been made about who will host the IRB, it is important to consider the financial structure of the IRB. Important questions to ask during this process include:

- How will the IRB be funded?
- What will be the IRB's primary expenses?
- Will the IRB charge fees? If so, how much will they be?
- Will IRB members be paid for their time spent reviewing applications?

- How will administrative tasks be completed? Will existing office or administrative staff assist with these tasks or will an administrative coordinator specific to the IRB need to be hired?
- How will the IRB's financial solvency be maintained over time?

For larger organizations, it may be feasible to allocate part of the organization's budget to fund the IRB. Smaller organizations may find this more challenging and may need to charge fees for IRB services to cover operating expenses. As previously mentioned, the BHRC IRB decided early on that the IRB would operate with as few expenses as possible in order to ensure a low-cost mechanism for IRB review (as high fees for private IRBs had been an obstacle to ethical review for some of the participating organizations). As a result, fees for applications were set fairly low ($250 for new applications, $50 for annual renewals, no fees for study modifications). It was also decided that IRB members would volunteer their time and that the only IRB staff who would be paid was an administrative coordinator. This individual's primary responsibilities include: management of all electronic application materials, taking minutes during IRB meetings, compiling IRB reviewer feedback and comments about study protocols prior to IRB meetings, and assisting with the creation of IRB forms. Other fixed annual costs for the IRB include business license fees, taxes, and liability insurance premiums. Additionally, the IRB elected to pay for the Chair to attend periodic IRB-related trainings and for one member of the IRB to join a professional association for individuals working in the area of research ethics. Whenever possible, the revenue from collected IRB fees are used to cover operating expenses. Expenses that cannot be covered by collected revenue (i.e., annual liability insurance premium) are divided among the participating organizations, thereby keeping the cost for each individual organization quite low. It should be noted that some of these expenses (business license fees, taxes) are a result of the decision to create a separate entity to host the IRB and would not be relevant for IRBs that are hosted by existing organizations that already have these expenses built into their operating budgets.

The decision about whether to obtain liability insurance to cover the work performed by the IRB will likely be influenced by a range of factors. First, if the IRB is hosted by a single organization, it is possible that the organization's existing liability policy may cover these activities and no additional policy may be needed. Second, liability insurance is technically not needed to operate an IRB and the decision about whether to obtain it is predicated somewhat on the level of risk tolerance of those involved. Although IRBs and IRB members have rarely been named in research-related lawsuits (Hoffman & Berg, 2005; Resnik, 2004), some risk is involved when providing ethical oversight of research involving human subjects and so having liability coverage can offer peace of mind, as well as the resources needed to pay for legal counsel if such action is taken. Third, although malpractice insurance may provide liability coverage for some individuals working with the IRB (e.g., clinicians, trainees), some IRB staff will not have such coverage (e.g., administrative staff) and thus, may have less liability protection in the event of a lawsuit.

Given that the BHRC IRB is hosted by a separate non-profit entity, the liability insurance policies of the participating organizations do not provide coverage for legal action taken against the IRB. Although the risk of legal action is low, the members of the IRB collectively felt that having liability protection was worth the peace of mind despite the cost. Thus, it was decided to obtain a liability insurance policy to cover the IRB's activities.[2] Identifying an insurance company that would write such a policy was challenging, given that many insurance companies are not familiar with IRBs. The BRHC ultimately opted for a liability policy only, and not a Director's and Officer's (D&O) policy, because it was believed that any potential legal risks, although negligible, were most likely to stem from the IRB's work itself and not the behaviors of the non-profit board of directors or officers. The cost of liability insurance represents the single largest item of the BHRC IRB's budget. However, because the annual premium is split between all participating institutions, the cost per organization is quite reasonable. In addition to this coverage, all members of the IRB have also notified their individual malpractice insurance carriers about their involvement with the IRB as an added layer of liability protection.

Registering the IRB with OHRP

An important decision to make during the early stages of forming an IRB is whether the IRB will register with the Office for Human Research Protections (OHRP), which is part of the U. S. Department of Health and Human Services (HHS). This decision is critical as it impacts whether the IRB can review certain types of grant-funded research, as well as the degree to which it will need to meet the regulatory standards for IRBs that are delineated by OHRP (often referred to as the "Common Rule" and are scheculed to be updated in 2018).

Any institution that conducts research with human subjects that is funded through HHS, which would include funding from the National Institutes of Health (NIH), Centers for Disease Control (CDC), and Federal Drug Administration (FDA), is required to submit an assurance of compliance to OHRP indicating that the institution agrees to comply with federal regulatory requirements regarding the protection of human research subjects (which are described in HHS Protection of Human Subjects, 2009). A document called a Federalwide Assurance (FWA) is the only type of assurance of compliance that OHRP will accept for these purposes. Furthermore, when preparing a FWA, an institution must designate the IRB that will provide ethical review of its studies and OHRP requires that this be an IRB that is registered with OHRP. Thus, even though the IRB itself does not file the FWA (it is filed by the organization conducting the research), the IRB must be aware of whether it will be reviewing studies that are funded through HHS in order to determine whether it will be necessary to register with OHRP. The earlier in the formation process the IRB is aware of this information the better, given that if the IRB registers with OHRP it will be required to meet all of the regulatory standards for the structure and function of an IRB (as set forth in HHS Protection of Human Subjects, 2009). As IRBs that are not registered with OHRP are not required to meet these standards, this has important implications for the drafting of the IRB's policies and procedures (see below).

IRBs that intend to register with ORHP can do so on the agency's website.[3] The process is relatively brief and involves providing basic information about the organization hosting the IRB, contact information for key leaders within the organization and the IRB (i.e., the Chair), as well as some information about the IRB members. There is no fee for registering an IRB with OHRP and registrations must be renewed at least every three years. After an IRB has registered with OHRP, it is then searchable in an online database of registered IRBs. The BHRC IRB chose to register with OHRP because at least one of the organizations involved when the IRB was created had grant funding through HHS and planned to pursue additional HHS funding over time. In order for this organization to designate the BHRC IRB in its FWA, it was necessary for the IRB to be registered with OHRP and also meet all related regulatory standards.

Drafting Standard Operating Procedures (SOPs) and Forms

One of the most time consuming steps in the process of forming an IRB involves writing SOPs and creating the necessary forms. Fortunately, many IRBs have their SOPs and forms publicly available on their websites and so there are numerous examples of these documents available to review and adapt. A helpful first step is to read through SOPs from two or three IRBs to get a sense of the scope of what these documents include, as well as to identify similarities and differences between IRBs.[4] When possible, selecting IRBs that review similar types of research as the newly forming IRB can be a useful strategy, as those SOPs are more likely to be relevant and beneficial as a model. For instance, an IRB that intends to review predominantly behavioral health research would not be helped much by reviewing SOPs for an IRB that reviews studies in the area of medicine or medical devices, as some of the policies needed for these types of studies will be quite different. This approach necessitates that those involved in creating the IRB first take time to consider the nature of the projects that are likely to be reviewed.

After several SOPs from other IRBs have been reviewed, the process of adapting existing policies from other IRBs to the new IRB can begin. If the IRB is planning to register with OHRP, it is essential to ensure that SOPs that are created are consistent with the regulatory standards for IRBs (available on the OHRP website). Due to the considerable work involved with drafting SOPs, it can be very helpful to hire administrative staff to assist with this task. In the case of the BHRC IRB, IRB members first identified several sets of SOPs from IRBs that were believed to be good models. One of the IRB members then enlisted the help of a postdoctoral fellow to adapt and draft a set of SOPs for the IRB. This draft was then reviewed and edited by the IRB members and final revisions were made by the IRB's administrative coordinator.

Similar to the process of drafting SOPs, IRB forms can also be created by adapting and modifying those from other IRBs. Again, having examples from multiple IRBs is very helpful as some will be more relevant and useful than others.[5] Although IRBs have numerous forms, a handful are used most frequently, including the IRB application for new studies, annual status report form, and study modification form. There is some variability in how IRBs design these forms and the information that they request from study investigators. It is therefore worth the time to review different models for these forms before making choices about the format and information that will be selected. The BHRC IRB took the approach of initially only creating forms that were certain to be used (as IRBs typically have numerous forms). Additional forms have been created along the way as needed. Drafts of all forms were first created by the IRB's administrative coordinator and then reviewed and edited by IRB members. Although having the administrative coordinator create these forms incurred some cost, this was more efficient and quicker than IRB members trying to find the time to complete this task. It also had a secondary benefit of helping the administrative coordinator become familiar with the IRB forms.

The process of drafting SOPs and forms took nine months for the BHRC IRB, in part because all of the IRB members also had full-time jobs in addition to putting time into forming the IRB. The process certainly could be completed more quickly, but it cannot be overstated that this is the most labor-intensive part of forming an IRB. Finally, it is important to note that SOPs are a "living document" and should be updated and revised over time along with changes in the IRB's structure and functions, as well as any regulatory changes (if applicable).

Staffing the IRB

IRBs are complex by nature and involve a range of responsibilities and duties. Decisions about who will fill various roles within the IRB are important, as how well the IRB functions will depend greatly on these decisions. There are several types of roles that will need to be staffed, including an administrative coordinator, the IRB Chair, full IRB members, and alternate IRB members.

The importance of the role of administrative coordinator for the IRB cannot be over-stated. This scope of this person's role can vary across IRBs, but typically this individual is responsible for the organization and management of the numerous documents and forms that are submitted to the IRB by study investigators. It is essential, for this reason, that this person is detail-oriented and possesses excellent organization skills. A background in working in research settings is also helpful, though not necessary. Other tasks the administrative coordinator might perform include: reviewing IRB applications for completeness, tracking when annual status reports are due, sending out notifications and materials for IRB meetings, and taking minutes at IRB meetings. The administrative coordinator for the BHRC IRB was hired because she had previously worked in a similar capacity on research studies that were run by several of the IRB members, making her background an excellent fit for the position. As the IRB is fairly small, this individual works, on average, a few hours per month and is hired as an independent contractor. The workload for this position fluctuates depending on the volume of submissions to the IRB. As the BHRC IRB uses an entirely electronic submission system, the administrative coordinator is able to work remotely and uses a web-based file storage system (box.com) to organize and store all IRB documents and study-related materials.

Another key decision is who will serve as the IRB Chair. The Chair has numerous responsibilities, including setting IRB meeting agendas, running IRB meetings, interfacing with the administrative coordinator, overseeing IRB members and onboarding new members, responding to questions from study investigators, and ensuring that the IRB is operating consistently with its own SOPs, as well as regulatory standards (if applicable). The role of Chair is the most extensive of all the IRB members and therefore, the individual who takes on this position will be taking on a disproportionate amount of IRB-related work. The degree to which the Chair is "hands on" vs. delegates' tasks certainly varies across IRBs, however, ideal characteristics of the Chair include being detail-oriented, timely in responding to communication, and an effective leader. As the majority of IRB Chairs have not served in this capacity prior to taking on the role, this position is likely to involve a fairly significant learning curve. Consequently, it is helpful if the Chair is someone who can commit to serving in the position for a period of time, both in order to provide continuity for the IRB, but also to help preserve accumulated knowledge that develops the longer one is in this position. Having said that, the IRB should also consider how the position of Chair will rotate over time and how such decisions will be made. In the case of the BHRC IRB, one of the individuals who was most involved with the formation of the IRB (the author) volunteered to serve as the Chair and made an initial commitment of five years to this position to provide the kind of stability the IRB needed when getting up and running.

The primary responsibilities of IRB members are to provide ethical review of study protocols and to attend IRB meetings and participate in discussions about these protocols. Members can serve in two main capacities—full member and alternate member. Full members are those who commit to serving on the IRB for a designated period of time and have consistent involvement with the IRB during that period. Alternate members are individuals who fill in for full members when they cannot participate in a study review or IRB meeting for some reason (i.e., conflicts of interest, scheduling conflicts, etc.). It is important for IRBs to have both full and alternate members to ensure that IRB activities can proceed when a full member cannot participate. All IRB members need to have a working knowledge of both research methodology and ethics. It is likely that IRB members will have different areas of expertise and knowledge and this is desirable as it leads to more comprehensive study reviews, as well as more rich discussions of ethical issues during IRB meetings.

If an IRB is registered with ORHP, there are several requirements for IRB membership that must be met (and are delineated in HHS Protection of Human Subjects, 2009). First, the IRB is required to have at least five members "with varying backgrounds to promote complete and adequate review of research activities commonly conducted by the institution." Second, every effort must be made to ensure that the IRB is not made up of members of only one gender. Third, the IRB must have at least one scientist member and at least one nonscientist member. Scientist members are individuals defined as those whose "primary concerns are in scientific areas." In many IRBs, individuals with MD or PhD degrees in behavioral or biomedical sciences serve in these roles. Nonscientist members are those whose "primary concerns are in nonscientific areas." Although the nonscientist member can have any professional background (aside from behavioral or biomedical sciences), a number of professions involve skillsets that are quite helpful for an IRB. For instance, the BHRC IRB's nonscientist member is a lawyer by training and this person's legal perspective is extremely useful, particularly when reviewing informed consent documents and HIPAA authorization forms. Given the increased use of electronic data collection and storage in many research settings, individuals with technology or technology security backgrounds would also be extremely valuable for an IRB to help ensure that proper standards are being met to ensure protection of confidentiality and data security. The nonscientist member role is particularly critical as IRB meetings cannot convene and conduct business (including reviewing or approving a study protocol) without a quorum and one of the stipulations for quorum is that a nonscientist member must be present. Lastly, the IRB must have at least one member who is not affiliated with the institution that hosts the IRB or who is a family member of someone affiliated with this institution. That individual could also have an overlapping role as a scientist or nonscientist member.

As BHRC IRB is registered with OHRP, it has to comply with the regulations described above. The IRB maintains a mixed-gender membership of at least five full members (including the Chair) and typically three to four alternate members. The IRB has one nonscientist member (a lawyer by training, as noted above) and the remaining members are all scientist members (individuals with graduate degrees in behavioral sciences). The nonscientist member is not affiliated with the organization that hosts the IRB and is also not related to anyone who is. In light of the fact that the IRB cannot conduct business if a nonscientist member is not present, the IRB is also in the process of adding a second nonscientist member to help ensure that at least one of these individuals can always be available for IRB meetings. All of the scientist members are asked to commit to two-year membership terms. The nonscientist member is asked to commit to a one-year membership term. Full members who decided to rotate off the board at the end of their terms are typically replaced by individuals who have been serving as alternate members. This system allows for fairly predictable staffing for the IRB and allows alternate members time to learn the IRB review process and how the IRB operates before transitioning into full member roles. Although all of the scientist members have a behavioral health background, their areas of specialty and research vary widely, which brings a range of perspectives and experiences to the IRB.

After an initial set of IRB members have been selected, they must then be trained. There is no consistent standard for the training of IRB members and IRBs vary widely in how members are oriented and trained before participating in reviews. The BHRC IRB developed its own training protocol that all members complete prior to joining the IRB and includes the following components:

- Completing a training on research involving human subjects, such as those provided by the NIH Office of Extramural Research or the Collaborative Institutional Training Initiative (CITI)
- Reading *The Belmont Report*[6]
- Reading *Institutional Review Board: Member Handbook, 3rd ed.* (Amdur & Bankert, 2011)
- Reading the BHRC IRB SOPs

After new IRB members have completed the required training, they fill out a training checklist documenting this and file it with the IRB. Additionally, they also sign and file several documents (all of which were modified from those of other IRBs), including (1) an appointment agreement that indicates the length of their appointment and describes the specific responsibilities of their role with the IRB; (2) a confidentiality agreement; and (3) a conflict of interest agreement (see the Appendix for copies of each of these documents). If members choose to recommit to a new term of service at the end of their appointment, each of these documents is signed and filed with the IRB anew. New members are also oriented by the Chair to the duties involved with their role and then "shadow" the review process for one or two reviews in order to learn the process and observe the structure of the IRB meeting. Following this period of observation, they begin full participation in the IRB.

In addition to initial training, ongoing continuing education for IRB members is also important to help these individuals stay up-to-date. The BHRC IRB has one member who is tasked with coordinating at least one continuing education activity per year for the board. Typically, these activities have included reading articles or chapters that pertain to specific issues that the IRB is faced with and that members need to learn more about. Additionally, the IRB has committed to paying for costs for the Chair to attend periodic trainings to stay abreast of regulatory requirements related to IRB operations and research involving human subjects. The IRB also pays to have members consult with topic experts when needed to help ensure that policies are drafted and decisions are made in ways that are consistent with best practices.

Conducting Reviews

After the IRB's SOPs and forms are finalized and members have been selected and trained, the IRB is ready to receive applications to review. How often the IRB meets may depend in part on how many applications are received. The BHRC IRB began with a system of scheduling meetings only when applications were submitted. Although this system helped to minimize the number of meetings per year to only those that were necessary, it was logistically challenging to identify meeting times that worked for all IRB members on an ad hoc basis. As a result, the IRB switched to having a set monthly meeting time. Study investigators who wish to have their applications reviewed must submit their materials at least 30 days prior to a meeting to allow sufficient time for materials to be distributed and members to complete their reviews. During the months when no applications are submitted, the IRB meets as needed to discuss any administrative or policy issues that need attention. To ensure that the workload for any given meeting is manageable, the BHRC IRB also limits the number of new applications that can be reviewed at any meeting to two. Other IRBs with different resources and volume of applications will likely operate differently.

Before conducting reviews, the IRB will need to select a reviewer system. IRBs differ with regard to how responsibilities for reviews are divided up. Some IRBs use a primary reviewer system in which one or more individuals (usually two or three) take the lead roles in reviewing a study protocol and guide the discussion about the protocol in the IRB meeting. These individuals also provide their recommendations about how the IRB should vote on the protocol. The remaining IRB members are also provided with the study materials in advance of the meeting and can participate in the discussion about the protocol in the IRB meeting to the extent that they feel necessary (Amdur & Bankert, 2006). Some IRBs use a primary and secondary reviewer system, in which one member is assigned as the primary reviewer and another is assigned as the secondary reviewer. These roles are similar to those described above for the primary reviewer system, with these individuals taking the lead on the review and meeting discussion and also making voting recommendations to the board. Regardless of which approach is taken, the implementation of a formal reviewer system can enhance the efficiency of the IRB and also help distribute the workload over time, as members typically rotate through primary (or secondary) reviewer roles.

The BHRC IRB initially took a slightly different approach to conducting reviews, in part to help all of the reviewers thoroughly learn the review process as all were new to serving on an IRB. When applications were submitted to the IRB for review, all reviewers were sent these materials and asked to provide written feedback to the Chair about any concerns or recommendations they had about the study. Thus, all reviewers completed reviews of every study protocol and essentially functioned as primary reviewers. Although this led to more work for the IRB members as a group, it also was helpful in training all members on the complexities of conducting reviews. This was particularly important because as a small IRB, applications were only reviewed five–six times per year. Now that the IRB has been in operation for several years and all reviewers have considerable experience reviewing study protocols, the IRB is in the process of transitioning to a primary reviewer system and clarifying expectations for members who are not serving in the primary reviewer role. This change will help decrease the intensity of the workload for IRB members and hopefully help the IRB be more sustainable over time.

During an IRB meeting in which a study protocol is being reviewed, a primary focus should be on discussing any key ethical concerns that have been identified by IRB members about the study. The goal of these discussions is to determine what changes or actions (if any) are needed in order to adequately address these concerns, with the protection of human subjects being the central guiding principle. The BHRC IRB invites study investigators to attend IRB meetings so that they can both hear and participate in the discussion about the ethical concerns related to their studies (all of the reviewers' feedback and questions about the protocol are sent to investigators prior to the meeting so they can prepare for this discussion). This model has been very effective in that it provides an opportunity for study investigators and IRB members to have a dialogue about any issues that have been raised. This real-time discussion is not only very efficient (as many questions or concerns can be easily cleared up by investigators once they are able to provide more information), but it also allows investigators and IRB members to brainstorm together about potential solutions for ethical dilemmas or concerns. These discussions often yield more effective solutions than IRB members or investigators would have come to separately. Study investigators have provided considerable positive feedback about their participation in these discussions and about their interactions with the IRB more broadly. Some IRBs may choose to operate in such a way that all questions about the study protocol are answered by investigators prior to the IRB meeting (Amdur & Bankert, 2006) so that meeting time can be preserved for decision making vs. discussion about specific study protocol issues. This is probably more necessary for IRBs with a high volume of studies to review. In the case of the BHRC IRB, this approach is not necessary as only one or two study protocols are ever reviewed during a single meeting.

After a study has been discussed in an IRB meeting, all IRB members then vote on whether to approve the study protocol. IRB members typically have five options of how they can vote on the protocol: (1) approved as submitted; (2) minor revisions required; (3) not approved (in the event that substantial revisions are necessary); (4) recuse (due to a conflict of interest); or (5) abstain (e.g., when the member does not feel that s/he has enough information to vote) (Amdur & Bankert, 2011). Study protocols are approved when the majority (more than half) of IRB members present in the meeting vote to approve them. Votes are also recorded in the meeting minutes (Amdur & Bankert, 2006).

Most IRBs provide a feedback document to study investigators detailing any revisions or questions that the IRB feels need to be addressed before final approval for the study can be given. How this feedback is organized can vary across IRBs. Some IRBs may choose to provide a document with feedback from different reviewers separated, similar to the feedback received from journal reviewers. The BHRC IRB chose to create an integrated feedback document to make it easier for both study investigators and the Chair, who works with study investigators to finalize all revisions, to track all issues that need to be addressed. Prior to the IRB meeting, reviewers provide their written comments and questions to the IRB's administrative coordinator, who then compiles the feedback into a single document that is organized by section of the IRB application. Reviewers can also make revisions and comments in electronic copies of study documents, such as informed consent documents or study fliers. It can be challenging and time consuming to merge several electronic copies of the same document to include all comments and revisions. Thus, the BHRC IRB is currently looking into web-based file-sharing tools to help streamline this process and would allow reviewers to all make revisions and comments in the same electronic document (i.e., Google docs, box.com).

After study investigators receive feedback from the IRB, they then revise the application and related study materials as needed to address the reviewers' concerns. Once all issues have been satisfactorily addressed, final study approval can be issued by the Chair and the study can begin recruitment. Any changes that are made to the study after this initial approval is given must be submitted to the IRB for review and approval before they can be implemented. This is typically done using a study modification form, in which study investigators detail the changes to the study being requested and indicate whether these changes alter the risk/benefit ratio of the study for participants. Additionally, studies must also be re-approved on an annual basis. To facilitate this review, study investigators are required to complete an annual status report that provides information about the progress of the research in the prior year, as well as any problems that have arisen or changes to the risk/benefit ratio that have emerged as the study has progressed. Ongoing oversight and approval of research protocols is an important aspect of the IRB's function.

Although a complete description of all aspects of operating an IRB are beyond the scope of this chapter, it is worth briefly mentioning that the regulatory standards describe several types of review that IRBs can conduct, predominantly based on the level of risk to human subjects inherent in the research. These categories include full board review, expedited review, and exempt (Bankert & Amdur, 2006). Full board review is appropriate for any study involving more than minimal risk and requires that the full IRB participate in the review, approval process, and ongoing review. Many studies however, particularly in the behavioral and social sciences, involve minimal to no risk to participants, and therefore do not necessitate that level of oversight. In such cases, expedited review or exempt classifications may be appropriate and the criteria for each are clearly delineated in the federal guidelines (HHS Protection of Human Subjects, 2009). Studies that qualify for expedited review and involve no more than minimal risk to participants, fall into one of a number of pre-defined categories of research (e.g., research using routinely collected medical information, research using survey, interview, focus group, program evaluation, or quality assurance designs), and only require review by one member of the IRB (i.e., the Chair or other designated IRB members) (Oki & Zaia, 2006). Research that is exempt from IRB review must involve minimal, if any, risk to participants and must also fall within one of several pre-defined categories (e.g., research conducted in typical educational settings, anonymous surveys or interviews when the data collected would not be harmful to participants if released, research involving existing records or data that are coded in such a way that participants cannot be re-identified) (Prentice & Oki, 2006). Best practice is for the IRB, not the investigator, to decide whether a project is exempt. Once the IRB has determined that a study qualifies for exempt status, the study is not required to undergo any additional continuing review by the IRB. It is important that IRB members take the time to learn and understand the details pertaining to these classifications of review to ensure compliance with regulatory standards. The BHRC IRB initially only conducted full board reviews of all studies regardless of level of risk (as described above) in order to help IRB members learn the review process. After all members were proficient in conducting reviews, the IRB phased in both expedited review and exempt processes and forms in order to provide less burdensome oversight (for the IRB and study investigators) for studies involving minimal or no risk.

Creating a Sustainable IRB

One of the considerable challenges of creating and running an IRB outside of the usual settings (i.e., university, medical center, private for-profit IRB) is developing a model that can be sustained over time. In most cases, the individuals who will be serving as IRB members will have other jobs and professional responsibilities. Depending on the financial structure of the IRB, many of these individuals may be donating their time as a form of professional service. Therefore, it is important to attend to factors that could contribute to burnout among IRB members, as this is likely one of the primary threats to the IRB's longevity.

There are a range of ways to help mitigate IRB member burnout. First, ensuring that the IRB has sufficient administrative support is key. As the IRB is forming, it is important to identify all tasks that can be performed by an administrative coordinator and to reserve tasks that require training in ethics and research design for IRB members. The BHRC IRB initially sought to limit the number of tasks assigned to the administrative coordinator in order to keep costs associated with the IRB low (as this individual was the only paid staff member of the IRB). However, over time it became clear that the IRB members, particularly the Chair, could not continue to complete the range of administrative tasks that they had taken on and several of these were reassigned to the administrative coordinator. This resulted in a small increase in IRB fees to offset this increased cost. The organizations that host the IRB felt this was worthwhile given that it increased the likelihood that the Chair would be able to continue in this role over a longer period of time.

A second way to help decrease IRB member burnout is to ensure that policies, procedures, processes, and forms are clear and easy to use in order to maximize efficiency. IRBs are complex organizations that can involve considerable regulatory language and requirements. Learning the ins and outs of being an IRB member can be taxing and additional burden is added to IRB members when the IRB does not run in a streamlined way. Investing sufficient time during the formation of the IRB to ensure that the organization is set up well will save IRB members considerable time and energy over the long-term. Additionally, IRB documents (SOPs, forms) should be living documents that are continually revised and improved to increase usability for both IRB members, as well as study investigators. As previously noted, the BHRC IRB invested nearly a year in creating policies and forms and did not begin to review protocols until these tools were in place. Additionally, SOPs and forms have continued to be revised over time in response to IRB member feedback. These changes have all increased clarity and efficiency, which in turn has saved IRB members time and energy when conducting reviews.

Third, it is important to recruit IRB members on an ongoing basis to ensure that the workload of running the IRB can be distributed over time. In the case of the BHRC IRB, senior clinician-researchers from each of the participating organizations were involved in the formation of the IRB and study reviews for the first several years. Over time, these individuals have brought in junior colleagues to first serve as alternate reviewers, and then as full IRB board members. This model allows for the possibility of IRB members rotating on and off the board over time, which will likely extend the life of the IRB by creating a larger pool of potential reviewers and contributors. This influx of new members over time must of course be balanced with maintaining a sufficient number of more senior members so that institutional knowledge and experience of how the IRB functions is not diminished.

Ongoing Training and Consultation

Due to the complexity of developing and maintaining an IRB, ongoing training and consultation is essential. Regarding training, several resources are particularly helpful. First, the books *Institutional Review Board: Management and Function, Second Edition* (Bankert & Amdur, 2006) and *Institutional Review Board: Member Handbook, Third Edition* (Amdur & Bankert, 2011) are essential resources for IRB professionals. Both provide detailed and easy to use information about a wide range of IRB-related functions and regulations and are an excellent first source to consult when forming the IRB and when questions arise. Second, OHRP offers education and outreach programs across the country that address a wide variety of topics that are relevant for IRB professionals (as well as study investigators). A list of upcoming programs is maintained on the organization's website and the fees associated with these workshops are relatively inexpensive. OHRP also provides numerous online resources and training materials covering a range of issues related to research ethics and regulations. Third, the professional association Public Responsibility in Medicine and Research (PRIM&R) offers resources and trainings for IRB professionals, including webinars, annual conferences, and workshops/trainings across the country. The organization also hosts an online IRB Forum that "promotes the discussion of ethical, regulatory, and policy concerns with human subjects research." Additionally, PRIM&R offers a certification program for IRB professionals who wish to pursue this level of credentialing.

As previously noted, the BHRC IRB requires that all IRB members read the *Institutional Review Board: Member Handbook* as part of the training process. The IRB has also used chapters from the *Institutional Review Board: Management and Function* text during the start-up phase of the IRB, as well as for ongoing continuing education materials. IRB funds have been used to pay for the Chair to attend workshops hosted by OHRP when they have been in the local area, as well as for one IRB member to join PRIM&R so this organization's resources can also be accessed to assist the IRB.

In addition to education and training, consultation with other professionals who are knowledgeable about specific research and IRB-related topics is extremely helpful. The BHRC IRB has consulted with a range of professionals over time in order to ensure that the organization is engaging in best practices. One helpful source of consultation is talking with other IRB professionals. Many of these individuals are willing to answer questions or discuss specific ethical or procedural issues free of charge. Another potentially invaluable source of information are private consultants who specialize in research ethics and compliance. A number of such consulting firms exist and offer a range of services to both researchers and IRB professionals. The BHRC IRB has hired such consultants on several occasions to provide guidance for creating specific procedures and policies. This consultation has saved considerable time and energy, as well as helped to ensure compliance with existing standards and regulations. Although these consultations required an investment of funds, the results were extremely worthwhile and moved the IRB forward in the development of these processes at a significantly faster pace than if IRB members had tried to figure these issues out on their own. Finally, consultation with lawyers who specialize in research and/or IRBs, as well as individuals who specialize in HIPAA regulations, can be important resources for addressing specific questions that required specialized knowledge or skillsets to answer. Information about several of the consultants used by the BHRC IRB is provided in the Appendix.

Final Thoughts

Creating an IRB is a significant undertaking that requires considerable patience, dedication, and work. At the same time, the benefits of a fully functional IRB that can provide ethical oversight to individuals who wish to conduct practice-based research are substantial at both the level of the individual professional (study investigator) and the field at large. Many mental health practitioners with research training have sufficient knowledge and skills to serve on an IRB. To date, however, there have been few models for how to create and run the type of IRB described here—one that operates outside of an academic center or for-profit IRB company. We hope that this step-by-step guide provides an initial jumping off point for people who are interested in doing similar work and that others can benefit from the lessons we have learned over the last number of years.

At the time of the publication of this chapter, the BHRC IRB had reviewed and approved nearly 30 research studies, many of which would not have been conducted without this mechanism for ethical oversight. The types of projects reviewed by the IRB have varied in nature and aims and have ranged from large, grant-funded randomized controlled trials examining innovative delivery models for mental health interventions, to non-funded studies examining outcomes data collected in clinical practice. Much of the data that has been collected across these studies has been from patients seeking services in mental health treatment settings, a significant strength in terms of the generalizability of findings to real-world clinical populations. Additionally, the IRB has enabled mental health professionals in primarily clinical settings and roles to design and carry out their own research studies and disseminate their findings. We believe this is a significant step in concretely addressing the practice-research gap in our field and hope this work inspires more individuals in clinical settings to get involved in conducting research and creating mechanisms, such as an IRB, to support these endeavors.

Notes

1. The founding organizations of the BHRC IRB include:
    Center for Cognitive and Dialectical Behavior Therapy, New York, NY
    Cognitive Behavior Therapy and Science Center, Oakland, CA
    Cognitive-Behavioral Therapy Center of Western North Carolina, PA, Asheville, NC
    Evidence-Based Practice Institute (EBPI), Seattle, WA
    Evidence Based Treatment Centers of Seattle (EBTCS), Seattle, WA
    Portland Psychotherapy Clinic, Research, & Training Center, Portland, OR
    The Center for Cognitive and Behavioral Therapy of Greater Columbus, Inc., Columbus, OH
2. BHRC IRB bought a liability policy through Sprague, Israel, Giles, Inc. insurance broker and the policy itself is underwritten by Hiscox. There are likely other brokers and insurers who can write such policies for IRBs, these are provided as an example.
3. www.hhs.gov/ohrp/register-irbs-and-obtain-fwas/index.html
4. The following web search engine terms will yield many examples: irb policies and procedures site:edu
5. The following web search engine terms will yield many examples: irb forms site:edu
6. The Belmont Report summarizes the basic ethical principles identified by the National Commission for the Protection of Human Subjects of Biomedical and Behavioral Research, which was created with the signing into law of the National Research Act in 1974. www.hhs.gov/ohrp/regulations-and-policy/belmont-report/index.html

References

Amdur, R. J. & Bankert, E. (2006). Guidelines for review, discussion, and voting. In E. A. Bankert & R. J. Amdur (Eds.), *Institutional review board: Management and function*, (2nd ed.) (pp. 187–190). Boston, MA: Jones and Bartlett Publishers.

Amdur, R. J. & Bankert, E. A. (2011). *Institutional review board: Member handbook*, (3rd ed.). Boston, MA: Jones and Bartlett Publishers.

Bankert, E. A. & Amdur, R. J. (2006). *Institutional review board: Management and function*, (2nd ed.). Boston, MA: Jones and Bartlett Publishers.

HHS Protection of Human Subjects, 45 C.F.R. 46 (2009).

Hoffman, S. & Berg, J. W. (2005). The suitability of IRB liability. *University of Pittsburg Law Review, 67*, 365–428.

Kazdin, A. E. (2008). Evidence-based treatment and practice: New opportunities to bridge clinical research and practice, enhance the knowledge base, and improve patient care. *American Psychologist, 63*, 146–159.

Oki, G. S. F. & Zaia, J. A. (2006). Expedited institutional review board review. In E. A. Bankert & R. J. Amdur (Eds.), *Institutional review board: Management and function*, (2nd ed.) (pp. 97–100). Boston, MA: Jones and Bartlett Publishers.

Osborne, T. L. & Luoma, J. B. (in press). Overcoming a primary barrier to practice-based research: Access to an institutional review board (IRB) for independent ethics review. *Psychotherapy*.

Prentice, E. D. & Oki, G. S. F. (2006). Exempt from institutional review board review. In E. A. Bankert & R. J. Amdur (Eds.), *Institutional review board: Management and function*, (2nd ed.) (pp. 93–96). Boston, MA: Jones and Bartlett Publishers.

Resnik, D. B. (2004). Liability for institutional review boards. *Journal of Legal Medicine, 25*, 131–184.

APPENDIX

IRB and Research Ethics and Compliance Resources

Office for Human Research Protections (OHRP)
www.hhs.gov/ohrp/
- Federal office that "provides clarification and guidance, develops educational programs and materials, maintains regulatory oversight, and provides advice on ethical and regulatory issues in biomedical and behavioral research." OHRP manages the registration process and oversight for federally registered IRBs, as well as sponsors numerous training programs throughout the country on research ethics and compliance.

Public Responsibility in Medicine and Research (PRIM&R)
www.primr.org
- Professional organization for individuals who are interested or engaged in research ethics and oversight. The organization provides a wide range of online educational resources (e.g., articles, webinars, and podcasts) and sponsors yearly research ethics conferences. PRIM&R also offers a certificate program in the Foundations of Human Subjects Protection, as well as a certification program for IRB Professionals.

IRB Forum (sponsored by PRIM&R)
www.irbforum.org
- Online discussion forum that "promotes the discussion of ethical, regulatory and policy concerns with human subjects research." The forum is free and is open to past and current members of various types of research ethics committees and review boards, as well as professionals involved in research activities.

NIH Office of Extramural Research, Protecting Human Research Participants Training
https://phrp.nihtraining.com/users/login.php
- Free online training that provides an overview of the primary ethical principles and issues related to the protection of human research participants. Individuals who pass the quizzes embedded in the training are provided with a certificate of completion.

© 2018, *Practice-Based Research: A Guide for Clinicians*, R. Trent Codd, III, Routledge.

Collaborative Institutional Training Initiative (CITI), Research Ethics Trainings
www.citiprogram.org/index.cfm?pageID=887
- Paid online trainings that cover a variety of topics related to research ethics, including human subjects research, responsible conduct of research, and IRB administration. Individuals who pass the quizzes embedded in the training are provided with a certificate of completion.

hrp Consulting Group
www.thehrpconsultinggroup.com
- Private consulting firm with expertise in research ethics and compliance, including IRB management and functions.

Apgar and Associates
www.apgarandassoc.com
- Private consulting firm with expertise in HIPAA privacy and information security, as well as regulatory compliance.

© 2018, *Practice-Based Research: A Guide for Clinicians*, R. Trent Codd, III, Routledge.

Behavioral Health Research Collective (BHRC) IRB

IRB Member Appointment Agreement

To: _____

Date: _____

Capacity: _____

_____

Term of Appointment: _____

_____

Introduction and Purpose

The BHRC IRB is a federally regulated entity with the mandate to review behavioral research studies that take place within or under the authority of BHRC. The purpose of this review is to determine if the proposed research meets certain established regulatory, policy, and ethical criteria to protect the rights and welfare of the human subjects of such research. The criteria used by the IRBs determine the acceptability of such research are based upon principles discussed in the Belmont Report, which include:

- The sum of the benefits to the subject and the importance of the knowledge to be gained so outweigh the risks to the subjects as to warrant a decision to allow the subject to accept these risks.
- Legally effective informed consent will be obtained from each subject, unless the requirements for waiver of informed consent are met, by adequate and appropriate methods in accordance with the provisions of applicable state and federal regulations.
- The conduct of the study will be reviewed at timely intervals.

© 2018, *Practice-Based Research: A Guide for Clinicians*, R. Trent Codd, III, Routledge.

Scope of Work

The IRB will review protocol and informed consent forms, and review or delegate the review of Investigator and site qualifications for the purpose of approving, recommending modifications to, or disapproving proposed research involving human subjects as required by regulations of the U.S. Department of Health and Human Services. Criteria to be used in reviewing protocols include minimization of risk, equitability of subject selection, adequacy of informed consent, and maintenance of subject confidentiality.

Regular Member:

As a regular member of the IRB your presence will be used to establish a quorum; therefore, you will be expected to attend regularly scheduled meetings, which will occur on as needed basis, but not more than once per month. All regular members receive a packet of material pertinent to the proposed research prior to the scheduled meeting. The packet will contain the meeting agenda, review information, the protocol(s), and informed consent form(s) submitted for review. You are expected to review this information prior to the meeting and participate in the review and ensuing discussion. You will be expected to serve as a primary reviewer on a rotating basis during your service to the IRB. The responsibilities of the primary reviewer are outlined in the BHRC Standard Operating Procedures (SOPs).

Alternate Member:

When you attend as an alternate member of the IRB, your presence will be used to establish a quorum. On occasion, you may be requested to serve as a substitute for a regular member or because of your unique qualifications. The IRB Chair will notify you well in advance of the meeting date to inform you about whether you will be filling in for a regular IRB member. Prior to each meeting you are asked to attend, you will receive a packet of material pertinent to the proposed research. The packet will contain the meeting agenda, review information, the protocol(s), and informed consent form(s) submitted for review. You are expected to review this information prior to the meeting and participate in the review and ensuing discussion.

Requirements

Prior to assuming responsibilities of an IRB member, new appointees will be expected to complete an NIH human subjects training (or comparable training), as well as other specified training tasks (see BHRC IRB Training Checklist and Documentation). IRB members are required to participate in continuing training and education during the term of their appointment.

© 2018, *Practice-Based Research: A Guide for Clinicians*, R. Trent Codd, III, Routledge.

Members are expected to agree to recuse themselves if they have a conflict of interest that could bias their consideration of research submitted for review and to document this agreement at the time they accept appointment to the IRB.

Term

The term for IRB members is at least two years of service and can continue via mutual decision between the IRB Chair and the IRB member. The only exception to this will be that the non-scientific member is expected to commit to at least a one-year term of service. Members who are unable or unwilling to fulfill their duties as IRB members may be removed from the IRB at any time by IRB Chair.

Please sign below if you agree to the terms described in the above.

_____
IRB Member   Date

_____
IRB Chair   Date

© 2018, *Practice-Based Research: A Guide for Clinicians*, R. Trent Codd, III, Routledge.

Behavioral Health Research Collective (BHRC) IRB

IRB Member Confidentiality Agreement

To: _____

Date: _____

I understand and agree that information disclosed orally or in written form or discussed at BHRC IRB meetings may include confidential information that is proprietary to commercial entities sponsoring the proposed research and/or involves the privacy rights of individuals.

I agree that I will not disclose or divulge in any manner any confidential or private information revealed at BHRC IRB meetings in any form or manner to any third party for any purposes whatsoever. "Confidential or Private Information" as used in this Agreement shall not include:

1. Information or knowledge in my possession prior to disclosure at a BHRC IRB meeting;
2. Information generally available to the public or thereafter becomes generally available to the public through a source other than BHRC IRB;
3. Information that was rightfully obtained by me from a third party, who, I believe, is under no obligation of confidentiality to BHRC IRB with respect to such information.

Acknowledged and Agreed:

_____
Signature   Date

_____
Printed Name

© 2018, *Practice-Based Research: A Guide for Clinicians*, R. Trent Codd, III, Routledge.

Behavioral Health Research Collective (BHRC) IRB

IRB Member (and Consultant) Conflict of Interest agreement

To: _____

Date: _____

I _____ certify that I shall recuse myself from deliberation and voting on any study submitted to the BHRC IRB in which I have a significant conflict of interest or the appearance of a significant conflict of interest concerning protocols reviewed by the board.

This would include:

Financial Interest:

Includes financial interests of immediate family members (at a minimum spouse/partner and each dependent child)

- Financial interests related to the research, product, or service being tested;
- Ownership interest (equity or stock options) or $10,000 or greater value when referenced to publicly traded prices or other measure of fair market value when aggregated for the immediate family;
- Ownership interest (equity or stock options) of any amount whose value could not be referenced to publicly traded prices or other measures of fair market value;
- Ownership interest (equity or stock options) of any amount when the value of the interest would be affected by the outcome of the research;
- Ownership interest (equity or stock options) whose value represented 5 percent or more interest in any one single entity;
- Compensation of $10,000 or more in the past year when aggregated for the immediate family.

- Compensation of any amount when the value of the interest would be affected by the outcome of the research;
- Proprietary interests related to the research of any value including, but not limited to, a patent trademark, copyright or licensing agreement;
- Board or executive relationship related to the research, regardless of compensation.

Non-Financial Interest:

- Involvement in the design, conduct, or reporting of the research;
- Involvement of immediate family in the design, conduct, or reporting of the research;
- Has an interest that the IRB members believe conflicts with his or her ability to objectively review a protocol; or
- Has an interest that the IRB members or others perceive may conflict with his or her ability to objectively review a protocol.

- I will make known any significant conflict of interest prior to the beginning of the IRBs discussion of any protocol under review.
- I will accept the assessment of the IRB Chair with respect to significant conflict of interest.

Acknowledged and Agreed:

_____   _____
Signature   Date

_____
Printed Name

© 2018, *Practice-Based Research: A Guide for Clinicians*, R. Trent Codd, III, Routledge.

CHAPTER 7

Using Social Enterprise Concepts to Create a Sustainable Culture to Fund Research in a Fee-For-Service Setting

Jenna T. LeJeune and Jason B. Luoma

Despite the dominance of the scientist-practitioner model in psychology training programs (Chang, Lee, & Hargreaves, 2008; O'Sullivan & Quevillon, 1992), most psychologists are unable to engage in the dual roles of both utilizing and producing scientific research. Psychologists entering the field are typically forced to choose between a research-focused career path, most commonly in an academic institution, in which they are largely, if not completely, removed from clinical practice or a clinically-focused career path where they rarely engage in research (Goldfried & Wolfe, 1996). As a result, most psychologists practice solely in the applied domain and few contribute to the body of scientific research after completing their dissertation (Cullari, 1996; Stewart & Chambless, 2007). This occurs despite the fact that conducting research in clinical practice not only contributes to the greater scientific community but also has the possibility of improving clinical outcomes (Lambert et al., 2003; Persons, 2007).

There are significant, and likely lasting, changes occurring in both academic institutions and funding agencies, which seem to indicate that psychosocial research will need to expand beyond traditional research settings in order to thrive. These changes include dramatic shifts toward more part-time faculty and fewer tenure track academic positions (U.S. Department of Education, 2013), policy shifts at the National Institutes of Mental Health (NIMH) that route funding away from psychosocial research and toward genetic/epigenetic, neuroscience and drug precursor research (NIMH, 2008), and an overall change in the cultural zeitgeist towards the medicalization of psychological suffering (Schomerus et al., 2012). This results in a decreased share of funding for psychosocial research, which is the kind of research that psychologists have excelled at and the kind of research which has direct implications for clinical practice. While these changes may result in a sense of uncertainty and anxiety for the academically-based psychosocial researcher, the uncertainty these changes bring may push people to look for ways to fund research. We suggest that private, fee-for-service clinical settings can provide a new way, provided they are structured appropriately.

In order for fee-for-service clinical practices to become productive research environments, they need to be structured differently than is typical. In particular, the positive effects of monetary contingencies need to be utilized and the negative effects controlled if we are to integrate clinical practice and research productivity under one roof. In this chapter, we offer one possible model called the "clinical-research social business model", that utilizes social enterprise concepts in order to support and fund psychosocial research inside a for-profit clinical setting (LeJeune & Luoma, 2015). We also provide an example of how our site has manifested this model, where profits from the income-generating activities of the business serve as a stable, internal funding source for in-house research endeavors. Organizing our fee-for-service clinic utilizing social enterprise concepts has allowed us to realize a possibility that seems to have been largely elusive to the field of psychology: a for-profit organization that allows for a fuller expression of both the scientific consumer and producer roles for which scientist-practitioners have been trained. In this chapter, we outline the advantages of doing research inside a fee-for-service setting, what social enterprise is and how social enterprise concepts can be implemented to overcome important barriers, and how this model has manifested at our site. We hope this gives readers some theory to guide implementation at their site as well as practical ideas on how to better organize a business to fund scientific research.

Why do Research in a Fee-For-Service Setting?

The most common worksite for applied psychologists is a group or individual for-profit fee-for-service practice (Cullari, 1996; Stewart & Chambless, 2007). Although no systematic data are available to our knowledge, our experience suggests these settings are very rarely involved in producing any significant amount of research. Nevertheless, we have found substantial benefits to doing so and review these below.

One major benefit of conducting internally funded research within a fee-for-service setting is the greater scientific freedom and flexibility afforded when funding is not dependent on external funding entities. Agency funding priorities are as much political as scientific and often impinge on grant-funded researchers' ability to pursue the topics they feel are most important to scientific advancement. Independence from funding agencies allows researchers to focus on lines of research that may be more innovative, have longer timelines, or do not conform to the dominant research paradigm. This may be particularly appealing to researchers working in areas that are not currently favored by funding agencies.

Embedding research inside a small business often allows for research monies to be utilized more efficiently than in traditional research settings. Most grant-funded researchers are familiar with the rapidly fluctuating funding levels that occur as grants come and go. It is common for research budgets to swing hundreds of thousands or millions of dollars over just a few months. This introduces significant waste into the system. Research skill takes time to develop and is lost when projects wrap up and employees or graduate students move on. Equipment often lays idle after a project is over. As funding priorities change, research protocols and guidelines that were painstakingly developed go unused, or subsequent research projects go unfunded. Our more stable funding lines allow us to focus on research with longer timelines. Overhead is lower. Projects begin more gradually and build more logically. Staff can be retained for longer periods. There is more continuity and integration within the research, with the first project flowing into the next, and protocols are reused repeatedly in a logical fashion. In addition, the relative lack of bureaucracy in a small business, as compared to in most academic, governmental, or medical settings, reduces the time, effort and frustration of jumping through bureaucratic hoops, and ultimately allows researchers to conduct more research on a smaller budget.

The ability to pursue a line of research that is independent of the priorities of external funders allows the clinician-researcher to focus on projects that have the potential for more immediate practice impact and more direct application to clinical work. Research that is not only conducted within, but is also directly supported by, clinical practice allows for a level of integration between science and practice that is rarely otherwise available. As such, direct ties to clinical practice may result in research that is more likely to be relevant to clinical practice and in interventions that are more likely to be usable in applied settings. This can help with the problem of researchers developing interventions that end up being impractical or difficult to use in applied settings. For example, much research on exposure therapy has been conducted using 90 to 120-minute therapy sessions (e.g., Foa, Yadin, & Lichner, 2012). However, as those who work in fee-for-service settings know, it is often challenging to get insurance companies to reimburse for the billing codes that apply to 90 or 120-minute sessions, making a direct extension of this research to its application limited. Because they are operating in these "real life" settings on a daily basis, a researcher in a fee-for-service setting would be much more likely to know of these logistical factors and take them into consideration when creating new interventions. Thus, these researchers would be more likely to design interventions, from the start, that could actually be used in the settings for which they were designed. Embedding research in the settings in which it is likely to be utilized may also result in environmental feedback that increases the relevancy of resulting innovations.

In addition to the benefits for researchers, nesting research inside a fee-for-service environment may offer significant benefits to one's clinical practice. Research suggests that clinicians who collect outcome data and conduct other research within their clinical setting have improved clinical outcomes (Lambert et al., 2003; Persons, 2007). The attention to detail, the meta-cognitive thinking and reflection, and the structured approach to learning that are part of research may also result in clinician skill gains over time. Nesting research within a practice can also help support a culture of ongoing learning and provide quicker access to, and adoption of, innovations occurring in the larger scientific community. Finally, conducting research within a clinical setting offers access to a variety of experiences and opportunities for collaboration that are typically absent for the clinician who is only focused on clinical work. Thus, conducting research in the fee-for-service setting not only contributes to the broader scientific literature, but can improve clinician quality of life and patient care.

Significant changes within the clinical practice landscape have resulted in an increasingly competitive fee-for-service practice environment. Many therapists, particularly those in the earlier stages of their career, struggle to get credentialed with insurance panels, as those panels are increasingly closed to new therapists (Lichtenberg, Goodyear, & Genther, 2008). Those who are able to get onto insurance panels have to contend with steady and significant decreases in reimbursement rates those insurance companies will pay (Goodheart, 2010). Conducting research can provide a way for fee-for-service settings to stand out in an increasingly competitive marketplace. As can be seen in the university teaching hospital model, there is prestige that comes from being recognized as a research institution. This prestige can generate increased revenue for the clinical practice. Clinical practices that are able to stand out from the crowd of private practices by distinguishing themselves as local or regional scientific leaders can garner higher profit margins for their clinical work. Essentially, research recruitment, and scientific presentations and publications indirectly serve as marketing and public relations.

Monetary Contingencies as a Barrier to Doing Research in Fee-For-Service Setting

While there are significant benefits to organizing fee-for-service practices in a way in that can support in-house research, common barriers often prevent individuals and organizations from doing so. Many of the logistical barriers, such as access to an institutional review board (IRB), research assistants and journals, are relatively straightforward to overcome and have been discussed in more detail elsewhere (see LeJeune & Luoma, 2015). However, the most significant and overarching barriers limiting research productivity in fee-for-service settings relate to money. The contingencies around money found in traditionally organized fee-for-service settings make it (very) difficult to do research in a sustainable or substantial way.

Money is a bully. The way that monetary contingencies function in traditional fee-for-service settings tend to shape clinicians to see increasing numbers of clients. These monetary contingencies are so tight and powerful that they are hard to overcome. Despite a desire to engage in other activities, such as conducting research, keeping up-to-date on the empirical literature, or advancing clinical skills through continuing education, the tight contingency between seeing a client and the extrinsic reward of receiving money, results in a relatively narrow focus of seeing increasing numbers of clients. This works fairly well if the focus is on the making the most money that one can with one's time. However, this same contingency is problematic if the goal is to engage in tasks that rely on intrinsic motivation, collaboration and creativity, as is the case with research (Hennessey & Amabile, 1998).

Research shows that external contingencies, such as money, tend to lead to a focus on goals resulting in short-term payoffs (Critchfield & Kollins, 2001). Money tends to motivate people to work harder, but it also tends to narrow their focus, thereby decreasing creativity and innovation (Hennessey & Amabile, 1998).

In addition, strong monetary contingencies tend to reduce sharing and cooperation (Lin, 2007). Being paid on a per-client basis tends to lead clinicians to be more "efficient" with their out-of-session time, more focused on getting the next client in the door, and more motivated to retain clients. Thus, monetary contingencies tend to work well, from a financial standpoint, in fee-for-service settings that are solely focused on clinical work.

However, these contingencies tend to work against scientific productivity, as this is an endeavor that requires innovation, creativity, collaboration and a willingness to delay reward. Without other structures in place, immediate monetary rewards present in clinical work will tend to trump the delayed intrinsic rewards present in research production (Critchfield & Kollins, 2001). We believe this a large part of the reason why there is little research productivity inside most clinical practices, despite many psychologists having solid training as researchers. In order to make research production viable in clinical practice, we need to think organizationally to alter the contingencies around money in the fee-for-service settings, such that research work is not in competition with clinical work.

Few psychologists receive any training in business during graduate school. We often feel uncomfortable about helping others in exchange for money, and, as a result, we tend to avoid thinking about it. It can be helpful to think of money as a tool. Tools can be used for both purposes that serve our values and for purposes that do not. The market economy, with its emphasis on making money, is one of the most powerful innovations in all of human history (Intriligator, 2004). Unless we completely exit the market economy, money is going to be a part of the picture. Rather than trying to ignore the monetary elephant in the room, it is essential to be intentional about the influence of money. Most researchers operate in the nonprofit world of government funding, nonprofit universities and nonprofit foundations. While this protects them from the pressures of competing in the commercial sector, it also means they lose out on the possible benefits of commercial enterprise.

Our goal was to harness the power of the market economy to fund substantial, ongoing and programmatic research, while simultaneously protecting our researchers from the negative effects of tight monetary contingencies. The result is a for-profit, fee-for-service business that uses social enterprise concepts to support broader social benefits, such as psychosocial research and environmental stewardship. This clinical-research social enterprise model generates income from the kinds of activities typically conducted in fee-for-service settings (e.g., provision of therapy, trainings offered to professionals, etc.) and uses a portion of these funds to support research through paying research staff a fixed, fair salary for research activities. The model is heavily influenced by social enterprise concepts (Yunus, 2011).

Introduction to Social Enterprise

A traditional for-profit company is organized with the primary goal of making money for the shareholders who own the business. In contrast, a nonprofit

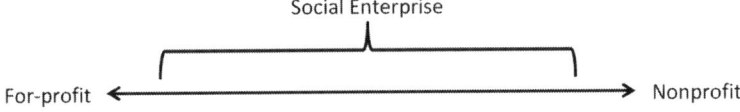

Figure 7.1 Spectrum of possible business

organization is concerned with money to the extent that it allows the organization to accomplish the social good for which it has been organized. Most nonprofits are generally not part of the commercial economy, but instead obtain their operating funds primarily through donations and grants.

If for-profits and nonprofits define the ends of a spectrum of possible business models (see Figure 7.1), then social enterprise refers to all business types that lie somewhere between these two ends. Social enterprises operate, at least partly, in the commercial sector, producing and selling a product to earn revenue, but also balancing this motive against other goals. One commonly used framework in the social enterprise world is the idea of the triple bottom-line. In for-profit accounting, the single bottom line refers to shareholder profit; it is the sole focus. In the triple bottom-line found in a social enterprise, this intention to be profitable is balanced against the desire to be environmentally responsible and produce social good. Social enterprises can be organized in many legal forms, including non-profits, for-profits, or newer entities, such as limited liability corporations (L3Cs) or B corporations. The legal organization does not define a social enterprise, but instead its goals and organizational structure do.

Social enterprises expanded in the 1970s and 1980s in Europe and America in response to economic downturns and cutbacks in government benefits. During this period, charities lost both government funding and individual donations, while at the same time need went up in many sectors. Some charities entered the commercial sector in an attempt to supplement their revenue. One of the most famous social enterprises, Grameen Bank, emerged during this period.

Grameen Bank is a microcredit bank that gives small loans, typically averaging around $100, to people starting or expanding businesses in low income countries. Grameen Bank targets the poorest of the poor and gives most of its loans to women. Most of its operating funds are provided by interest payments on the loans it provides. Through leveraging the commercial sector, this social enterprise has been able to provide billions of dollars to those in most need who otherwise would not have access to credit. Our organization takes inspiration from organizations, such as Grameen Bank, that attempt to harness the power of the commercial sector in order to do good in the world.

An Example of Social Enterprise: The Clinical-Research Social Business Model

In this section, we describe the reasoning behind and the development of our clinical-research social business model (LeJeune & Luoma, 2015). We also outline some of what we have learned through our experience of developing and testing our model.

The clinical-research social business model emerged out of our several years of experience in more traditionally structured settings, including solo private practice and grant-funded academic positions. Until this point, money had never been much of our motivation for working, but instead a byproduct; we did good work and were reimbursed sufficiently for that work. However, as we began to explore social enterprise models, we wondered if it could be possible to actively use commercial activity as a tool to maximize our ability to do "good" (as defined by our values, which we will discuss more in a subsequent section). In creating this model, we were essentially trying to find the convergence of three realms: 1. What we do well, 2. What we can get paid to do, and, most importantly, 3. What values we most want to stand for (see Figure 7.2). Those values we wanted money to serve included generosity, community and relationships, stewardship of the natural environment, compassion and play.

As clinical psychologists trained in the scientist-practitioner model, both of us had a value of contributing to our broader community by using science to address the problems of human suffering. We wanted more integration between the science and practice of our craft than we had experienced in other settings. We hoped for a setting in which individual work with clients directly contributed to something broader than the lives of the two people in the therapy room and also one in which the research we conducted could be both more directly applicable to and potentially influenced by those it was intending to benefit.

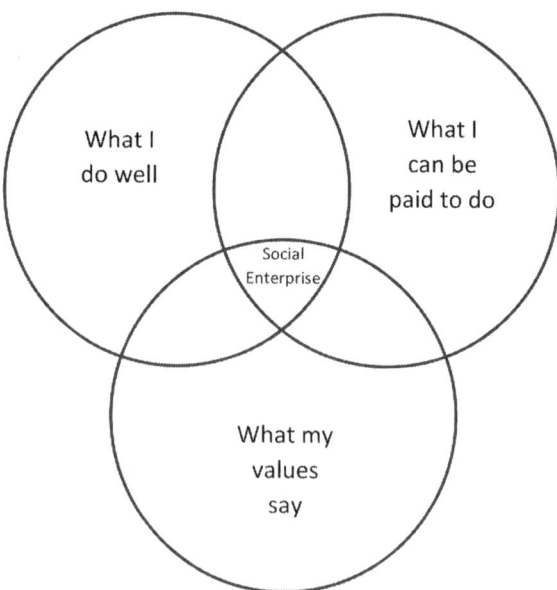

Figure 7.2 Three guiding considerations in building a social enterprise.

Using Social Enterprise to Fund Research 115

We also wanted to make choices about where we lived based on our values rather than out of necessity. Our strong desire to be in the community we loved near family took priority over pursuing an academic position wherever that might be available. A significant benefit of housing a research career within a fee-for-service setting is that one is not geographically constrained by the pursuit of the increasingly limited number of academic or research positions available at any given time (U.S. Department of Education, 2013).

At the time we were considering forming a social enterprise to fund research, it was becoming increasingly apparent that the funding of psychosocial research was on a significant decline and that all signs suggested that trend would continue into the foreseeable future. At the time we were considering this shift (2009), we noted that funding success rates at the National Institutes of Health (NIH) had dropped precipitously and alternate forms of research funding might be worth exploring. NIH funding rates remain historically low to this day (see Figure 7.3).

From its inception, it was clear that Portland Psychotherapy (which, at the time, consisted of the two authors and a postdoctoral fellow) would need to develop different contingencies around money. We felt that simply attempting

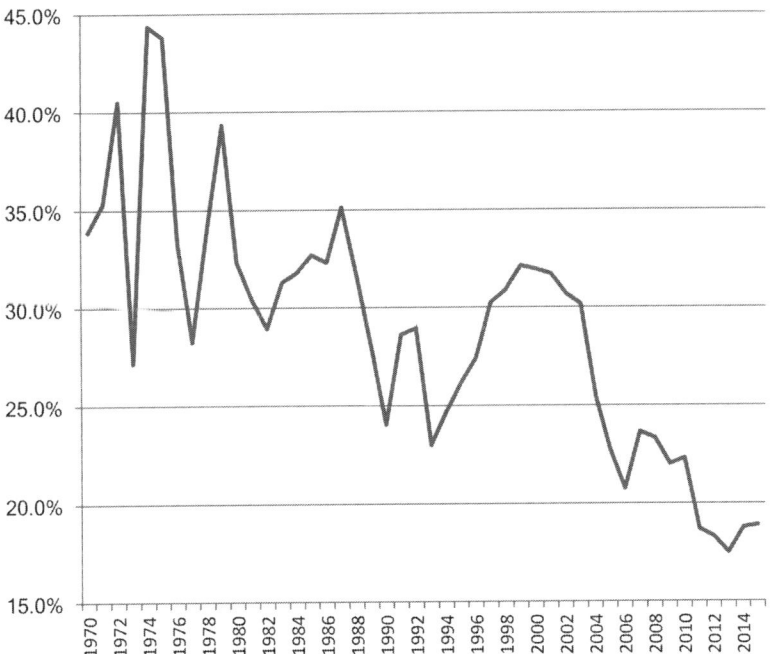

Figure 7.3 Success rate of R01 equivalent grants by year at the NIH. Changes in NIMH funding rates track overall funding rates quite closely. Graph generated from data from "Research Project and R01-Equivalent Grants: Success Rates, 1970 to Present". National Institutes of Health Office of Extramural Research, 2013. Retrieved from: http://report.nih.gov/success_rates/index.aspx

to carve out time from clinical work for research without pay for that time was a significant factor in why clinical settings rarely produced much research. Without other contingencies to support it, over time, dedicated research time would be eroded by encroaching pressures to engage in more clinical work, since that work is supported by the immediate, extrinsic reinforcement of earning money, and also, of course, by the immediate reinforcement of helping a particular client. As such, we needed a model that would be able to pay staff a fair, fixed and stable salary for research pursuits that would not generate any immediate or direct profits.

Because maximizing shareholder benefit was not the singular goal in our social enterprise, which was instead based on a triple bottom line, we decided to create a model where the profits would fund in-house research endeavors, rather than go directly to the shareholders (the owners, in this case), as would be the case in traditional fee-for-service settings. Based on these organizing concepts, our clinical-research social business model was born; we would create a for-profit fee-for-service clinic and training center in which the profits from money-making activities would serve as a stable, internal funding source for our research program. Portland Psychotherapy Clinic, Research, and Training Center (Portland Psychotherapy) was formed as a test of this model. Below, we outline the main steps we went through in order to build our current organization and then we briefly review our outcomes.

Have a Plan to Generate an Adequate Profit Margin

In order to fund in-house research, one must generate an adequate profit margin. As we considered various business models that would allow us to increase the profit margin of our income-generating activities, we also wanted to ensure our model would reflect our chosen values. Core values around community and generosity meant that increasing our profit margin by being a "boutique" clinic with dramatically increased fees that served only wealthy clients was not the choice we wanted to make. Instead, we sought to sustain an adequate profit margin by minimizing health insurance panel participation, which allows us to avoid the artificially depressed reimbursement rates insurance companies dictate to their in-network providers. In order not to limit our services to only those who are able to bypass using their insurance altogether, we chose to continue to accept insurance and provide those billing services for our clients. However, the majority of our clinical services are provided as out-of-network providers, thereby allowing us to regularly receive our full fee from insurance companies, rather than from the significantly lower in-network rates.

In order to able operate largely out-of-network, our center needed to be one in which clients saw our services as containing added value beyond what they might find in other in-network settings. Although not directly affiliated with any academic institution, our center is similar in many ways to the university teaching hospital model. Many individuals will seek out and spend more of their disposable income on receiving care from exceptional teaching and research hospitals because of the perceived expertise of their staff, access to the latest scientific advances, opportunities for more specialized care, and access to the latest diagnostics and treatment technologies. Our goal was to develop a center that had similar resources, expertise and access to scientific advances, but with a focus on the provision of mental health services.

The research and training parts of our mission ensure that ongoing learning and training is built into our model. We are intentional about hiring and retaining staff who provide specialty care and have expertise in a particular area of focus. We do not try to provide care to everyone that comes through our door, but instead try to focus on what we are excellent at and attempt to refer out those potential clients who are not a good fit for our services. We seek to be regarded as a center of excellence with services that are worth paying a bit extra for. In our metropolitan area of two million people, there are many people who have the extra income that allows them to pay another $20–$60 per session if they see value in the service they are receiving for that extra money. Certainly, not every client we serve can pay extra for our specialized services and for those clients we offer a sliding scale and reduced fees. However, for many people, the choice in spending the extra $20–$60 isn't so much a question of "Can I?" but rather "Is it worth it?", and for those people, being able to receive exceptional care from specialists at our center often results in a "yes" to the "Is it worth it?" question. According to data we have collected at our center, one of the most common reasons clients endorse for having come to our center is our reputation for emphasizing scientific research and evidence-based specialty care.

Be a Good Community Member

Some people will also seek to support businesses they see as being good members of the community. Many people, for example, will pay a little bit extra to shop at stores that provide their employees with a fair wage and good working conditions, or will spend more to buy locally grown produce at a farmers' market rather than support "big agriculture." Similarly, we have sought to communicate to potential clients that, if they choose our services, they are supporting a business that cares about more than just a financial bottom line. Their choice to work with us is a choice to support scientific research, to support diversity, and to support a company that tries to maximize social and environmental benefit above shareholder profit.

Be Guided by your Values

Privilege allows some people the ability to choose to pay more for perceived value, but not all are able to make those choices. We wanted evidence-based services to be available to *all* in our community, regardless of privilege. Because of this, we have also set up a structure that allows us to provide significant sliding scale and lower fee services for those who are not able to afford our standard out-of-network rates. Licensed providers also participate on a limited number of insurance panels, which allows us to provide even more moderate fee services and also helps with overall client flow. Our postdoctoral fellowship program was founded in 2008 primarily as a way to provide affordable, sliding scale services. This program has also been a key lever for growth within the organization and an integral part of our research production, as most fellows also assist with research. Recently, we also started a practicum program, allowing us to provide even more sliding scale services. Neither the postdoctoral fellowship nor the practicum program would likely be programs we would choose to fund if the organization was focused on the single-bottom line of profit, as they are not generally effective income generators. However, these programs do benefit our goal of contributing to the social good and help us move towards our values of generosity and community. Thus, these programs are a highly valued part of our organization.

Develop Infrastructure

In addition to developing the postdoctoral fellowship program, two other fundamental tasks were essential to attend to as Portland Psychotherapy was developing: developing the infrastructure needed to conduct research and making financial investments in the organization that would drive down overhead over the longer term. For example, in 2011 we began exploring how to set up an independent IRB to review our research and helped spearhead the development of a nonprofit corporation that now reviews our research along with those of other member organizations (see Chapter 6). We also reached out to local academicians and universities as we developed a research assistant program that has allowed us to gain high quality assistance with our research while simultaneously serving our training mission by offering mentorship to numerous research assistants, several of whom later got into graduate school in part because of the research experience they gained at Portland Psychotherapy. Additionally, by 2012, the revenue generated from the business provided the cash flow needed to allow the purchase of a 16-office building that has already decreased the overhead costs associated with office space.

Develop Business Skill

As the organization continued to grow, it soon became evident that we needed to develop expertise in how to successfully run and manage a small business. Over the past several years, JBL has dedicated much of his professional efforts to developing skills in all aspects of small business through a combination of reading, consultation and formal coursework at the local small business resource center. We developed relationships with excellent consultants to tap for expertise when needed. Our marketing program was developed, expanded and routinized with a goal to become particularly strong on internet-based marketing, as fit with our goal to be regional leader. We gradually expanded our administrative staff one hire at a time. We spent many unpaid hours developing our methods for management, our organizational culture, and clinical and administrative procedures.

Outcomes

This combination of business development, intentional hiring, internal development and marketing has resulted in a 29 percent annual revenue increase since 2008, when we hired our first postdoc. Our staff has increased from two (the authors) to 15, including nine full-time clinical and clinical-research staff, two part-time clinicians, a full-time research coordinator, and three administrative staff, plus several contractors. This growth allows us to serve over 100 individual therapy clients per week, including many reduced-fee and sliding scale clients, in addition to meeting other clinical needs through the various groups and classes we run.

In addition to the fixed, paid research time that our clinician-researchers receive, Portland Psychotherapy has recently started an internal grant program through which any of our clinical staff can apply for additional research funds and have thus far distributed approximately $20,000 through that grant program. In the years 2013–2015, approximately 16 percent of the total revenue generated by the center went to fund our research program, mostly to pay employee salaries. We currently fund approximately one full-time equivalent of research time for doctoral staff. In addition, we were recently able to hire a full-time research coordinator to manage most of the day-to-day aspects of our research studies. The current research program consists of more than ten ongoing research projects and has resulted in the publication of more than two dozen peer-reviewed articles in addition to numerous other publications in non-reviewed outlets (e.g., book chapters). Several articles are in preparation or under review at any given time. The research conducted at Portland Psychotherapy ranges from basic to applied, and includes topics such as perspective taking, evidence-base therapy training, social signaling behavior in high self-critics, longitudinal research on substance misuse, and development of interventions for chronic shame and self-criticism. All of that research productivity has been accomplished without any outside grant funding and would not have been possible in a fee-for-service setting organized as a traditional for-profit company with a single bottom line.

Our Triple Bottom Line

A fundamental concept in social enterprise is the idea of a triple bottom line, which consists of balancing "social benefit", "environmental benefit" and "shareholder benefit" (i.e. profit). This triple bottom line guides every decision we make within the organization. Without significant intentionality, it is easy to revert back to focusing primarily on the single bottom line of maximizing shareholder profit. As such, we have been explicit in articulating the balance of benefits we seek to provide through the business, and have institutionalized these in our administrative systems, in our organizational culture and through decision-making process.

Social Benefit

All decisions made within the organization weigh the social or community benefit, which includes the welfare of Portland Psychotherapy employees, our local community, the broader professional community and the global community. A singular focus on maximizing shareholder profit can result in traditionally structured for-profit companies emphasizing employee productivity (i.e., profit per unit of effort) at the cost of employee quality of life. A traditional for-profit model puts employee satisfaction and quality of life in a subordinate position to profitability. In the single-bottom line model, employee quality of life is primarily important to the extent to which it predicts retention and productivity and, thus, pencils out financially. However, for a social enterprise like ours, optimizing for employee benefit and quality of life becomes an end goal in and of itself, at least on par with profitability. At a structural level, our model supports 15 well-paid jobs with benefits. All staff members have a great deal of flexibility and autonomy in terms of schedules, tasks they engage in and number of hours they work. However, we would contend that quality of life is defined not only by having a well-paying job with flexibility and autonomy, but also one that includes explicit support for both individual and group-level values.

As we define them, values are freely chosen qualities of action that are intrinsically reinforcing. Put more simply, they are our personal and subjective sense of what we would choose to make important and what we stand for in this world (and, in this case, in our professional lives). Staff are encouraged to and supported in identifying what values they would want their work at Portland Psychotherapy to be in the service of. The organization is then tasked with supporting the staff in moving towards those values. For example, a staff member may say that they would choose to value "mastery" in their job and the organization would then put resources (both financial and interpersonal support) toward helping that individual move towards mastery.

In addition to these individual values, we have also worked to identify group values we wanted to be reflected by our internal culture. Over the course of a year, we identified four overarching values, each containing several related values. The values we chose to make important in our organization were: 1. **Play**, which includes fun, adventure, delight and spontaneity; 2. **Community**, which includes genuineness, connection, generosity and cooperation; 3. **Growth**, which includes beauty, challenge, creativity, and curiosity, and, finally; 4. **Love**, which includes support, security and nurturance. We reference these values when considering decisions we make in the organization. These group values also guide how we interact as a group as the internal culture we strive to create at Portland Psychotherapy are defined by these group values.

The social benefit we seek to provide also includes benefitting our local community in Portland, Oregon. We accomplish this through some of the more obvious means that would be expected from any fee-for-service setting, including our clinical services, sliding scale and reduced fee therapy options, and by offering various groups and classes for the community. We also seek to foster evidence-based practices and support our local community of mental health professionals.

Private practice can be very isolating and so we wanted to provide a source of community and connectedness for people in that position. We do this through hosting a no-cost peer consultation group, organizing social gatherings for local providers, and offering affordable trainings on topics the professional community asks for. The trainings we offer are primarily intended to provide a social benefit to local professionals with profit being a secondary consideration (i.e. they do not fall under the "shareholder benefit" bottom line). A side benefit of these trainings, however, is that they also serve a marketing function by keeping our center in mind and building goodwill with other providers who might be potential referral sources.

The broadest social benefit on which we focus is contributing to the body of scientific research. We view research as an altruistic act; the primary goal is the betterment of the whole rather than the betterment of the person who produces the scientific research. Scientific research progresses when scientists openly share their results in a manner that others can learn from and replicate. At the heart of why we developed this clinical-research social business model is a desire to contribute to scientific research that would not otherwise get funded, thereby benefitting our community and our world.

Environmental Benefit

Social enterprises employing a triple bottom line also attend to their environmental footprint. Every business has an environmental footprint to be managed, which can be done in a less or more responsible manner. Perhaps the largest way in which we have tried to be responsible in our environmental impact has to do with our office building. In 2012, we purchased a worn down 1889 Victorian home that would have otherwise almost certainly been torn down to make room for new construction. Because much of the lifetime environmental cost of a building is found in its construction, we chose to renovate an old building, rather than build a new structure. It was clear that this was not the cheapest way to get workable office space, but it was the more environmentally responsible choice. This choice also served a social good by preserving a historic home that helped to maintain a higher quality of life in the neighborhood. During that rehab, we sought to preserve and reuse as much of the original building material as possible. For things that could not be preserved, we generally selected the most environmentally friendly building materials we could afford at the time.

Since renovating and moving into our building in 2013, we have continued to implement policies designed to maximize environmental benefits. We have installed solar panels in the building. We incentivize employees to take public transportation or bike to work. We have developed an office supply policy that prioritizes purchasing supplies that are recycled, "cruelty free", or otherwise more environmentally friendly, and we buy most of our office supplies from a local business that specializes in green office supplies. These choices cost somewhat more and would not make sense in a structure set up to only maximize profits. However, the choices do make sense within our triple bottom line structure.

Shareholder Benefit

The final component to our triple bottom line is shareholder benefit. Unlike a non-profit organization, a social enterprise such as ours does have as part of its structure the goal of making a profit for the shareholders, in this case, the two owners. In addition to our employees being paid well, we as owners also benefit from having relatively well-paying jobs. Although the income we receive from the organization has been somewhat less than we would probably have earned if we were working solely for ourselves, or if we were seeking to solely maximize our financial gains, the business nonetheless meets our financial needs.

It is important, however, to also recognize that shareholder benefit not only includes financial benefits, but also, and we would argue even more importantly, includes the non-monetary benefits we receive through the business. At the most fundamental level, we have been able to carve out a work life that allows us to live many of our values and engage in the work tasks we want to be engaging in, in the location and environment we love. We are able to do meaningful work with a short bicycle commute in a beautiful setting surrounded by a wonderful community of friends and colleagues. In addition, as it is for our employees, our work is flexible and can, and has over the years, shifted with our changing interests and life circumstances.

Key Strategies to a Successful Clinical-Research Social Enterprise: What we have Learned

Over the years since we first started implementing our model, we have learned a tremendous amount, largely through trial and error. There have been some key business strategies that have been essential to the success of our clinical-research social business model. We have a strong interest in doing work that has scope and we sincerely hope that the model we have developed at Portland Psychotherapy can be generalizable to settings beyond ours. Consistent with our core value of generosity, we are interested in sharing what we have learned with the hope that others find them beneficial and, to the extent to which they are helpful, utilize them in their own settings, such that the world may benefit from having more scientific research.

Hire for Synergy

Anyone who has spent time in an academic department knows that creating cooperation among a group of highly achieving, driven professionals is often challenging. Our thinking about fostering cooperation has been highly influenced by multilevel selection theory from evolutionary science (Turchin, 2016). According to multilevel selection theory, groups with higher levels of within-group cooperation and altruism are generally more successful, whereas groups with higher levels of within-group conflict and selfishness are generally less successful over time. In line with these ideas, our attention is focused on group-level dynamics and individual tendencies toward cooperation, so that together, our organization will be more successful than any of us could be alone.

As a consequence of focusing on cooperation and the good of the whole, we prioritize candidates who are highly collaborative over those who appear more interpersonally competitive or self-focused. When hiring new staff, consideration is also given to diversity of skill and complementarity with current staff. One way we are able to obtain the somewhat higher profit margin that is required for our business model to work is that we are able to market ourselves as specialists. Although all of our clinical staff are expert in the particular area in which they focus (e.g. shame, interpersonal trauma, anxiety disorders, etc.), we try to reduce the extent to which our areas of expertise overlap so as to reduce within-group competition. When we are seeking to expand our staff, we hire individuals whose expertise complements, but does not generally compete with, current staff. As a result, we have been able to create a team whose members are (very) skilled, high achieving, and are among the best at what they do. However, at the same time, we feel incredibly fortunate to have built a culture in which we all genuinely care for and enjoy one another, and in which everyone looks out for the good of the group, not just their self-interest.

Have a Training Program

We have observed several benefits in having a postdoctoral fellowship program. First, a postdoctoral fellowship program can be a great way to hire new staff and expand. The training year allows us to get to know the individual in a deeper way than would be possible through even the most extensive hiring interview. The temporary nature of the postdoc year allows for an extended period of assessment of fit and reduces the pressure of trying to "make it work" even if the fit is not good. Also, from a financial perspective, it is less expensive to have turnover of postdocs than it is of licensed staff, so the direct economic cost of a failed match is reduced. The economics of having postdocs providing most of our sliding scale services means we can provide much more of those services than if our licensed staff were the only ones providing reduced fee services. Finally, even though our postdoctoral program loses some money each year, we get a large number of hours of research assistance from highly qualified staff. As such, we feel our postdoctoral program has largely been a big success even though it does not directly contribute in a positive way to the clinic's financial bottom line.

Support Staff in Identifying their Individual Values and Develop Group Values to Motivate and Guide Behavior

In typical for-profit businesses, money is often the primary reinforcer used to motivate and retain employees. However, it is clear that finding meaning or having a sense of purpose in one's work significantly predicts overall job satisfaction and performance (Bond & Bunce, 2003; Cartwright & Holmes, 2006; Pink, 2011). From our framework, values are what provide that sense of meaning and purpose.

Values, as they are thought of in this context, are inherently reinforcing qualities of action that are freely chosen by either the individual, or in this case, the group. As noted above, we have put considerable effort into, and have spent significant resources on, helping our staff identify their own individual values that can guide their work, as well as a shared set of values for the whole group. These values are, by their very nature, intrinsically meaningful/reinforcing to those who choose to work here. We use the intrinsic reinforcement of values as a way to recruit and retain quality staff, and to balance out the problematic effects of monetary contingencies. Our staff could likely get paid somewhat more in other settings because of their level of training and expertise. The shareholders/owners would certainly make more money if the corporation were set up as a traditional for-profit business in which all profits were retained by the shareholders/owners. However, in the social enterprise structure, monetary reinforcement is only one of several consequences that sustain the behavior of both staff and shareholders.

Maximize Autonomy

In addition to a sense of purpose, having a sense of control or autonomy is one of the most significant predictors of job satisfaction and increased quality of life (Bond & Bunce, 2003). As such, we have found it essential in our business strategy to increase staff's autonomy to the greatest extent possible. We strive to support staff in having a great deal of choice over their work lives, including hours worked, financial targets they set for themselves, types of clients they want to see, and the kinds of specialties they wish to develop. This works in our organization, in large part, because we have selected staff to fit organizational needs. Focusing on shared group values, in addition to their own individual values, also helps staff focus on the good of the organization in addition to their own individual interests.

Be Generous

Our social mission means that we make many decisions that are in the service of our broader community and our employees that we would likely not have made had we focused solely on maximizing shareholder benefit. We strive for generosity across multiple levels. We try to make generous interpretations of colleagues' and clients' behavior, assuming they have the best intentions at heart and are doing their best. Our employees are not coerced to sign non-compete provisions or other restrictive contracts, but instead we rely on them to be fair and honest should they choose to leave the organization. In our newsletter where we announce training events, we don't only announce our events, but share any training events that we know of that are relevant to the topic of the newsletter. We offer workshops for well below the going rate of similar workshops. We give a steep discount on workshops for students and charge a reduced fee for any clinician that needs it. We offer several of our groups on a sliding scale so that no client is excluded for financial reasons. We offer sliding scale services when we could charge higher fees for our postdoctoral fellows. We give away our research without expecting any direct remuneration. Our decision to write this paper was also based, in large part, on our value of generosity. Even though we feel some anxiety at disclosing our strategies that have led to a successful business, we feel it is more important to spread these ideas so that other similar businesses might flourish than it is for us to try to minimize potential competition.

While generosity is a value in and of itself, it may also be an effective business strategy. Multi-level selection theory suggests that, at least in certain contexts, altruism often pays off for those who are good group members through reputational gains and through others wanting to repay the generosity (Sober & Wilson, 1999). We want to create a world where generosity is the norm and where people (and organizations) that are generous thrive and are willing to take the risk that they may be taken advantage of at times.

Develop a Robust Marketing Program

Developing a solid marketing plan and implementing it reliably is an essential aspect of generating a sufficient profit margin. Skill in marketing needs to be built, either by hiring staff and contractors or through owner self-study. While many mental health professionals are uncomfortable with marketing, it can be done in an ethical fashion and an argument can even be made that it's the ethical course of action. If you truly believe that the services your organization provides are beneficial, then it could be argued that it is important to maximize the number of people who have access to them. Marketing is an important way to spread the message of evidence-based practice to people who might not otherwise seek treatment and it can be done in a way that is neither coercive nor deceptive. Indeed, it is essential that your marketing is done ethically, as your reputation depends on it. We have developed expertise in, and marketing plans relating to, many different lines of both online and offline marketing. We spend significant financial resources maintaining our marketing program.

Considerations and Action Steps to Implementing the Clinical-Research Social Business Model to Fund Research

All business models have their pros and cons, and the clinical-research social business model is no exception. This model will not be a great fit for everyone. When considering whether or not to use social enterprise concepts to fund research in your setting, you may want to consider some of the following factors.

Money

Are you comfortable thinking about and discussing money and the role it has in your life and your career choices? When it comes to money, can you think long-term, make financial sacrifices in the present in the service of future goals, and focus on your long-term financial health? If not, then this is probably not a good direction for you.

Autonomy

Are you someone who is comfortable going your own way and blazing new trails or do you seek the comfort of well-trodden paths? Do you do well being self-directed or do you prefer to have an already identified set of tasks laid out for you? Do you seek independence in your research? This is a setting, at least in our experience, for those who appreciate independence and who are willing to tolerate the uncertainty in forging new paths.

Isolation

If you are currently in a private practice, are you feeling isolated and wish to have more community in your work life? In our experience, the clinical-research social business model is best suited for someone who is largely self-directed and enjoys a great deal of autonomy. However, autonomy is not the same as isolation. This model not only allows for, but also thrives on strong community and collaboration. Thus, we have found this model to be an excellent way to increase community and decrease the isolation associated with private practice while still maintaining the independence that many people like about private practice.

Strategic planning

Are you someone who likes to think of the bigger picture of where you want to go in your life? Can you think strategically and organizationally or, if not, are you interested in and motivated to develop that ability? If, in your business, you are going to expand your focus beyond the more immediate, extrinsic reinforcer of money, you will need to be able to do some strategic planning that will allow you to focus on the long game and you will need to be clear about what you are playing for.

What social impact do you want to have?

How intrinsically rewarding do you find research and learning? Do you see research as more of a means to the end or do you find the process rewarding in and of itself? Do you think scientific progress is important enough that you would be willing to sacrifice some of your income to make a contribution to it? If so, how much of your income would you be willing to sacrifice in order to contribute to science? There are many ways to contribute to the broader social good. The clinical-research social business model is designed, specifically, for those who want to make that contribution, at least in large part, through adding to the scientific literature. If you would prefer to contribute to the broader social good in a different way, then you may want to consider exploring other social enterprise models.

Research

Is the kind of research you want to do best conducted inside a clinical setting? What kinds of funding would be best for the kinds of research you want to do? How much do you value choice over the type of research you do versus involvement in the process of research itself? This setting allows for a lot of choice over the research you do, but if you are more interested in participating in the process of science versus any particular topic, then melding your work to current funding priorities and following the traditional route may be the better bet.

Are you Ready to do this?

Embarking on this clinical-research social business endeavor is a huge investment of time and resources and is not well financially compensated immediately. It's important to consider your current financial situation and whether you have the resources and willingness to invest in this kind of a business. The returns are not as quick as a traditional job and the early years are likely to be somewhat leaner than if you took a more traditional path.

Consider your Values

As you consider this endeavor, it can be important to consider three factors: 1. What you do well, 2. What you can get paid to do, and most importantly, 3. What values you most want to stand for. We'd suggest doing some writing about each of the three factors and plot out the places they intersect (see Figure 7.2). In particular, consider whether there is enough overlap between these three areas such that a reasonable amount of your time could be spent in the middle sector, because that is what a well-functioning social enterprise requires. If there is more than one person involved in your organization, then each person will want to consider this for themselves in terms of how they might contribute to the organization.

Profit Margin

What can you sell that could generate enough of a profit margin to pay for activities that would not be directly funded? If you don't have anything currently that could generate that kind of margin, what is your plan for getting there? How does this plan fit your values?

Resources/Skills Needed

In order to create an organization similar to ours, you need to either build the following skills yourself or assemble the right team of contractors, consultants and employees. Most likely it will need to be a combination of both. Deciding which of the skills to develop yourself and which to build a team to provide is part of the learning process. Needed skills include the following:

- *Small Business skills*—Do you know how to run a small business? If not, where can you acquire the needed business skills? Your local small business development center can help you develop skills needed to run a small business, provide you with coaching and help you find relevant contractors.
- *Ability to manage and supervise*—Managing employees requires a different set of skills than working with clients. How will you acquire these skills if you do not have them?
- *Research abilities*—Are you a strong researcher already? If not, how will you acquire the collaborators and mentors you will need to be effective?
- *Strategic planning*—It's imperative that someone on the team has a vision, is able to set long term goals, and can help others break down those goals into actionable projects and steps. In addition, learning at least a little about social enterprise can greatly help you in organizing your thinking and gaining clarity about your goals.
- *Marketing skills*—Marketing is a huge field with a tremendous amount to learn about. Small business marketing books like *Duct Tape Marketing* (Jantsch, 2011) can be a helpful resource. However, you will likely need some help setting up and implementing a solid marketing program. Having a reliable marketing strategy, plan, calendar, and the staff to carry it out is essential.

Conclusion

Social enterprise models can offer an important and viable alternative to the traditional for-profit versus non-profit dichotomy. In this chapter, we have outlined one such model, the clinical-research social business model which offers a way for those looking to contribute through both provision of clinical services and production of scientific research to do both in a more integrated and symbiotic manner. If you are choosing to operate in the money-making economy, as nearly all of us in fee-for-service settings have chosen to do, then we encourage you to consider how that money could serve your values. The clinical-research social business model is our way of ensuring that we aren't just working for money, but that money is being put to work in the service of our chosen values.

References

Bond, F. W. & Bunce, D. (2003). The role of acceptance and job control in mental health, job satisfaction, and work performance. *Journal of Applied Psychology, 88*(6), 1057–1067.

Cartwright, S. & Holmes, N. (2006). The meaning of work: The challenge of regaining employee engagement and reducing cynicism. *Human Resource Management Review, 16*(2), 199–208.

Chang, K., Lee, I. L., & Hargreaves, T. (2008). Scientist versus Practitioner–An abridged meta-analysis of the changing role of psychologists. *Counseling Psychology Quarterly, 21*(3), 267–291.

Critchfield, T. S. & Kollins, S. H. (2001). Temporal discounting: Basic research and the analysis of socially important behavior. *Journal of Applied Behavior Analysis, 34*(1), 101–122.

Cullari, S. (1996). Psychotherapy practice questionnaire. *The Independent Practitioner, 16,* 140–142.

Foa, E. B., Yadin, E., & Lichner, T. K. (2012). *Exposure and response (ritual) prevention for obsessive compulsive disorder: Therapist guide.* Oxford, UK: University Press.

Goldfried, M. R. & Wolfe, B. E. (1996). Psychotherapy practice and research: Repairing a strained relationship. *American Psychologist, 51*(10), 1007–1016.

Goodheart, C. D. (2010). Economics and psychology practice: What we need to know and why. *Professional Psychology: Research and Practice, 41*(3), 189–195.

Hennessey, B. A. & Amabile, T. M. (1998). Reality, intrinsic motivation, and creativity. *American Psychologist, 53*(6), 674–675.

Intriligator, M. D. (2004). Globalization of the world economy: Potential benefits and costs and a net assessment. *Journal of Policy Modeling, 26*(4), 485–498.

Jantsch, J. (2011). *Duct tape marketing: The world's most practical small business marketing guide.* Nashville, TN: Thomas Nelson Inc.

Lambert, M. J., Whipple, J. L., Hawkins, E. J., Vermeersch, D. A., Nielsen, S. L., & Smart, D. W. (2003). Is it time for clinicians to routinely track patient outcome? A meta-analysis. *Clinical Psychology: Science and Practice, 10*(3), 288–301.

LeJeune, J. T. & Luoma, J. B. (2015). The integrated scientist-practitioner: A new model for combining research and clinical practice in fee-for-service settings. *Professional Psychology: Research and Practice, 46*(6), 421–428.

Lichtenberg, J. W., Goodyear, R. K., & Genther, D. Y. (2008). The changing landscape of professional practice in counseling psychology. In S. D. Brown & R. W. Lent (Eds.) *Handbook of counseling psychology,* (pp. 21–37). Hoboken, NJ: John Wiley & Sons.

Lin, H. F. (2007). Effects of extrinsic and intrinsic motivation on employee knowledge sharing intentions. *Journal of Information Science, 33*(2), 135–149.

National Institute of Mental Health (2008). *The National Institute of Mental Health strategic plan.* Retrieved from: www.nimh.nih.gov/about/strategic-planning-reports/index.shtml

O'Sullivan, J. J. & Quevillon, R. P. (1992). 40 years later: Is the Boulder model still alive?. *American Psychologist, 47*(1), 67–70.

Persons, J. B. (2007). Psychotherapists collect data during routine clinical work that can contribute to knowledge about mechanisms of change in psychotherapy. *Clinical Psychology: Science and Practice, 14*(3), 244–246.

Pink, D. H. (2011). *Drive: The surprising truth about what motivates us.* New York: Penguin.

Schomerus, G., Schwahn, C., Holzinger, A., Corrigan, P. W., Grabe, H. J., Carta, M. G., & Angermeyer, M. C. (2012). Evolution of public attitudes about mental illness: a systematic review and meta-analysis. *Acta Psychiatrica Scandinavica, 125*(6), 440–452.

Sober, E. & Wilson, D. S. (1999). *Unto others: The evolution and psychology of unselfish behavior.* Cambridge, MA: Harvard University Press.

Stewart, R. E. & Chambless, D. L. (2007). Does psychotherapy research inform treatment decisions in private practice? *Journal of Clinical Psychology, 63*(3), 267–281.

Turchin, P. (2016). *Ultrasociety.* Chaplan, CT: Beresta Books.

United States Department of Education. (2013). *Tabulation by AAUP Research Office of trends in instructional staff employment status, 1975–2011.* Retrieved from: www.aaup.org/sites/default/files/files/AAUP_Report_InstrStaff-75-11_apr2013.pdf

Yunus, M. (2011). *Building social business: The new kind of capitalism that serves humanity's most pressing needs.* New York: Public Affairs.

CHAPTER 8

Research in Private Practice Settings

Travis L. Osborne

Much has been written about the science-practice gap in the field of psychology and how to address it (e.g., Kazdin, 2008; Teachman, Drabick, Hershenberg, Vivian, Wolfe, & Goldfried, 2012). Practice-based research is one solution to this problem, but in order for it to truly have a meaningful and broad impact, it must extend to clinicians in solo and group private practice. Large scale surveys have shown that for the last several decades, the majority of clinical psychologists have identified primarily as clinical practitioners and that private practice is the most common employment site for these professionals (Norcross, Karpiak, and Santoro, 2005). Private practice clinicians have considerable expertise and wisdom that could help inform and advance the science of psychology and psychological treatments, however, most of this knowledge is not represented in the academic literature (Kazdin, 2008). Instead, the vast majority of the science generated by clinical psychologists is done by a relatively small number of individuals (Norcross et al., 2005), many of whom are either not clinicians or engage in relatively limited clinical work. Increasing research productivity by private practice psychologists has the potential to make significant contributions to the extant literatures on treatment effectiveness, treatment dissemination, mechanisms of action in psychotherapy, and a wide range of topics that could help improve treatment outcomes and service delivery, as well as strengthen the reputation of our field as being rooted in science.

Although private practice-based research holds considerable promise, it is also not without numerous challenges. The primary objective of this chapter is to describe common barriers to conducting research in private practice settings, as well as discuss potential solutions for these barriers. This chapter will also describe various ways that research can be structured and conducted in private practice, including the types of research that are a natural fit for this setting. Specific studies will be highlighted that represent useful models of this type of work. Lastly, when relevant, examples will be provided from the practice-based research program at the Evidence Based Treatment Centers of Seattle (EBTCS), given the author's involvement with this program over the last decade.

Practice-Based Research at EBCTS

EBTCS is a specialty outpatient practice that was founded in 2002 by three psychologists and one psychiatrist, with an initial focus on providing dialectical behavior therapy (DBT). Over time, the center has grown to roughly 30 providers and in addition to providing comprehensive DBT services, it also provides treatment for pediatric and adult anxiety and related disorders, as well as pediatric and adult eating disorders. Despite being a practice setting that is not directly affiliated with an academic institution, a commitment to the science of psychology and the scientist-practitioner model has been a fundamental value of the organization since its inception.

This value on science has been manifest in the following key ways. First, a high priority is placed on providing high-fidelity, evidence-based treatment. Whenever possible, providers select their interventions based on the best available scientific data for the specific problems being addressed. To assist with treatment fidelity, all services are organized around treatment teams for specific clinical populations or problems (i.e., DBT, adult anxiety disorders, pediatric anxiety disorders, and eating disorders). Clinicians attend weekly team meetings to get consultation with problems encountered in their work with specific clients, as well as help with staying adherent to treatment protocols and principles. Second, the organization has an APA approved continuing education (CE) program. A primary aim of this CE program is to help clinicians stay up-to-date with changes in the field, including staying abreast of new research that has implications for treatment outcome and delivery. Third, EBTCS has an active postdoctoral training program, one purpose of which is to help disseminate empirically supported treatments by providing specialty training to early career professionals. Fourth, early on the organization developed an outcomes monitoring program in order to collect data on clients' symptoms during the course of treatment. Outcomes monitoring is an important component of evidence-based practice (Persons, Koerner, Eidelman, Thomas, & Liu, 2016) and provides clinicians and clients with ongoing data about symptom change and treatment effectiveness. Finally, the organization developed a practice-based research program, with the intent of contributing to the scientific literature in the field of psychology. One objective of this research program is to work to address the practice-research gap in the field by disseminating research that is developed and conducted by clinicians in a practice setting.

The practice-based research program at EBTCS has been up and running for over ten years. The author has been actively involved with this program since the beginning stages of development and currently oversees all of the program's activities. The author and his colleagues have learned a considerable amount over the last decade about the barriers facing clinicians who want to conduct research in private practice and developing solutions to address some of these problems. The specific barriers affecting clinicians may vary somewhat depending on the unique context of their practice settings. However, it is hoped that the information presented here about how many of these barriers have been successfully addressed can be helpful to those looking to incorporate or expand research activities in private practice (solo or group) settings.

Common Barriers to Conducting Research in Private Practice and Potential Solutions

Although there are numerous challenges facing clinicians who wish to conduct practice-based research (see also Koerner & Castonguay, 2015; LeJeune & Luoma, 2015), this chapter will focus on the following barriers: (1) lack of a researcher identity among clinicians; (2) lack of a research culture in clinical settings; (3) contingencies that undermine research involvement; (4) challenges with research staffing; (5) gaps in research-related skills; (6) lack of access to IRB review; and (7) costs associated with conducting research.

Lack of a Researcher Identity Among Clinicians

One significant barrier to private practice clinicians conducting research has to do with the way that training programs, particularly doctoral training programs in clinical psychology, socialize trainees to think about careers in psychology. Despite the adoption by most clinical psychology programs of the scientist-practitioner (or "Boulder") model (Chang, Lee, & Hargreaves, 2008) and the provision of both clinical and research training, the strong message that many students in these programs receive is that they need to choose a career *either* as an academic (scientist) *or* a practitioner (clinician). Given this message and that the majority of clinical psychologists choose career paths in practice settings vs. academia or research settings (Norcross & Karpiak, 2012), it is not surprising that the modal number of publications for clinical psychologists is zero (Norcross et al., 2005). Simply put, there is ample evidence to suggest that clinical psychology graduate programs are not succeeding in training most psychologists to *concurrently* function as both clinicians and researchers (Chang et al., 2008). Additionally, although there are certainly high-profile models of researchers who do clinical work (i.e., most of the major treatment developers from the last several decades, including Marsha Linehan, Steven Hayes, David Barlow, etc.), there are substantially fewer visible models of clinicians who conduct research. Thus, for the majority of psychologists who work in clinical settings, it is likely that the concept of being a researcher is not part of their professional schema or identity.

Addressing this barrier on a larger scale will require changes to how clinical psychologists and other mental health professionals are trained, in order to foster the development of professional identities and skill sets that more tightly integrate research and practice. On an individual level, however, this can start to be accomplished via several potential solutions. First, clinicians who are interested in conducting research would benefit from reading studies that have been published by other clinicians; examples of such publications will be presented later in this chapter. Having models is an important component of professional identity development and becoming familiar with research by other practitioners is one way to start envisioning being able to do this work oneself. Second, clinicians with strong research interests are encouraged to network and affiliate with other like-minded clinicians. As most clinicians do not engage in research activities, or necessarily want to, such networks can be challenging to develop and access.

However, local, state, and national professional associations are one good way to seek out individuals with similar interests and developing networks with other practice-based researchers can help to strengthen this professional identity. Third, attending presentations at professional conferences on conducting research in practice settings can be a helpful way to learn information about how this is done in other settings. For instance, there have been several such symposia and workshops at the annual convention for the Association of Behavioral and Cognitive Therapies (ABCT) in recent years (e.g., Koerner, Persons, Luoma, & Osborne, 2011; Persons, 2014; Persons, Eidelman, & Hong, 2014). Lastly, it can be beneficial to become familiar with the range of ways that research can be conducted in practice in order to develop an expanded view of how one could contribute to the empirical literature as a clinician (multiple examples will be described later in this chapter).

Clinicians at EBTCS employed a number of these strategies when working to develop their research program. For instance, several of the therapists were familiar with the practice-based research published by Jacqueline Persons, PhD (see below) and thus, reviewing her work served as a starting point for conceptualizing how clinicians could participate in the creation of science. Additionally, several clinicians attended workshops by Dr. Persons at professional conferences on this topic, which further enhanced both learning about how to conduct practice-based research, as well as providing a model for a professional identity as a clinician-researcher. Lastly, clinicians at EBTCS developed ongoing relationships with other individuals who conduct practice-based research through their involvement in helping to create an Institutional Review Board (IRB) to support this type of work (see Chapter 6 of this book). These relationships have helped to solidify professional identities as clinicians who create and disseminate research.

Lack of a Research Culture in Clinical Settings

In part due to the false dichotomy perpetuated in our field between practice and research, most clinical settings do not have a culture of research or empiricism. This is perhaps nowhere more true than for the clinician in solo or group private practice. In fact, many psychologists in private practice likely chose to work in this setting *specifically because they did not want careers in research*. Not surprisingly then, a major obstacle to conducting research in this setting is the lack of a culture to promote research development and productivity. Once clinicians develop a sense of professional identity as a researcher, work will be needed to develop a culture that supports this work.

How a research culture is developed will depend on the nature of the clinical setting. In a solo practice setting, a clinician who is interested in conducting research would benefit from teaming up with other like-minded clinicians in order to develop a community to support these activities. Designing, conducting, and disseminating research is a complex process that involves a range of skills and a significant commitment of time. Solo practitioners may find it daunting to complete all the tasks involved in conducting research (i.e., design the research protocol, consent clients, collect data, analyze data, write up findings for presentation or publication) and thus, collaborating with other professionals will likely increase the chances of success. Similar teams are needed in group practice settings for the same reasons, but may be somewhat easier to form given the built-in network of colleagues. Once a team of colleagues is assembled, regular meetings about research projects (similar to those that would occur in an academic research lab) can be used to brainstorm research ideas, determine the specific details of a research protocol, troubleshoot obstacles to research implementation, address ethical issues that arise when conducting research, and help with accountability and motivation when working on writing manuscripts for publication. The importance of such a team cannot be overstated given how challenging it is to conduct research in an ongoing way in isolation. Meetings can be conducted virtually (via teleconference or videoconference) for individuals whose colleagues and collaborators may not be in the same locale. In group practice settings, it is important to include individuals from all levels of the organization (i.e., front office staff, administrative staff, clinicians) so that investment in a culture of research is fostered across the practice.

When the practice-based research program at EBTCS was first developed, an intentional effort was made to create a culture throughout the organization that supported research involvement. A research team was created that included senior clinicians/administrators who headed up the research program, individual clinicians who wanted to participate in research, postdoctoral fellows who had protected time to work on research, as well as front office staff. By creating the team and including such a wide range of individuals, this helped to send a strong message that research was an important part of the organization's mission, culture, and values. Additionally, all members of the team took on specific roles related to the research program in order to foster active involvement in a culture of research. For example, senior clinicians/ administrators developed the overarching research priorities and plan, postdoctoral fellows and office staff prepared poster presentations for conferences, clinicians conducted statistical analyses and assisted with writing manuscripts for publication, and office staff managed the informed consent process and completed data entry and database management tasks. After ten years, some of the members of this team have changed as various staff and trainees have come and gone, but the team continues to meet on a consistent basis to address issues related to research implementation, as well as to spearhead efforts to disseminate research findings at conferences and via publications. Additionally, the successes of the research team are publicized to the larger organization as they occur, creating opportunities to highlight the benefits of having an active research program in a clinical setting, as well as opportunities for social reinforcement of those participating in these efforts.

Contingencies that Undermine Research Involvement

In private practice settings, contingencies are set up to promote revenue generating activities (i.e., individual psychotherapy, psychotherapy groups, consultation), as these are directly tied to income and profit. As a result, the likelihood of investing significant time and energy in non-revenue generating activities, such as research, is diminished for most private practitioners. LeJeune and Luoma (2015) describe these problematic contingencies, as well as the successful implementation of a model of practice-research integration that is designed to address them. These issues are also described in another chapter in this book (Chapter 7), and thus, will not be addressed extensively here. In short, how clinicians manage these contingencies will likely play an important role in the success or failure of practice-based research activities.

EBTCS has addressed the challenges posed by these contingencies in a few ways. Funds from the clinic's revenue are set aside to pay for part of the salary of a senior clinician who serves as the Director of Research. This individual has a somewhat reduced clinical load in order to preserve time to oversee the research program. Additionally, all postdoctoral fellows have 25 percent of their time set aside for participation in research activities and they play a significant role in the ongoing maintenance of the research program, as well as with disseminating research findings. Research activities (such as, consenting clients to research, participating in the research team, etc.) are also integrated into the job duties of front desk staff. As highlighted by LeJeune and Luoma (2015), solutions like these require a willingness to invest revenue back into research activities, thereby reducing potential profit. Such a decision requires a shift in values and mindset from a traditional business approach, which would be to maximize profit and income. A detailed example of such a model is described further in Chapter 7.

Challenges with Research Staffing

As noted above, research is very difficult to carry out in isolation. Typically, some staff are needed to support research activities if they are to be successful and sustainable. Many solo practitioners do not have office staff and even group practices may have very little office or administrative support, depending on the nature of how the practice is structured. Given that it is unrealistic to think that busy providers are going to be able to carry out all roles and responsibilities of a research study, staffing issues need to be addressed. A range of different solutions are described below that will be more or less applicable depending on the nature and size of the practice setting.

One potential solution for staffing problems is to hire a part-time research assistant to help with various aspects of running a study. These tasks could include consenting clients to the research study, tracking and managing study-related materials and files, collecting or recording study data, and managing datasets. For many studies, particularly in relatively small clinical settings, only a few hours per week of help may be needed, which may be affordable. Good candidates for such a position include psychology or social science undergraduate students or recent graduates who may be looking for research experience to help enhance qualifications for graduate school. If the costs of hiring a research assistant are too burdensome, students might also be willing to fill such roles in exchange for course credit. Many psychology departments have mechanisms for students to volunteer in research settings to fulfill credit hours. Establishing relationships with local psychology departments can create a mechanism for identifying interested students, as well as provide the university with much needed external placements for these students. Practice-based research opportunities, in particular, are quite unique and may be of interest to students who are interested in research outside of traditional academic settings.

Another solution if a practice has administrative support staff, is to incorporate research support activities into the job descriptions for these individuals. Many of these tasks, such as consenting clients to research or collecting client outcomes data, can be incorporated into existing workflows without significant burden. Integrating these individuals into research activities has the added benefit of strengthening a culture of research (as discussed above). Lastly, for those with more ambitious research goals, hiring a postdoctoral fellow may be an ideal solution, particularly for clinicians with a specialty practice that could lend itself to specialized clinical training that might be of interest to early career professionals. Many graduates of doctoral programs in clinical psychology have strong research skills and a subset are interested in the integration of practice and research. The opportunity to receive advanced clinical training and supervision, as well as participate in real-world psychological research, may be appealing to many individuals, particularly those with an evidence-based background. Although offering a postdoctoral fellowship also involves work on the part of the clinician (i.e., getting additional client referrals, providing training and supervision), this can also be very professionally rewarding on many levels.

EBTCS employs all three of the above strategies. Many years ago, the organization established a working relationship with staff within the psychology department of a large, local university, who oversee placement of students in organizations in the community for course credit. At any given time, EBTCS has had between one to five students working as volunteers in exchange for course credit. These individuals typically work a limited number of hours per week (usually less than 10) and assist with a range of research-related activities (data entry, scoring client outcome measures, participating in research team meetings), in addition to other office administration tasks. These students receive the benefit of experiencing what it is like to work in a mental health setting, while also getting to be part of the research team and interact with practicing psychologists. In addition to students receiving course credit, EBTCS has also had students and recent graduates serve as volunteers even without receiving course credit, as this was helpful in rounding out experiences as preparation for graduate school.

Office staff at EBTCS are also integral to the organization's research activities. Most of these individuals have undergraduate degrees in psychology (or a related social science field) and have elected to take time off before applying to graduate school. Typically, they would like to use this time to gain experience that will make them more competitive for that process. As a result, EBTCS has integrated these individuals into the research structure of the organization as it benefits both the organization and these staff. These individuals participate in several aspects of the research process, including approaching new clients about the research program, overseeing all aspects of the research consent process, assisting with some aspects of data collection, creating datasets, participating in research team meetings, and serving as co-authors on poster presentations of research findings at national professional conferences.

As previously mentioned, EBTCS also has an active postdoctoral training program and typically takes one to three new fellows each year. A quarter of fellows' time is set aside for research and related activities, including overseeing data collection, participating in the design of specific research projects, creation of datasets, analyzing data, and assisting with dissemination of research findings via conference presentations and publications. Fellows have some flexibility with how much they participate in research-based on their interests, although many choose EBTCS because of the mix of clinical and research opportunities. Fellows also mentor office staff in the research process, particularly when developing poster presentations for conferences.

Gaps in Research-related Skills

Many graduates of doctoral programs in clinical psychology have considerable training in research methods and statistics and have experience working on research studies and designing and running their own research studies (e.g., thesis and/or dissertation projects). However, research-related skills, like all skills, have to be practiced regularly to be maintained and this practice does not continue for many who go on to work in clinical settings. Additionally, it can be difficult after leaving graduate school to keep up with changes in analytic methods, as well as to stay current with new statistical software packages. Finally, no one individual typically has all of the skills needed to execute all aspects of every research study.

In academic settings, researchers usually have numerous resources available to them that allow them to address gaps in skills or knowledge. For instance, these individuals almost always work in teams with other researchers and statisticians. As a result, they can assemble teams that collectively have the expertise and skills needed to carry out a study. Additionally, grant funding often provides the means for study investigators to get training in particular research or statistical methods, or pay for consultants to assist with areas where certain skills are lacking. Moreover, working in an academic environment allows for easier access to other researchers and mentors with whom one can collaborate and learn from. Clinicians conducting practice-based research often do not have easy access to any of these resources to help address gaps in skills. However, much can be learned from how research is conducted in academic settings and translated to clinical settings.

As previously highlighted, creating teams to support research productivity is essential and in particular, is critical for addressing gaps in research-related skills. A natural starting place to building such a team is by including others who have experience conducting practice-based research. In some cases these individuals may be interested in ongoing collaboration and consultation, in others they may only be able or interested in providing one-time consultation about specific problems or questions. Regardless, tapping into the skills and wisdom of those who conduct this kind of research can be invaluable. One example of this kind of collaboration would be to seek out practice-based researchers with expertise in specific kinds of research designs (i.e., single-case designs, longitudinal studies). Those who have experience conducting similar types of studies will be able to provide information and advice about challenges inherent with specific types of studies and can help with assessing the knowledge and skills gaps that will need to be addressed for a project to be successful.

In addition to including other practice-based researchers, these teams can also include researchers working in academic settings. For instance, collaborating with researchers who specialize in quantitative methods and analysis (most academic psychology departments have faculty members with this specialty) can be extremely helpful for clinicians whose statistics skills are rusty or out of date. Some collaborations may involve paying these individuals to provide statistics consultation and services, whereas others may be arranged in which these individuals get authorship credit on a publication in lieu of payment. Similarly, collaborating with advanced graduate students who have expertise in up-to-date analytic methods and software would serve the same purpose and could be very beneficial to professionals who are early in their careers.

Aside from addressing skill deficits by creating teams of individuals with complementary skills and seeking consultation, at times formal training will be needed. For instance, it may be necessary to take a class on particular statistical procedures or software packages. Some universities may allow individuals with adjunct faculty appointments to audit courses. Online courses are also increasingly offered by both universities and private companies on a range of related topics.

The research team at EBTCS is comprised of individuals with varying research backgrounds, which helps bring different sets of skills to the research program. Over time, several of these individuals have had considerable training in analytic methods and have been able to conduct statistical analyses of data for presentations or publications. When this has not been the case, the team has sought statistical consultation, typically from individuals at a local university. In some cases this consultation has been paid for, in others it has been provided for free through on-campus resources that EBTCS staff were able to access due to having adjunct faculty appointments. Additionally, at one point in time the individual at EBTCS serving as the Director of Research took a class at the university on a specific statistical analysis software package to help address particular needs for these skills. Finally, consultation has been sought from other practice-based researchers to gain more information about the types of models for practice-research integration that have proven successful.

Lack of Access to IRB Review

Although not all research requires review by an IRB from a regulatory standpoint (e.g., only research that is conducted or supported by a federal department or agency is required to undergo IRB review per HHS Protection of Human Subjects

(2009); see Chapter 6 for a more detailed discussion of this issue), ethical review and oversight of psychological research is desirable for many reasons (i.e., external checks on protections of human subjects, it is often necessary to present data at conferences or publish data in scientific journals, some grant funding mechanisms require it). Unfortunately, the majority of clinicians in private practice do not have easy or affordable access to an IRB. Osborne and Luoma (in press) describe a variety of ways that clinicians in practice settings have attempted to address this barrier, as well as the limitations of each. Two strategies for accessing university or medical center-based IRBs include seeking an adjunct faculty appointment (which *may* open up access to the institution's IRB) and collaborating on research projects with faculty or graduate students at academic institutions, who can then have studies reviewed by their IRBs. The former strategy can be tenuous as IRBs can change their policies about whether they will review studies by adjunct faculty (as has been experienced by the author), and the latter strategy can limit autonomy and the development of independent research questions and lines of research. Numerous private IRBs are also available, however, the costs associated with their services may be prohibitive for many clinicians, particularly those working without grant funding for their studies. Finally, some practice-based researchers can also avoid the need for IRB review by designing studies and data collection and storage procedures in such a way that it is not necessary. For instance, if the identity of participants cannot be determined by the researchers and the data collected cannot be linked to specific individuals, then such projects to do not meet the federal definition of human subjects' research and are, therefore, not required to undergo IRB review (Amdur, Speers, & Bankert, 2006). There are some drawbacks to these kinds of datasets (i.e., they may limit the possibility of longitudinal research), but they may be suitable in some settings. Additionally, case studies and case series typically do not require IRB review (Amdur et al., 2006).

EBTCS initially sought approval for its research program from a local university, as several clinicians had adjunct faculty appointments with the department of psychology given their roles as clinical supervisors for doctoral students in clinical psychology. The university agreed to review the research protocol, but several problems were encountered. To begin, the approval process took several years (much longer than is standard), in part due to a lack of understanding on the part of the IRB about the specifics of conducting research in practice settings. Additionally, after a few years of providing ethical oversight, the IRB decided that because clinicians at EBTCS were not direct employees of the university, it would no longer be able to provide ethical review given staffing constraints related to budget cuts. Fortunately, during the several years that the university IRB was reviewing EBTCS' study protocol, clinicians from the organization teamed up with other practice-based researchers from across the country to form an independent IRB that specializes in the review of practice-based research. Thus, EBTCS was able to transfer its research protocol to this IRB after oversight was ended by the university IRB. Chapter 6 of this book describes a step-by-step approach to creating an IRB for this purpose.

Costs Associated with Conducting Research

Conducting research can involve a number of expenses, including:

- Pay for research staff.
- Equipment—computers and other devices used for data collection and analysis.
- Software—statistical software packages, software for managing research paper citations.
- Measures—some psychological symptom measure are free, though many are not.
- Consultation—funds may be needed to pay for statistical or research consultation.
- Conferences—costs associated with staff attending conferences to present research data.
- Trainings or classes to address skill deficits.
- Fees for IRB review.

In academic research settings, the costs for conducting research are built into the grant budgets that typically fund these projects. Such funding is much less common for research in clinical settings and thus, the expenses associated with carrying out research activities will typically need to come from the revenue generated by clinical services. As discussed above, this requires a shift in mindset away from a primary goal of running a business (solo or group practice) to maximize profit. Instead, some profit will need to be set aside to fund research activities and this necessitates a shift in values and priorities. However, there are also numerous ways to minimize costs associated with research, many of which have been mentioned above (i.e., hiring undergraduate volunteers to help with data collection and data entry, integrating research tasks into the job duties of existing staff, offering authorship credit on a manuscript in exchange for assistance with data analysis, using measures that are in the public domain).

The research program at EBTCS is self-funded and not support by grants. As a result, some clinic revenue is set aside each year for a research program budget to cover the costs of research-related expenses. Over the years, these funds have been used to purchase a laptop for the research program, tablets for data collection, statistical analysis software (SPSS), and software to help manage research citations in manuscripts (Endnote). Some funds have also been used to purchase psychological measures that are not in the public domain, however, to help minimize costs, the majority of measures used are in the public domain and are free (see resources for low cost and free measures at the end of this chapter). As previously mentioned, staffing costs are kept low by hiring undergraduate volunteers to help with data entry and some research tasks are integrated into the jobs of existing front office staff (i.e., approaching clients about research participation, consenting clients to research). Some funds are also set aside each year to help pay for conference-related expenses for staff who present research data at these meetings. Whenever possible, decisions are made to minimize research costs. However, some level of financial investment in the research program is necessary to make it viable and sustainable.

Models for Conducting Research in Private Practice

There are numerous ways that clinicians in private practice can participate in and produce research, however, examples of this type of work are less prominent in the field and often not highlighted in training programs. Below, a number of research projects conducted entirely, or in part, by private practitioners are described in order to provide much needed models of practice-based research. The examples provided here are by no means exhaustive, but are meant to showcase the variety of ways that clinicians in practice can engage in research and make significant contributions to the knowledge base in our field. Due to space constraints, the descriptions that follow are not intended to be so comprehensive as to review all aspects of how the studies were conducted. Instead, studies are described in enough detail to illustrate key points and readers are encouraged to read the original studies for more in-depth descriptions of their methodologies.

Case Studies

The case study is one of the most natural ways that clinicians in practice can engage in research. Case studies have a long tradition in the mental health literature and have the potential to contribute significantly to the science of clinical psychology. For instance, case studies can be a very effective way of examining the feasibility of new treatments, application of existing treatments to new populations, and mechanisms of change in psychotherapy. Depending on the type of case study being conducted, practitioners may need very little research training (a case in which a treatment and its outcomes are described), or a more sophisticated knowledge of single-case experimental research methods (such as those described in Chapter 4). Evidence-based practitioners are particularly well suited to conducting and publishing this kind of research, as most evidence-based practice involves the collection of data throughout treatment about specific symptoms, behaviors, or processes being targeted. As this data is already incorporated into routine clinical care, much of the "scaffolding" for a research project is already in place.

An example of a case study that involved the application of a new treatment to a novel population was published by Welch and Kim (2012). The case study described the treatment of hair pulling in an adolescent girl using a DBT-enhanced cognitive behavioral therapy (CBT) treatment protocol. The protocol had been previously evaluated in an open trial with adults and had shown promising results. However, no data were available for its use with adolescents and the literature on the treatment of hair pulling in adolescents more broadly was fairly minimal at that time. The case study was informative in several key ways. First, it provided a detailed description of an emerging treatment (DBT-enhanced CBT for hair pulling) and how it was applied to a new population (adolescents). Second, it included data that were collected throughout the course of treatment (measures of hair pulling severity, emotion regulation, anxiety and mood), that allowed for reporting on the effectiveness of the treatment for this client. Finally, the study included supplemental video demonstrations of several components of the treatment, a feature not common in published studies, thereby providing clinicians with a useful resource for learning and adopting this treatment approach. Although a case study such as this alone does not provide sufficient data to determine the treatment's potential effectiveness on a broader scale, it does provide initial data of such effectiveness and feasibility, as well as justification for more rigorous testing of this treatment approach with adolescents.

Experimental single-case research designs are another important method by which clinicians in practice can conduct case studies in a way that helps advance the empirical literature. Examples of these types of case studies are not discussed here as they are the focus of another chapter in this book (Chapter 4).

Case Series

Similar to case studies, case series describe the use of specific treatment methods, or the treatment of specific clinical problems, but across a number of clients vs. a single client. The benefits of such an approach include both a more extensive dataset from which to draw potential conclusions, as well as more clinical examples, which can help with dissemination of treatment methods.

Codd, Twohig, Crosby, and Enno (2011) published a case series in which three clients with anxiety disorders (panic disorder with agoraphobia; social anxiety and generalized anxiety disorder; posttraumatic stress disorder) were treated by a single clinician (Codd) using acceptance and commitment therapy (ACT). The case series was designed to address several important questions: (1) Can a unified/transdiagnostic ACT protocol be effective across anxiety disorders?; (2) Is ACT effective for treating anxiety when exposure therapy components are excluded (as exposure strategies are effective for treating anxiety and are often included in ACT)?; and (3) What are the processes of change in ACT treatments for anxiety? Each of these questions are clinically and empirically important, as their answers have the potential to improve treatments for individuals with anxiety-related problems. Validated measures of anxiety disorder symptoms and psychological inflexibility (a mechanism targeted in ACT) were administered at pre-treatment, post-treatment, and follow-up (ranging from 8–17 months post-treatment). Additionally, daily ratings of anxiety and avoidance were collected throughout treatment. Results showed that a relatively brief ACT intervention (ranging 9–13 sessions) that excluded exposure (1) was effective in treating multiple anxiety disorders (none of the clients met criteria for an anxiety disorder at post-treatment), (2) increased psychological flexibility in two of the three clients (a primary aim of ACT), and (3) led to decreases in avoidance behaviors for all three clients even though anxiety severity ratings did not significantly decrease. This latter finding was particularly important as it provided support for a key theoretical underpinning of ACT (i.e., that targeting the functional impact of anxiety—avoidance—is effective even if anxiety severity does not change). This case series is an excellent example of how tightly integrated clinical work and research can be in a private practice setting and how this integration can help address critical questions that inform our understanding of if and how treatments work.

Similarly, Persons, Beckner, and Tompkins (2013) published a case series that described the use of a case formation approach to psychotherapy to treat two clients with anxiety symptoms. In this transdiagnostic approach to treatment, "the therapist, in collaboration with the patient, develops a hypothesis (formulation) about the psychological mechanisms that cause and maintain the patient's difficulties, uses the formulation to guide intervention, and collects data to test the formulation and evaluate the effectiveness of the intervention plan" (Persons et al., 2013, p. 399). A case study or case series is the ideal way to evaluate the effectiveness of this approach to therapy, given that testing this kind of idiographic treatment via a tightly controlled research trial could be exceedingly difficult. In this case series, the clients were treated by different therapists, both trained in the same treatment methodology. As with the case series by Codd et al. (2011), collection of relevant data was integrated into treatment, making it substantially more feasible to turn this work into a publication. The case series also provided much needed clinical guidance on a critical topic in psychotherapy: how to respond to initial poor response to treatment. Very little is included in published treatment manuals about how to conceptualize and respond to treatment non-response and/or failure. Thus, the case formulation approach, because of its reliance on testing out hypotheses that are part of the case formulation via the inspection of empirical data (symptom measures, indicators of functioning), is ideally suited to target this clinically important problem. The authors describe how, in both cases, the therapist and client were able to use the case formulation to identify potential reasons that treatment was not working, revise hypotheses about what was maintaining symptoms, make changes to interventions based on this revised conceptualization, and ultimately generate a positive outcome. This case series is not only an outstanding model for how to implement this approach to clinical work, but also how to integrate clinical practice and science in a way that is seamless and can lead to generalizable knowledge.

Effectiveness Studies

The gold-standard research methodology for establishing the efficacy of psychotherapy interventions is the randomized controlled trial (RCT). The random assignment of participants to treatment conditions, the hallmark of RCTs, helps to minimize population bias in order to maximize the likelihood that observed group differences are due to the variable(s) being studied (typically a treatment or intervention) and not other sources of variance. Common criticisms of this approach include that study settings (usually academic research labs), strict inclusion and exclusion criteria, as well as reliance on highly standardized treatment protocols, often do not mirror the conditions under which most providers deliver these treatments (e.g., Kazdin, 2008). As a result, effectiveness studies, which involve evaluating the benefits of established psychotherapies in clinical settings and without the controls imposed by RCTs, are needed to inform the extent to which the results of RCTs are generalizable to the "real world." In this way, RCTs and effectiveness studies work hand in hand to advance the science of psychotherapy.

Private practice clinicians are uniquely poised to make significant scientific contributions via their involvement in effectiveness studies, given that they work in the very settings where much of psychotherapy is delivered. Again, evidence-based practitioners, in particular, are an excellent fit for this type of research given that data collection and outcome monitoring are frequently a core part of treatment delivery. There are numerous models of effectiveness studies in the literature, many of which have been conducted by, or in conjunction with, individuals in private practice. Two such studies are described below, both by Persons and colleagues, given Person's pioneering work in this area.

Persons, Bostrom, & Bertagnoli (1999) published a study that compared the outcomes of 45 depressed clients who were treated in private practice (all by Persons) with either cognitive therapy or cognitive therapy in addition to pharmacotherapy, to the outcomes for depressed clients who received the same treatments from a published RCT (Murphy, Simons, Wetzel, & Lustman, 1984). Because most effectiveness studies, unlike most RCTs, do not include control or alternative treatment conditions to allow for group comparisons of outcome, "benchmarking" techniques can be used to address this issue. Benchmarking involves selecting appropriate comparison conditions and outcome measures from RTCs, to which the results from clinical practice can be compared (e.g., Houghton, Saxon, Bradburn, Ricketts, & Hardy, 2010; Minami, Serlin, Wampold, Kircher, & Brown, 2008). In essence, the aim is to determine whether outcomes in clinical settings are comparable to those observed in RCTs, thereby substantiating the generalizability of RCT findings. Persons et al. used the data from the Murphy et al. (1984) study as the benchmark for their data from clinical practice. This was possible because the same validated symptom measures that were used to track progress in treatment were the same as those used to assess outcomes in the RCT. Additionally, the authors noted that therapy was implemented more flexibly in practice than in the RCT due to the needs of "real world" clients, and that treatment length was open-ended for each client vs. a designated number of sessions (the latter of which is typical in RCTs). Persons and colleagues found that depressed clients in private practice improved significantly during treatment and that outcomes were comparable to those from the RCT, despite the fact that the private practice sample was more heterogeneous than the RCT sample and that there was more variability in treatment delivery.

In a similar study, Persons, Roberts, Zalecki, and Breechwald (2006) examined the outcomes for 58 clients with anxiety and depression who were treated in a private practice setting (by multiple therapists). All clients met criteria for a mood disorder, anxiety disorder, or both and reported symptoms of both depression and anxiety at intake. Clients were treated using CBT that was guided by a case formulation approach (described above). The purpose of the study was to evaluate whether this approach led to both statistically and clinically significant changes in symptoms, as well as to compare treatment outcomes to those from RCTs for empirically supported treatments for depression and anxiety. These benchmarking data were taken from two sources, a meta-analysis (Westen & Morrison, 2001) and a review paper (Barlow & Lehman, 1996). As with the study by Persons et al. (1999), clients in private practice received a more flexible treatment in terms of the application and timing of specific interventions, as well as treatment duration. Results indicated that clients treated in private practice did make significant improvements with symptoms of both depression and anxiety and that those improvements were comparable to those from published RCTs. These results are compelling because the treatment was targeting co-morbidity specifically (symptoms of depression and anxiety), whereas RCTs generally only target symptoms of a single disorder or problem. Given that clients in clinical practice frequently present with co-morbid conditions, these findings are particularly valuable in demonstrating treatment effectiveness with clients who more closely resemble those seen in clinical practice.

Both studies by Persons and colleagues (1999, 2006) are excellent examples of effectiveness studies. They also serve as models for uncontrolled open trials, which are frequently conducted as a precursor to RCTs to establish the feasibility and acceptability of a treatment. Both employed benchmarking techniques, which address an important limitation of this kind of research, which is the lack of a control condition. As opposed to case studies or case series, the data derived from the larger sample sizes in these studies allow for more sophisticated data analysis techniques, as well as more potential generalizability of the findings. Many clinicians in private practice, particularly those with a specialty practice and/or who practice evidence-based treatment, likely have the types of data needed to conduct and publish similar studies.

Psychometric Studies

At first glance, psychometric studies may not seem like a natural fit for clinicians in private practice. When new psychological measures are created to assess symptoms or specific constructs, the psychometric properties of the scales (e.g., reliability, validity, factor structure) are frequently evaluated using large samples of college students. This methodology is understandable given that most researchers conducting these studies work in academic settings and have relatively easy access to this population and large samples are needed for some of the statistical analyses used in this research (i.e., factor analysis). Unfortunately, many scales then start to be widely used with clinical populations, often without much published data supporting the psychometric properties of the scales for these groups. Private practice clinicians are in a unique position to be able to assist with this problem given that they have access to clinical populations. This is particularly true for clinicians in group practice settings, in which data could be collected from large groups of clients in a relatively short period of time. Given that many clinicians include symptom measures as part of the intake process, this kind of research is relatively easy to integrate into practice settings with minimal additional burden on providers or clients. Two examples of psychometric studies conducted in a group practice setting (EBTCS) are described below.

The Overall Anxiety Severity and Impairment Scale (OASIS; Norman, Cissell, Means-Christensen, & Stein, 2006) is a five-item measure that can be used to assess anxiety severity and functional impairment across anxiety disorders. The measure has potentially broad utility in both mental and physical health care settings given that it only takes a few minutes to administer and can be used across all anxiety disorder presentations (including subclinical presentations). As is typically the case, the first psychometric evaluation of the scale was conducted with college students (Norman et al., 2006). Subsequent psychometric evaluations were conducted using samples of college students (Norman et al., 2011), primary care patients referred to a treatment study for anxiety disorders (Campbell-Sills et al., 2009), and women with and without posttraumatic stress disorder (PTSD) related to intimate partner violence (Norman et al., 2013). Unfortunately, none of these studies included a population of anxiety disorder clients seeking outpatient mental health treatment, one of the primary groups for whom the use of this scale might be most useful. As a result, clinicians at EBTCS published a psychometric evaluation of the OASIS that included data from 347 clients who sought specialty care for anxiety and related disorders (Moore et al., 2015). This study provided much needed information substantiating the reliability, validity, and factor structure of the scale in a transdiagnostic group of individuals with anxiety problems, thereby filling an important gap in the empirical literature.

In a similar study, clinicians at EBTCS examined the psychometric properties of the Difficulties in Emotion Regulation Scale (DERS; Gratz & Roemer, 2004), a widely used measure of problems with emotion regulation. As with the OASIS, the scale was initially developed with a large sample of college students. Although numerous psychometric studies were published on the DERS in the decade after it was created, all but two were with non-clinical samples and the two studies that included clinical samples were both conducted in inpatient psychiatric settings (Fowler et al., 2014; Perez, Venta, Garnaaz, & Sharp, 2012). Therefore, no data were available for the use of this scale with outpatient populations. Osborne and colleagues (Osborne, Michonski, Sayrs, Welch, and Karwoski-Anderson, 2017) investigated the psychometric properties of the DERS in a sample of 344 clients seeking comprehensive outpatient DBT, a treatment that was developed to target underlying problems with emotion regulation (Linehan, 1993). The findings contributed to the literature on the DERS by providing data about the properties of the scale in a sample previously not studied (outpatients seeking DBT), as well as utilizing analytic methods not previously used with this measure that were more appropriate for addressing concerns about the scale.

The studies by Moore et al. (2015) and Osborne et al. (2017) highlight how clinicians in private practice can make important scientific contributions precisely *because* they work in real-world clinical settings and have access to data that is often challenging to come by in academic settings. Both studies also demonstrate how a relatively simple procedure—administering a few symptom measures during the intake process—can provide the basis for a meaningful practice-based research project.

Studies Targeting Therapist-related Variables

Although research on client outcomes and client-related data are certainly a natural fit for practice-based researchers, clinicians who want to conduct research are not limited to research questions that focus on clients. In fact, private practice clinicians may also be in a unique position to study therapist-related variables in order to help enhance treatment delivery and outcomes.

Luoma and Vilardaga (2013) described the results of a pilot RCT that was designed to increase therapist psychological flexibility following a two-day ACT training. Despite the fact that ACT trainings often include experiential exercises in order to target psychological flexibility in the attendees (just as various ACT interventions are designed to target the same process in clients), no research had previously examined whether this outcome is achieved. Luoma and Vilardaga randomly assigned 20 ACT training participants to one of two conditions: (1) a no further contact condition or (2) a phone consultation condition that consisted of six, 30-minute phone sessions over a three-month period of time. The phone consultation sessions included a range of interventions, including experiential exercises to improve psychological flexibility. Results indicated that psychological flexibility three months after the ACT training was significantly greater in the phone coaching condition than the no contact condition. The groups were similar in terms of conceptual knowledge of ACT and burnout at three-month follow-up, suggesting that the phone coaching had a unique impact on psychological flexibility above and beyond the initial training, but not on the other variables examined. This study illustrates how clinicians in practice (Luoma) can use gold-standard research methods (RCT) to answer interesting and useful research questions about psychotherapy training.

A recent study by Persons, Koerner, Eidelman, Cannon, and Liu (2016) exemplifies how clinicians can produce innovative research outside of more traditional research settings. Persons and colleagues designed an online progress monitoring tool that enabled therapists to administer symptom measures to their clients throughout treatment. In addition to this tool, they also developed an online training series to teach therapists how to integrate progress monitoring and the online tool into their clinical work. The purpose of the study was to test the effectiveness of an intervention (online tool + training) that could help address barriers that clinicians encounter when trying to adopt evidence-based practices (in this case, progress monitoring). Results indicated that among the 26 therapists who participated in the study, use of progress monitoring was significantly greater following the training, as well as 12-months after the training, as compared to baseline. Additionally, and perhaps even more importantly, the findings at 12-months were most pronounced for any type of progress monitoring, not just the measure that had been included as part of the online tool that participants had access to for the duration of the study. Thus, the intervention led to behavior change that was generalized to progress monitoring broadly. This study was supported by grant funding (something that is relatively uncommon in practice-based settings), leveraged technology in innovative ways, and demonstrated how targeting therapist behaviors could potentially lead to better psychotherapy outcomes, as progress monitoring has been linked to improved outcomes in a range of studies (e.g., Lambert, 2015). Though not all private practice clinicians will be able to conduct such research, this study provides an aspirational model for the caliber of science that can be generated by clinicians in practice.

Studies Focusing on Non-clinical Samples

One final example of research conducted by private practice clinicians illustrates how such researchers are also not restricted to investigating questions that focus solely on data from the therapy context (i.e., from clients or therapists). Luoma and colleagues (Luoma, Guinther, & Vilardaga, 2016) conducted a study examining the relationships between shame, guilt, and drinking behaviors in a sample of community dwelling drinkers. Although shame and guilt have been proposed to be factors associated with problematic drinking, minimal research has studied these associations in fine detail. This study examined data from 88 participants who completed baseline measures of shame, guilt, negative affect, drinking behaviors, and negative impacts related to drinking, as well as daily diary ratings (for 21 days) of variables such as day and nighttime drinking, shame, and negative affect. The results indicated that shame and guilt accounted for more variance in problems related to drinking than amount of drinking. Additionally, daily diary data indicated that when people chose to drink, *how much* they drank was related to how much shame they felt that day. However, *whether or not* they drank, was more related to whether they drank the prior day. These findings highlight the nuanced relationships between these variables and may have utility for designing more effective treatments for problematic drinking behaviors. They also highlight how investigation of such important questions are not uniquely the domain of academic researchers.

Summary

The artificial divide in the field of psychology between research and practice has many adverse impacts, not the least of which is the underrepresentation of clinicians in the scientific community. Though many private practice clinicians may not have the interest or training to conduct research, many do and these individuals have the potential to address a range of important questions that can help advance the field in countless ways. Dissemination research, as one example, could likely be improved and expedited with greater inclusion of clinician-researchers in this process. Practice-based researchers also have the potential to bring new perspectives to the empirical literature given their extensive experience with delivering treatments to real-world clients in real-world settings.

Many obstacles are present for individuals who wish to conduct research in private practice. This chapter highlights some of these challenges, as well as describes potential solutions and different models of this type of research. This chapter also describes the practice-based research program at EBTCS, a large outpatient specialty practice. The clinicians who conduct research at EBTCS have faced all of the obstacles described here and continue to learn about and refine processes for producing high-quality research in a practice setting. To date, this program has generated 16 poster presentations at professional conferences, as well as three published manuscripts (Moore et al., 2015; Osborne et al., 2017; Welch and Kim, 2012), with several more currently in preparation.

Hopefully, the information presented here makes it apparent that research in private practice is feasible and can be carried out in many different ways; practitioners with sufficient research training and experience can conduct their own projects from start to finish, whereas others may benefit from consulting or partnering with other practice-based researchers or academia-based researchers to round out specific skillsets needed to complete projects (i.e., knowledge of specific research methods or statistical analyses). Regardless, clinician-researchers can play a vital role in all aspects of the research process and those who are interested in doing this work are encouraged to seek out like-minded professionals for both collaboration and mentorship. These professional networks will be essential for advancing work in this area, particularly until clinical psychology graduate programs begin to emphasize the importance of this type of research.

References

Amdur, R. J., Speers, M., & Bankert, E. (2006). Identifying intent: Is this project research? In E. A. Bankert & R. J. Amdur (Eds.) *Institutional review board: Management and function*, (2nd ed.) (pp. 101–105). Boston, MA: Jones and Bartlett Publishers.

Barlow, D. H. & Lehman, C. L. (1996). Advances in the psychosocial treatment of anxiety disorders. *Archives of General Psychiatry, 53*, 727–745.

Campbell-Sills, L., Norman, S. B., Craske, M. G., Sullivan, G., Lang, A. J., Chavira, D. A., Bystritsky, A., Sherbourne, C., Roy-Byrne, P., & Stein, M. B. (2009). Validation of a brief measure of anxiety-related severity and impairment: the Overall Anxiety Severity and Impairment Scale (OASIS). *Journal of Affective Disorders, 112*, 92–101.

Chang, K., Lee, I. L., & Hargreaves, A. T. (2008). Scientist versus Practitioner–An abridged meta-analysis of the changing role of psychologists. *Counseling Psychology Quarterly, 21*(3), 267–291.

Codd, R. T., Twohig, M. P., Crosby, J. M., & Enno, A. (2011). Treatment of three anxiety disorder cases with acceptance and commitment therapy in a private practice. *Journal of Cognitive Psychotherapy: An International Quarterly, 25*, 203–217.

Fowler, J. C., Charak, R., Elhai, J. D., Allen, J. G., Frueh, B. C., & Oldham, J. M. (2014). Construct validity and factor structure of Difficulties in Emotion Regulation Scale among adults with severe mental illness. *Journal of Psychiatric Research, 58*, 175–180.

Gratz, K. L. & Roemer, L. (2004). Multidimensional assessment of emotion regulation and dysregulation: Development, factor structure, and initial validation of the Difficulties in Emotion Regulation Scale. *Journal of Psychopathology and Behavioral Assessment, 26*, 41–54.

HHS Protection of Human Subjects, 45 C.F.R. 46 (2009).
Houghton, S., Saxon, D., Bradburn, M., Ricketts, T., & Hardy, G. (2010). The effectiveness of routinely delivered cognitive behavioral therapy for obsessive-compulsive disorder: A benchmarking study. *British Journal of Clinical Psychology, 49*, 473–489.
Kazdin, A. E. (2008). Evidence-based treatment and practice: New opportunities to bridge clinical research and practice, enhance the knowledge base, and improve patient care. *American Psychologist, 63*, 146–159.
Koerner, K. & Castonguay, L. G. (2015). Practice-oriented research: What it takes to do collaborative research in private practice. *Psychotherapy Research, 25*, 67–83.
Koerner, K., Persons, J. B., Luoma, J. B., & Osborne, T. L. (2011, November). *Practice-based research: How to conduct meaningful research in clinical practice*. Symposium conducted at the Association for Behavior and Cognitive Therapies Annual Convention, Toronto, Canada.
Lambert, M. J. (2015). Progress feedback and the OQ-system: The past and the future. *Psychotherapy, 52*, 381–390.
LeJeune, J. T. & Luoma, J. B. (2015). The integrated scientist-practitioner: A new model for combining research and clinical practice in fee-for-service settings. *Professional Psychology: Research and Practice, 46*(6), 421–428.
Linehan, M. M. (1993). *Cognitive behavior therapy for borderline personality disorder*. New York: Guilford.
Luoma, J. B., Guinther, P., & Vilardaga, R. (March, 2016). *A Multimethod Investigation of Shame as an Antecedent for Problem Drinking*. Poster presented at the Annual Conference of the Society for Affective Science in Chicago, IL.
Luoma, J. B. & Vilardaga, J. P. (2013). Improving therapist psychological flexibility while training acceptance and commitment therapy. *Cognitive Behaviour Therapy, 42*, 1–8.
Minami, T., Serlin, R. C., Wampold, B. E., Kircher, J. C., & Brown, G. S. (2008). Using clinical trials to benchmark effects produced in clinical practice. *Quality and Quantity, 42*, 513–525.
Moore, S. A., Welch, S. S., Michonski, J., Poquiz, J., Osborne, T. L., Sayrs, J., & Spanos, A. (2015). Psychometric evaluation of the Overall Anxiety Severity and Impairment Scale (OASIS) in individuals seeking outpatient specialty treatment for anxiety-related disorders. *Journal of Affective Disorders, 175*, 463–470.
Murphy, G. E., Simons, A. D., Wetzel, R. D., & Lustman, P. J. (1984). Cognitive therapy and pharmacotherapy. *Archives of General psychiatry, 41*, 33–41.
Norcross, J. C. & Karpiak, C. P. (2012). Clinical psychologists in the 2010s: 50 years of the APA Division of Clinical Psychology. *Clinical Psychology: Science and Practice, 19*, 1–12.
Norcross, J. C., Karpiak, C. P., & Santoro, S. O. (2005). Clinical psychologists across the years: The division of clinical psychology from 1960 to 2003. *Journal of Clinical Psychology, 61*, 1467–1483.
Norman, S. B., Allard, C. B., Trim, R. S., Thorp, S. R., Behroozia, M., Masino, T. T., & Stein, M. B. (2013). Psychometrics of the Overall Anxiety Severity and Impairment Scale (OASIS) in a sample of women with and without trauma histories. *Archives of Women's Mental Health, 16*, 123–129.
Norman, S. B., Campbell-Sills, L., Hitchcock, C. A., Sullivan, S., Rochlin, A., Wilkins, K. C., & Stein, M. B. (2011). Psychometrics of a brief measure of anxiety to detect severity and impairment: the Overall Anxiety Severity and Impairment Scale (OASIS). *Journal of Psychiatric Research, 45*, 262–268.
Norman, S. B., Cissell, S. H., Means-Christensen, A. J., & Stein, M. B. (2006). Development and validation of an Overall Anxiety Severity and Impairment Scale (OASIS). *Depression and Anxiety, 23*(4), 245–249.

Osborne, T. L. & Luoma, J. B. (in press). Overcoming a primary barrier to practice-based research: Access to an institutional review board (IRB) for independent ethics review. *Psychotherapy*.

Osborne, T. L., Michonski, J., Sayrs, J., Welch, S. W., & Karwoski-Anderson, L. (2017). Factor structure of the Difficulties in Emotion Regulation Scale (DERS) in adult outpatients receiving dialectical behavior therapy (DBT). *Journal of Psychopathology and Behavioral Assessment, 39*, 355–371.

Perez, J., Venta, A., Garnaat, S., & Sharp, C. (2012). The Difficulty in Emotion Regulation Scale: Factor structure and association with nonsuicidal self-injury in adolescent inpatients. *Journal of Psychopathology and Behavioral Assessment, 34*, 393–404.

Persons, J. B. (2014, November). *How to do research in your private practice*. Workshop conducted at the Association for Behavior and Cognitive Therapies Annual Convention, Philadelphia, PA.

Persons, J. B., Beckner, V. L., & Tompkins, M. A. (2013). Testing case formulation hypotheses in psychotherapy: Two case examples. *Cognitive and Behavioral Practice, 20*, 399–409.

Persons, J. B., Bostrom, A., & Bertagnoli, A. (1999). Results of randomized controlled trials of cognitive therapy for depression generalize to private practice. *Cognitive Therapy and Research, 23*, 535–548.

Persons, J. B., Eidelman, P., & Hong, J. (2014, November). Research at the Cognitive Behavior Therapy and Science Center. In J. B. Persons (Chair), *Overcoming obstacles to doing research in a private practice setting*. Clinical Roundtable conducted at the Association for Behavior and Cognitive Therapies Annual Convention, Philadelphia, PA.

Persons, J. B., Koerner, K., Eidelman, P., Thomas, C., & Liu, H. (2016). Increasing psychotherapists' adoption and implementation of the evidence-based practice of progress monitoring. *Behaviour Research and Therapy, 76*, 24–31.

Persons, J. B., Roberts, N. A., Zalecki, C. A., & Brechwald, W. A. G. (2006). Naturalistic outcome of case formulation-driven cognitive behavior therapy for anxious depressed clients. *Behaviour Research and Therapy, 44*, 1041–1051.

Teachman, B. A., Drabick, D. A. G., Hershenberg, R., Vivian, D., Wolfe, B. E., & Goldfried, M. R. (2012). Bridging the gap between clinical research and clinical practice: Introduction to the special section. *Psychotherapy, 49*, 97–100.

Welch, S. S. & Kim, J. (2012). DBT-enhanced cognitive behavioral therapy for adolescent trichotillomania: An adolescent case study. *Cognitive and Behavioral Practice, 19*, 483–493.

Westen, D. & Morrison, K. (2001). A multidimensional meta-analysis of treatment for depression, panic, and generalized anxiety disorder: An empirical examination of the status of empirically supported therapies. *Journal of Consulting and Clinical Psychology, 69*, 875–899.

Resources

Books and Articles for Identifying Free and Low-cost Psychological Symptom Measures

Antony, M., M., Orsillo, S. M., & Roemer, L. (2001). *Practitioner's Guide to Empirically Based Measures of Anxiety*. Springer.

Beidas, R. S., Stewart, R. E., Walsh, L., Lucas, S., Downey, M. M., Jackson, K., et al. (2015). Free, brief, and validated: Standardized instructions for low-resource mental health settings. *Cognitive Behavioral Practice, 22,* 5–19. www.ncbi.nlm.nih.gov/pmc/articles/PMC4310476/

Corcoran, K. & Fisher, J. (2013). *Measures for Clinical Practice and Research, Volume 1: Couples, Families, and Children, Fifth Edition.* Oxford University Press.

Corcoran, K. & Fisher, J. (2013). *Measures for Clinical Practice and Research, Volume 2: Adults, Fifth Edition.* Oxford University Press.

Nezu, A., M., Ronan, G. F., Meadows, E. A., & McClure, K. S. (2000). *Practitioner's Guide to Empirically Based Measures of Depression.* Springer.

Online Tools

Mendeley (*www.mendeley.com*)—Free software for managing references and citations, as well as other research-support tools.

CHAPTER 9

Simultaneous Practice and Research: A Model for Conducting Research in Private Practice

Jacqueline B. Persons

My idea of heaven is: I am sitting in my office conducting a therapy session with a patient and, *as I do that*, I am collecting data that simultaneously aid my treatment of that patient and contribute to research that advances knowledge. In this chapter, I describe a model for conducting research in a private practice setting that I call *simultaneous practice and research*, because many elements of the research and practice happen simultaneously. The model is founded on a very tight integration of the practitioner's clinical work and the research s/he conducts. I describe the elements of the model, beginning with a description of the idiographic case formulation approach to clinical practice that is the foundation of the model, and ending with an account of the ways the research and clinical work feed and support each other.

The simultaneous-practice-and-research model I describe here, in which the research enterprise is founded on data collected for clinical purposes, is certainly not the only way to conduct research in a private practice setting, as some of the other chapters in this volume show (Castonguay & Youn, Osborrne, and Juoma). I made up the simultaneous model as I went along, over the course of many years, and I adopted it because it addresses many of the impediments to conducting research in a clinical practice setting. The model's conceptual clarity and elegance also strengthen its appeal. The model underpins most of my own research contributions, and has made it possible for me to have a research career in a private practice setting. I describe it here with the hope that it might be helpful to others.

The Simultaneous Practice and Research Model

The simultaneous-practice-and-research model requires a high degree of overlap of the practitioner's clinical skills and research interests. The practitioner must be interested in questions that can be addressed using the types of data collected in his/her clinical practice. Or, stated the other way around, the practitioner must have the clinical skills to treat the types of symptoms and problems that s/he wants to study. The model won't support the practitioner who, for example, has an outpatient practice treating childhood anxiety disorders and a research interest in psychotic disorders.

In addition to the overlap of clinical and research interests, in order to implement the model described here, the practitioner must have: a case formulation-driven approach to clinical work, research skills and training, library access, collaborators and helpers, statistical assistance and software, a treatment agreement in which the patient provides informed consent for research, access to an institutional review board or some other review mechanism to address ethical issues, collegial support, and solutions to the problems of time and money. I describe each of these elements here.

A Case Formulation-driven Approach to Clinical Work

An essential element of the simultaneous practice and research model for doing research in clinical practice is a case formulation-driven approach to clinical work. In a case formulation-driven approach to psychotherapy, the clinician collects data from each patient, in order to develop an idiographic formulation or case conceptualization. The formulation is a hypothesis about the mechanisms that cause and maintain the symptoms and problems of the unique individual who is in the clinician's office at that moment. The clinician uses the formulation to develop interventions and guide clinical decision-making, collecting data as the treatment proceeds to evaluate whether the treatment is effective in helping the patient achieve his or her treatment goals and whether the formulation hypothesis that guides the treatment appears to be correct (Persons, 2008). In this approach to psychotherapy, the clinician is using the same hypothesis-testing and data collection mode of working that scientists use, treating each case as an N = 1 experiment (Sackett, Richardson, Rosenberg, & Haynes, 1997). The therapist also draws on a wide range of types of scientific evidence, including evidence from randomized controlled trials of treatments, basic science findings, studies of the process of change in psychotherapy, and evidence collected from the patient himself. Thus, the case formulation approach to psychotherapy relies on both the *products* and the *methods* of science.

The case formulation-driven approach to clinical work promotes scientific thinking and curiosity, facilitates the use of evidence from multiple sources, and requires extensive data collection. All of these support the research enterprise. I discuss each of these in turn, giving particular emphasis to the data collection piece.

Curiosity and Scientific Thinking

The case formulation-driven approach promotes curiosity and scientific thinking because the clinician is constantly asking questions and testing hypotheses about what is going on in the clinical work (rather than turning to the next page in the empirically-supported treatment (EST) protocol). Shiloff (2015) describes the way training students to use ESTs teaches them to use some of the *products* of the clinical science enterprise, but does not train them in the *methods* of clinical science, does not train them to think or operate like clinical scientists. A case formulation approach to psychotherapy, in contrast, calls for constant hypothesis-testing.

Reliance on Multiple Types of Evidence

To develop a case formulation and carry out a treatment based on it, the therapist draws on multiple sources of evidence from the scientific literature, including evidence-based formulations of disorders and symptoms, basic science findings, and on evidence from the patient at hand, such as information about typical events that trigger symptoms for this patient. The therapist also relies on evidence-based assessment tools. The therapist draws on the basic science and psychotherapy literatures, including, for example, findings about the maladaptive effects of suppression (e.g., Rosenthal, Cheavens, Lejuez, & Lynch, 2005), about the role of imagery in depression (Holmes, Blackwell, Heyes, Renner, & Raes, 2016), about the role of memory enhancement strategies in improving psychotherapy outcome (Harvey et al., 2014), and evidence that the trajectory of change in psychotherapy is generally non-linear, with early rapid improvement typically followed by a slower rate of change (Lutz, Martinovich, & Howard, 1999). The therapist is often developing a formulation based on transdiagnostic mechanisms such as perfectionism, intolerance of uncertainty, anxiety sensitivity, and similar, and drawing on the basic science findings about these phenomena as she does so. The focus on transdiagnostic mechanisms aligns with current thinking in the research community (Sanislow, Pine, Quinn, Kozak, & Garvey, 2010), and thus enhances the potential for the clinician to make a contribution to research.

Extensive Data Collection

The case formulation-driven approach requires extensive data collection that provides a strong support for both the clinical work and for research. To develop a formulation and get the progress monitoring started right away, the clinician collects a lot of data *at intake*. To test hypotheses (formulations) and monitor the patient's progress in treatment, the practitioner collects data *at every session* (and indeed, at every moment (e.g., monitoring the patient's nonverbal and verbal responses to the therapist's behavior and interventions)). I discuss each of these in turn.

ASSESSMENT AT INTAKE

When I meet with a new patient at intake, I ask them to complete and bring to the session a large packet of questionnaires asking about their symptoms, treatment history, and family and social history. These tools aid with the initial tasks of developing a problem list, obtaining diagnosis and formulation hypotheses, and setting treatment goals.

Patients complete an Intake Questionnaire that provides extensive information about current symptoms and treatment and family history, and a Diagnostic Screening Tool, a self-report measure that my colleagues and I developed that includes screening questions (e.g., questions about substance use) that help the clinician identify areas where additional diagnostic assessment is needed. These measures are available at: https://oaklandcbt.com/forms-and-tools-for-clinicians/. Patients also complete the *Depression Anxiety Stress Scales* (DASS; (S. H. Lovibond & P. F. Lovibond, 1995), a self-report measure with three subscales assessing symptoms of depression anxiety (panic and physiological arousal, and stress). Patients complete the *Patient Health Questionnaire-9* (PHQ-9; Kroenke, Spitzer & Williams, 2001), a 10-item self-report measure designed for screening, diagnosing, and/or monitoring depressive symptoms over a two-week period. The measure is available copyright-free at www.phqscreeners.com. They also complete the *Perseverative Thinking Questionnaire* (PTQ; Ehring et al., 2011), a 15-item self-report scale that assesses content-neutral repetitive negative thinking, including rumination and worry. The PTQ is reproduced in the appendix of Ehring et al. (2011), which is available online at www.sciencedirect.com/science/article/pii/S000579161000114X. Clicking the link within the text that reads "under a creative commons license" on that webpage will give you access to the PTQ through the creative commons. I collect information about perseverative thinking using the PTQ at intake because I have learned in my experience, and there are data indicating that patients who have a lot of perseverative thinking do not respond well to standard CT (Watkins, 2016) so I collect this measure to help me identify when perseverative thinking is a treatment target, and also because I hope to be able to do a piece of research to test the hypothesis that patients who score high on this measure are less likely to respond to treatment unless the clinician explicitly targets it in treatment. Patients also complete the *Obsessive Beliefs Questionnaire-44* (OBQ-44); (Obsessive Compulsive Cognitions Working Group, 2005), a 44-item self-report scale that assesses beliefs about over-responsibility and perceived threat of harm, assessing perfectionism and intolerance of uncertainty, and assessing over-importance of thoughts and of controlling thoughts, that are common in patients with OCD and other anxiety disorders. The OBQ-44 is copyright-free, available at https://oaklandcbt.com/forms-and-tools-for-clinicians. There is evidence that patients high on perfectionism have worse outcome of treatment of depression, so collecting these data will allow for a future test of that hypothesis. Patients also complete the *Difficulties in Emotion Regulation Scale* (DERS; Gratz & Roemer, 2004), and the *Medical Outcomes Study Social Support Survey* (Sherbourne & Stewart, 1991), a 19-item self-report measure of perceived social support in several domains, including emotional/informational support, tangible support, affectionate support, and positive social interaction. Finally, they complete the *Work and Social Adjustment Scale*, a self-report measure of functional impairment due to a problem (e.g., depression) identified by the patient (Mundt, Marks, Shear, & Greist, 2002). The scale consists of five questions that ask the patient to rate the degree of impairment caused by their problem in five domains of life: work, home manage-ment, social/leisure activities, private leisure activities, and close relationships. The measure can be obtained from the author, Isaac Marks, for use in research free of charge.

PROGRESS MONITORING

Collecting data to monitor progress is an essential element of the case formulation approach. In an ideal world, the practitioner collects data to monitor both the *outcome* (symptoms, functioning, patient progress toward idiographic goals) and *process* of treatment (including changes in the transdiagnostic mechanisms described in the case formulation, the quality of the patient-therapist relationship, homework compliance, patient learning, and patient satisfaction with treatment).

To monitor outcome, I try to assess outcome with at least one standardized measure to monitor symptoms for every patient at every session. The most common measures I use are the Depression Anxiety Stress Scales, the Yale-Brown Obsessive-Compulsive Scale, the Perseverative Thinking Questionnaire the PHQ-9, and the GAD-7. The PHQ-9 is useful because it includes an item that measures functioning, which is under-studied and yet of great importance to patients and clinicians. The study of changes in functioning due to psychotherapy is an area where the practitioner can make a research contribution. The weakness of the PHQ-9 for progress monitoring purposes is that it assesses symptoms over a two-week period; a measure that assessed symptoms over the one week that is typical between therapy sessions would be more useful for monitoring progress.

I use the DASS for most patients because it assesses symptoms that are problematic for the majority of my patients, and I have found it to be sensitive to change during treatment. Although there are some data in the literature documenting the sensitivity to change of the DASS (Ronk, Korman, Hooke, & Page, 2013), my colleague Lance Rappaport pointed out that this issue has not much been studied, and so he and I are considering undertaking a study of the DASS's sensitivity to change. As Osborne (this volume) points out and the study by Ronk et al. (2013) illustrates, studies of the properties of assessment tools are an area where the practitioner can make a research contribution.

Despite my best efforts, I can only find a standardized measure for only about 75 percent of my patients. There are inevitably some patients who do not report easily-assessed distress and I am unable to identify a standardized measure to track outcome. In some of these cases, I track progress via a self-monitoring log, sometimes a shared google form on which the patient tracks number of minutes spent worrying daily, for example.

To assess process, I am using two assessment measures. One is a standard progress note that I developed with the help of two colleagues, Polina Eidelman, and Janie Hong. We used Google Forms to develop a progress note that assesses key aspects of psychotherapy process that we need to track for clinical purposes and that we believe are related to outcome and can allow for a research study. The data are stored in a secure site in the cloud that is encrypted and HIPAA compliant, and can be exported from the google form into an excel document that can easily be converted to or used in statistical packages. Amy Sanchez, a clinical science graduate student at UC-Berkeley, is leading a study of the role of patient skill learning and practice in symptom change during therapy that we hope to conduct in our clinical practice setting, collecting data using the standard progress note that we use for clinical purposes.

The second process measure that I use routinely is the Session Assignment and Feedback Form (SAFF), a measure developed by Janie Hong, Polina Eidelman, Victoria Lemle Beckner, and Daniela Owen, local psychotherapists and clinician-researchers, to track homework assignments and compliance, patient learning in the session, the quality of the alliance, and several other aspects of process (Persons, Hong, Lemle Beckner, Owen, & Eidelman, 2012). It is available at https://oaklandcbt.com/forms-and-tools-for-clinicians/. One of our very talented research assistants, Alexandra Jensen, has studied SAFF data that all these collaborators collected in routine clinical practice, and found that when the patient's homework assignments are closely related to the material the patient reported was helpful in the session, homework compliance was greater (Jensen et al., 2017).

When tracking outcome and process, I strive to select measures that are sensitive to change, allow me to efficiently keep tabs on important phenomena (e.g., suicidality), are not copyright-protected, help the patient and therapist know if the patient is making progress toward his/her treatment goals, give information about whether the mechanisms that the therapist proposes are underpinning and maintaining the symptoms are in fact changing in treatment, can be used in a software or online format, and give the therapist some feedback about the relationship and other aspects of process. Another key criterion is that the measure is used in the research literature, in order to strengthen the research contribution that our clinical data can make.

Although I am striving to shift from paper-and-pencil to online data collection mechanisms, I am only at the beginning of that process. So, for many measures, I am still using paper and pencil. I store measures in a box in waiting room and I ask the patient to come five minutes early for the session, grab a measure and clipboard and complete the measure in the waiting room and bring it to me. Then I score the measure at the beginning of the session, plot the score, review the plot with the patient, and use the data to inform the agenda session. A large change in the patient's score since the previous session is always worth an agenda item as the more we can understand the factors that push the patient's scores up and down, the more we understand the mechanisms driving symptoms and driving improvement in symptoms, and the more effective we can be in treatment.

Research Skills and Training

To conduct research, the clinician must have skills in formulating a good research question, designing a study to test the question, collecting data in a systematic way, handling and storing and analyzing data, presenting the paper at a conference, writing the paper, and submitting the paper for publication and navigating the revision process. Good research training is needed; this generally means a PhD in clinical psychology or a similar field.

The most important research skill is the skill of choosing a good question. To choose a good question, pay attention to your observations and insights, and take them seriously. Don't assume that Tim Beck knows everything there is to know about cognitive therapy or that Marsha Linehan knows everything there is to know about borderline personality disorder. Notice the questions that concern you in your clinical work, that take up your time and energy, that aid or impede your ability to help your patients. Focus on those.

Many clinicians are super-talented and have fabulous ideas. The field needs them to publish their ideas and clinical experiences and successes. Notice that we have do not yet have ESTs for many disorders and problems that talented clinicians treat every day, including autism spectrum disorders in adults, most personality disorders, dissociative disorders, alexithymia, cyclothymia, anorexia nervosa in adults, and misophonia, among others. Related, the response rates even for the disorders where we have the best treatments are roughly 50 percent to 60 percent (Westen & Morrison, 2001). Clinicians who are working every day with these patients, and learning about and having some success with them, can make an important contribution to the field. If the clinician has a treatment success with any of these types of cases, s/he who has collected extensive data of the sort described here will be in the position to publish a single case study or case series that can make a useful contribution to literature.

Questions about the process of change in psychotherapy are of central interest to the clinician and they are also of central interest to the field (Persons, 2007). An example is the study I conducted with David Burns (Persons & Burns, 1985) when I was an intern, titled "Mechanisms of action of cognitive therapy: The relative contributions of technical and interpersonal interventions." This study consisted of data collected during the course of completing Thought Records from 17 patients whose therapy session entailed completing a Thought Record during the session. We also asked the patient to complete a ten-item scale assessing the quality of the alliance. My husband (Jeffrey M. Perloff, a co-author on several of my other papers — but not this one!), an econometrician, conducted the data analysis for us, and we showed that, as predicted by Beck's cognitive model, change in intensity of emotions during the therapy session was a function of the change in degree of belief in the patient's automatic thoughts during the session and the strength of the patient-therapist relationship; both factors made independent contributions to emotion change during the session. This paper is an example of a study that cost nothing to conduct and that addressed questions about the mechanism of action of cognitive therapy that remain important to this day.

My experience has been that if you study a good question, journal editors and reviewers will be interested in publishing your work even if the study has flaws as a result of the fact that the data were collected in a clinical setting. An example is a single case study I published with Amori Mikami, showing that when the initial treatment of the patient's hypochondriasis failed, the process of collecting additional assessment data and using the data to develop a new formulation of the case led to an improved treatment plan that led to a successful outcome (Persons & Mikami, 2002). In that study, I measured symptoms of hypochondriasis by simply asking the patient at the beginning of each session to report how many bouts of hypochondriasis he had had during the preceding week!

It is important to acknowledge that the method I advocate here of doing research by studying data that are collected during the routine clinical enterprise does not always match up well with the dictum to identify a good question. That is because the simultaneous practice and research method leads to the collection of a lot of data without a good question having been formulated. So that leads to time spent asking: What research questions can I answer with the data I have collected? This is not a very elegant or efficient way to do research. That said, creativity, or in my case, creative collaborators, can save the day. My collaborator Cannon Thomas very creatively identified two questions in the literature that could be addressed with the dataset available to us that consisted of weekly Beck Depression Inventory scores collected during the course of routine treatment for mood and anxiety disorders. In one study, Thomas conducted data simulations and used other methods to test the hypothesis that sudden gains (large reductions in BDI score from one session to the next) were not necessarily evidence of a qualitative change in the change process, as the primary account of sudden gains proposed, but could simply be a very large instance of gradual change (Thomas & Persons, 2010). In a second study, we used the same dataset and also studied datasets we obtained from investigators who collected the data in randomized controlled trials, to show that depressed patients who remain severely symptomatic at week four of cognitive therapy for depression are very unlikely to remit from their depression at the end of their treatment (Persons & Thomas, 2016).

Library Access

To make a research contribution, the simultaneous practice and research must stay up to date with the current state of the field. Library access is essential. Often clinical psychologist practitioners can get a clinical faculty appointment at a local university that will give them library access. However, there are other options for solving this problem. If you yourself do not have access to a university library, you may be able to get it by working with collaborators or even research assistants who have access. LeJeune and Luoma (2015) point out that public libraries can often provide access to journals or databases. Google Scholar can be surprisingly helpful. Another option is that if you know the author's name you can go to his/her university webpage or send a request via e-mail for the article. Research that is federally funded is available online at the pubmed website, located at: www.ncbi.nlm.nih.gov/pmc/about/public-access-info/. Go to the website and enter the author name or topic into the search window at the upper right. Another resource is ResearchGate, which offers investigators access to members' work via a self-archiving mechanism. An online library resource is Deepdyve (go to www.deepdyve.com/). For about $40/month, it provides full online access to all their journals, and this appears to include a large number in clinical psychology and CBT.

In addition to getting access to the literature, the clinician faces the daunting challenge of keeping up with the literature. I find it useful to get journal alerts, so that I get an e-mail that tells me about the newest papers that are appearing in the journals of greatest interest to me. I often ask my research assistants to download papers that come to me via the alerts that are useful to my clinical and research work, and then enter them into the tool I use to manage references, which is easily searchable. That way I have a chance of finding an article that is now filed in my articles folder on my desktop by the last name of the author and can easily get lost or forgotten there. If I find an article that is immediately relevant to a project I'm working on, I dump the pdf of the article in the folder (a google drive folder or a dropbox or box.net folder) for that project.

Collaborators and Helpers

It is difficult to impossible for a single person to have all of the skills and resources I list here as needed to carry out research in a clinical practice settings. Even clinicians who have excellent research training often need help in one or more of these areas, often in the area (my own weak link) of statistics and data analysis, where skills go out of date quickly and abilities get rusty. Even management of the database that results when the simultaneous practice and research collects data from his or her patients in a routine way, is a challenging task, and the clinician will want help with it. In addition, research often involves many hours of detailed work entering data, cleaning data, preparing tables and Powerpoint slides, doing literature searches, organizing references, formatting tables, and more. Assistance with these tasks is invaluable to all researchers, especially the busy clinician.

The clinical psychologist researcher who is located near a college or university can reach out to recruit collaborators and volunteer research assistants there. Psychology students who aspire to a degree in clinical psychology often want research assistant work to help them sort out their career goals and interests and to accrue valued experience (and a letter of recommendation) to support their applications to graduate school in clinical psychology. The students will be eager to help and provide useful assistance, and have an invaluable learning experience, so that is a win-win for all. I purposely located my office within easy access to UC-Berkeley, and I find I do not have any difficulty recruiting talented undergraduates or post-undergraduates who are willing to volunteer their time one day a week as research assistants (RAs) in exchange for training in research and research experience. And when I was able to contribute to the design of a new space, I arranged a larger-than usual common area that would hold a table for the RAs and a nearby storage closet for materials. Before I had this space, I had to organize my clinical schedule so as to not have patients during the time my RAs were on site; occasionally when the schedule broke down, the RAs were relegated to doing their work in the coffee shop down the street!

Statistical Assistance and Software

Occasionally, especially when using a single case research design, a simple plot or report of summary statistics is sufficient to present the results of a study. More commonly, a more formal data analysis is required. Excel can conduct several basic calculations and statistical analyses. Most practitioners likely have Microsoft Office and may not need anything beyond what Excel can offer. Free or inexpensive data analytic software, such as R, are also an option.

The clinician who has a university affiliation can sometimes obtain otherwise-costly data analytic software such as SPSS and SAS through the university. Collaborators, and students who can assist, are another valuable resource to solve this problem. The Clinical Research Methods and Statistics Special Interest Group at the ABCT is a useful resource. Its members are skilled methodologists and statisticians who can be tapped to provide consultation and collaboration.

A Treatment Agreement in which the Patient Provides Informed Consent for Research

The clinician who wishes to use data obtained from the patient during the treatment process for research purposes must obtain the patient's written permission to do so. I seek my patient's written permission using this material in the Treatment Agreement that each patient signs, and I ask the patient to initial this paragraph if she gives permission.

RESEARCH, TRAINING, WRITING: Dr. Persons conducts research and training, and she writes for professional and lay audiences. Your initials here give Dr. Persons permission to use information about you and your treatment in any of these ways, provided that she takes reasonable efforts to protect your identity. If you do not initial, Dr. Persons understands that she does not have your permission to use de-identified information about you in research, training, or writing. Declining to give permission will not affect your treatment with Dr. Persons in any way.

My experience is that the large majority of patients will give permission for use of data from their treatment in research. I do view the clinical care as primary, and thus the request for research permission is optional and the care provided does not depend on the patient giving permission for data to be used in research.

I am working to establish a data repository for my clinical data, and so I have established an additional consent mechanism for the data repository. For details about that, see my Treatment Agreement, which is available at https://oaklandcbt.com/intake-forms/.

Access to a Review Mechanism to Address Ethical Issues

The therapist who is collecting data from his/her patients for both clinical and research purposes has a dual relationship with the patient. The clinician has both a treatment provider-patient and a researcher-research participant relationship with the same patient. APA ethical principle 3.05 (cite the 2002 code) states: "(a) A psychologist refrains from entering into a multiple relationship if the multiple relationship could reasonably be expected to impair the psychologist's objectivity, competence, or effectiveness in performing his or her functions as a psychologist, or otherwise risks exploitation or harm to the person with whom the professional relationship exists. Multiple relationships that would not reasonably be expected to cause impairment or risk exploitation or harm are not unethical." Other applicable codes include the privacy and confidentiality codes of the APA Ethics code. Of course, clinicians from other disciplines may have other ethics codes for their professional discipline.

To address these ethical issues, and to protect him or herself and the clinician's practice (her livelihood!) in the event of a disgruntled subject/patient, the practitioner will want to obtain some sort of review of his/her research project.

If the data that are collected do not differ from those collected for clinical purposes, the review may not be needed until the project moves to the stage where the practitioner begins to pull the data together to make a contribution to science, that is, to generalizable knowledge. Pulling the data together for evaluation purposes, to evaluate the quality of one's work, is not research. But when the practitioner writes up the data for publication or presentation at a conference, for contribution to generalizable knowledge, s/he is conducting research and will want to obtain some sort of ethical review from an outsider.

The practitioner can follow any of several strategies to obtain a review of his/her research. One is consultation with another professional, as we have all been trained to do when handling other ethical issues that arise in practice. This consultation might be an informal one from a colleague with whom we trade consultation, so no money might be exchanged. Or it might be a more formal, hands-off consultation so to speak, for which the practitioner pays the consultant, who is not a friend or close colleague, for his/her time. To guide the review, you might ask the reviewers to review the research using the principles outlined in the Belmont Report (posted at www.hhs.gov/ohrp/regulations-and-policy/belmont-report/index.htmlxx), a short document that outlines principles underpinning ethical research that was published in 1979 by the National Commission for the Protection of Human Subjects of Biomedical and Behavioral Research. I once hired a local colleague who was both a psychologist and an attorney and who held multiple posts in our local professional community, including serving as chair of the IRB at one of the local professional schools, to review my project.

The practitioner can also elect to obtain a formal review of his/her study from an institutional review board (IRB). An IRB review is only legally required for studies that are supported by federal funding. However, if the practitioner has access to an IRB, perhaps through a university adjunct appointment or via collaborators, an IRB review is a good idea. Another option is to work with a freestanding IRB in the community that will review your projects in exchange for a fee. The fees can be sizeable, up to several thousand dollars for an initial review, and additional fees to review revisions. A final option, one that involves a major investment of time and energy, is to establish your own cooperative institutional review board (IRB) following the model described by Travis Osborne in this volume.

When conducting research in your clinical setting, it is a good idea to consult with your malpractice insurance company to be sure that they will cover your research work in the case of any adverse events. It is also a good idea to identify whether your state has regulations governing research that you must attend to (California does not).

To assure that you are aware of federal standards guiding research and are using them, you and the members of your research team can complete online training in the conduct of research. A useful resource for providing that training is the Collaborative Institutional Training Initiative (CITI), which was established in 2000 with the mission "To promote the public's trust in the research enterprise by providing high quality, peer reviewed, web based, research education materials to enhance the integrity and professionalism of investigators and staff conducting research." The CITI online training program in human subject research can be accessed at: www.citiprogram.org/. It offers access to independent learners who aren't affiliated with a subscriber organization. The cost to take a course in Social Behavioral Human Subjects Research appears to be $100 and the clinician can get CEU credits for completing the training.

A strategy for minimizing the need for IRB review is to create a data repository. The data repository is a de-identified database of clinical data, and no IRB review is required for research conducted using de-identified data. The data are de-identified in that they do not include any information that would uniquely identify each patient, such as date of birth, name, etc. And the simultaneous practice and research must not be able to identify patients in the database simply because of his/her familiarity with the patients. A de-identified database has no master identifying list or key to link the data to a patient name or identity. However, even though IRB review is not needed for research conducted using the data repository data, the clinician will want to obtain the patient's written consent for his/her data to be entered into the repository, and may want to get an IRB or some sort of review of the policies and procedures, consent document, and ongoing activity of the data repository mechanism itself. Regulations to be attended to when developing all these things (consent, procedures, oversight) include: the federal Office of Human Research Protection (OHRP), HIPAA, and state medical record regulations, and your state's IRB, if there is one (California does not have one).

Collegial Support

Collegial support is essential to a successful research career. It is easy, as a clinician, to feel like a fish out of water when thinking about research and interacting with the practitioners you work with every day who live in the clinical world. To develop an identity as a researcher, it is essential to join and participate in communities of fellow-researchers. The Association of Behavioral and Cognitive

Therapies (ABCT) has been my primary community, and since I joined the ABCT as a postdoctoral fellow more than 30 years ago, I have made it a point to submit to and present at and attend every annual conference of the ABCT. Other groups that have been important to my development as a simultaneous practice and research are the Anxiety and Depression Association of America (ADAA), the Society for Psychotherapy Research (SPR), the Society for a Science of Clinical Psychology, Division 12 (Society of Clinical Psychology) of the American Psychological Association, and the Society for a Science of Clinical Psychology (SSCP). The practitioner will want to identify professional organizations that focus on his/her area of interest and can support the research work.

Participating in a professional community of colleagues can add invaluable interpersonal and other reinforcers. Learning at a conference or from a colleague that someone has read your work and used what s/he learned to guide his or her own work is a huge positive reinforcement, in an environment where reinforcers of this sort are few and far between. And it is the stray conversations at conferences, the e-mail dialogue in the process of putting together a symposium, which yield tiny diamond-like bits of reinforcement that will carry the simultaneous practice and research through many long lonely hours when you are doing the hard slogging work required to compile or clean the dataset or your data analysis is failing to produce the desired results.

Participating in a professional community of researchers can also magnify the contribution you can make. If you sit in your office and write your papers and get them published in journals, you can make a certain contribution, but if you go to conferences, present your work, interact with others who are doing similar work and exchange ideas, your influence and learning and thus your contribution can be greater.

In fact, participation in the community of scientists is not only a help to the practitioner, but really a requirement for the practitioner who wants to contribute to science. Clinical work is usually very private. Science is public. No matter how smart the clinician's ideas are, unless he or she publishes them and sends them out into the world, she is not able to make a contribution to knowledge.

Local support is also important. Collegial relationships with other local practitioners who do research, and with students and faculty at local universities, and with the undergraduate research assistants, can also provide a solid foundation for the clinician's research activities. I hold a monthly research meeting with all of my (usually one or two, sometimes three) research assistants to build a local sense of community and support.

Solutions to the Problems of Time and Money

Research requires time and therefore money. The biggest cost of the research is the investigator's time. The main cost of research is the foregone income—that is, money not collected from clients because the practitioner spent the time on research activities, including collecting data, meeting with assistants and collaborators, and going out of town to a conference to present the research. And there can be other expenses as well, for statistical software or consultation, for equipment, books, conference registration fees and travel expenses.

Of course, one solution to the time and money problem is to seek grant funding and that certainly can be done. My own experience is that obtaining grant funding is a large amount of work, and I'd rather put the work into the research itself. So one of the main reasons I set up or established the highly overlapping clinical and research model of working that I present here is to try to fold the research as much as possible into the clinical operation, so that the research can be self-funded rather than supported by grant funding.

In the simultaneous-practice-and-research model, the high degree of overlap of the clinical and research tasks addresses several of the issues that arise with time and money. In that model, the research relies on data collected during the clinical enterprise addresses this problem in part. The time required to establish and implement a mechanism for data collection is time that the simultaneous practice and research is already expending to support his/her clinical practice. Similarly, much of the time required to keep up with the literature, necessary for doing research, is also necessary for a high quality evidence-based practice. And the time required and the fees expended to attend conferences serve joint clinical and research purposes in that the practitioner attends conferences to learn about the latest findings in the field, both basic science and clinical applications, and to present his/her research and clinical offerings. Books that the researcher wants to read are also useful clinically. And, at least in my community in the San Francisco Bay Area, the clinician who is attending to the literature and providing high quality evidence-based care can establish a fee for service practice (rather than participating on insurance panels that often impose paperwork burdens) and to set a high fee that allows him/her to reduce his/her caseload to allow time for research and to pay for costs of the research.

The main solution to the problems of time and money is intrinsic motivation. The clinical researcher puts in the time (unpaid) to do the research because s/he enjoys doing it. He enjoys learning and working hard, enjoys making a contribution. My typical week includes about ten hours for patient visits and five hours for consultation to clinicians, some time spent returning calls, handling clinical record-keeping, and managing my practice. The rest of the time I spend on my my projects, including one or two committees I serve on — and my research and writing projects. I generally work from eight or nine in the morning until 6 p.m. Monday through Friday and I like to spend the hours of 9:30 to 10 a.m. until 3 or 4 p.m. on Saturday in my office.

As the work hours I just described indicated, the simultaneous-practice-and-research model only works for the individual who is intrinsically motivated to do the work. Many hours are unpaid. The tight integration of research and clinical work increases the intrinsic reward, as the clinician is tackling research questions that are also intriguing clinically. However, the intrinsic reward of contributing to knowledge is also an essential piece of the puzzle.

Synergy of the Elements of the Simultaneous Practice and Research Model

I've described a mode of clinical work and practice that tightly links the clinical work to research. However, the sequential description above of the list of elements of the integrated approach does not quite capture the synergy that results from using these same core elements as the foundation of practice and science, and I'll try to say a bit here to capture that magic that glues everything together. It's the clean, coherent, elegant seamlessness of the whole thing that makes it work. Because the researcher studies the same phenomena that s/he treats clinically, the reading and library work you do to improve your patient care aids your research, and the library work you do to advance my research improves your patient care. The overlap of clinical and research interests means that the conference talks you attend (and give) to improve your research also improve your patient care, and the conference talks and clinical training and consultation you do to improve your patient care also contribute to your research. The overlap of research and practice helps you select good research questions, because the questions that the clinician wants to answer in order to help her patients are frequently questions that the scientific literature also wants to answer. The tight link between research and clinical practice gives the practitioner multiple vantage points of viewing research questions, as the practitioner sees the same question from the vantage point of the research literature and interactions with and data collected from patients in the office.

Another benefit of the tight links is the excitement of producing a piece of research that has both clinical and research implications. This type of project is super-exciting to me! An example is the study I described earlier in which Cannon Thomas and I showed that remission from depression can be very strongly predicted by examining the patient's BDI score at week four of treatment. This study tells clinicians that it is important to consider making a change to the treatment plan of the depressed patients who remains severely depressed at week four of treatment, as this patient is highly unlikely to remit. And the study also has implications for treatment developers, encouraging them to stop writing fixed treatment protocols that are 16 to 18 or 20 sessions in length, and instead to write flexible protocols that encourage therapists to make changes in the treatment plan when the patient continues to be severely ill after several weeks of treatment.

Doing clinical work and research simultaneously, using the tightly integrated model for clinical work and research that I describe here, can make the difficult task of conducting research in a clinical setting a manageable and rewarding part of the clinician's daily practice experience, while simultaneously improving the quality of the practitioner's clinical work.

Acknowledgements

Many contributed to the methods and work I describe here, including my patients, who have given me permission to use data I collect from them during treatment in research and taught me as much or more as I learned in my formal training;

my teachers, especially Jonathan Baron, Aaron T. Beck, David D. Burns, Edna B. Foa, Ralph M. Turner, and Joseph Wolpe; many colleagues from whom I have learned along the way, including Polina Eidelman, Janie Hong, Kelly Koerner, Jeffrey M. Perloff (my husband), Michael Tompkins and Joan Davidson and my colleagues at the San Francisco Bay Area center for Cognitive Therapy, Kimberly Wilson, Cannon Thomas, Travis Osborne and the Behavioral Health Research Collective; my many research collaborators; and many research assistants who have helped along the way, with one, Corey Pallatto Hughan, making particularly huge contributions.

References

Ehring, T., Zetsche, U., Weidacker, K., Wahl, K., Schönfeld, S., & Ehlers, A. (2011). The Perseverative Thinking Questionnaire (PTQ): Validation of a content-independent measure of repetitive negative thinking. *Journal of Behavior Therapy and Experimental Psychiatry, 42*(2), 225–232.

Gratz, K. L. & Roemer, L. (2004). Multidimensional assessment of emotion regulation and dysregulation: Development, factor structure, and initial validation of the difficulties in emotion regulation scale. *Journal of Psychopathology and Behavioral Assessment, 26*(1), 41–54.

Harvey, A. G., Lee, J., Williams, J., Hollon, S. D., Walker, M. P., Thompson, M. A., & Smith, R. (2014). Improving outcome of psychosocial treatments by enhancing memory and learning. *Perspectives on Psychological Science, 9*(2), 161–179.

Holmes, E. A., Blackwell, S. E., Heyes, S. B., Renner, F., & Raes, F. (2016). Mental imagery in depression: phenomonology, potential mechanisms, and treatment implications. *Annual Review of Clinical Psychology, 12*, 249–280.

Jensen, A. S., Persons, J. B., Miles II, A. L., Hong, J. J., Beckner, V. L., Eidelman, P., & Owen, D. (2017). *Patients are more likely to complete psychotherapy homework assignments that are closely related to what they learned in session.* Paper presented at the Association for Behavioral and Cognitive Therapies, San Diego.

Kroenke, K., Spitzer, R. L., & Williams, J. B. W. (2001). The PHQ-9: Validity of a Brief Depression Severity Measure. *Journal of General Internal Medicine, 16*(9), 606–613.

LeJeune, J. T. & Luoma, J. B. (2015). The integrated scientist-practitioner: A new model for combining research and clinical practice in fee-for-service settings. *Professional Psychology: Research and Practice*, no pagination specified.

Lovibond, P. F. & Lovibond, S. H. (1995). The structure of negative emotional states: Comparison of the Depression Anxiety Stress Scales (DASS) with the Beck Depression and Anxiety Inventories. *Behavior Research and Therapy, 33*(3), 335–343.

Lovibond, S. H. & Lovibond, P. F. (1995). *Manual for the Depression Anxiety Stress Scales* (2nd ed.). Sydney: Psychology Foundation.

Lutz, W., Martinovich, Z., & Howard, K. I. (1999). Patient profiling: An application of random coefficient regression models to depicting the response of a patient to outpatient psychotherapy. *Journal of Consulting and Clinical Psychology, 67*, 571–577.

Mundt, J. C., Marks, I. M., Shear, M. K., & Greist, J. M. (2002). The Work and Social Adjustment Scale: A simple measure of impairment in functioning. *The British Journal of Psychiatry, 180*(5), 461–464.

Obsessive Compulsive Cognitions Working Group. (2005). Psychometric validation of the obsessive belief questionnaire and interpretation of intrusions inventory—Part 2: Factor analyses and testing of a brief version. *Behaviour Research and Therapy, 43*, 1527–1542.

Persons, J. B. (2007). Psychotherapists collect data during routine clinical work that can contribute to knowledge about mechanisms of change in psychotherapy. *Clinical Psychology: Science and Practice, 14*(3), 244–246.

Persons, J. B. (2008). *The case formulation approach to cognitive-behavior therapy.* New York: Guilford.

Persons, J. B.,& Burns, D. D. (1985). Mechanisms of action of cognitive therapy: The relative contributions of technical and interpersonal interventions. *Cognitive Therapy and Research, 9,* 539–551.

Persons, J. B., Hong, J., Lemle Beckner, V., Owen, D., & Eidelman, P. (2012). *Monitoring therapy process at every session: Development of a new tool and clinical examples of its utility.* Paper presented at the Association for Behavioral and Cognitive Therapies, Naval Harbor, MD.

Persons, J. B. & Mikami, A. Y. (2002). Strategies for handling treatment failure successfully. *Psychotherapy: Theory/Research/Practice/Training, 39,* 139–151.

Persons, J. B. & Thomas, C. (2016). *BDI score at week 4 of cognitive behavior therapy predicts depression remission.* Paper presented at the Association for Behavioral and Cognitive Therapies, New York.

Ronk, F. R., Korman, J. R., Hooke, G. R., & Page, A. C. (2013). Assessing clinical significance of treatment outcomes using the DASS-21. *Psychological Assessment, 25*(4), 1103–1110.

Rosenthal, M. Z., Cheavens, J. S., Lejuez, C. W., & Lynch, T. R. (2005). Thought suppression mediates the relationship between negative affect and borderline personality disorder symptoms. *Behaviour Research and Therapy, 43,* 1173–1185.

Sackett, D. L., Richardson, W. S., Rosenberg, W., & Haynes, R. B. (1997). *Evidence-based medicine: How to practice and teach EBM.* New York: Churchill Livingstone.

Sanislow, C. A., Pine, D. S., Quinn, K. J., Kozak, M. J., & Garvey, M. A. (2010). Developing constructs for psychopathology research: Research Domain Criteria. *Journal of Abnormal Psychology, 119,* 631–639.

Sherbourne, C. D. & Stewart, A. L. (1991). The MOS social support survey. *Social Science and Medicine, 32*(6), 705–714.

Shiloff, N. (2015). The scientist-practitioner gap: A clinical supervisor self-discloses. *Clinical Science, 18*(3), 21–23.

Thomas, C. & Persons, J. B. (2010). *Sudden gains can occur in psychotherapy even when the pattern of change is gradual.* Manuscript submitted for publication.

Watkins, E. R. (2016). *Rumination-focused cognitive behavioral therapy for depression.* New York: Guilford Press.

Westen, D. & Morrison, K. (2001). A multidimensional meta-analysis of treatments for depression, panic, and generalized anxiety disorder: An empirical examination of the status of empirically supported therapies. *Journal of Consulting and Clinical Psychology, 69,* 875–899.

CHAPTER 10

Practice-Based Scholarship

Amy Wenzel

All too often, a sharp distinction is drawn between science and practice in clinical psychology. Some clinical scientists hold the view that practitioners ignore or dismiss science, favoring unsubstantiated clinical judgment instead. Some practitioners hold the view that results from clinical research that examines aspects of mental health disorders or psychotherapy, usually conducted in academic settings, are not relevant to the issues that they typically see in their everyday practices (Lilienfeld, Ritschel, Lynn, Cautin, & Latzman, 2013; Persons & Silberschatz, 1998). This divide is unfortunate, as the most well-known and comprehensive model of training in clinical psychology (i.e., the Boulder model, or scientist-practitioner model) clearly outlines the importance of clinical psychologists (a) having a strong foundation in scientific methods, (b) using these methods to contribute to the advancement of the field, and (c) applying these methods in making health care decisions (Raimy, 1950).

Although many leaders in the field will argue that the ideals of the Boulder model are not typically reflected in most training programs today or in the activities of most clinical psychologists (e.g., Strickler, 2000), there is, nonetheless, a substantial contingency of clinical psychologists who, indeed, embody the Boulder model's tenets. Many academic clinical psychologists maintain a clinical practice. Moreover, many clinical psychologists who function primarily as practitioners, value and wish to contribute to the science of clinical psychology. The conduct of practice-based research is one way for practitioners to live out the aims of the Boulder model.

As you will likely see from the other chapters in this volume, practice-based research can indeed be conducted in an array of clinical settings. Many practitioners who engage in practice-based research find it to be tremendously gratifying, as it is a way to measure tangible progress in their clients, test the effectiveness of innovative interventions, and maintain a "foot" in the research world while doing meaningful clinical work. At the same time, practice-based research requires persistence, patience, and ingenuity. Tasks that clinical scientists in large research settings need not think twice about, such as finding undergraduate research assistants to assist with data collection and data entry in exchange for course credit or securing approval from an institutional review board (IRB), can pose formidable challenges in a practice setting. When practice-based researchers face these and other challenges as they are initiating a program of research, it is understandable that there is the potential to become discouraged.

However, take heart, as in this chapter, I argue that there are *many* ways to engage in practice-based research. In fact, I encourage clinicians in practice to expand their view from a narrow focus on *research*, per se, to a broader focus on *scholarship*. A quick Google search on the definition of scholarship indicates that it is "academic study or achievement; learning at a high level." I would add to this definition that it is also *contribution* to a field of study, whether that contribution be through the direct collection and analysis of data for a research report, writing a review article that synthesizes research or advances a theory, writing or editing a book, or training personnel who are part of a research team. I even view an informal activity like blogging to be scholarship if it is grounded in the scientific literature and advances a unique idea. In other words, I believe that there are many ways to contribute to a field of study—and hence, engage in scholarship and embody the spirit of the Boulder model—that go beyond the collection of original data.

This chapter describes many types of practice-based scholarship. It is divided into four major sections. First, I tell the "story" of my graduate and early career to set the context for understanding how and why various practice-based scholarship opportunities have presented themselves to me. Second, I describe the wide array of practice-based scholarship with which I have been involved during the time I have been in private practice, including collaborations with investigators at research institutions, analysis of archival data, training and supervision of clinicians in research studies, writing and editing of books, and blogging. Third, I identify ways to initiate and execute practice-based scholarship, discussing potential obstacles that you might encounter and providing suggestions of ways to overcome them. I end this chapter with a reflection on themes that pervade the development of my practice-based scholarship and ways in which practice-based scholarship has enhanced my career, with the hope that these insights will be useful for others who hope to establish a program of practice-based scholarship.

My Story

I entered the University of Iowa's clinical psychology graduate program in 1994, bound and determined to establish a career in which I would conduct cutting-edge research as a faculty member at a reputable research institution. My initial interest was geared toward understanding the psychopathology and treatment of survivors of torture—a direct outgrowth from my days as a human rights activist at my undergraduate institution, Duke University. When I interviewed at Iowa, I was gently informed that there were likely to be few (if any) survivors of torture in Iowa City, IA (audiences to whom I lecture generally laugh out loud at this part of my story). However, there was a young faculty member who was recruiting a graduate student interested in the broader study and treatment of anxiety disorders. I jumped on the opportunity to work with him.

I met with my mentor, Craig Holt, the day after I made the trek from Durham, NC to Iowa City, eager to begin developing a program of research in advance of the first day of classes. He assigned me my first (formidable) task—to read the recent literature on anxiety disorders and identify areas of inquiry that could form the basis of a program of research. As I poured through thousands of abstracts, I was consistently drawn to studies that provided evidence for cognitive biases in anxiety disorders, such as attentional and memory biases toward (or in some cases, away from) threat, which turned out to be a "hot topic" in the mid-1990s. This attraction can likely be attributed to my honor's thesis project at Duke, which was supervised by a premier cognitive psychology researcher, David Rubin, and was later published in the American Psychological Association journal, *Psychological Review* (Rubin & Wenzel, 1996). Having identified a more realistic program of research, I was raring to go.

During my five years at the University of Iowa, I established my own research laboratory with eager undergraduate research assistants who were willing to help me with my research, and I conducted at least ten studies on cognitive biases associated with various types of anxiety (e.g., Wenzel & Holt, 2003). Along the way, I was recruited and mentored by another faculty member, Michael O'Hara, to serve as a graduate research assistant on a study funded by the National Institute of Mental Health (NIHM) examining the efficacy of interpersonal psychotherapy (IPT) for postpartum depression (O'Hara, Stuart, Gorman, & Wenzel, 2000). It was through this experience that I established a second area of scholarly inquiry—perinatal distress, which is one that continues to be the subject of a great deal of my practice-based scholarship today. Toward the end of my graduate career, I was given the phenomenal opportunity by yet another faculty member, John Harvey, to assist him in editing a book (which turned into two edited books) on close, romantic relationships (Harvey & Wenzel, 2001, 2002). It was this opportunity that solidified my true love contributing or writing and editing books. Even during my one-year clinical psychology internship at the University of Wisconsin Medical school, when I carried a hefty clinical caseload, I managed to find ways to engage in research when my duties were primarily clinical in nature, such as by analyzing data from a study by Roseanne Clark evaluating a novel treatment for postpartum depression (Clark, Tluczek, & Wenzel, 2003) and receiving a small grant to examine close, romantic relationships in people with social anxiety disorder (Wenzel, 2002).

My first job out of graduate school (2000) was as an assistant professor in the Department of Psychology at the University of North Dakota (UND). There, I established a research laboratory composed of graduate and undergraduate students in which I continued the studies of cognitive biases in anxiety (e.g., Wenzel, Finstrom, Jordan, & Brendle, 2005), perinatal distress (e.g., Wenzel, Haugen, Jackson, & Brendle, 2005), and close, romantic relationships in social anxiety (e.g., Wenzel, Graff-Dolezal, Macho, & Brendle, 2005). In other words, I continued to develop the trajectories of scholarship that I had established during graduate school. I continued to edit volumes on close romantic relationships (Harvey, Wenzel, & Sprecher, 2004; Sprecher, Wenzel, & Harvey, 2008), and I gained experience as lead editor on a volume on research methods to study cognitive biases (Wenzel & Rubin, 2005). I maintained a small private practice outside of the University, and not only was I pleasantly surprised that I received a similar amount of professional gratification from my clinical work as I did from my research and writing, I saw many ways in which my research influenced my clinical work and vice versa. In 2004, I left UND after four years to pursue a tremendous opportunity to serve as an assistant professor in Aaron T. Beck's Psychopathology Research Unit (now called Aaron T. Beck Psychopathology Research Center) at the University of Pennsylvania School of Medicine, with the aim of maximizing the amount of time I could devote to research, writing, and application to clinical practice.

If my experiences in graduate school and in my first job at UND provided the foundation for my current practice-based scholarship, my experience at Penn with Aaron "Tim" Beck served as the catalyst. I received tremendous supervision in cognitive therapy from Tim and Cory Newman (director of Penn's Center for Cognitive Therapy) to bring my therapeutic skills to a new level, which, though clinical in nature, provided essential experience that afforded many practice-based scholarship opportunities today. I focused many of my research efforts on the adaptation of cognitive therapy to various populations (e.g., suicidal clients, clients with addictions who are treated in a group setting), and as a result, I was granted opportunities to co-author books with Tim on these treatment approaches (Wenzel, Brown, & Beck, 2009; Wenzel, Liese, Beck, & Friedman-Wheeler, 2012). I also secured grants from the American Foundation for Suicide Prevention and the National Association for Research on Schizophrenia and Depression (now called Brain and Behavior Research Association) to examine cognitive biases in suicidal clients, which has provided a rich archival data set from which to work even after I have left my full-time job at Penn (Jager-Hymen et al., 2014).

I left my job at Penn in 2008 to pursue a unique combination of professional activities, such as clinical practice; training, consultation, and supervision, and practice-based scholarship. In fact, the opportunity to pursue independent practice-based scholarship was one of the main reasons that drove this decision, as I discovered that I thrived on the creativity and autonomy that it afforded me. I found myself in a place in which I received more personal gratification from writing and editing books than from writing grant applications and publishing short empirical articles in peer-reviewed journals. Today, I devote about half my time to clinical practice, approximately 40 percent of my time to practice-based scholarship, and the remaining time to training, consultation, and supervision. In the sections that follow, I provide examples of the types of practice-based scholarship in which I have been engaged.

Types of Practice-Based Scholarship (Broadly Speaking)

Collaboration with Investigators at Research Institutions

Even if you do not have access to a means for collecting original data, collaboration with investigators at research institutions can fulfill a desire to make a scientific contribution to the field. Many investigators at research institutions find that they are spread so thin that they would welcome assistance in writing up their data and submitting for publication in a timelier manner than they would if they were left to do it on their own. Tasks that you could take on in such an arrangement include a literature review, analysis of results, and/or the writing of the manuscript itself—all of which are sufficient to deserve authorship on the resultant publication.

I have several examples of successful collaborations of this nature, as I have assisted investigators in many capacities and have been named as an author on their articles since I left my full-time academic position at Penn. For example, I regularly write manuscripts with Irismar Reis de Oliveira from the Federal University of Bahia in Brazil. Because he, his colleagues, students, and trainees are non-native English speakers, I oftentimes will write the introduction and discussion sections of the manuscripts on which we collaborate so that they are appropriate for journals that are published in English (e.g., de Oliveira et al., 2012; Rodriques et al., 2011). Moreover, because I developed expertise in research methodology from my experiences at Iowa, UND, and Penn, I make contributions to his method and results sections as well. In another example, I was approached by a colleague with whom I have a distant relationship—she worked with one of my graduate school mentors (Dr. Michael O'Hara) soon after I graduated from Iowa—to assist with a series of studies in which she adapted and validated a measure that I developed over ten years ago. I made a significant contribution to this line of research by, of course, having developed the measure. However, I also contributed to her program of research by making intellectual contributions to her studies' research designs and by assisting with the writing of the manuscripts (Moran, Polanin, & Wenzel, 2014; Moran, Segre, Polanin, & Wenzel, 2014).

The take-away message from this section is that by initiating and accepting collaborations with investigators at research institutions, you can be actively involved in empirical research even if there are significant barriers to collecting data on your own. Such collaboration may not result in many first-authored publications, as usually you will be invited to participate after the research idea has already been developed by the investigator. As can be seen from the citations provided above, I did not assume first-author status on any of these collaborations. However, such collaborations allow you to make meaningful intellectual contributions to research and obtain the tangible and gratifying result of being included as an author on a publication. From a personal standpoint, I have found that involvement in such collaboration allows me to keep current with the literature, which enhances my clinical and supervision work, the lectures and trainings that I deliver, and the books that I write.

Analysis of Archival Data

Participation in practice-based research is not limited to the collection of new data; you can also conduct research by analyzing archival data sets associated with projects that have yet to be written up for population. In addition, you can devise new hypotheses and conduct secondary analyses on archival data sets associated with projects for which the main aims have already been published in peer-reviewed journals. You might have your own archival data sets from your dissertation project or from other projects in which you served as investigator. As stated previously, even now I continue to publish manuscripts from my large data set I collected at Penn in the second half of the 2000s on cognitive biases in suicidal clients (Jager-Hymen et al., 2014). In addition, you can collaborate with other investigators who have archival data sets. For example, after I left my full-time position at Penn, I continued to collaborate with members of Tim Beck's group to analyze and write up data on impulsivity in suicidal patients, which had been collected many years before I had even started my position there (Spokas, Wenzel, Brown, & Beck, 2012).

Supervision of Clinicians in Research Studies

Many clinicians are simply interested in being a part of empirical research studies, even if their names are not necessarily included on resulting publications. One way to do this is to provide supervision over research activities that are integral to a research project. A natural avenue for clinicians to achieve this aim is to provide supervision of clinicians who are providing psychotherapy in clinical trials. Thus, if you have expertise in a particular approach to treatment, such as (but not at all limited to) cognitive behavioral therapy (CBT), acceptance and commitment therapy, IPT, short-term psychodynamic therapy, or motivational interviewing, you may be able to serve as a supervisor of clinicians who are delivering a treatment that is being evaluated in a clinical trial. Once you provide supervision for one study, it is likely that you have a "foot-in-the-door" to provide supervision for additional studies.

I have provided a great deal of supervision for clinical trials over the past decade. Soon after I left my full-time job at Penn, I was recruited to provide oversight of clinicians who worked in Veterans' Affairs (VA) Hospitals who were aiming to achieve competency in the delivery of CBT for depression (CBT-D). My duties included review of recorded CBT sessions, rating of CBT sessions per the Cognitive Therapy Rating Scale (Young & Beck, 1980), and holding weekly conference calls with groups of therapists to whom I was providing consultation and feedback on sessions. At any one time across the span of approximately five years, I carried between one and six groups, each composed of four or five clinicians who were enrolled in the CBT-D program. Although the primary focus of this endeavor was clinical in nature, I was fortunate to be asked to author the manual that guided the delivery of the treatment (Wenzel, Brown, & Karlin, 2011), and data collected during the course of the program were evaluated to determine its effectiveness (Karlin et al., 2012).

Participation in this project opened the door for me to assume supervision duties in other research studies, including National Institute of Mental Health (NIMH)-sponsored clinical trials designed to evaluate the effectiveness of CBT for depression in a community mental health setting and CBT for suicide prevention to homeless youth who seek services at a homeless shelter. Although I do not expect to be included as an author on manuscripts based on these projects that will ultimately be submitted to publication, I regard them as highly enriching and worthwhile experiences because I have learned a great deal about the delivery of CBT to clients who presented to a very different type of treatment setting than my own private practice setting, and I have expanded my own flexibility in the delivery of CBT to racially, ethnically, and socioeconomically diverse clientele. Moreover, results from these endeavors will advance the overall literature on the effectiveness of CBT in and its dissemination to community mental health agencies—issues that are regarded by leading scholars and clinicians as paramount in ensuring that all people have access to evidence-based mental health treatments (Shafran et al., 2009).

Clinicians who have advanced training in psychological assessment may also provide valuable supervision and oversight to ongoing research. For example, on the basis of my experience over 15 years ago in graduate school, in which I administered hundreds, if not thousands of Hamilton Rating Scales for Depression (HAM-D; Hamilton, 1960) to postpartum women, I am currently serving as a consultant on a project in which the HAM-D will be administered to postpartum women to evaluate the course of depressive symptoms as they receive a novel treatment for depression. My responsibilities in this study are to develop training materials and to provide training to study assessors and monitor their adherence to administration guidelines. This opportunity presented itself not because the principal investigator happened to contact the lead author of a manuscript on which I collaborated (Allison, Wenzel, Kleiman, & Sawrer, 2011)—another piece of practice-based scholarship—and the lead author was unable to provide consultation and instead recommended that he talk with me. I was willing to take a half hour to speak with the principal investigator of the current project about my experiences in administering the HAM-D to postpartum women, and he offered me the opportunity to contribute to the project as a consultant overseeing HAM-D training and administration. This example illustrates that taking time informally to provide consultation to a study investigator who would like to "pick your brain" can open doors for practice-based scholarship in the future. It also illustrates that opportunities for practice-based research can be quite serendipitous and that you might have something to offer on the basis of previous clinical and research experience that you did not realize would be of value. I say more about the serendipity of these opportunities in the final section of this chapter.

It is not difficult to imagine ways in which clinicians' backgrounds in assessment could lead to practice-based scholarship opportunities. For example, if you have extensive training in the administration of inventories like the Minnesota Multiphasic Personality Inventory-2 (MMPI-II; Butcher, Dahlstrom, Graham, Tellegen, & Kaemmer, 1989) or the Revised NEO Personality Inventory (NEO-PI-R; Costa, & McCrae, 1992), you might supervise its scoring and interpretation if the measure is being used in a research study. If you have extensive training in neuropsychological assessment, you might provide training and supervise clinicians in the administration, scoring, and interpretation of neuropsychological tests to assess cognitive function in children, people who have experienced traumatic brain injury, and/or older adults. Thus, I encourage you to think broadly about your psychotherapy and assessment background and be alert for opportunities to contribute this expertise.

Conducting a Meta-Analysis

A *meta-analysis* is a study in which a person aggregates data from many individual research studies to calculate an effect for a question of interest. For example, if a person wants to know the degree to which CBT is more efficacious than a control condition such as usual care for the broad category of eating disorders, he or she could gather all available studies that examine this issue, extract relevant data from the research reports (e.g., means, correlations, standard deviations, sample sizes, reliabilities of measures used to evaluate outcome), and subject them to statistical analysis. Many meta-analysis software programs are readily available to facilitate the types of calculations that are typically reported in manuscripts that describe meta-analyses. The "data" used in the meta-analysis are the descriptive statistics that have been reported in previous studies; thus, meta-analyses can be an attractive option for clinicians who find it challenging to collect original data in their practice.

Although meta-analyses are not free from controversy (e.g., Greco, Zangrillo, Biondi-Zoccaai, & Landoni, 2013), they can make a major contribution to a field because, when conducted thoughtfully and skillfully, they provide a more stable estimate of the true population effect than can any one individual study (for one example of a meta-analysis, see Cuijpers, Geraedts, van Oppen, Andersson, Markowitz, & van Straten, 2011). Moreover, they can resolve inconsistent results found in individual studies by identifying moderating variables that may affect outcome. Many meta-analyses in clinical psychology are highly cited, which means that their impact on the field is significant.

Writing Review Articles and Reviews of Books

As stated previously, a central part of my definition of practice-based scholarship is that the scholarly activity contributes to the field at large. To this point in the chapter, I have discussed innovative ways to engage, specifically, in empirical research efforts. However, it is important to remember that practice-based scholarship extends beyond participation in empirical research efforts. An alternative way to contribute to the field is to publish pieces that do not rely on original, archival, or meta-analytic data.

The quintessential example of such a contribution is a review article. As is the case when conducting a meta-analysis, people who write review articles have a specific question in mind and then critically review the literature to address the question. The question could be as broad as whether a particular type of psychotherapy is efficacious or effective, or as specific as the effects of a particular common factor, such as the working alliance, on outcome in a particular type of clinical population, such as clients with borderline personality disorder who have already participated in multiple courses of mental health treatment. Some review articles are simply compilations of the extant literature, which contributes significantly to the field because it assembles all known available research in one location (e.g., Miniati et al., 2014). Other review articles are written to describe a clinical phenomenon, such as specific psychotherapeutic approach (e.g., Stuart, 2012). Still other review articles are written to compare and contrast constructs or ideas, or to advance an argument, such as the degree to which two separate therapeutic approaches are similar or distinct (e.g., Markowitz, Svartberg, & Swartz, 1998).

The best example of a clinical psychology journal that publishes review articles is *Clinical Psychology Review* (www.journals.elsevier.com/clinical-psychology-review/). However, many other journals relevant to clinical psychology will publish review articles on a case-by-case basis (e.g., *Behavior Therapy*; www.abct.org/Journals/?m=mJournal&fa=BT). Moreover, journals are being developed that advance the practice of clinical psychology and bridge the gap between research and practice, such as *Cognitive and Behavioral Practice* (www.abct.org/Journals/?m=mJournal&fa=CBT). Journals like this one invite authors to submit articles on the implementation of various psychotherapeutic approaches. At times, authors report data collected from their clinical practices, but the inclusion of data is not usually a requirement for these types of articles.

One journal that has particular relevance to the practicing clinician is *Professional Psychology: Research and Practice*, published by the American Psychological Association. According to the journal's website (www.apa.org/pubs/journals/pro/):

> Articles that present assessment, treatment, and practice implications are encouraged. Both data-based and theoretical articles on techniques and practices used in the application of psychology are acceptable. Specifically, this journal is an appropriate outlet for articles on
>
> - State-of-the-art literature reviews of clinical research on specific high-incidence disorders specifically written so as to draw out the implications for assessment and/or treatment.
> - Research and theory on public policy as it affects the practice of psychology.
> - Current advances in applications from such fields as health psychology, community psychology, psychology of women, clinical neuropsychology, family psychology, psychology of ethnicity and culture, forensic psychology, and other areas.
> - Standards of professional practice and delivery of services in a variety of contexts—industries, institutions, and other organizations.
> - Research and theory as they concern the interests of those who practice psychology.

Thus, clinicians who have innovative ideas about the practice of psychology can make scholarly contributions to the field at large through a journal such as this one.

Submitting a review article to a peer-reviewed journal can be a daunting task if one is "out of practice" with scholarly writing. One way to gain experience with writing thoughtful pieces on specific topics is to draft shorter articles for newsletters or publications associated with a professional society. For example, as a member of my state psychological association, the Pennsylvania Psychological Association, I receive a monthly publication called *The Pennsylvania Psychologist*. Many clinicians contribute short pieces on a diverse array of topics such as ethics, training, and/or the changing climate of private practice. As another example, the national organization in which I am most active—the Association for Behavioral and Cognitive Therapies (ABCT)—publishes *the Behavior Therapist* eight times a year. Submissions are typically six to 12 double spaced pages and are meant to focus on the timely communication of news, new ideas, and innovations in the field (www.abct.org/Journals/?m=mJournal&fa=SubmissionInfo). Thus, publishing smaller pieces in newsletters and other publications associated with a professional society could pave the way to develop a lengthier, sophisticated review article that can be submitted to a more selective peer-reviewed journal.

Yet another way to make a scholarly contribution to the field is to write a book review for PsycCRITIQUES, an online database of reviews of books, films, and videos published by the American Psychological Association (www.apa.org/pubs/databases/psyccritiques/). If you are interested in taking on a review, you can contact the editorial staff and make known your interest. If selected, they will supply you with a free copy of the book or video, and you will be expected to supply your review within a short period of time (e.g., 30 days). These reviews are typically short—reviewer guidelines state that pieces that are longer than 2,000 words will be returned to authors. Although PsycCRITIQUES is perhaps the most comprehensive and well-known repository of reviews, oftentimes journals, newsletters, and other publications associated with professional societies will publish reviews. Thus, if you notice that reviews of books, films, and videos are printed in publications that you read regularly, you can contact the editorial office to inquire about serving in this capacity. As with submitting a short review article to a newsletter associated with a professional society, writing reviews allows clinicians outside of academia to gain confidence in their writing and ability to make a scholarly contribution, setting the stage for even greater contributions in the future.

Authoring or Editing Books

My personal favorite avenue for engaging in practice-based scholarship is to author or edit books. An *authored book* is a volume that contains original writing by one or more scholars. An *edited book* is a volume in which chapters are written by experts in the field, who are hand-picked by the scholar or scholars who are assembling the book. Books are typically much lengthier than articles submitted to a peer-reviewed journal; in my experience, a common length of submissions is 350 pages using 12-inch font and one inch margins. As a result, authors and editors of books have room for creativity and innovation, and the length allows them to fully develop unique ideas that contribute to the field. Although authored and edited books require a substantial amount of effort—usually a year or more depending on the nature of the topic and the agreed-upon length with the publisher—the gratification that one can achieve at the completion of such a project is unmatched.

In order to secure a book contract from a publisher, you must have an idea for a topic that fulfills a unique niche in the market. Some scholars develop topics for books by developing their ideas in shorter pieces, such as in review articles. Others stumble upon book ideas by chance, searching for a particular topic and realizing that nothing of the sort has been written about the topic to date. Next, you would develop a proposal that you can submit to one or more publishing houses. Proposals typically include a general description of the book, an argument for why the book would advance the field, a listing of proposed chapters and a description of each chapter's contents, a description of competing books that have already been published, a proposed timeline for completion, and a biography of each author or editor. If the proposed book is an edited volume, the proposal might include names of respected scholars who have agreed to contribute, although there is usually not a need to secure a contributor for every chapter before a proposal is submitted to a publisher. The publisher typically sends the proposal to several peer reviewers, who comment on the book's merits and make a recommendation for publication. The publisher will then make the final decision as to whether to offer you a contract.

Authors who receive contracts typically work in whatever style works best for them to submit books to the publisher by the agreed-upon deadline. Editors who receive contracts typically ask contributors to submit their chapters several months in advance of the deadline so that they can review submissions, recommend changes, and allow ample time for a resubmission. Editors typically write brief introductions to edited books, and at times, they also draft brief conclusions that assimilate the main themes evident across chapters.

Earlier in the chapter, you saw that I was introduced to the world of editing books when a graduate school professor (John Harvey) afforded me the generous opportunity to assist him in editing two volumes on close, romantic relationships (Harvey & Wenzel, 2001, 2002). My collaboration with him continued naturally as we identified other ways to extend scholarship on the topic and involved a third collaborator, Susan Sprecher (Harvey, Wenzel, & Sprecher, 2004; Sprecher, Wenzel, & Harvey, 2008). I built upon this experience in editing volumes by forging a relationship with American Psychological Association Books (APA Books) to publish my first edited book in the mid-2000s (Wenzel & Rubin, 2005). My relationship with APA Books continues to this day, which has allowed me to publish authored books on cognitive behavioral therapy (Wenzel, Brown, & Beck, 2009; Wenzel, Dobson, & Hays, 2016; Wenzel, 2013) and perinatal distress (Wenzel & Stuart, 2011; Wenzel, 2014). Moreover, I was introduced to another publisher, Routledge (the publisher of this volume, in fact), through practice-based collaboration with Karen Kleiman, an expert in perinatal distress and author of the premier book on postpartum depression, *This Isn't What I Expected:*

Overcoming Postpartum Depression (Kleiman & Raskin, 1994, 2013). Karen has had a longstanding relationship with Routledge, and she invited me to collaborate with a Routledge book on "scary thoughts" (Kleiman & Wenzel, 2011). That project subsequently led to two additional collaborations on aspects of postpartum adjustment, both of which were also published by Routledge (Kleiman, with Wenzel, 2014; Wenzel, with Kleiman, 2015). Because my work with Karen allowed me to develop a close working relationship with Routledge, I was in a position to take on my own additional Routledge projects, including a forthcoming book on innovations in CBT (Wenzel, in press) and a book under contract that will describe a learning program for clinicians who hope to develop competency in CBT. Along the way, I also developed working relationships with Guilford Press (Wenzel et al., 2012), Oxford University Press (Wenzel, 2016), and SAGE Publications (Wenzel, in press), all of which came about because these publishers reached out to me on the basis of my previous writing and editing experiences.

Thus, the writing and editing of books allows clinicians to make thoughtful, creative, and meaningful scholarly contributions to the field. Although an authored or edited book project may sound daunting to you, it has the potential to be one of the most fulfilling accomplishments of your career. Moreover, my experience is that once you have completed a book and have developed a relationship with a publisher, doors may open for additional opportunities.

Blogging

Blogging is an activity in which a writer regularly posts short articles on a website about a topic of current interest. Although blogs are less formal than peer-reviewed articles and published books, they are an easy avenue to advance new ideas and perspectives and share your writing. I believe that they represent practice-based scholarship, particularly when they are grounded in psychological science, describe relevant research, and offer unique ideas. Perhaps the most well-known platform for blogs related to clinical psychology is *Psychology Today* (www.psychologytoday.com/). There are literally hundreds of mental health professionals who have established unique *Psychology Today* blogs on topics as diverse as relationships, parenting, and stress management. Many bloggers are people who function primarily as practitioners. I was recently asked to establish a *Psychology Today* blog, now entitled, "Beyond the Baby: Complexities of Fertility, Pregnancy, Childbirth, Parenthood, and Balance in Life" (title subject to change!) (www.psychologytoday.com/blog/beyond-the-baby).

You need not be limited to *Psychology Today* if you wish to blog—anyone who has "liked" news outlets on social media can see hundreds of platforms for blogging. Some platforms invite you to submit blogs if you pay a membership fee (e.g., Your Tango; www.yourtango.com/). Other platforms are geared toward relatively targeted issues, such as grief (e.g., Open-to-Hope Foundation; www.opentohope.com/), and often welcome guest bloggers to contribute ideas. You can even start archive blog posts on your own website, as I have done on a couple of occasions (http://dramywenzel.com/blog/). Blogging allows you to write and publish posts as frequently or as infrequently as you see fit. However, the more you post, the more you will increase your social media presence, which can bring a host of opportunities such as your blog posts being syndicated to national new sites, new clients, and other writing opportunities.

Initiating and Executing Practice-Based Scholarship: Barriers and Solutions

Values Clarification

The first step in initiating practice-based scholarship is to make a commitment to it. You must critically evaluate whether you value practice-based scholarship enough to pursue it and, once an opportunity has been identified, devote time to it. Indeed, a therapeutic task that is often implemented by clinicians with their clients these days is *values clarification*, which is the process by which people decide what is truly important to them. You can apply the process of values clarification to your own professional activities to determine whether the value of making a scholarly contribution to the field is strong enough to devote time and effort. If it is, then that value can guide your behavior, even when the path to finding and executing practice-based scholarship opportunities is unclear.

Even in instances in which you identify scholarly contribution to the field as an important value, "life" could pose a significant barrier to its pursuit. Salaried clinicians who work in agencies and organizations might experience externally-imposed pressure to meet the number of clinical contact hours that they are expected to meet. Salaried clinicians who work in agencies and organizations might be faced with other externally-imposed demands, such as the expectation that they will supervise interns, attend meetings, or handle crises when they are on call. Clinicians in a private practice setting might feel an internally-imposed pressure to see a large number of clients, as foregoing clinical work for research activities might mean a reduction in salary. Regardless of whether you work in salaried or private practice settings, you also have a personal life that is separate from your professional life—there are children to raise, older parents to care for, a house to maintain, and mundane tasks of daily living that cannot be ignored.

How do you commit to practice-based scholarship in the face of these professional and personal demands? First, I encourage you to keep in the forefront of your mind that making scholarly contributions to your field is a value that you have identified. I often say to my clients that living a valued life, or allowing one's values to guide behavior as much as is possible, is potentially associated with fulfillment, satisfaction, and wellbeing. This observation holds true for all people—clients and clinicians alike. Keeping this "big picture" in mind can be difficult, but as the saying goes, the more sacrifices a person makes to obtain something of value, the sweeter the victory will taste in the end.

In addition, if you are struggling with finding time for practice-based scholarship, I encourage you to identify any thoughts, beliefs, expectations, or attitudes that might decrease commitment or motivation to pursue it. For example, I have heard clinicians say, "If I'm not seeing clients, then I should be devoting my free time to my family." This is an artificial (and dichotomous) social construction that has been put in place, rather than a true fact. Many clinicians, particularly those who practice from a cognitive behavioral standpoint, often work with their clients to identify, evaluate, and modify thoughts, beliefs, expectations, and attitudes that are untrue, exaggerated, or simply unhelpful. Many clinicians also work with their clients to take time for themselves so that they can engage in personally meaningful pursuits. We must live by the same suggestions that we make to our clients.

Finally, you might have to sharpen your problem solving, organizational, and prioritization skills to work practice-based research into an otherwise cramped schedule. This might involve carving out a period of time during the work week that is devoted (no matter what) to practice-based scholarship, such as by blocking out one or two hours a week that would otherwise be devoted to clinical work. It could involve an adjustment in efficiency, such as by minimizing time spent on the Internet and social media. It could involve doing work toward practice-based scholarship during (relative) down time like waiting at the gym during a child's gymnastics class (as I often do side-by-side with a Villanova University Associate Professor of Counselor Education, Krista Malott). Or, it could involve working collaboratively with your partner to re-negotiate division of labor and child care in order to find a chunk of time on an evening or weekend to devote to practice-based scholarship.

Identifying Opportunities

The second step in initiating practice-based scholarship is identifying opportunities for it. I can imagine readers of this chapter saying to themselves something like, "The opportunities that the author describes are all well and good, but she already *had* connections to many investigators and publishers. I don't have any of those connections and don't know where to start." This section addresses these concerns.

First, I encourage you to think broadly about your connections. You probably developed relationships with some faculty members in your graduate program, many of whom maintain active programs of research. You might know peers from graduate school who pursued academic careers. You can contact those individuals to inquire whether they have any available research opportunities, archival data sets, or other writing opportunities (e.g., contracts for book chapters) on which they would be interested in collaborating.

Second, do not limit yourself only to potential collaborators with whom you have some sort of connection. For example, you might live in an area in which there are research universities, medical schools, or other training programs. Use the Internet to get a sense of the types of ongoing programs of research that exist in institutions in your area. Reach out to the principal investigator or laboratory coordinator. As stated previously, research teams often welcome individuals who are willing to denote time and effort, as it helps them complete projects and write up data quicker than would happen otherwise.

Third, connect with scholars who conduct research of interest to you at local and national conferences. Attend their talks at these meetings, and ask thoughtful questions in the question and answer period. Invite them out for coffee to talk more about the direction in which their research program is going and ways you might get involved. Although some of these scholars might be booked with meetings, participation in other conference events, and social gatherings, having even one meeting with a potential collaborator could open the door for years of practice-based scholarship.

Fourth, remember that you need not "shoot for the stars" on your first attempt at practice-based scholarship. Rather than proposing a sole-authored book, team up with a friendly colleague with whom you have a strong working relationship to spread out the workload. Submit a book proposal to a publisher that might not be as well-known as the major publishers in the field. For example, there is an excellent group called The Practice Institute (http://thepracticeinstitute.com/) that was established to coach practitioners in the business of behavioral health practice. It recently established its own press (i.e., TPI Press; www.tpishop.com/product-category/tpi-press/), and at the time of this writing, it had published four practice-oriented books. Publishing a book with this press would be a tremendous opportunity to form a solid relationship as it becomes established and expands its reach.

Overcoming Obstacles

Even the most seasoned academics face many roadblocks in completing their empirical and scholarly projects. My rule of thumb is to double the amount of time that I think it will take to complete a project when I estimate deadlines (to which the editor of this volume can attest!). There will inevitably be days in which you have the best of intentions to write a certain number of pages, or to complete a task associated with a research project, only to find that you must address an unavoidable clinical emergency, that you must retrieve a sick child from school, or that it just simply was not coming together as smoothly as you would have hoped. Accept that those days happen, practice self-compassion rather than self-flagellation, and know that there will be a "clean slate" the next time you can work on the project.

However, if you repeatedly find that you have difficulty the motivation of execution of practice-based scholarship, it is time to make some creative adjustments. As stated in the previous section, working with a colleague with whom you have a sound working relationship will decrease your own workload, and it could also add an extra layer of accountability. Another way to increase accountability is to join a writing group that meets on a regular basis (e.g., monthly) and has a mechanism in place for critique. Moreover, you can implement any number of creative reward or punishment systems to stay on track. For example, stickK (www.stickk.com/) is a free platform developed by behavioral economists at Yale University that enables you to sign a commitment contract with yourself and uses loss aversion as a motivator to stick with goals. If you knew, for instance, that you had to donate $10 to a cause with which you vehemently disagree (i.e., an "anti-charity") each time you fail to meet a goal, then you will likely do everything in your power to achieve it.

An additional obstacle often encountered by practitioners who do not have university affiliations involves access to scholarly articles published in peer-reviewed journals. Although the number of "open-access" journals is growing tremendously, most seminal articles are published in journals that do not have open access. If you are affiliated with a university, you can access the university library's databases like PsycINFO and PubMed and download the articles for free. But if you do not have such an affiliation, the journal requests a fee to access the article. It is not difficult to imagine that expenses would quickly accumulate if you must pay for each article that you acquire. Fortunately, most members of the academic community are very interested in disseminating their work, and they will likely supply you with aa PDF of their article if you contact them directly. If you are conducting a meta-analysis or writing a review, you can make requests for articles on the topic on listserv associated with professional organizations. At times, you can "Google" the article and locate it online, even if it is not published in an open-access journal. Finally, you can take steps to access a university library system, such as by attaining a visitor's pass, inquiring as to whether you can access your undergraduate or graduate school's library as an alumnus, or working with a colleague who does have access to a university library system.

Although I am hopeful that these suggestions for identifying collaborators, building and maintaining motivation and commitment, and accessing scholarly articles are helpful, you still might find yourself in a position in which you are "hitting a brick wall" as you attempt to cultivate practice-based scholarship. If you find yourself in this position, I encourage you to take on small projects that you can complete relatively independently. Publish a blog post (or series of blog posts) on your website. Look into guidelines for submitting small pieces to a newsletter associated with a local professional society. Begin to outline ideas for a sole-authored article to be submitted to a professional practice journal, like *Professional Psychology: Research and Practice.* And, while doing so, know that this is just the beginning or your program of practice-based scholarship. I elaborate more on this notion next, in the final section of this chapter.

Summary and Conclusion

As I hope was evident in this chapter, there is a vast array of opportunity for clinicians to make contributions to the field, especially when one expands the view of contribution from *practice-based research* to *practice-based scholarship*. Although it can help to have connections with scholars who have access to data or who have strong publication records, by no means is it essential. With good ideas, creativity, persistence, and follow-through, you can develop a program of practice-based scholarship even if you have not published a single piece to this point. In this final section of the chapter, I outline four themes that pervade my own trajectory of practice-based scholarship and that can serve as guiding principles for your own practice-based scholarship.

THEME 1: Pursue areas of scholarship where you have already had success or have developed some sort of expertise. Your previous experiences and successes will provide a platform from which you can extend your scholarship. By building on these previous experiences and successes, you will not be starting from "square one," as you will already have some sense of the literature on the topic and will have formulated unique ideas and insights. In my case, I was immersed in a program of research on IPT for postpartum depression during graduate school, found a collaborator who was doing similar work while on internship, collected data on perinatal distress during my first full-time academic job, and, using these experiences as a platform, have written or edited six books on the topic in the years since I have left academia and have pursued practice-based scholarship. Now, I am regularly asked to provide workshops and keynote addresses in this area of study, *Psychology Today* has recently asked me to blog on the topic, and I am serving as a consultant on a project evaluating a novel treatment for postpartum depression.

THEME 2: Say yes to opportunities. If an opportunity for practice-based scholarship comes your way, I encourage you to seize the moment. Of course, take care to clarify your role in the project and be sure that your role will allow you to achieve the goal for which you are aiming (e.g., being included as an author on a publication). However, assuming that you have confidence that your collaborators will follow through with the project to its completion, taking on the opportunity will give you (a) research experience (or experience, more broadly, with scholarship); (b) exposure to the process of implementing and publishing research or scholarship, which will be invaluable as you continue to pursue practice-based scholarship on your own; (c) the opportunity to establish a strong reputation with collaborators or publishers; and (d) the opportunity to become familiar with the literature on a field of study in a way that is intellectually stimulating and that generates new ideas.

THEME 3: Opportunities beget other opportunities. I cannot state this point enough. If you do a good job on a research or scholarly project, additional opportunities will undoubtedly come your way. Personally, I am at a place (for which I am flattered and grateful) that I rarely need to submit proposals to publishers for book ideas, as they now come to me with ideas and ask me to write them.

However, you need not have a track record of multiple publications on your curriculum vitae for this notion to hold true. You will be presented with opportunities for practice-based scholarship even if your writing primarily consists of blogging. For example, I recently completed a stint as the General Editor of SAGE Publication's seven-volume *Encyclopedia of Abnormal and Clinical Psychology* (2017), which includes 1,406 encyclopedia entries on topics relevant to these fields. There were many, many instances in which I conducted "Google" searches on these topics, which led me to blog posts and other clinically relevant articles (versus more academic articles published in peer-reviewed journals) that were published by practitioners. I invited many of these practitioners to contribute to the *Encyclopedia*, and they were thrilled to do so. Now, I have a relationship with these clinicians, and if I am in a position in which I am looking for contributors for future projects, they will be on my "radar," and I might very well contact them with another practice-based scholarship opportunity.

THEME 4: Opportunities for practice-based scholarship arise from professional activities when you least expect them. For example, they can arise from a workshop you give on a topic relevant to clinical practice. In but one instance, I met Trent Codd, the editor of this volume, several years ago when I presented a CBT workshop in his hometown of Asheville, NC. He and I "hit it off" and remained in touch. Over five years later, I provided him with a practice-based scholarship opportunity to contribute to the *Encyclopedia* that I mentioned in the previous section, and he provided me with the opportunity to write this chapter. Neither of us knew we would have these opportunities to present to one another when we first met. Practice-based scholarship opportunities can also arise when you spend just a small amount of time providing consultation, as one did for me when I had a telephone conversation with an investigator who had questions about administering the HAM-D to women with postpartum depression who were undergoing treatment. They can arise from a mere happenstance conversation with a colleague about an issue of interest to you both, as one did for me when I met my ongoing collaborator, Karen Kleiman, many years ago through mutual colleagues. Now, Karen and I have authored four books together, have recently contributed a theoretical article to a special issue in the nursing journal, *JOGNN*, and will co-present a keynote address at the annual meeting of Postpartum Support International in July 2017.

To provide another example of the serendipity of practice-based scholarship opportunities, I will describe a sequence of events that I experienced during the time in which I was drafting this chapter. I was asked to review a book proposal for the publisher of this volume (Routledge)—a task that you, also, might very well be asked to do once you have authored or edited a book. Reviewing a book proposal could be considered practice-based scholarship in and of itself, as you are critically evaluating the merits and drawbacks of a potential scholarly contribution to their field. However, it is within the realm of possibility that the review could lead to another book opportunity in the future. In fact, the last question on the review template asked whether I had any ideas for future books of my own. Although my response to that question was, "Routledge will kill me if I propose any additional books until I finish the ones for which I already have contracts!", you certainly could take that opportunity to describe another idea. I had thought the submission of that proposal review to Routledge was the end of my brief involvement with that project. However, the author of the proposal was quite taken with my review and suggestions of ways to strengthen his book—I had *a lot* to say because it was quite an innovative and exciting proposal on a subject that, in retrospect, I wish I would have thought of myself! He asked for permission to contact me to talk more about my ideas. We spoke on the telephone, and he offered me co-editorship of his proposed book—an opportunity that I could not pass up regardless of all that is on my plate. Serendipity indeed.

Thus, practice-based scholarship has the potential to add a dimension to your career that is meaningful, creative, and intellectually stimulating. It can come about with ingenuity and perseverance, and it can also "fall into your lap." The more you are open to opportunities and the more you pursue them, the more will come your way. I have found that practice-based scholarship allows me to have a firm grasp of "cutting-edge" research, which not only contributes greatly to my writing, but that also enhances my clinical practice. I believe that these experiences allow me to function as a scientist-practitioner (or perhaps practitioner-scientist) and that I am, therefore, conducting my professional self in the spirit of the Boulder model. However, I also believe that pursuing practice-based scholarship outside the walls of academia can allow freedom and autonomy in choosing valued pursuits that are not dependent on grant funding or other restrictions of an academic department. I have had the freedom to steer away from areas of inquiry in which I have become less interested, such as cognitive biases in anxious and suicidal individuals, and I have embraced areas of inquiry with more clinical relevance, such as novel approaches to the treatment of perinatal women and the strategic delivery of CBT. Now that I have left my full-time university-level position, I have even come full circle and, at least from a clinical standpoint, have gone back to my interest from my undergraduate days in working with survivors of torture and political persecution. Stay tuned for ways I will turn that meaningful clinical experience into a practice-based scholarship opportunity.

References

Allison, K. C., Wenzel, A., Kleiman, K., & Sawrer, D. B. (2011). Development of a brief measure of postpartum distress. *Journal of Women's Health, 20,* 617–623.

Butcher, J. N., Dahlstrom, W. G., Graham, J. R., Tellegen, A., & Kaemmer, B. (1989). *The Minnesota Multiphasic Personality Inventory-2 (MMPI-2): Manual for administration and scoring.* Minneapolis, MN: University of Minnesota Press.

Clark, R., Tluczek, A., & Wenzel, A. (2003). Psychotherapy for postpartum depression: A preliminary report. *American Journal of Orthopsychiatry, 73,* 441–454.

Costa, P. T. & McCrae, R. (1992). *Revised NEO Personality Inventory (NEO-PI-R) and NEO Five Factor Model (MEO-FFI) professional manual.* Odes, FL: Psychological Assessment Center.

Cuijpers, P., Geraedts, S., van Oppen, P., Andersson, G., Markowitz, J. C., & van Straten, A. (2011). Interpersonal psychotherapy for depression: A meta-analysis. *American Journal of Psychiatry, 168,* 581–592.

de Oliveira, I. R., Powell, V. B., Wenzel, A., Caldas, M., Seixas, C., Almeida, C., Bonfirm, T., Grangeon, M. C., Castro, M., Galvão, A., Moraes, R. D., & Sudak, D. (2012). Efficacy of the Trial-Based Thought Record: A new cognitive therapy strategy designed to change core beliefs in social phobia. *Journal of Clinical Pharmacy and Therapeutics, 37,* 328–334.

Greco, T., Zangrillo, A., Biondi-Zoccaai, G., & Landoni, G. (2013). Meta-analysis: Pitfalls and hints. *Heart, Lungs, and Vessels, 5,* 219–225.

Hamilton, M. (1960). A rating scale for depression. *Journal of Neurology and Neurosurgical Psychiatry, 23,* 56–62.

Harvey, J. H. & Wenzel, A. (Eds.) (2001). *Close relationships: Maintenance and enhancement.* Mahwah, NJ: Lawrence Erlbaum Associates.

Harvey, J. H. & Wenzel, A. (Eds.) (2002). *A clinician's guide to maintaining and enhancing close relationships.* Mahwah, NJ: Lawrence Erlbaum Associates.

Harvey, J. H., Wenzel, A., & Sprecher, S. (Eds.) (2004). *Handbook of sexuality in close relationships.* Mahwah, NJ: Lawrence Erlbaum Associates.

Jager-Hymen, S., Cunningham, A., Wenzel, A., Mattei, S., Brown, G. K., & Beck, A. T. (2014). Cognitive distortions and suicide attempts. *Cognitive Therapy and Research, 38,* 369–374.

Karlin, B. E., Brown, G. L., Trockel, M., Cunning, D., Zeiss, A. M. & Taylor, C. B. (2012). National dissemination of cognitive behavioral therapy for depression in the Department of Veterans Affairs Health Care System: Therapist and patient level outcomes. *Journal of Consulting and Clinical Psychology, 80,* 707–718.

Kleiman, K. R. & Raskin, V. D. (1994). *This isn't what I expected: Overcoming postpartum depression.* New York: Bantam Books.

Kleiman, K. R. & Raskin, V. D. (2013). *This isn't what I expected: Overcoming postpartum depression* (2nd ed.). Boston, MA: De Capo Press.

Kleiman, K. & Wenzel, A. (2011). *Dropping the baby and other scary thoughts: Breaking the cycle of negative unwanted thoughts in motherhood.* New York: Routledge.

Kleiman, K. with Wenzel, A. (2014). *Tokens of affection: Reclaiming your marriage after postpartum depression.* New York: Routledge.

Lilienfeld, S. O., Ritschel, L. A., Lynn, S. J., Cautin, R. L., & Latzman, R. D. (2013). Why many clinical psychologists are resistant to evidence-based practice: Root causes and constructive remedies. *Clinical Psychology Review, 33,* 883–900.

Markowitz, J. C., Svartberg, M., & Swartz, H. A. (1998). Is IPT time-limited psychodynamic psychotherapy? *The Journal of Psychotherapy Practice and Research, 7,* 185–195.

Miniati, M., Callri, S., Calugi, S., Rucci, P., Savino, M., Mauri, M., & Dell'Osso, L. (2014). Interpersonal psychotherapy for postpartum depression: A systematic review. *Archives of Women's Mental Health, 17*(4), 257–268.

Moran, T. E., Polanin, J. R., & Wenzel, A. (2014). An initial validation of the Postpartum Worry Scale—Revised. *Archives of Women's Mental Health, 17,* 41–48.

Moran, T. E., Segre, L., Polanin, J. R., & Wenzel, A. (2014). The Postpartum Worry Scale—Further validation with a sample of NICU mothers. *Archives of Women's Mental Health, 17,* 41–48.

O'hara, M. W., Stuart, S., Gorman, L. L., & Wenzel, A. (2000). Efficacy of interpersonal psychotherapy for postpartum depression. *Archives of General Psychiatry, 57*(11), 1039–1045.

Persons, J. B. & Silberschatz, G. (1998). Are results of randomized controlled trials useful to psychotherapists? *Journal of Consulting and Clinical Psychology, 66,* 126–135.

Raimey, V. (1950). *Training in clinical psychology.* New York: Prentice-Hall.

Rodrigues, E., Wenzel, A., Ribeiro, M. P., Quarantini, L. C., Mirnada-Scippa, A., de Sena, E. P., & de Oliveira, I. R. (2011). Hippocampal volumes in borderline personality disorder with and without comorbid posttraumatic stress disorder: A meta analysis. *European Psychiatry, 26,* 452–456.

Rubin, D. C. & Wenzel, A. E. (1996). One hundred years of forgetting: A quantitative description of retention. *Psychological Review, 103,* 734–760.

Shafran, R., Clark, D. M., Fairburn, C. G., Arntz, A., Barlow, D. H., Ehlers, A., . . ., & Wilson, G. T. (2009). Mind the gap: Improving the dissemination of CBT. *Behaviour Research and Therapy, 47*(11), 902–909.

Spokas, M., Wenzel, A., Brown, G. K., & Beck, A. T. (2012). Characteristics of individuals who make impulsive suicide attempts. *Journal of Affective Disorders, 136,* 1121–1125.

Sprecher, S., Wenzel, A., & Harvey, J. H. (Eds.) (2008). *Handbook of relationship initiation.* New York: Psychology Press.

Strickler, G. (2000). The scientist-practitioner model: Gandhi was right again. *American Psychologist, 55,* 253–254.

Stuart, S. (2012). Interpersonal psychotherapy for postpartum depression. *Clinical Psychology and Psychotherapy, 19,* 134–140.

Wenzel, A. (2002). Characteristics of close relationships in individuals with social phobia: A preliminary comparison with nonanxious individuals. In J. H. Harvey & A. Wenzel (Eds.) *A clinician's guide to maintaining and enhancing close relationships* (pp. 199–213). Mahwah, NJ: Lawrence Erlbaum Associates.

Wenzel, A. (2013). *Strategic decision making in cognitive behavioral therapy.* Washington, DC: APA Books.

Wenzel, A. (2014). *Coping with infertility, miscarriage, and neonatal loss: Finding perspective and creating meaning.* Washington, DC: APA Books (LifeTools Division)

Wenzel, A. (Ed.) (2016). *Oxford handbook of perinatal psychology.* New York: Oxford University Press.

Wenzel, A. (2017). *Innovations in cognitive behavioral therapy: Strategic interventions for creative practice.* New York: Routledge.

Wenzel, A. (Editor-in-Chief) (2017). *SAGE encyclopedia of abnormal and clinical psychology, Vols 1–7.* Thousand Oaks, CA: SAGE Publications.

Wenzel, A., Brown, G. K., & Beck, A. T. (2009). *Cognitive therapy for suicidal patients: Scientific and clinical applications.* Washington, DC: APA Books.

Wenzel, A., Brown, G. K., & Karlin, B. E. (2011). *Cognitive behavioral therapy for depressed veterans and military servicemembers: Therapist manual.* Washington, DC: U.S. Department of Veterans Affairs.

Wenzel, A., Dobson, K. S., & Hays, P. A. (2016). *Cognitive behavioral therapy techniques and strategies.* American Psychological Association.

Wenzel, A., Finstrom, N., Jordan, J., & Brendle, J. R. (2005). Memory and interpretation of visual representations of threat in socially anxious and nonanxious individuals. *Behaviour Research and Therapy, 43,* 1029–1044.

Wenzel, A., Graff-Dolezal, J., Macho, M., & Brendle, J. R. (2005). Communication and social skills in the context of close relationships in socially anxious and nonanxious individuals. *Behaviour Research and Therapy, 43,* 505–519.

Wenzel, A., Haugen, E. N., Jackson, L. C., & Brendle, J. R. (2005). Anxiety disorders at eight weeks postpartum. *Journal of Anxiety Disorders, 19,* 295–311.

Wenzel, A. & Holt, C. S. (2003). Social-evaluative threat and cognitive performance in socially anxious and nonanxious individuals. *Personality and Individual Differences, 34,* 283–294.

Wenzel, A. with Kleiman, K. (2015). *Cognitive behavioral therapy for perinatal distress.* New York: Routledge.

Wenzel, A., Liese, B. S., Beck, A. T., & Friedman-Wheeler, D. (2012). *Cognitive therapy addictions groups.* New York: Guilford Press.

Wenzel, A. E. & Rubin, D. C. (2005). *Cognitive methods and their application to clinical research.* American Psychological Association.

Wenzel, A. & Stuart, S. C. (2011). *Anxiety in childbearing women: Diagnosis and treatment.* Washington, DC: American Psychological Association.

Young, J. E. & Beck, A. T. (1980). *Cognitive Therapy Scale rating manual.* Unpublished manuscript, University of Pennsylvania, Philadelphia, PA.

PART IV

Practice-Based Research in Other Clinical Settings

CHAPTER 11

Implementation Science at the End-Point: A New Approach for Researchers in Primary Care

Jodi Polaha and Ivy Click

Mental health professionals who are providing services in collaboration with primary health care are well-positioned to contribute to science in this burgeoning area. This chapter is written for the clinician-scientist who is engaged in such collaborative practice regardless of model (e.g., distinct but collaborative practices, co-located practice, fully integrated, etc.), and whose primary responsibility is clinical service delivery. This chapter explores and discusses the utility and application of Implementation Science (IS) methods in addressing key questions in this area. In addition, this chapter discusses pragmatics regarding data collection strategies, IRB and HIPAA concerns, publication outlets, and creating clinical release time to do research.

A Prime Opportunity

There is a significant and distinct opportunity for mental health providers working in primary care to contribute to the scientific literature. In fact, such professionals' position could be viewed as an advantage, or perhaps even an imperative for conducting research, for at least three reasons. First, policy changes within the Affordable Care Act have opened doors to the import of mental health into primary care on a significant scale in recent years (Beacham, Kinman, Harris & Masters, 2012; Nash, Khatri, Cubic, & Baird, 2013). For example, integrated behavioral health care has been identified as an essential feature of ground-level policies such as the Patient Centered Medical Home (Working Party Group on Integrated Behavioral Healthcare, 2014) and many large health care networks and even entire state-wide programming is shifting to integrated models (e.g., see Hunter et al., 2017). As a result of this shift, behavioral health technology is now available to patients who could or would not seek it elsewhere (Polaha, Williams, Heflinger, & Studts, 2015). However, with this rapid advance, the field has made ad hoc adaptations to its empirically-supported treatments to "fit" a new setting—but leaving a gap in the literature around whether the treatments, as applied in primary care, are effective or impactful. Thus, mental health providers in primary care have the opportunity to develop science around the portability of interventions with a long-standing evidence base in specialty mental health.

Another reason why mental health professionals in primary care are poised to conduct research is because, with policy changes, primary care settings are increasingly under pressure to produce the evidence that their interventions work. As payments for value (rather than fee-for-service) become more common, practices have focused on demonstrating the Triple Aim, including patient experience, cost effectiveness, and improved population health (Berwick, Nolan, & Whittington, 2008). Individual practices, often in coordination with the accountable care organizations to which they belong, are beginning to develop skills and systems for collecting metrics on their patients and practice processes and outcomes. These data are at the fingertips of mental health providers in primary care and can be leveraged to close essential gaps in the scientific literature.

Finally, mental health professionals who are working day-to-day in primary care have front row seats to "action" at the end-point. This perspective is an essential one; without it, our field struggles to implement empirically-supported treatments in a way that truly has impact. Consider this: Impact = Effectiveness X Reach (Miller, Munoz, & Christensen, 2010). While the behavioral health field has made a significant dent in the *effectiveness* element in this equation, it has had little *impact*, because it lacks *reach*. Reach is defined as the extent to which a given intervention or program attracts its intended audience (Klesges, Estabrooks, Glasgow, & Dzewaltowski, 2005), and "boots on the ground" providers have an excellent vantage on that variable. Indeed, providers at the end-point have the opportunity to publish work that asks the questions and points the directions for the many other scientists in the field who are one, two, or more degrees of separation from the end-point itself, but who aim to develop treatments that will have traction in that setting.

Asking the Right Questions

It is our contention that, in order for busy mental health providers in primary care to best leverage their position for research purposes, they should ask the right questions. For many, this will require a significant shift in perspective. Mental health professionals are often trained in the tradition of asking research questions around the efficacy and effectiveness of interventions, and using labor-intensive study designs, such as randomized controlled trials, to answer them. These questions and methods are certainly relevant in primary care; however, the execution of such projects is extremely challenging (Peek, Cohen, & DeGruy, 2014) and the logistics will set the embedded clinician at odds with practice contingencies, potentially causing conflict.

More importantly, however, it can be argued that questions about the effectiveness of interventions are not the most essential questions for integrated care at this time. The questions and answers generated by scientific endeavor has been likened to a "bridge" (Zerhouni, 2003; see Figure 11.1). Science "translates" study outcomes from the left end, where researchers ask basic questions about etiology and then develop methods, specifying technology or equipment, to the center, where researchers ask questions about efficacy (questions about treatment

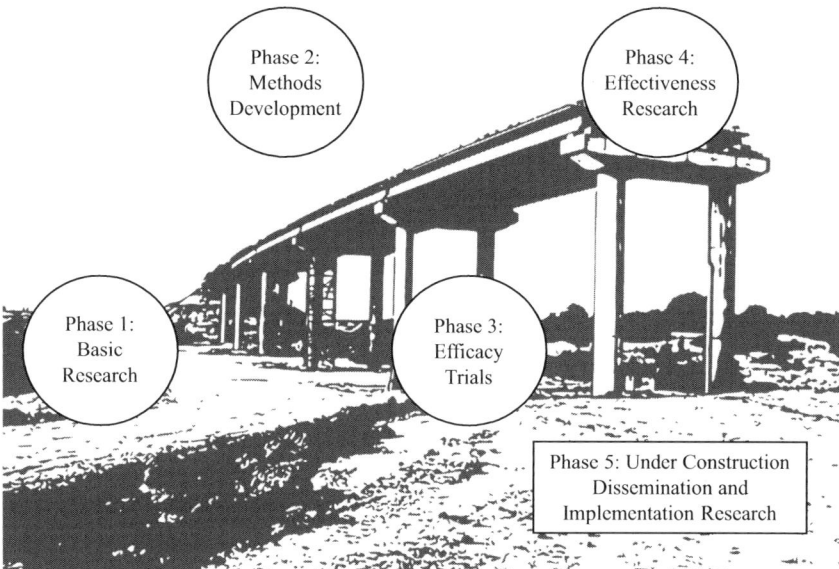

Figure 11.1 Five phases of research depicted along the translational bridge

outcomes under ideal or laboratory conditions) and then effectiveness (treatment outcomes under real or usual conditions) (Sussman, Valente, Rohrbach, Skara, & Pentz, 2006). Finally, effective treatments are translated to the end-point, where final phase research evaluates dissemination and implementation questions. These final phases ask essential questions about whether and how the interventions can gain traction or have utility in real-world settings.

As depicted in Figure 11.1, scientific methods and the literature base in mental health is strong in stages one and two, but less so as the bridge articulates into the final phases at the end-point. An excellent analogy (Brown, Smith, Villamar, & Benbow, 2016) is research on immunization for life-threatening diseases. Presently, research has advanced basic science to the point of highly effective vaccines for diseases like measles, chicken pox, and tuberculosis. These medicines are well-understood, and backed by rigorous, large-scale studies including controlled trials. But if research around dissemination and implementation of the vaccines is not conducted, these vaccines will have little reach, and ultimately, little impact. Consider the transport and distribution of these vaccines to a poorly developed country where there are few trained health professionals, scarce refrigeration units, and remote villages that are hard to access. In this scenario, much like moving extant mental health treatments to primary care, many essential questions arise about how best to implement and disseminate the intervention.

Indeed, the growth and drive of evidence-based medicine has been strong across all health services (Claridge & Fabian, 2005), and, especially in the field of mental health, where "EBTs" (empirically-supported treatments) are well-known and accepted within the guild. As the field extends to new end-point settings, we contend that clinician-scientists should ask questions about implementation. The arguments for this contention mirror our rationale as to why mental health professionals are so well poised to do research in primary care: 1) the largest gap in our science is around how impactful our interventions are at the endpoint (Dodge, 2011; Hoagwood & Olin, 2002; Proctor et al., 2009); 2) studies of implementation will closely align with ongoing demand in primary care for data around the Triple Aim (quality improvement); and 3) the intimate understanding of the nuanced aspects of the end-point will make for better informed questions and measures. Our contention that implementation questions have significant value to integrated care at this point in time is supported by a number of scholars, policy analysts, and researchers working in this field (e.g., Hunter et al., 2017; Miller, Mendenhall, & Malik, 2009; Peek, 2008).

Dissemination and Implementation Science

Dissemination and Implementation Science (D&I Science) is a growing field of research models and methods designed to answer the essential questions at the end-point (Brownson, Colditz, & Proctor, 2012). This burgeoning area has its own journals, funding programs, scientific meetings, and training programs. *Dissemination Science* is focused on evaluating the complex factors that influence the speed at which, and the likelihood that, interventions are taken up by a broad audience (Greenhalgh, Robert, MacFarlane, Bate, & Kyriakidou, 2004). In contrast, *Implementation Science* addresses "reach" by employing approaches to introduce or change evidence-based health interventions within human service settings in a way that helps them gain better traction and follow-through. The National Institute of Health has called for implementation research looking at how service systems and setting characteristics influence prevention and treatment program implementation, as well as strategies to improve the adoption and implementation of evidence-based treatment innovations.

Polaha and Nolan (2014) summarize several key characteristics of D&I Science. First, this work focuses on stakeholders in the context where the treatment or service is to be delivered. For the clinician-scientist in collaborative primary care practice, these are the patients, physicians, clinical staff, and administrative personnel they are surrounded by every day. In fact, this includes the researcher and his or her behavioral health colleagues as well! Second, D&I Science engages transdisciplinary teams, getting the development and product of science out of the "silo" of mental health journals and into the minds and hands of physician, nursing, business, and public health professionals. Again, clinicians in collaborative practice are ideally situated to engage colleagues from other disciplines comprising such research teams. Third, D&I Science is characterized by the incorporation of novel partners and methods. Examples include having informatics experts who design electronic health records weigh in on relevant retrievable variables for a study, or using company marketing professionals to design high quality materials as part of a new intervention. Finally, a key characteristic of D&I Science is an

Implementation Science at the End-Point 197

emphasis on scaling-up and sustainability. It is in this domain that the clinician-scientist has particular savvy about what can be reimbursable, fit into the space and time-demands of primary care, and meets the mission, culture, or values inherent in a given practice. Indeed, clinicians in primary care, in collaboration with their colleagues and patients, are well-positioned to make strong predictions about what new treatments, programs, or services can realistically be delivered practice-wide and will have staying-power.

The entire field of D&I Science technology has significant applicability to the translation of EBTs in mental health to primary care. The reader is directed to more in-depth content in a chapter with a broad overview developed for mental health professionals by Polaha & Nolan (2014) or one of the seminal texts in this area by Brownson et al. (2012). That said, we believe the busy clinician-scientist is best positioned for engaging implementation research using methods that resemble quality improvement and program evaluation initiatives already used within primary care (Chambers, Wang, & Insel, 2010). The remainder of this chapter digests tangible implementation outcomes that may be accessible and have the potential to answer critical gaps in the field.

Implementation Outcomes

Many quality improvement projects and "demonstration studies" articulate variables relevant to implementation, however, if such work is guided by theory and developed with rigorous design and methods, it is better positioned to move not only internal knowledge about what works but can also lead to generalizable knowledge (Brown et al. 2017). One comprehensive guide for the selection and harmonization of relevant implementation outcomes is provided by Proctor et al. (2011). This taxonomy distinguishes between *client outcomes* (the areas of focus in traditional clinical research, such as satisfaction, functioning, and symptomatology)—the furthest downstream from the implementation process—and *implementation outcomes*. The latter are the most proximal outcomes and include acceptability, adoption, appropriateness, costs, feasibility, fidelity, penetration, and sustainability. Other models serve a similar purpose, such as the widely used RE-AIM model, which focuses on reach, efficacy, adoption, implementation, and maintenance (Glasgow, Vogt, & Boles, 1999). The following section details key implementation outcomes identified by Proctor and her colleagues, and crosswalks them with suggested primary care variables, providing examples and direction for future research. For easy reference, a summary is provided in Table 11.1.

Acceptability

"Acceptability" refers to the stakeholders' perception of whether a given intervention, practice, or service, is agreeable, palatable, or satisfactory based on their direct experience with it. In primary care, "stakeholders" can include patients, providers (behavioral health, medical, or other), clinical staff, office staff and administration, or even payer and policy professionals. Importantly, this variable

Table 11.1 Implementation Outcomes from Proctor et al. (2011): Application to Primary Care

Outcome	Definition	Application to Primary Care	Data Source/Measures
Acceptability	Stakeholders' perception of whether a given intervention, practice, or service, is agreeable, palatable, or satisfactory based on their direct experience with it	Self-reported "fit" of intervention from medical providers, clinical staff, behavioral health professionals, patients and their families, office staff and administration	Rating scales Interviews Focus groups
Adoption	Uptake of a treatment of service, or, providers' intent to engage it	Behavioral measure of "fit" particularly from those in the clinic context who are expected to alter their practice to engage the new service such as medical providers, clinical staff, behavior health professionals, and office staff	Electronic Health Records (EHR) showing a task was completed (e.g., referral made; screening collected) Administrative data (e.g., scheduling, billing) Observations Surveys Interviews
Fidelity	The degree to which an intervention was implemented as it was prescribed	A fidelity measure for an existing EBT that has been adapted for primary care; A fidelity measure for a service delivery model that has articulated components in the literature	Electronic Health Records (EHR) showing a task was completed (e.g., referral made; screening collected) Administrative data (e.g., scheduling, billing) Observations Rating Scales

Cost	The cost impact of delivering an intervention or service; varies by the complexity of the intervention and by the setting in which it is offered.	Return on investment, cost benefit, or cost effectiveness with particular consideration for staffing time and health/system impacts that go beyond the immediate impact of the treatment (e.g., the presence of a behavioral health provider impacting the costs/time for health care visits more broadly in the practice).	Administrative data (e.g., scheduling, billing) Observation
Penetration	The extent to which an intervention or service "reaches" the people that it intends to reach.	Access/uptake of behavioral health services in coordination with primary care, particularly in groups not targeted by specialty mental health who are at risk of not accessing treatment in that setting (e.g., prevention efforts or behavioral health technology impact on a chronic illness such as diabetes).	Electronic health records especially behavioral health providers' notes Follow-up interviews or surveys with patients
Sustainability	The extent to which a new intervention or service is maintained within a system's infrastructure over time.	The durability of a new intervention/system of behavioral health care in primary care after a certain passage of time (e.g., one year) or a critical incident such as a new EHR system, new residents starting, changes in management, or to address an ACO initiative.	EHR Administrative data Follow-up interviews or surveys with patients, provider, or administration

is dynamic, changing as stakeholders gain experience with a given intervention, process or service. For example, providers may describe a new innovation in their clinic as highly acceptable initially based on perceived need or potential for revenue generation; however, they may describe it as less acceptable, over time, if it places significant demand on their workload. An inverse scenario has played out this way in the area of telemental health, where patients who have not experienced the service do not see it as an acceptable treatment (Polaha, Williams, Heflinger, & Studts, 2015), but patients who do contact the service rate it as highly acceptable (e.g., Jacob, Larsen, & Craighead, 2012).

There is a significant gap in the literature around the acceptability of interventions adapted for collaborative practice as well as the model of integrated or collaborative care itself. For example, in studies of the Primary Care Behavioral Health Model (PCBH) of integrated care researchers have developed fairly targeted satisfaction surveys for providers and patients (e.g., Funderburk, Fielder, DeMartini, & Flynn, 2012; Runyan et al., 2003). According to Proctor et al. (2011), however, acceptability differs from satisfaction in that the former assess very specific experiences with a given process, treatment, or change, whereas the latter generally refers to global experiences measured through consumer surveys. Thus, to conduct a true acceptability study for PCBH, potential questions should target key aspects to the model including the patient/provider's perceptions of the visit length, the visit being incorporated into the primary care milieu, and the visit being triggered by a specific screening tool. The clinician-researcher who is engaged in the implementation of a new service, intervention, or program in primary care is ideally situated to collect acceptability data from one or more stakeholders in a way that informs the literature.

Adoption

"Adoption" refers to the uptake of a treatment of service, or, providers' intent to engage it (Proctor et al., 2011). It is an essential element of implementation success; the behavioral expression of acceptability. Without adoption, the most efficacious intervention has little chance of public health impact.

Much of the extant literature in integrated care has measured adoption indirectly via studies of referrals to mental health services. Indeed, providers' referrals can be an indicator of their adoption of a service; however, many studies lack rigor in this regard. One example of weak measurement are demonstration studies which show total referrals post implementation. Another example are studies which show a correlational and indirect change in referral practice after an integrated practice was initiated, such as providers making fewer referrals to specialty mental health after fully integrated services are implemented (Brawer et al., 2010; Felker et al., 2004).

A more rigorous way to measure adoption is as a ratio of the total number of patients who *should have been referred* to the number who *were referred*. This ratio can be expressed as a percentage—in other words, the percent of referrals made from that targeted group. As an example, Smith and Polaha (2017), evaluated the adoption of a family-centered evidence-based parent training program in two different primary care clinics. A parent-completed screening measure of child psychosocial concerns was used to identify families who should be referred to the service based on the severity of their score. Adoption outcomes were reported as the percentage of children who were referred to the service, calculated by dividing the total number referred by the total number who scored above the cutoff on the screening measure. As with acceptability, adoption can be dynamic and should be measured at intervals. Smith and Polaha found that high rates of adoption in the first few months of implementation (around 85 percent) began to flag (as low as 70 percent) when new medical residents began serving the clinic and had not been trained appropriately to use the screener to make referrals.

Adoption can be measured using other indicators as well, and mental health providers with a close view of the clinical landscape can be creative about measuring this variable. For example, in our recent development of a new multi-component intervention to change physicians' management of chronic heart failure in primary care, pharmacists worked with nurses attending twice-daily huddles to track the frequency of staff "check-ins" (part of the articulated process) around patients coming in with heart failure who might benefit from the new intervention. Our measurement of adoption was the number of staff "check-ins" during huddle divided by the total number of patients identified by the pharmacy technician as needing the new treatment (i.e., those who should have had a check-in during huddle).

Fidelity

Fidelity refers to the degree to which an intervention was implemented as it was prescribed (Proctor et al., 2011). Fidelity is a particular strength for the field of mental health in that many EBTs are manualized or protocol-driven interventions which have complementary fidelity measures. For example, the Coping Cat, a cognitive-behavioral treatment for children with anxiety, has published strategies for measuring fidelity including an expert rating using video tapes and a less intensive rating form strategy (Shoenwald, Mehta, & Shernoff, 2013). A primary care-based clinician who adapted the Coping Cat for a new setting or model could demonstrate fidelity using one of these established and accepted strategies to provide a convincing case that the key aspects to the treatment are the same in its new iteration. In fact, leaders in the field of implementation science, Chambers and Norton (2016), argue that, given the extant strength of the evidence base for interventions like the Coping Cat, the demonstration of fidelity constitutes a satisfactory end-point for science and clinicians need not continue to produce effectiveness studies. To date, very few studies of fidelity to EBTs in adapted-for-integrated care versions have been published (e.g. Kolko & Perrin, 2014).

While methodologically demonstrating fidelity to existing treatments may be a strength in the context of mental health, demonstrating fidelity to models of collaborative practice is a significant weakness. To date, models of collaborative care are broadly described on a continuum that ranges from distinct practices with some collaborative communication, to fully integrated practices where patients are seen for behavioral health concerns in the exam room as part of their primary care visit. An improvement is represented by various taxonomies of integrated practice such as Peek's (2013) lexicon which operationalizes various aspects to integration (e.g., pathways, electronic health records, patient perceptions of the experience, etc.) and has been converted for measurement by the Practice Integration Profile (PIP; Kessler, 2015), however, to date it is unknown what scores on the PIP are associated with better or specific outcomes in integrated practice. Other specific models of integration are beginning to articulate fidelity criteria. For example, within the PCBH model, Funderburk et al. (2010) provided an easy-to-use provider rating scale to assess fidelity of implementation to that particular model. Likewise, an operationalized fidelity criterion for PCBH has been articulated, however, there are no published studies on adherence to this model in its entirety (Hunter et al., 2017). This is an area where clinician-scientists can fill a significant gap in the literature, not only by collecting real-world data on these new measures but also by identifying strategies for acquiring fidelity data in a low-impact way (e.g., through the EHR or scheduling databases) so that it can be readily and frequently assessed for drift and in response to programming changes.

Cost

"Cost" refers to the cost impact of delivering a particular intervention, which can vary by the complexity of the intervention and by the setting in which it is offered. For a detailed summary of conceptual issues relevant to measuring cost within the field of mental health, see Goodheart (2010). To date, much of the research related to cost in collaborative practice is represented by large-scale or system wide studies of cost-offset in which it is well-established that the costs associated with delivering behavioral health services (e.g., the cost of the provider, fee for the service, etc.) are returned to the system by overall savings in reduced medical visits (Chiles, Lambert, & Hatch, 1999). These data tend to "speak" to systems and insurers more than providers or individual practices.

While studies of this nature certainly have importance in showing the broad impact of integrated behavioral health care, there are at least two other ways to measure cost that are imperative for the field and are more accessible to those engaged in clinic settings. First, the measuring costs of implementing EBTs adapted for collaborative practice will be essential to their uptake. These costs might include the cost of the provider who is implementing the treatment, the cost of his or her training and maintaining fidelity, and the cost of materials or equipment. Second, measuring the costs of service delivery models is another important need. Recently, Gouge, Polaha, Rogers and Harden (2016) showed that a rural, stand-alone pediatric practice generated over $1,200 more on days when the BHC was on site as compared to days when she was not. The increased revenue is attributed to providers' time savings by using warm hand-offs, allowing them to see more patients by double-booking and treating more walk-ins.

Penetration

"Penetration" refers to the extent to which an intervention or service "reaches" the people that it intends to reach, or, its uptake. It is best described as the percentage of those who received the treatment out of the total population of patients who were targeted for the intervention. Along with fidelity, penetration could be seen as one of the high bars of all of the implementation outcomes and is incorporated into the widely disseminated RE-AIM model of implementation study which is carefully articulated in Kessler et al. (2013).

Measuring penetration in primary care can be challenging. An illustration is found in the use of a brief screening tool to identify patients in need of treatment for depression. The Patient Health Questionnaire-9 (Kroenke, Spitzer, & Williams, 2001) has broad uptake for this purpose and many clinics have established the two-item version as a gatekeeper for the administration of the nine-item version, which triggers treatment if the score is significant. Many practices are motivated to track and bill for their use of this measure by their association with an Accountable Care Organization and/or specific payers. Thus, a clinician can access electronic health record (EHR) and billing data from within their practice for measures of whether the screening tool was administered and to some extent this assesses its reach to the patient; however, it could also be considered adoption (i.e., the provider, nurse, front desk adopted the practice of administering the screening tool). A more explicit measure of penetration would be the percent of patients who received treatment for depression of all patients who scored above the cutoff on the screening tool. In other words, of those targeted for treatment by the screening (patients who score high), what percent actually received the treatment? To assess this outcome, the clinician would have to have data showing the patient followed through with treatment which, if at an alternate site, could be a logistical challenge. Fully integrated mental health providers, however, may be able to tap treatment notes as measures of attendance to treatment, although, depending on the format of the records, this may remain quite challenging.

Sustainability

"Sustainability" is the extent to which a new intervention or service is maintained within a system's infrastructure over time. This could be the least-developed area in terms of the study of collaborative practice models, mostly because the field is still new and working to describe the start-up of models and their feasibility as described in the outcomes above. The health care system, however, is an incredibly dynamic system with continually evolving contingencies resulting from changes in public policy (and then billing/payment models), scientific advances and profession best-practices, and inner context fluctuations such as staffing, space, and EHR software use. Importantly, the measure of a new intervention's sustainability over time should not be considered as its adherence to the static model that was first introduced, but the way in which that model is able to—or unable to—adapt to changing contingencies in the inner and outer settings.

Strategy

To this point we have provided the rationale and scientific technology for conducting implementation research. In the following sections we discuss logistics and strategies for doing this work. Indeed, there are a number of barriers to producing research for anyone in a clinical position: time, low priority, limited support, and administrative hurdles. Again, we argue these could be diminished in primary care because there is an expectation for quality improvement initiatives requiring data collection, analysis, and internal dissemination. For the motivated clinician, this "expectation" can be made more rigorous and with greater planning including a review of the literature, consideration of the ethics of human subjects, and the collection of the right data using the strongest possible design. With that additional effort, findings can be disseminated beyond the practice.

Design a Low Impact Strategy

One way to overcome the barriers of conducting research as a busy primary care clinician is to design a research strategy that has low impact on the on the practice providers, clinical staff, and research participants. Overly burdensome research methodologies that disrupt clinical activity decrease buy-in from administrators, providers, and staff and may affect the implementation outcomes in which you are interested. By designing and conducting research using low impact methodologies by "boots on the ground" clinicians in real world practice settings, primary care researchers can reduce time away from clinical duties, increase support from providers and administrators, and ensure realistic, translatable outcomes.

As previously mentioned, several external motivators such as PCMH, Meaningful Use, and ACOs have made it increasingly likely that your organization or practice is already in the process of one or more quality improvement initiatives. Many health care organizations have full-time staff dedicated to these efforts such as care coordinators, informatics personnel, and practice facilitators. Aligning your own research interests with that of your organization's may allow you to turn an ongoing process into a research project without much disruption to the rest of the practice. Furthermore, you may be able to negotiate your own and/or dedicated staff time with your administration toward research efforts as they align with and inform ongoing quality improvement processes. When designing your low impact research strategy, consider ahead of time the resources you will need for data collection, IRB and HIPAA, evaluation, and dissemination of your findings.

Data Collection

Collecting data can be time and labor intensive, however, there are many ready data sources in busy practice settings. As depicted in Table 11.1, the electronic health record (EHR) and various administrative records (electronic schedules, billing, referral paperwork, etc.) can be leveraged to assess several implementation outcomes. The advent of electronic health records (EHR) has increased access to robust data for both retrospective and prospective research studies, however your system may not be designed to readily assay these data. Informatics personnel can be essential stakeholders as a project is developed to negotiate the establishment of retrievable fields that satisfy both clinician and researcher needs.

You may find the data you need are not accessible via the EHR or any other permanent product in the clinic. In these cases, alternative data collection means may be necessary, such as paper and pencil measures or observational data collection. There are many evidence-based measures for implementation research, summarized by Rabin et al., 2016, including a number of web-based repositories. Direct observation of patient interactions, clinical staff, etc. can be time and labor intensive, but increasingly can be done through technological means such as CCTV, smart phones, and small cameras such as GoPros. Gouge et al., (2016) demonstrate a strong method for measuring cost using observation by volunteer undergraduate research assistants.

IRB

An Institutional Review Board (IRB) is a committee that performs ethical review of proposed research. The purpose of an IRB is to ensure that humans involved in research are afforded protection in accordance with funding and regulatory agencies. Most institutions engaged in research will have their own IRB; however, some smaller organizations or practices may have agreements in place to use an outside established IRB to oversee ethical human subjects research. It is beyond the scope of this chapter to discuss in detail the IRB approval process or the levels of IRB review, however, many high quality primary care research projects may meet the qualifications for exempt or expedited review, which are generally more straight-forward proposals with quicker turn-around times for approval. Importantly, considering the IRB rules when designing the study can eliminate this potential barrier. Studies designed to have data assessed in aggregate via information technology (i.e., no tapping individual records and no identifiable information) are often not considered human subjects research at all.

If you are directly observing research participants or are collecting data from questionnaires or surveys, you will likely need to provide informed consent to participate in research. Informed consent is a process, not just a document, which includes disclosing that the study involves research and is voluntary, the purpose of the research, describes in layperson terms the procedures to be followed, and any potential risks and benefits to the participant. Completely retrospective EHR data collection often does not require informed consent of participants and prospective EHR data collection sometimes does not require informed consent. Your IRB will determine whether informed consent is necessary.

Quality improvement projects that are intended only for internal use (i.e, not to be disseminated outside the practice) are not subject to the IRB, however, sometimes it is only after completing a strong quality improvement project that clinician-scientists realize they could disseminate the work through presentation or publication. It is always better to engage with the IRB from the outset, however under these circumstances the investigator should retrospectively engage the IRB for review and approval. When approaching the IRB with this type of project, focus on the fact that this will be secondary data analysis of an existing internal process. It may be helpful to explain that this quality improvement initiative took place as routine practice improvement and that the research will only examine the implementation outcomes of the process.

HIPAA

The HIPAA Privacy Rule provides federal protections for Protected Health Information (PHI) and provides patients with rights with respect to that information. It also permits the disclosure of personal health information needed for patient care and other important purposes. If your research project accesses identifying health information through the EHR, patient surveys, observation, or any means, you will need to consider whether you need to make accommodation for HIPAA. Under the Privacy Rule, researchers are permitted to use PHI for research with individual patient authorization or without authorization if permitted a waiver from an IRB. There are three criteria which must be met in order for an IRB to approve a waiver of authorization under the Privacy Rule: 1) the use or disclosure of PHI involves no more than minimal risk to the privacy of individuals; 2) the research could not be practicably conducted without the waiver; and 3) the research could not be conducted without access to and use of the PHI. (DHHS [45 CFR 164.501, 164.508, 164.512(i)]).

Many research investigations may be conducted without the use of PHI. Informatics or QI personnel can often provide a de-identified data set, which may not be considered research on human subjects by your IRB, eliminating the need for the approval process. Regardless of the details of your project, you should consider whether you need to access PHI and be prepared to answer questions regarding this usage from your IRB.

Design and Evaluation

Designing a low impact research methodology takes more than deciding to collect data from the EHR or using data from an ongoing QI process for research purposes; care must be taken to choose a feasible research design and evaluation strategy. Although randomized controlled trials are considered the gold standard of research, they can be costly, time consuming, confusing, and not well-liked by providers or participants. Additionally, there are many examples in which it is not possible, or would be unethical, to randomly assign participants to different groups. In order to increase buy-in from administrators and providers, choose other rigorous, but less demanding designs.

Quasi-experimental designs evaluate interventions, but do not include randomization. A commonly used quasi-experiment is the prettest-posttest design. In this design outcomes are evaluated prior to and following an intervention. Adding a control group to your design reduces threats to validity, but is not always possible in a clinical setting. It may be possible to compare a non-equivalent group in another part of the practice or organization who were not exposed to the intervention.

Stepped wedge designs are another alternative to individual randomization. In the stepped wedge design, providers (or units or clusters) are randomly assigned to an *order* and assigned a step based on that order. Units are measured over time, with more units added to the intervention as time progresses. In the first time block all units are in the control phase, but by the end of the study all units will have received the intervention. The advantages to a stepped wedge design include: 1) alleviates some ethical concerns as all groups eventually receive the treatment and it is not removed part way through the study; 2) efficiency, as units act as their own controls, so fewer units are needed; 3) it is possible to study effects over time on intervention effectiveness; and 4) may be logistically or financially attractive to not introduce an intervention to all units at once.

Dissemination

Research efforts are only as valuable as they are useful. It has been demonstrated that it takes an average of 17 years for research evidence to translate to clinical practice (Green, Ottoson, Garcia, & Hiatt, 2009; Morris, Wooding, & Grant, 2011; Westfall, Mold, & Fagnan, 2007), a finding that supports the "imperative" of dissemination of findings. This chapter has focused on asking relevant research questions for the endpoint, and dissemination of those findings should "speak" to those at the endpoint (who might readily adopt demonstrated practices or interventions). For fellow clinicians, publish in newsletters, websites and training initiatives, taking care to include tools, work flows, or templates. Providing practical resources for applying evidence-based practices increases the likelihood of uptake. There are several excellent resources and toolkits to assist with planning application and dissemination of findings (AHRQ *www.ahrq.gov/professionals/quality-patient-safety/patient-safety-resources/resources/advances-in-patient-safety/vol4/planningtool.html*; PHCRIS *www.phcris.org.au/guides/dissemination.php*; UCSF *https://accelerate.ucsf.edu/research/community-pubs*).

The product of work in a clinical setting should also "speak" to scientists working in other places on the translational bridge who can utilize the new knowledge to develop interventions or study causes in a way that is more sensitive to the "real world" needs identified in your work. While most researchers are familiar with traditional academic dissemination outlets, such as peer-reviewed journals and professional conference presentations, deGruy et al. (2015) recommend tailoring your message to specific audiences and seeking alternative dissemination means to accompany publications, such as social media, public relations experts, and impact statements. Interprofessional collaboration can also be helpful to get your findings to a broader audience. In addition to traditional mental health journals and conferences, your interprofessional colleagues may know of alternative conferences and journals to which to submit your work.

Conferences focusing on practice improvement are excellent venues for this type of work. You may be able to put several different "spins" on your work for different audiences, resulting in multiple publications from one project. Collaborating with colleagues can also reduce the burden of writing. Leveraging interprofessional colleagues' discipline specific knowledge adds value to the final product.

Becoming the Clinician-Scientist

While this paper argued for many efficiencies and overlap in the conduct of research in primary care, there are several activities that the clinician-scientist must engage for which there is no apparent return on investment in a primary care environment. For many individuals, this work is simply a passion they follow for personal reasons, working on papers, data analyses, or collaboration with other researchers during their time outside work. Depending on the specific contingencies in your practice, however, you may be able to creatively negotiate protected time to do engage these activities. For example, to the extent that your research has a strong overlap with the targets of clinical operations, implementation outcomes may serve as data for use in ACO reporting. You may even be able to demonstrate a return on investment for your time on implementation projects that drive efficiencies, making a case for more protected time to do such work. In addition, you may consider partnering with research-focused agents outside your clinic. University partnerships, for example, can be particularly symbiotic. Alternately, you may be able to enhance your research efforts by joining a practice-based research network (PBRN; see chapter on this topic in this book). Primary care PBRNs focus on answering questions central to primary care clinical practice. Increasingly PBRNS are supporting quality improvement activities. The Agency for Healthcare Research and Quality (AHRQ) has stated that PBRNs are "uniquely positioned for dissemination and implementation research," (AHRQ, 2012). Joining a PBRN may allow others to do the heavy lifting of data collection and evaluation, while providing you with experience implementing a research project in your practice. Some PBRNs provide staff support in the form of practice facilitators or practice enhancement assistants to assist with research consultation, implementation, and data collection.

References

Agency for Healthcare Research and Quality. (2012, December). Primary care practice-based research networks. Retrieved from: www.ahrq.gov/research/findings/factsheets/primary/pbrn/index.html

Beacham, A. O., Kinman, C., Harris, J. G., & Masters, K. S. (2012). The patient-centered medical home: Unprecedented workforce growth potential for professional psychology. *Professional Psychology: Research and Practice, 43*(1), 17–23.

Berwick, D. M., Nolan, T. W., & Whittington, J. (2008). The triple aim: Care, health, and cost. *Health Affairs, 27*(3), 759–769.

Brawer, P. A., Martielli, R., Pye, P. L., Manwarning, J., & Tierney, A. (2010). St. Louis initiative for integrated care excellence (SLI²CE): Integrated-collaborative care on a large scale model. *Families, Systems, & Health, 28,* 175–187.

Brown, C. H., Curran, G., Palinkas, L. A., Aarons, G. A., Wells, K. B., Jones, L., . . . Cruden, G. (2017). An overview of research and evaluation designs for dissemination and implementation. *Annual Review of Public Health, 38*(1), null.

Brown, C. H., Smith, J. D., Villamar, J. A., & Benbow, N. (2016, December). *Implementation Science: An Introductory workshop for researchers, clinicians, policy makers, and community members.* Workshop conducted in collaboration between the Center for Prevention Implementation Methodology for Drug Abuse and HIV and the Third Coast Center for AIDS Research, Chicago, IL.

Brownson, R. C., Colditz, G. A., & Proctor, E. K. (2012). *Dissemination and Implementation Research in Health: Translating Science to Practice.* New York: Oxford Press.

Charach, A., Carson, P., Fox, S., Ali, M. U., Beckett, J., & Lim, C. G. (2013). Interventions for preschool children at high risk for ADHD: A comparative effectiveness review. *Pediatrics, 131,* e1584; originally published online April 1, 2013.

Chambers, D. A. & Norton, W. E. (2016). The adaptome: Advancing the science of intervention adaptation. *American Journal of Preventative Medicine, 51*(42S), S124–S131.

Chambers, D. A., Wang, P. S., & Insel, T. R. (2010). Maximizing efficiency and impact in effectiveness and services research. *General Hospital Psychiatry, 32*(5), 453–455.

Chiles, J. A., Lambert, M. J., & Hatch, A. L. (1999). The impact of psychological interventions on medical cost offset: A meta-analytic review. *Clinical Psychology Science and Practice, 6,* 204–220.

Claridge, J. A. & Fabian, T. C. (2005). History and development of evidence-based medicine. *World Journal of Surgery, 29,* 547–553.

deGruy, F. V., Ewigman, B., DeVoe, J. E., Hughes, L., James, P., Schneider, D., . . . Peek, C. J. (2015). A plan for useful and timely family medicine and primary care research. *Family Medicine, 47*(8), 636–642.

Dodge, K. A. (2011). Context matters in child and family policy. *Child Development, 82,* 433–442.

Fabiano, G. A., Pelham, Jr., W. E., Coles, E. K., Gnagy, E. M., Chronis-Tuscano, A., & O'Connor, B. C. (2009). A meta-analysis of behavioral treatments for attention-deficit/hyperactivity disorder. *Clinical Psychology Review, 29,* 129–140.

Felker, B. L., Barnes, R. F., Greenberg, D. M., Chaney, E. F., Shores, M. M., Gillespie-Gateley, L., . . . Morton, C. E. (2004). Preliminary outcomes from an integrated mental health primary care team. *Psychiatric Services, 55,* 442–444.

Funderburk, J. S., Fielder, R. L., DeMartini, K. S., & Flynn, C. A. (2012). Integrating behavioral health services into a university health center: Patient and provider satisfaction. *Families, Systems & Health, 30,* 130–140.

Funderburk, J. S., Sugarman, D. E., Maisto, S. A., Ouimette, P., Schohn, M., Lantinga, L., . . . Strutynski, K. (2010). The description and evaluation of the implementation of an integrated healthcare model. *Families, Systems & Health, 28,* 146–160.

Glasgow, R. E., Vogt, T. M., & Boles, S. M. (1999). Evaluating the public health impact or health promotion interventions: The RE-AIM framework. *American Journal of Public Health, 89,* 1322–1327.

Goodheart, C. D. (2010). Economics and psychology practice: What we need to know and why. *Professional Psychology: Research and Practice, 41*(3), 189–195.

Gouge, N., Polaha, J., Rogers, R., & Harden, A. (2016). Integrating behavioural health into pediatric primary care: Implications for provider time and cost. *Southern Medical Journal, 109*(12), 774–778.

Green, L. W., Ottoson, J. M., Garcia, C., & Hiatt, R. A. (2009). Diffusion theory and knowledge dissemination, utilization, and integration in public health. *Annual Review of Public Health, 30,* 151–174.

Greenhalgh, R., Robert, G., MacFarlane, R., Bate, P., & Kriakidou, O. (2004). Diffusion of innovations in service organizations; Systematic review and recommendations. *Milbank Quarterly, 82,* 581–629.

Hoagwood, K. & Olin, S. S. (2002). The NIMH blueprint for change report: Research priorities in child and adolescent mental health. *Journal of the American Academy of Child and Adolescent Psychiatry, 41,* 760–767.

Hoffman, S. G. & Smits, J. A. (2008). Cognitive-behavioral therapy for adult anxiety disorders: A meta-analysis of randomized placebo-controlled trials. *Journal of Clinical Psychiatry, 69,* 621–632.

Hunter, C. L., Funderburk, J. S., Polaha, J., Bauman, D., Goodie, J. L., & Hunter, C. M. (2017). Primary Care Behavioral Health Model (PCBH) research: Current state of the science and a call to action. *Clinical Psychology in Medical Settings.* Online only. https://doi.org/10.1007/sl0880-017-9512-0.

Jacob, M. K., Larson, J. C., & Craighead, W. E. (2012). Establishing a telepsychiatry consultation practice in rural Georgia for primary care physicians: A feasibility report. *Clinical Pediatrics, 51,* 1041–1047.

Kessler, R. (2015). Evaluating the process of mental health and primary care integration: The Vermont Integration Profile. *Family Medicine and Community Health, 3*(1), 63–65.

Kessler, R. L., Purcelll, E. P., Glasgow, R, E., Klesges, L, M., Benkeser, R. M., & Peek, C. J. (2013). What does it mean to "employ" the RE-AIM model? *Evaluation & the Health Professions, 36*(1), 44–66.

Klesges, L. M., Estabrooks, P. A., Glasgow, R. E., & Dzewaltowski, D. (2005). Beginning with the application in mind: Designing and planning health behavior change interventions to enhance dissemination. *Annals of Behavioral Medicine, 29,* 66S-75S.

Kolko, D. J. & Perrin, E. (2014). The integration of behavioral health interventions in children's health care: Services, science, and suggestions. *Journal of Clinical Child and Adolescent Psychology, 43*(2), 216–218.

Kroenke, K., Spitzer, R. L., & Williams, J. B., (2001). The PHQ-9: Validity of a brief depression severity measure. *Journal of General Internal Medicine, 16*(9), 606–613.

Miller, B. F., Mendenhall, T. J., & Malik, A. D. (2009). Integrated primary care: An inclusive three-world view through process metrics and empirical discrimination. *Journal of Clinical Psychology in Medical Settings, 16*(1), 21–30.

Miller, W., Munoz, R., & Christensen, C. (November, 2010). *Expanding evidence based psychological services: From traditional therapy to self-help books to internet interventions.* Clinical Round Table presented at the annual meeting of the Association for Behavioral and Cognitive Therapies. San Francisco, CA.

Morris, Z. S., Wooding, S., & Grant, J. (2011). The answer is 17 years, what is the question: Understanding time lags in translational research. *Journal of the Royal Society of Medicine, 104*(12), 510–520.

Nash, J. M., Khatri, P., Cubic, B. A., & Baird, M. A. (2013). Essential competencies for psychologists in patient centered medical homes. *Professional Psychology: Research and Practice, 44*(5), 331–342.

Peek, C. J. (2008). Planning care in the clinical, operational, and financial worlds. In *Collaborative Medicine Case Studies* (pp. 25–38). Springer: New York.

Peek, C. J. (2013). Lexicon for behavioral health and primary care integration: Concepts and definitions developed by expert consensus. *AHRQ Publication* No. AHRQ 13-IP001-EF.

Peek, C. J., Cohen, D. J., & deGruy, F. V. (2014). Research and evaluation in the transformation of primary care. *American Psychologist, 69*(4), 430–442.

Polaha, J. & Nolan (2014). Dissemination and implementation science: research for the real world medical family therapist. In J. Hodgson, T. Mendenhall, & A. Lamson (Eds.) *Medical Family Therapy*. Switzerland: Springer International.

Polaha, J., Williams, S. L., Heflinger, C. A., & Studts, C. R. (2015). The perceived stigma of mental health services among rural parents of children with psychosocial concerns. *Journal of Pediatric Psychology, 40*(10), 1095–1104.

Proctor, E. K., Landsverk, J. A., Aarons, G. A., Chambers, D., Glisson, C., & Mittman, B. (2009). Implementation research in mental health services: An emerging science with conceptual, methodological, and training challenges. *Administration and Policy in Mental Health and Mental Health Services Research, 36*(1), 24–34.

Proctor, E. K., Silmere, H., Raghavan, R., Hovmand, P., Aarons, G. A., Bunger, A., ... Hensley, M. (2011). Outcomes for implementation research: Conceptual distinctions, measurement challenges, and research agenda. *Administration and Policy in Mental Health and Mental Health Services Research, 38*(2), 65–76.

Rabin, B. A., Lewis, C. C., Norton, W. E., Neta, G., Chambers, D., Tobin, J. N., Brownson, R. C., & Glasgow, R. E. (2016). Measurement resources for dissemination and implementation research in health. *Implementation Science, 11*, 42.

Runyan, C., Fonseca, V. P., Meyer, J. G., Oordt, M. S., & Talcott, G. W. (2003). A novel approach for mental health disease management: The Air Force Medical Service's interdisciplinary model. *Disease Management, 6*, 179–187.

Schoenwald, S. K., Mehta, T. G., Frazier, S. L., & Shernoff, E. S. (2013). Clinical supervision in effectiveness and implementation research. *Clinical Psychology: Science and Practice, 20*(1), 44–59.

Smith, J. D. & Polaha, J. (2017). Using implementation science to guide the integration of evidence-based family interventions into primary care. *Families, Systems, & Health, 35*(2), 125–135.

Sussman, S., Valente, T. W., Rohrbach, L. A., Skara, S., & Pentz, M. A. (2006). Translation in the health professions: Converting science into action. *Evaluation & the Health Professions, 29*(1), 7–32.

Westfall, J. M., Mold, J., & Fagnan, L. (2007). Practice-based research – "Blue Highways" on the NIH Roadmap. *Journal of the American Medical Association, 297*(4), 403–406.

Working Party Group on Integrated Behavioral Healthcare (2014). The development of joint principles: Integrating behavioral health care into the patient-centered medical home. *Annals of Family Medicine, 12*(2), 183.

Zerhouni, E. (2003). The NIH Roadmp. *Science, 302*(5642), 63–72.

CHAPTER 12

Research in Partial Hospital Settings

*Marie Forgeard, Courtney Beard,
Norik Kirakosian, and Thröstur Björgvinsson*

Partial hospitals provide an intermediate level of care for patients needing intensive treatment beyond what can be offered in outpatient settings. A partial hospital program (PHP) is defined by the code of federal regulations as "a time-limited, ambulatory, active treatment program that offers therapeutically intensive, coordinated, and structured clinical services within a stable therapeutic milieu" (Office of the Federal Register, 2005, p. 172). PHPs are generally based at hospitals or community mental health centers. Partial hospitals were designed to provide care in lieu of inpatient hospitalization and, therefore, address two needs. First, when patients are "stepped up" from outpatient care delivered in the community following worsening of symptoms, PHPs provide timely services to help avoid a crisis and inpatient hospitalization. Second, when patients are "stepped down" from inpatient hospitalization, PHPs can help further stabilize symptoms and prevent relapse (Leung, Drozd, & Maier, 2009). To be eligible for partial level of care, patients must not pose immediate risks to themselves or others. They are, however, at high risk for worsening or relapse of acute symptoms, and their concerns often include non-immediate risks to themselves or other (e.g., patients with moderately severe passive suicidal ideation without immediate intent or plan to harm themselves). PHPs therefore provide an important "bridge" level of care that allows patients to maintain independence and return home at the end of the day, while also receiving intensive treatment and support.

To achieve the goals of stabilization and transition to outpatient treatment, PHPs provide intensive day treatment in a structured fashion. Although PHPs may differ in the kind of care provided, patients' days are typically organized with a schedule that incorporates a number of therapeutic modalities including case management, individual therapy, group therapy, and consultations with psychopharmacologists and other providers (e.g., occupational therapists, vocational counselors, etc.) (Commission on Accreditation of Rehabilitation Facilities, 2016). Treatment may be delivered by a range of mental health providers, including psychiatrists, psychologists, social workers, licensed mental health counselors, community residence counselors, and trainees.

Why Conduct Research in Partial Hospitals?

Although there are currently over 400 partial hospitals operating in the United States, and although these provide services at a critical junction in the care provided for patients suffering from psychopathology, these settings remain relatively understudied (Kiser et al., 2010). Clinicians who work at PHPs may be interested in conducting research for a number of important reasons. First, incorporating a research infrastructure will help with effective and informative program evaluation. As explained below, informing clinical practice with structured measures of relevant clinical characteristics (such as symptom severity and psychosocial functioning) as well as treatment response can provide evidence for or against the effectiveness of implemented interventions, and highlight directions for enhancing treatment at both individual and group levels. Second, patients presenting for treatment at PHPs often have heterogeneous and comorbid psychiatric concerns. These features make them a unique sample in which to study psychopathology and generate new knowledge regarding psychiatric heterogeneity and comorbidity. Third, considering that individuals in partial care represent two acute clinical populations (individuals stepping up from community care, and those recently discharged from inpatient units), research in this setting can help generate important clinical knowledge on what constitutes effective treatment at this critical junction specifically. Because existing research in PHPs is limited, future scholarship in this area will not only help improve intervention strategies targeting the specific needs of this clinically understudied population, but also help update the literature on acute psychopathology and high-risk populations in general (for reviews of research conducted in PHPs see Horvitz-Lennon, Normand, Gaccione, & Frank, 2001; Ogrodniczuk & Piper, 2001; Schene, 2004; Zipfel et al., 2002). For these reasons, conducting research in partial hospital settings provides an interesting window into factors that predict and foster crisis stabilization during a period of high risk for relapse and re-hospitalization (Beard et al., 2016).

In the present chapter, we review practical considerations for setting up a research infrastructure within partial hospital settings, drawing on our experience conducting research at McLean Hospital's Behavioral Health Partial Hospital Program (BHP). We begin by providing a brief description of the program, its setup, and logistics for conducting research. We then detail how the research infrastructure can be integrated into the clinical care provided, by organizing treatment around evidence-based principles. Additionally, we provide information about how specific research projects can be designed and carried out, and discuss examples of projects successfully conducted at the BHP. We end by discussing potential obstacles that may be encountered in the process of conducting research in partial hospital settings, and propose solutions we have used to overcome them.

Setting up a Research Infrastructure

Program Description

The Behavioral Health Partial Hospital Program (BHP) at McLean Hospital provides intensive treatment for adults (18 years and older) experiencing acute symptoms of psychopathology, including symptoms of mood, anxiety, personality, psychotic, and substance use disorders. Patients attend the program five days a week from 8:30am to 3pm, with a one hour break for lunch from 12 to 1pm. Treatment consists of case management (provided by a Clinical Team Manager who coordinates services and plans aftercare), group therapy, individual skills-based therapy, psychopharmacology consultation, and other appointments as needed (occupational therapy, vocational counseling, etc.). Our team consists of clinical psychologists and psychology trainees, including practicum students, doctoral interns, and post-doctoral fellows, social workers, psychiatrists, nurses, and bachelor-level counselors. Multiple groups are offered every hour to meet the needs of a diverse patient population; approximately 100 groups are offered per week, with the number of individuals per group ranging from two to 20 (group sizes are determined based on content; for example, core cognitive-behavioral skills groups typically have a large number of participants while groups geared towards individuals actively experiencing psychotic symptoms are much smaller).

Approximately 50 percent of patients in our program are "stepped up" by providers from the community; the other 50 percent are "stepped down" from inpatient hospitalization and use the BHP for further stabilization of symptoms before returning to outpatient care. The BHP admits approximately 850 patients per year. As an example, from December 2015 to July 2016, the average number of days from admission to discharge (including weekend days) at the BHP was 12 ($SD = 5$). Examination of demographic information showed the following patient profile. The BHP patient population is predominately White (85 percent), well-educated (51 percent have a four-year college degree), and approximately half are female (52 percent). Half are unemployed, and most are single/never married (65 percent). The average number of prior psychiatric hospitalizations is two, and approximately one-third of patients are categorized as being at high risk for suicide (defined as thoughts of specific suicide plans, difficulties restraining oneself from suicidal impulses, and suicidal gestures or attempts in the past month). Our patient population presents with high levels of acuity and comorbidity (determined by a structured interview, as described below). Approximately three quarters of individuals admitted to the BHP present within the context of a Major Depressive Episode (full blown or in partial remission); 57 percent also meet criteria for Major Depressive Disorder, 25 percent for Bipolar Disorder (20 percent Bipolar I, 5 percent Bipolar II). At the time of admission, 42 percent of patients also meet criteria for current Generalized Anxiety Disorder, 35 percent for Social Anxiety Disorder, 21 percent for panic disorder, 18 percent for Alcohol Dependence or Abuse, 16 percent for Posttraumatic Stress Disorder, 11 percent for Obsessive-Compulsive Disorder, 8 percent for Body Dysmorphic Disorder, and 6 percent for a Psychotic Disorder (including schizophrenia, delusional disorder, schizoaffective disorder, etc.). In our patient population, comorbidity is the rule, not the exception: 70 percent of our patient population meets criteria for two or more of the disorders listed above.

Treatment Philosophy

Our treatment philosophy, which is founded upon evidence-based principles, sets the stage for the integration of clinical practice and research. Patients learn about, and practice, skills from empirically supported modalities of treatment including Cognitive-Behavioral Therapy (CBT; Beck, Rush, Shaw, & Emery, 1979), Dialectical Behavior Therapy (DBT; Linehan, 1993), and Acceptance and Commitment Therapy (ACT; Hayes, Strosahl, & Wilson, 2012). Examples of skills include behavioral activation, cognitive restructuring, self-assessment, mindfulness, distress tolerance, emotion regulation, and interpersonal effectiveness (among others). Patients are introduced to these skills in a way that encourages them to emulate the scientific approach. For example, patients are encouraged to practice self-assessment by collecting data about their own symptoms (e.g., monitoring mood and activity levels at regular intervals using a worksheet designed for this purpose) in order to increase awareness of factors promoting or impeding their mental health. Patients are also encouraged to conduct behavioral experiments to assess how activities affect mood and cognitions, and to record prior expectations and evidence obtained during behavioral experiments. In summary, using empirically supported principles provides an excellent opportunity to not only deliver the best care available within the context of a brief program, but also to familiarize patients with the importance of thinking about their own treatment using a scientific approach.

Managing the Research Team and Research Projects

Our approach to managing research activities is grounded in our understanding of the challenges and opportunities presented by the integration of research and clinical practice. Our research mission informs our clinical care both in the short-run and in the long-run, and nurtures the talents of young clinical scientists. Given that our team members have important time constraints, we offer them the autonomy to carry out independent projects and complete research-related activities within flexible timeframes, while at the same time ensuring close regular supervision and guidance. In our experience, this careful balance between providing autonomy and support leads to the best outcomes, both in terms of training and productivity. For example, we have noticed that goals that are too ambitious or rigid lead to unnecessary anxiety for trainees who are juggling other important responsibilities. However, goals that are too imprecise (or absent) also lead to frustration if trainees do not find a way to prioritize their research activities. Thus, realistic goals help ensure that adequate progress is made, and that project leaders are able to ask for the guidance they need at every step.

Our team maintains a flow of research projects by meeting once a week to discuss progress and address pressing issues. Once a month, we also review a project list which summarizes all data collection efforts (as described below) as well as manuscripts in preparation. A regular meeting allows the team to discuss progress, adjust expectations for balancing clinical and research duties, and provide support and help with projects. Our research team includes members with a wide range of experience, and mentorship of younger clinicians/researchers is a very important component of our approach. The Director and Assistant Director of Research lead and plan research efforts. The post-doctoral fellow also plays an important role in deciding major directions for the research agenda during their fellowship. The research coordinator assists with all efforts and is first in line to maintain the integrity of the data collected. Doctoral interns and practicum students participate in research by meeting with members of the research team to propose projects, develop them, and carry them out (sometimes as part of their dissertation work, sometimes as additional independent projects). Volunteer undergraduate research students also provide important support with activities such as data entry, participant recruitment and data collection for ancillary studies.

Regular meetings and supervision for all individuals is important to maintain a cohesive team. Our research benefits from this highly collaborative approach. To maintain enthusiasm, all students are encouraged to work on their own projects (poster presentations or manuscripts depending on current knowledge, interest, and involvement) alongside their support activities within the research program. Our program has been very productive in publishing findings from our setting: since 2010, we have published 40 manuscripts in peer-reviewed journals, have another ten under review, 12 in preparation, and more than 100 conference presentations (symposia and posters).

Carrying out Data Collection and Research Activities

Data Collection

Data are collected in several ways, through (1) daily progress monitoring, (2) a structured diagnostic assessment, (3) extraction of information from clinical charts and (4) ancillary studies. We explain below how these serve the purpose of both treatment planning and research. Patients are provided with information about our treatment philosophy and about the purpose of data collection efforts during their initial orientation with a counselor when they start the program. Counselors also offer patients the option of providing informed consent for their clinical data to be used for research purposes. All data collection procedures (including administration setup and specific measures) are approved by our institution's Institutional Review Board (IRB). Any changes in these procedures are reflected in amendments to our research protocols.

Progress Monitoring

Patients are asked to complete surveys every day during their stay in the program. The primary purpose of progress monitoring is to monitor their symptoms. Our program has designated a room only used for this purpose. This room contains 6–8 laptop computers so that several patients can complete surveys at the same time. Data is collected through REDCap, a secure and HIPAA-compliant survey-administration platform (Research Electronic Data Capture; Harris et al., 2009). Clinical team managers obtain patients' scores in real time through the use of automated reports that can be downloaded from a shared secure server.

Given the demands that are put on our staff that are involved in providing clinical care, we have learned through experience that it is imperative to have one person (either part- or full-time) assigned to data collection and management—or as we like to call it, to preserve the integrity of the data. Hence, the BHP has one full-time staff member who serves as the main person in charge of data collection and management. This research coordinator is the first point of contact with all patients during the day, and patients report great benefit in the simple interaction of being greeted by the same welcoming person every day, in addition to having the opportunity to practice self-assessment through progress monitoring.

ADMISSION AND DISCHARGE MEASURES

On their first day in the program (admission) patients fill out a 30-minute survey that enables us to provide a comprehensive assessment of their current symptom severity on a number of important dimensions. The length of the survey was determined through iterations—we have found that our patients can tolerate up to 200 items at one time point, although there are individual differences. We utilize a core measure battery (approximately 100 items) which forms the foundation of the clinical summary reports that aid with treatment planning. In addition, we rotate in and out another 100 items every three to four months. This allows us to attempt to answer different relevant and interesting research questions, as well as to engage our trainees (who rotate through our program each year) by enabling them to incorporate assessments of constructs of interest to them. This is a unique system that can truly be useful in any PHP research program, as we have found this approach to be inclusive, generative and rewarding.

Our primary measures are the Patient Health Questionnaire 9 (PHQ-9; Kroenke, Spitzer, & Williams, 2001) to assess current symptoms of depression, and the Generalized Anxiety Disorder Questionnaire 7 (GAD-7; Spitzer et al., 2006) to assess current symptoms of anxiety. Patients also complete the Behavior and Symptom Identification Scale (BASIS-24; Cameron et al., 2007), a scale that assesses symptoms and functioning in six domains: depression/functioning, relationships, psychosis, emotional lability, self-harm, and substance use. Patients also complete the Mental Health Continuum—Short Form (MHC-SF; Lamers, Westerhof, Bohlmeijer, ten Klooster, & Keyes, 2011) to assess well-being. Other measures include the McLean Screening Instrument for Borderline Personality

Disorder (MSI-BPD; Zanarini et al., 2003), the Inventory of Statement about Self-Injury (ISAS; Klonsky & Glenn, 2009), as well as the Childhood Trauma Questionnaire (CTQ; Bernstein et al., 2003). These were selected following literature reviews and clinician feedback about the type of information that is most important and useful for the purpose of treatment planning. As explained below, we utilize REDCap to create automated reports that flag high risk issues (such as suicidal ideation) and summarizes results of core measures effectively (see Appendices A and B for examples of reports).

On the day of discharge, patients complete most of those measures again as a gauge of how much symptoms have changed, and in addition answer questions about their perceptions of the care they received, as well as how much they think they improved as a result of treatment (among other measures). Patients also complete other rotating measures depending on ongoing research projects; all research projects are carefully selected so that they have the potential to improve clinical care (see below for examples of completed projects).

DAILY PROGRESS MONITORING MEASURES

One of the main advantages of conducting research in a PHP is the opportunity to track symptoms every single day while patients are engaging in intensive treatment. Thus, finding ways to track symptom trajectories (and potential predictors and/or mechanisms of change) allows researchers to best capitalize on the richness of the data available in naturalistic clinical settings. To ensure patient acceptability as well as practical feasibility, daily progress monitoring surveys are much shorter than those completed at admission and discharge.

Every day the patients attend our program (except the first and last day, as described above), they fill out a five-minute survey between 8:30 and 9am (before the first group starts) that mainly assesses primary symptoms of depression and anxiety (using the PHQ-9 and the GAD-7, as described above), as well as levels of suicidal ideation (using item nine of the PHQ-9). These short, validated instruments are used to facilitate efficient daily assessment of patients' severity of symptoms and level of functioning. A standardized and efficient assessment is particularly important in a partial hospital setting because of the high volume and brief length of stay, as well as the high severity and comorbidity of the patient population served.

Structured Diagnostic Interviews

Clinical assessment by a multidisciplinary competent clinical team is a cornerstone of most PHP programs. At the BHP, we employ a rigorous and comprehensive evaluation approach implemented by an experienced team led by a psychiatrist and a case manager. We added a reliable structured interview to the assessment for two reasons. First, a structured interview enhances the validity of our clinical assessment and makes sure previously undisclosed or unknown areas of concerns are revealed. Second, a structured interview serves important research purposes, by allowing us to characterize all of the diagnoses for a patient (rather than only the primary diagnosis assigned by the treatment team) and to write research papers where we can verify that our structured diagnostic evaluation of our patients corresponds to the team's diagnosis. This was an important challenge to implement in our program, but we folded this into the standard program therapy that is provided by our psychology trainees.

In the first individual program therapy meeting, usually on their second day in the program, the patient completes the *Mini International Neuropsychiatric Interview* (MINI; Sheehan et al., 1998) administered by a clinician. The MINI is a structured interview assessing for DSM-IV Axis I disorders. We have continued to use the DSM-IV version of the MINI after the publication of the DSM-5 to ensure continuity of diagnostic procedures for ongoing research projects. However, as these projects end, we are now transitioning to the most recent version of the MINI, which assesses for DSM-5 disorders (Sheehan et al. 2015). The MINI is administered by interns and doctoral practicum students in clinical psychology who receive weekly supervision by a postdoctoral fellow. Training includes reviewing administration manuals and completing mock interviews. All clinicians are required to pass a final training interview with their supervisor before administering MINIs for the program. MINI raters meet bi-annually to rate an audio recording of a MINI interview. The MINI has strong reliability and validity in relation to the Structured Clinical Interview for DSM-IV (SCID-IV; First et al., 1997), with inter-rater reliabilities ranging from *kappas* of .89–1.0 (Sheehan et al., 1998). The MINI was chosen in order to balance coverage of a number of different disorders in a relatively short period of time. Administration of the MINI generally ranges from 20 to 60 minutes in our program.

Clinical Chart Information

The program records and aggregates data pertaining to treatment that may be used for research purposes (in addition to program evaluation). Information recorded includes referral source (e.g., inpatient unit), discharge outcome (e.g., planned discharge, inpatient hospitalization), medication changes made as a result of psychopharmacology consultations with psychiatrists, number and types of groups attended, height, weight, and blood pressure at admission, primary diagnosis assigned by the psychiatrist.

Ancillary Studies

Patients may enroll in optional research studies conducted by our team outside of program hours (e.g., at lunch time or after 3pm). Studies include investigations of adjunctive treatments, collaborative and multi-site research, and other studies covering the range of interests of members of the research and clinical teams. Ancillary studies typically involve computerized or behavioral tests and/or additional questionnaires that were not administered during progress monitoring. These studies may also use data from the progress monitoring surveys.

Uses of Data Collected

The BHP utilizes data collected to benefit (1) the individual patient by informing treatment planning and monitoring progress, (2) the BHP and future patients by facilitating program evaluation and development, and (3) the broader scientific and clinical community by answering important research questions.

Treatment Planning and Progress Monitoring

The data collected are first used for the clinical purpose of informing treatment. In and of itself, a patient's ability to complete assessments and their adherence with daily progress monitoring can be clinically informative. For example, factors including the speed and rate of completion, along with other observations made by the research coordinator during progress monitoring can provide information regarding a patient's levels of motivation, anxiety, and/or cognitive functioning.

Once admission assessments are completed, REDCap automatically generates a summary report for each patient, which the clinical team managers review and discuss regularly during rounds with the patients' treatment team. We use data from these reports in a dynamic fashion: reports are updated daily with current symptom levels, and are projected on a large screen during clinical rounds, allowing the entire treatment team to incorporate these data into case conceptualization and treatment planning. Two versions of these summary reports become part of the patient's medical record, namely the admission report and the discharge report which summarizes each patient's symptom trajectory during treatment (see Appendices A and B). The research coordinator also promptly informs clinical team managers of urgent concerns that are flagged automatically on the reports (e.g., an increase in suicidal ideation). Admission screening measures alert the treatment team to clinical issues that may need further assessment (e.g., substance use). Daily scores from the PHQ-9 (including suicidal ideation) and GAD-7 are presented in graph form so the clinical team can see symptom trajectories and adjust treatment as needed. For example, additional appointments may be scheduled to check in with someone experiencing a sudden increase in symptoms; a patient may be asked to attend a group addressing current immediate concerns; additional risk assessments may be conducted to determine if a person might need to be hospitalized, etc. Patients have access to their scores, and these can form the basis for fruitful discussions with their clinical team managers and individual program therapists. Finally, clinicians often find other ways to use these patient-reported data, such as using depression scores and suicide risk in negotiation with insurance companies or to help explain the patient's current clinical status to a family member.

On the flip side, some patients also report they find completing these measures helpful. Patients generally report understanding the purpose of a "daily check-in" and appreciate having a structured way to practice self-assessment. Seeing their data displayed graphically, and getting to review it with their clinicians can also be beneficial. Sometimes, incremental change may be occurring, and patients may not recognize it before discussing results of their assessments with the team; this process therefore validates their efforts and can instill hope. Moreover, reviewing the results of assessment through psychoeducation is a valuable form of intervention in itself.

Results from the structured interviews are communicated back to the treatment team on the second day of treatment and are the basis for a separate initial evaluation. The diagnostic information provided by the MINI can then be compared to the "program diagnosis" assigned by the psychiatrist and the clinical team manager on the first day of treatment (before the MINI is conducted). We have found adequate inter-reliability between MINI diagnoses and program diagnoses (Kertz, Bigda-Peyton, Rosmarin, & Björgvinsson, 2012). In addition, findings from the structured interview often reveal areas of concern patients may not have disclosed to the treatment team, thus enhancing the assessment. These findings may also help with differential diagnoses questions faced by the treatment team.

Completing a comprehensive set of measures that covers a wide array of symptom domains and areas of functioning allows patients to feel better understood, and clinicians to better target interventions. Perhaps counter-intuitively, patients often report appreciating being asked sensitive questions during their admission survey, as they may not always have the opportunity to bring up all areas of concern in the context of short-term treatment, and sometimes feel more comfortable answering a survey on the computer than sharing this sensitive information face to face. Thus, although patients will often work with their clinicians on addressing their most pressing concerns, they can still provide a more thorough and accurate picture of factors that may influence their acute concerns on our self-report measures. For instance, we have recently added the Childhood Trauma Questionnaire (CTQ; Bernstein et al., 2003) in our admission survey, as patients do not always share histories of childhood trauma, but such information is often very important in planning current and future treatment interventions.

Program Evaluation and Development

The data we collect help us evaluate the effectiveness of our program and determine whether the type of care we offer (short-term cognitive-behavioral treatment) shows reliable benefits for our patients. Although our naturalistic settings do not allow us to have a control group, we have been able to investigate the effectiveness of our program using a benchmarking strategy to compares changes seen in our sample with changes observed in randomized controlled trials (which can, through the use of control groups and random assignment, establish the efficacy of a treatment; see Bateman & Fonagy, 1999, 2008, for an example of a randomized controlled study in a PHP). Results indicate that our brief program leads to comparable and reliable improvements in depressive symptoms, worry, self-harm, emotional lability, substance abuse, interpersonal relationships, and well-being (Björgvinsson et al., 2014; see Harris et al., 2015; Thatte, Makinen, Nguyen, Hill, & Flament, 2013 for examples of program evaluation conducted in other PHPs).

In addition, we are currently examining effects of specific groups by administering questionnaires before and after a group of interest (e.g., to assess changes in affect or other psychological processes), as well as by looking at relationships between group attendance and treatment outcomes.

Additional projects (as further described below) complement these examinations of our program's effectiveness by investigating the role of predictors of treatment response, including demographic factors (e.g., age, sex, gender identity, sexual orientation, employment status, education level, disability status, etc.), symptom severity and type (e.g., severity of suicidal ideation), expectations for treatment, specific cognitions, alliance with the program, or use of cognitive-behavioral skills, among others. For example, we have found that LGBQ+ patients report being less satisfied with treatment overall, and show less improvement on some outcomes (Beard et al., 2017). Results of program evaluation such as these directly inform our approach to treatment. Thus, we have developed a new group designed to address issues surrounding patients' identities. Related to this, patient feedback obtained through our perceptions of care survey is reviewed quarterly by all program staff. We have, for example, created an introductory group about Dialectical Behavior Therapy (DBT) based on patient comments indicating that introductory information presented in other DBT informed groups felt repetitive.

Clinical Research

The main aim of our research program, as we assume is also true for any PHP research program, is to contribute knowledge on the nature of psychopathology and treatment outcomes as they unfold in naturalistic settings, where patients present with high levels of severity as well as comorbid concerns. As explained above, patients are given the opportunity to provide informed consent on their first day of treatment for their data to be used for research purposes. All patients complete the same set of progress monitoring measures regardless of their consent status, since data are used for clinical purposes as well. However, we only use de-identified data from patients that have provided informed consent giving us permission to use the data for research. Projects conducted for program evaluation purposes can however be given an exemption from informed consent from Institutional Review Boards. We provide here examples of projects carried out successfully within our research program as a template of some projects that could be successfully implemented in other PHP research programs.

UNDERSTANDING PSYCHOPATHOLOGY

Conducting research in practice settings provides invaluable insight into psychopathology in the real world. We are interested in the classification, assessment, and mechanisms underlying psychopathology.

PSYCHOMETRICS Large samples of individuals with high levels of symptomatology provide an excellent opportunity to validate measures used in other samples before. For example, our clinic has validated two measures used as screeners in primary care settings, the PHQ-9 and the GAD-7 (Beard & Björgvinsson, 2014; Beard, Hsu, Rifkin, Busch, & Björgvinsson, 2016; for an example of an instrument validation within a different day treatment setting, see Fergus et al., 2009). In addition to establishing the reliability and validity of these measures in a sample high in acuity and comorbidity, these psychometric studies also allowed us to establish the appropriateness of using modified versions of these measures to track patients' symptoms over time on a daily basis, and assess relationships between symptom changes and participation in intensive psychological treatment. Thus, this kind of research benefits both our program, and other programs that may need to use brief measures to track patient outcomes. We have also conducted similar psychometric studies to examine instruments assessing the use of empirically-supported skills during treatment. For example, our team has validated the use of the Dialectical Behavior Therapy Ways of Coping Checklist (Neacsiu, Rizvi, Vitaliano, Lynch, & Linehan, 2010), which showed adequate reliability, validity, and sensitivity to change in our heterogeneous sample of patients learning skills in different modalities (including DBT) (Stein, Hearon, Beard, Hsu, & Björgvinsson, 2016).

NETWORK ANALYSIS In contrast with the traditional psychometric approach, we have also been involved in projects that study new ways of understanding psychopathology by examining relationships (and possible causal influences) between symptoms. Traditional psychometric analyses such as the ones described above implicitly reflect a medical disease model, in which an underlying entity (e.g., "depression") causes observable symptoms (e.g., "sad mood," "decreased appetite," "insomnia"). Network analysis, a set of procedures based on the modeling of dynamical systems, turns this assumption on its head by instead proposing that symptoms co-occur not because they are caused by a similar root, but because they influence each other. Following the approach described by Borsboom and Cramer (2013; see also Cramer et al., 2010; McNally et al., 2014), we have recently examined relationships between symptoms of Major Depressive Disorder (MDD) and Generalized Anxiety Disorder (GAD) using data from the PHQ-9 and GAD-7. We found that individual symptoms of anxiety and depression were generally more related to other symptoms within each disorder (MDD and GAD) than between disorders, and that "sad mood" and "worry" were the symptoms that were most strongly connected to all other symptoms (i.e., the most "central" symptoms, in network analysis parlance). In addition, we found that the network structure was stable at admission and discharge, though the strength of the relationships between symptoms increased as symptom severity decreased over the course of treatment (Beard et al., 2016). As an example of implementing technology into clinical care, we are currently in the process of designing a longitudinal study that will utilize ecological momentary assessments (EMA) through smartphones and that will allow us to more closely look at the causal influence of symptoms on other symptoms over time. Such research can eventually help determine whether targeting certain symptoms in a particular individualized order may prove useful to address psychopathology strategically and effectively in the age of personalized medicine.

TRANSDIAGNOSTIC PROCESSES One of the main advantages of conducting research in naturalistic settings is access to a heterogeneous sample with high levels of acuity and comorbidity. Such a sample allows us to examine transdiagnostic processes that help maintain psychopathology across disorders, an initiative in line with the Research Domain Criteria (RDoC) put forward by NIMH (Insel et al., 2010). The RDoC framework encourages researchers to examine basic dimensions of functioning that cut across diagnostic categories using different levels of information or analysis (e.g., from genes, to cells, to behaviors, to self-reports, etc.). We are very interested in understanding transdiagnostic processes across disorders given that such processes may constitute strategically efficient targets for treatment, or to the development of transdiagnotic treatments (e.g., Barlow, Allen, & Choate, 2004; Mansell, Harvey, Watkins, & Shafran, 2009).

In a recent study, we found that the relationship between deficits in attentional control and symptoms of depression and anxiety was explained by increased rumination (i.e., the tendency to engage in repetitive thinking about self-relevant negative information or symptoms) (Hsu et al., 2015). In a related study, we found that improvements in repetitive negative thinking associated with cognitive-behavioral treatment accounted for a significant amount of improvements in depression and anxiety (Kertz et al., 2015). In another study, we found that reductions in distress intolerance (i.e., the perceived inability to manage negative emotional and somatic states) were associated with improvements in depression and anxiety symptoms (McHugh et al., 2014). These findings suggest that targeting processes such as repetitive negative thinking and distress intolerance may be especially important in order to best address comorbid psychopathology.

TREATMENT OUTCOMES

PREDICTORS OF TREATMENT OUTCOMES In addition to establishing the effectiveness of short-term cognitive-behavioral treatment in real-world settings (as described above), PHP research programs, provide a unique opportunity to better understand predictors of treatment outcomes. Such studies can help us understand what factors maximize the likelihood of treatment success, and what pre-existing characteristics may affect the degree to which individuals benefit from treatment (for examples of studies assessing predictors of treatment outcomes in other PHPs, see Drymalski & Washburn, 2011; Joyce, Ennis, O'Kelly, Ogrodniczuk, & Piper, 2009; Tasca et al., 2004). For example, in our program, we have found that higher treatment outcome expectations (i.e., believing that treatment will be helpful) and fewer past hospitalizations are associated with clinically significant improvements in depressive symptoms (Beard et al., 2016). We have also found that certain patient characteristics measured at baseline predict inpatient hospitalization (rather than discharge to outpatient care). Among patients stepped down from inpatient care, higher levels of suicidal ideation and psychotic symptoms predicted re-hospitalization. Among patients stepped up from outpatient care, higher levels of suicidal ideation and poor relationship functioning predicted hospitalization (Beard et al., 2016). Findings pertaining to suicidal ideation and psychotic symptoms were in line with expectations given the relevance of these variables to immediate risk considerations. Findings pertaining to relationship functioning were somewhat less intuitive and highlight the importance of taking into account patients' support systems and interpersonal stressors and skills when assessing patients.

We have also been interested in understanding the types of cognitions that are associated with treatment outcomes in our program. We have, for example, found that internalized stigma of mental illness (awareness of, and agreement with, negative stereotypes about mental illness) is associated with worse self-reported mental and physical health at the beginning of treatment; internalized stigma, however, decreases during brief treatment and this decrease is associated with improvements in outcomes (Pearl et al., 2017). Similarly, positive beliefs about mental illness (i.e., believing that one's illness is associated with advantages or positive consequences, such as increased imagination or strength) are associated with better treatment outcomes, with one exception: positive beliefs were associated with decreased emotional lability in all participants except those diagnosed with bipolar disorder (Forgeard et al., 2016).

In another study, we assessed whether the therapeutic alliance (in this case, defined as the relationship between a patient and the program) predicted depressive symptom improvement in our sample. Our findings indicated that, although the therapeutic alliance is related to treatment outcomes, improvements in the alliance tended to follow, rather than precede, symptom change (Webb et al., 2014). In other words, high levels of treatment alliance appeared to result from effective treatment, as opposed to predict it. Such research sheds light on factors at play in treatment effectiveness.

Finally, we have also examined whether self-reported changes in the use of specific skills learned in our program predict symptom improvement. We found that the use of behavioral activation strategies predicted improvement in depressive symptoms (especially for patients with high baseline levels of depression), while the use of Dialectical Behavior Therapy skills predicted improvements in anxiety symptoms (Webb et al., 2016). In contrast, the use of cognitive restructuring skills was not associated with outcomes. Such findings help us understand how treatment works, and what skills may be most beneficial for patients during their participation in short-term intensive treatment for acute psychopathology. For example, cognitive restructuring skills may be somewhat more complex to acquire and may require more time before benefits become apparent.

NOVEL INTERVENTION APPROACHES We have also been able to test the effectiveness of novel intervention approaches and determine which ones may be useful to incorporate in short-term treatment. We are for example testing whether repeated computerized training to address biased interpretations leads to enhanced treatment outcomes. Such research can help translate findings on the efficacy of cognitive bias modification to "real-world" settings. Preliminary findings from our sample already suggest that a brief daily interpretation training protocol might constitute an acceptable, feasible, and potentially useful adjunctive intervention during partial hospitalization. Such studies constitute a promising way to examine whether and how technology-based interventions can potentially be used effectively to augment existing treatments.

Our program's focus on group therapy as a modality has also allowed us to examine whether short-term group-based interventions on a variety of topics are helpful. We have, for example, found that more than half of our patients report an interest in discussing issues related to spirituality during psychiatric care (Rosmarin et al., 2015). Current depression as well as religious affiliation were associated with greater interest, though many unaffiliated patients still reported interest. These findings highlight the importance of providing space for patients to discuss such challenging issues as spirituality in their care. Offering a group on spirituality can be a very relevant topic during periods of crisis in patients' lives, both as something they struggle with and as a potential source of strength. It is important to note that we only made this group available to patients who self-selected to attend the group. We are also in the process of assessing whether a once weekly gentle yoga protocol is beneficial for our patients. Preliminary findings indicate that such a group is acceptable and feasible for patients, and is associated with improvements in affect over the course of an hour of practice (McHugh et al., 2016).

Barriers to Research in a Partial Hospital Program

Conducting research in a partial hospital requires flexibility, compromise, and significant investment by the researchers. Many of the challenges faced are common to any practice setting, such as finding funding to support research activities. The BHP does not have specific research funding, and our activities therefore operate on a very limited, shoe-string budget. We started our research program with very limited funding and equipment, only purchasing six used laptop computers for the purpose of data collection. After a few years, and given the success of our initial research efforts, our institution, which understands the importance of evidence-based care and monitoring patient outcomes, made funds and resources available so we could automate summary reports. In addition to funding, partial hospitals have specific characteristics that are associated with unique barriers. In this section, we highlight three main challenges, as well as examples of potential solutions that have worked in our program.

Naturalistic Treatment

Research Design

Naturalistic settings pose constraints on treatment outcome research for reasons related to the naturalistic treatment itself. First, it is often difficult to use "gold standard" research designs, such as randomized controlled trials (RCT). Thus, almost all PHP research programs will focus on utilizing effectiveness research designs, with potentially great generalizability, but limited internal validity. RCT designs are needed to establish the efficacy of a treatment with high levels of internal validity (Chambless & Hollon, 1998). Without a control group, it is impossible to determine whether patients are improving due to the treatment itself, or to other factors (e.g., time). Most PHPs will not be able to compare their treatment to a control group, as all patients need urgent care (by definition a requirement for partial hospital eligibility) and cannot be randomly assigned. Even a wait-list control would not be feasible or acceptable because half of our patients are referred directly from inpatient hospitalization and need further stabilization immediately; the other half of patients have varying waits depending on the clinic census. In the absence of a control group, PHPs may use other approaches to test effectiveness. For example, as described above, we have demonstrated our program's effectiveness using a benchmarking approach (Björgvinsson et al., 2014), in which we compared our effect sizes to those obtained in RCTs and calculated the number of patients achieving a reliable and clinically significant change. Additionally, although we are unable to compare standard partial hospital treatment to a control, we have been able to rigorously test augmentation strategies by randomly assigning patients to receive an adjunct to standard treatment or to treatment as usual (e.g., the computerized training targeting interpretation bias described above).

The Nature of Treatment

Sound intervention research requires scientists to know exactly what treatment is being implemented, how it is being implemented, and whether it is implemented with fidelity. In RCTs, researchers may therefore use a treatment manual, ensure appropriate therapist training and competence, and assess therapist adherence (Chambless & Hollon, 2012). These procedures ensure the construct validity of the study, and may allow researchers to determine which component(s) of treatment are driving improvement (e.g., by comparing the intervention of interest to another intervention that does not include specific component(s), etc.). In partial hospital settings, it is challenging to both deliver a similar treatment to all patients, as well as to determine which component(s) of partial hospital treatment is driving improvement. PHPs generally deliver multiple types of treatment (e.g., CBT, DBT, pharmacotherapy, peer support groups) across multiple modalities (individual and group). Additionally, partial hospitals involve increased structure and social contact, which may be more important than any particular therapeutic technique. Moreover, each individual patient receives a different treatment experience, depending on the specific groups they attend, providers on their treatment team, and number of days in the program. Over time, even patients who attend the same type of therapy groups may receive different treatment due to different staff members delivering the treatment (though adherence to group protocols should minimize differences in group delivery).

In an attempt to account for heterogeneity in treatment content, we track which groups patients attend, as well as medication changes from admission to discharge, using our clinical chart database. Although this information may help in controlling for different treatment exposures, the nature of the treatment delivered inherently poses important challenges for research. Although, on the one hand, naturalistic treatment is "messier" to study, our study design also provides fertile ground for hypothesis generation and the assessment of relationships among various forms of treatment and outcomes. Thus, research in partial hospital settings both provides an interesting opportunity to apply insights from controlled research to the "real world," but also a unique space to generate new ideas to be tested in controlled research.

Treatment Duration

Additional challenges are related to the brief and intensive nature of treatment provided by partial hospitals. For example, patients attend our program for an average of 12 days from admission to discharge (including weekends). This obviously may limit the type of research questions and designs that require longer term follow-up. In addition, patients attend group or individual treatment appointments from nine until three with a one-hour break for lunch. Any research activities must be conducted outside of treatment hours, to ensure that patients receive adequate clinical care. Thus, any research procedures must be squeezed either before 9am (when patients complete progress monitoring surveys), or into 30 minute sessions during the lunch break or after program hours (when we conduct ancillary studies). This short window of time requires streamlined assessments, and we often cannot include all the measures we desire or gold-standard interviews.

Missing Data

Research conducted in PHPs will always have a certain amount of missing data for practical reasons. For example, 8 percent of patients in our program are discharged to inpatient hospital care ("stepped up") during partial hospitalization, and consequently do not complete discharge assessments given their urgent need for more intensive care. Additionally, many of our patients unexpectedly discharge from home. Sometimes, patients may also already have too many clinical appointments on their discharge day to complete discharge assessments. We have attempted to minimize the amount of missing data by assessing patients' depression and anxiety symptoms daily. Thus, even when a patient is unable to complete a longer discharge assessment on the very last day of treatment, we have their symptom ratings on primary outcomes (depression, anxiety) from the day prior to discharge.

Acuity of Patient Symptoms

Individuals requiring a partial hospital level of care are in general experiencing acute symptoms, suicidal ideation, and poor functioning. Many patients may be experiencing active symptoms of mania and psychosis, which poses challenges to informed consent, accurate self-report, and ability to complete even basic research procedures. Moreover, patients experiencing symptoms of paranoia are less likely to consent to research, leading to selection biases. Patients are also typically fatigued due to psychiatric symptoms, medication side-effects, and/or the intensive treatment itself. Additionally, many patients may be unable to complete research procedures due to acute distress related to symptoms and personal crises. Our staff is trained to encourage patients to complete our assessment while respecting that clinical concerns and other factors sometimes make data collection impossible. Gaining the expertise to appropriately recognize when to encourage participation vs. when to acknowledge limitations takes time and support from other staff members. We encourage collaborative and transparent communication between staff members, and between staff and patients, to make these decisions effectively.

In addition, some research procedures may be upsetting (or "triggering") for patients with trauma histories (or for patients with acute symptoms of anxiety). For example, we have recently added a childhood trauma questionnaire to our standard clinical assessment. Our decision to assess childhood trauma was based on the importance of such experiences for treatment outcomes. We attempted to reduce any potential distress by using a well-validated measure that has been used in many other psychiatric studies. To verify whether the benefits of assessing past trauma outweighed the risks involved in assessing it, we began by conducting pilot interviews with ten patients. Pilot patients completed the measure, and then completed a brief semi-structured interview to assess their reaction to the measure, the degree to which they found the measure acceptable and feasible, and the degree to which they agreed that assessing past trauma may generate useful insights for clinical care and research, and is worth the potential costs of being reminded of past trauma. Pilot participants overwhelmingly thought that this was important to assess, and had helpful suggestions with regard to how to implement it. We now present a disclaimer before the questionnaire that lets patients know that the next set of questions will ask about childhood trauma. Patients can choose to skip the entire questionnaire by clicking a button. Even with these precautions, we have had several patients complete the measure and then report increased dissociation and emotional dysregulation. Temporary increases in symptoms are not in themselves indicative of the need to remove a measure, as patients may also react similarly to other daily events. However, it is our responsibility to ensure that staff is adequately trained to help patients cope with symptom exacerbation if it occurs. When this has happened, staff have helped patients use skills learned in the program (e.g., distress tolerance skills) to manage temporary increase in symptoms, the clinical team is informed, and the patient receives extra check-ins.

Staff Attitudes and Program Culture

The successful implementation of research studies within partial hospital settings requires that research be viewed favorably by staff members, even those not directly involved in research. In our program, almost all of our research staff also assumes a clinical role (e.g., group and/or individual therapists, among other clinical roles). Undergraduate research students are the only exception to this, as they are not allowed to assume clinical duties. Thus, the people in charge of deciding and implementing research directly understand how their decisions will affect clinical care and clinical staff. Most of our clinical staff does not directly participate in the design/implementation of research.

The degree to which staff attitudes and program culture pose a challenge to research will likely depend on how and when research is introduced, as well as the purpose of the research. New programs that from the beginning incorporate evidence based assessments used for clinical care and research will likely not encounter much concern from staff. However, established programs that introduce new assessments as part of a programmatic shift should be prepared to address staff concerns about making important changes in the way care is delivered and assessed using a research-informed perspective. As explained above, research staff should always consider the degree to which findings from a research project will impact patient care when planning.

Partial hospital staff may include psychiatrists, psychologists (PhD or PsyD), social workers, licensed mental health counselors, nurses, occupational therapists, bachelor level counselors, administrative assistants, and trainees (e.g., medical residents, psychology interns). These various backgrounds vary greatly in their research training, which may impact staff attitudes toward the value of research in general, expectations for results, and use of empirically supported assessments and treatments. Additionally, staff who are naive to research procedures may express concern over routine, benign procedures.

Clinical staff that do not conduct research may have a higher bar for judging the value of research, and whether the importance of the knowledge to be gained outweighs potential risks and inconveniences. Related to this, there may a conflict between the importance of conducting basic science studies, or incremental research that makes small but meaningful contributions, and staff's expectation that results will make an immediate and significant clinical impact. There may also be tension between the aim of research to benefit society at large, and the aim of the clinician to benefit the individual patient. Studies that offer additional treatment or unique clinical information for the treatment team will obviously be most appealing and obtain consensus. We recommend that clinical staff be included in the entire research process (idea formation, selection of measures, protocol development) in order to develop a transparent and effective research culture. We make sure to disseminate findings regularly to staff verbally at staff meetings, as well as by distributing published manuscripts. Staff consultation of course takes time and skill, and the research team should therefore plan ahead to have enough time to design and implement research accordingly.

It is important to note that partial hospital programs have the unique challenge of treating extremely high risk patients during the day who then go home at night and on weekends. Staff do not have the security of inpatient units and must constantly assess whether patients are safe to go home. Consequently, staff may be concerned about any research procedures that could possibly upset patients. To the researchers, some of these concerns may seem unfounded. However, it is important to realize that normal, routine research procedures used in outpatient settings may cause more distress in individuals experiencing acute psychiatric distress.

Given the number of parameters to consider when planning research projects in high acuity naturalistic settings, it is crucial to remember that compromises will need to occur to find the best balance between research rigor, clinical care, practical constraints, and other considerations. Nonetheless, having staff "buy-in" ensures that the research procedures will be feasible and acceptable to both staff and patients, and makes the research process an exciting opportunity for the program as a whole. In our experience, having transparent discussions about the nature of research projects in question, as well as the risks and benefits involved, is crucial to successful implementation and to obtaining a reasonable buy-in by the entire clinical team.

Conclusions

The challenges inherent in conducting research in partial hospital settings require that staff approach this initiative with patience, persistence, creativity, and a highly collaborative spirit. However, these same challenges explain why conducting research in such settings can produce invaluable insights: to better understand the nature of acute psychopathology, and to improve treatment as patients go from crisis to stabilization. Our experience leads us to believe that the benefits are well-worth the efforts. Partial hospitals are an important level of care helping individuals at high risk for suicide, relapse, and re-hospitalization. It is therefore crucial to conduct research to better understand these patients' psychopathology and improve treatment—a goal that patients, clinicians, and researchers share. In addition to the benefits we have discussed and highlighted above, our patients report being interested in contributing to research, and appreciating the opportunity to give back. Many patients are willing to participate in studies that might advance our scientific knowledge and lead to better treatments, and report enthusiasm about being involved in research that may help others experiencing similar difficulties.

References

Barlow, D. H., Allen, L. B., & Choate, M. L. (2004). Toward a unified treatment for emotional disorders. *Behavior Therapy*, 35, 205–230.

Bateman, A. & Fonagy, P. (1999). Effectiveness of partial hospitalization in the treatment of borderline personality disorder: A randomized controlled trial. *American Journal of Psychiatry*, 156, 1563–1569.

Bateman, A. & Fonagy, P. (2008). 8-year follow-up of patients treated for borderline personality disorder: Mentalization-based treatment versus treatment as usual. *American Journal of Psychiatry*, 165, 631–638.

Beard, C. & Björgvinsson, T. (2014). Beyond generalized anxiety disorder: Psychometric properties of the GAD-7 in a heterogeneous psychiatric sample. *Journal of Anxiety Disorders*, 28, 547–552.

Beard, C., Hearon, B. A., Lee, J., Kopeski, L. M., Busch, A. B., & Björgvinsson, T. (2016). When partial hospitalization fails: Risk factors for inpatient hospitalization. *The Journal of Nervous and Mental Disease*, 204, 431–436.

Beard, C., Hsu, K. J., Rifkin, L. S., Busch, A. B., & Björgvinsson, T. (2016). Validation of the PHQ-9 in a psychiatric sample. *Journal of Affective Disorders*, 193, 267–273.

Beard, C., Millner, A. J., Forgeard, M. J. C., Fried, E. I., Hsu, K. J., Treadway, M. T., . . . Björgvinsson, T. (2016). Network analysis of depression and anxiety symptom relationships in a psychiatric sample. *Psychological Medicine, 46,* 3359–3369.

Beard, C., Kirakosian, N., Silverman, A. L., Winer, J. P., Wadsworth, L. P., & Björgvinsson, T. (2017). Comparing treatment response between LGBQ and heterosexual individuals attending a CBT- and DBT-skills-based partial hospital. *Journal of Consulting and Clinical Psychology, 85,* 1171–1181.

Beck, A. T., Rush, A. J., Shaw, B., & Emery, G. (1979). *Cognitive Therapy of Depression.* New York: Guilford Press.

Bernstein, D. P., Stein, J. A., Newcomb, M. D., Walker, E., Pogge, D., Ahluvalia, T., . . . Zule, W. (2003). Development and validation of a brief screening version of the Childhood Trauma Questionnaire. *Child Abuse & Neglect, 27,* 169–190.

Björgvinsson, T., Kertz, S. J., Bigda-Peyton, J. S., Rosmarin, D. H., Aderka, I. M., & Neuhaus, E. C. (2014). Effectiveness of cognitive behavior therapy for severe mood disorders in an acute psychiatric naturalistic setting: A benchmarking study. *Cognitive Behaviour Therapy, 43,* 209–220.

Borsboom, D. & Cramer, A. O. J. (2013). Network analysis: An integrative approach to the structure of psychopathology. *Annual Review of Clinical Psychology, 9,* 91–121.

Cameron, I. M., Cunningham, L., Crawford, J. R., Eagles, J. M., Eisen, S. V., Lawton, K., . . . Hamilton, R. J. (2007). Psychometric properties of the BASIS-24© (Behaviour and Symptom Identification Scale–Revised) Mental Health Outcome Measure. *International Journal of Psychiatry in Clinical Practice, 11,* 36–43.

Chambless, D. L. & Hollon, S. D. (1998). Defining empirically supported therapies. *Journal of Consulting and Clinical Psychology, 66,* 7–18.

Chambless, D. L. & Hollon, S. D. (2012). Treatment validity for intervention studies. In H. Cooper, P. M. Camic, D. L. Long, A. T. Panter, D. Rindskopf, & K. J. Sher (Eds.) *APA handbook of research methods in psychology, Vol 2: Research designs: Quantitative, qualitative, neuropsychological, and biological* (pp. 529–552). Washington, DC: American Psychological Association.

Commission on Accreditation of Rehabilitation Facilities (CARF) International (2016). *Partial hospitalization.* Available from: www.carf.org/Programs/ProgramDescriptions/BH-Partial-Hospitalization/

Cramer, A. O. J., Waldorp, L. J., van der Maas, H. L. J., & Borsboom, D. (2010). Comorbidity: a network perspective. *Behavioral and Brain Sciences, 33,* 137–193.

Drymalski, W. M. & Washburn, J. J. (2011). Sudden gains in the treatment of depression in a partial hospitalization program. *Journal of Consulting and Clinical Psychology, 79,* 364–368.

Fergus, T. A., Valentiner, D. P., McGrath, P. B., Stephenson, K., Gier, S., & Jencius, S. (2009). The Fear of Positive Evaluation Scale: Psychometric properties in a clinical sample. *Journal of Anxiety Disorders, 23,* 1177–1183.

First, M. B., Spitzer, R. L., Gibbon, M., & Williams, J. B. (1997). *User's guide for the Structured clinical interview for DSM-IV axis I disorders SCID-I: clinician version.* Arlington, VA: American Psychiatric Press.

Forgeard, M. J. C., Pearl, R. L., Cheung, J., Rifkin, L. S., Beard, C., & Björgvinsson, T. (2016). Positive beliefs about mental illness: Associations with sex, age, diagnosis, and clinical outcomes. *Journal of Affective Disorders, 204,* 197–204.

Harris, J. I., Farchmin, L., Stull, L., Boyd, J., Schumacher, M., & Drapalski, A. L. (2015). Prediction of changes in self-stigma among veterans participating in partial psychiatric hospitalization: The role of disability status and military cohort. *Psychiatric Rehabilitation Journal, 38,* 179–185.

Harris, P. A., Taylor, R., Thielke, R., Payne, J., Gonzalez, N., & Conde, J. G. (2009). Research electronic data capture (REDCap)—A metadata-driven methodology and workflow process for providing translational research informatics support. *Journal of Biomedical Informatics, 42*, 377–381.

Hayes, S. C., Strosahl, K. D., & Wilson, K. G. (2012). *Acceptance and commitment therapy: The process and practice of mindful change* (2nd ed.) New York: Guilford Press.

Horvitz-Lennon, M., Normand, S.-L. T., Gaccione, P., & Frank, R. G. (2001). Partial versus full hospitalization for adults in psychiatric distress: A systematic review of the published literature (1957–1997). *American Journal of Psychiatry, 158*, 676–685.

Hsu, K. J., Beard, C., Rifkin, L., Dillon, D. G., Pizzagalli, D. A., & Björgvinsson, T. (2015). Transdiagnostic mechanisms in depression and anxiety: The role of rumination and attentional control. *Journal of Affective Disorders, 188*, 22–27.

Insel, T., Cuthbert, B., Garvey, M., Heinssen, R., Pine, D. S., Quinn, K., ... Wang, P. (2010). Research domain criteria (RDoC): toward a new classification framework for research on mental disorders. *The American Journal of Psychiatry, 167*, 748–751.

Joyce, A. S., Ennis, L. P., O'Kelly, J. G., Ogrodniczuk, J. S., & Piper, W. E. (2009). Depressive manifestations and differential patterns of treatment outcome in an intensive partial hospitalization treatment program. *Psychological Services, 6*, 154–172.

Kertz, S., Bigda-Peyton, J., Rosmarin, D. H., & Björgvinsson, T. (2012). The importance of worry across diagnostic presentations: Prevalence, severity, and associated symptoms in a partial hospital setting. *Journal of Anxiety Disorders, 26*, 126–133.

Kertz, S. J., Koran, J., Stevens, K. T., & Björgvinsson, T. (2015). Repetitive negative thinking predicts depression and anxiety symptom improvement during brief cognitive behavioral therapy. *Behaviour Research and Therapy, 68*, 54–63.

Kiser, L. J., Lefkovitz, P. M., Kennedy, L. L., & Knight, M. A. (2010). *Continuum of ambulatory behavioral health services. Association of ambulatory behavioral health services (aabh.org).* Available from: www.aabh.org/content/continuumambulatory-behavioral health-services

Klonsky, E. D. & Glenn, C. R. (2009). Assessing the functions of non-suicidal self-injury: Psychometric properties of the Inventory of Statements About Self-injury (ISAS). *Journal of Psychopathology and Behavioral Assessment, 31*, 215–219.

Kroenke, K., Spitzer, R. L., & Williams, J. B. (2001). The PHQ-9: Validity of a brief depression severity measure. *Journal of General Internal Medicine, 16*, 606–613.

Lamers, S. M. A., Westerhof, G. J., Bohlmeijer, E. T., ten Klooster, P. M., & Keyes, C. L. M. (2011). Evaluating the psychometric properties of the Mental Health Continuum-Short Form (MHC-SF). *Journal of Clinical Psychology, 67*, 99–110.

Leung, M. Y., Drozd, E. M., & Maier, J. (2009, February). *Impacts associated with the Medicare psychiatric PPS: A study of partial hospitalization programs.* Waltham, MA: RTI International.

Linehan, M. (1993). *Cognitive-behavioral treatment of Borderline Personality Disorder.* New York: Guilford Press.

Mansell, W., Harvey, A., Watkins, E., & Shafran, R. (2009). Conceptual foundations of the transdiagnostic approach to CBT. *Journal of Cognitive Psychotherapy, 23*, 6–19.

McHugh, K. Buchholz, Chad-Friedman, S., Borkum, D., Kopeski, L., Forgeard, M., Beard, C., & Björgvinsson, T. (2016, September). *Integrating yoga with cognitive-behavioral therapy: Perceived benefits, acceptability, feasibility, and associated changes in mood in a partial hospital setting.* Poster presented at the 2016 Symposium on Yoga Research, Stockbridge, MA.

McHugh, R. K., Kertz, S. J., Weiss, R. B., Baskin-Sommers, A. R., Hearon, B. A., & Björgvinsson, T. (2014). Changes in distress intolerance and treatment outcome in a partial hospital setting. *Behavior Therapy, 45*, 232–240.

McNally, R. J., Robinaugh, D. J., Wu, G. W. Y., Wang, L., Deserno, M. K., & Borsboom, D. (2014). Mental disorders as causal systems a network approach to posttraumatic stress disorder. *Clinical Psychological Science, 3,* 836–849.

Neacsiu, A. D., Rizvi, S. L., Vitaliano, P. P., Lynch, T. R., & Linehan, M. M. (2010). The dialectical behavior therapy ways of coping checklist: development and psychometric properties. *Journal of Clinical Psychology, 66,* 563–582.

Office of the Federal Register (2005). *The code of federal regulations of the United States of America.* Washington, DC: United States Government Printing Office.

Ogrodniczuk, J. S. & Piper, W. E. (2001). Day treatment for personality disorders: A review of research findings. *Harvard Review of Psychiatry, 9,* 105–117.

Pearl, R. L., Forgeard, M. J. C., Rifkin, L., Beard, C., & Björgvinsson, T. (2017). Internalized stigma of mental illness: Changes and associations with treatment outcomes. *Stigma and Health, 2,* 2–15.

Rosmarin, D. H., Forester, B. P., Shassian, D. M., Webb, C. A., & Björgvinsson, T. (2015). Interest in spiritually integrated psychotherapy among acute psychiatric patients. *Journal of Consulting and Clinical Psychology, 83,* 1149–1153.

Schene, A. H. (2004). The effectiveness of psychiatric partial hospitalization and day care. *Current Opinion in Psychiatry, 17,* 303–309.

Sheehan, D., Janavs, J., Baker, R., Sheehan, K. H., Knapp, E., & Sheehan, M. (2015). *MINI international neuropsychiatric interview–version 7 for DSM-5.*

Sheehan, D. V., Lecrubier, Y., Sheehan, K. H., Amorim, P., Janavs, J., Weiller, E., . . . Dunbar, G. C. (1998). The Mini-International Neuropsychiatric Interview (M.I.N.I.): The development and validation of a structured diagnostic psychiatric interview for DSM-IV and ICD-10. *The Journal of Clinical Psychiatry, 59,* 22–33.

Spitzer, R. L., Kroenke, K., Williams, J. B. W., & Löwe, B. (2006). A brief measure for assessing generalized anxiety disorder: the GAD-7. *Archives of Internal Medicine, 166,* 1092–1097.

Stein, A. T., Hearon, B., Beard, C., Hsu, K., & Björgvinsson, T. (2016). Properties of the Dialectical Behavior Therapy Ways of Coping Checklist in a diagnostically diverse partial hospital sample. *Journal of Clinical Psychology, 72,* 49–57.

Tasca, G. A., Taylor, D., Ritchie, K., & Balfour, L. (2004). Attachment predicts treatment completion in an eating disorders partial hospital program among women with anorexia nervosa. *Journal of Personality Assessment, 83,* 201–212.

Thatte, S., Makinen, J. A., Nguyen, H. N. T., Hill, E. M., & Flament, M. F. (2013). Partial hospitalization for youth with psychiatric disorders: treatment outcomes and 3-month follow-up. *The Journal of Nervous and Mental Disease, 201,* 429–434.

Webb, C. A., Beard, C., Auerbach, R. P., Menninger, E., & Björgvinsson, T. (2014). The therapeutic alliance in a naturalistic psychiatric setting: temporal relations with depressive symptom change. *Behaviour Research and Therapy, 61,* 70–77.

Webb, C. A., Beard, C., Kertz, S. J., Hsu, K. J., & Björgvinsson, T. (2016). Differential role of CBT skills, DBT skills and psychological flexibility in predicting depressive versus anxiety symptom improvement. *Behaviour Research and Therapy, 81,* 12–20.

Zanarini, M. C., Vujanovic, A. A., Parachini, E. A., Boulanger, J. L., Frankenburg, F. R., & Hennen, J. (2003). A screening measure for BPD: the McLean Screening Instrument for Borderline Personality Disorder (MSI-BPD). *Journal of Personality Disorders, 17,* 568–573.

Zipfel, S., Reas, D. L., Thornton, C., Olmsted, M. P., Williamson, D. A., Gerlinghoff, M., . . . Beumont, P. J. (2002). Day hospitalization programs for eating disorders: A systematic review of the literature. *International Journal of Eating Disorders, 31,* 105–117.

APPENDIX A

Sample De-Identified Admission Report

Admission Report: BHP Patient Name: DOB:
  MRN: Date/Time:

Thoughts of Death/Suicide

Survey	Question	Response
Basis 24 #20	Think about hurting yourself?	Sometimes

PHQ-9 Depression

- Pt Score
- BHP Average Admission Score (14.0)

Timeframes
Adm. Past 2 Wks
Ints or D/D: Past 24 Hrs

Interpretative Norms
0–4: Minimal
5–9: Mild
10–14: Moderate
15–19: Moderately severe
20+ Severe

Th-Adm 10-13

GAD-7 Anxiety

- Pt Score
- BHP Average Admission Score (14.0)

Timeframes
Adm. Past 2 Wks
Ints or D/D: Past 24 Hrs

Interpretative Norms
0–4: Minimal
5–9: Mild
10–14: Moderate
15+: Severe

Th-Adm 10-13

Basis 24 — Basis 24 Scores (BHP Average Admission Scores / Pt Admission Scores)

Category	BHP Avg	Pt
Depression/Functioning	2.3	3.2
Relationships	1.4	0.4
Psychosis	0.5	0.0
Substance Abuse	0.5	0.5
Self-harm	0.8	1.5
Emotional Liability	1.7	2.7

Admission Scores: Screening Surveys

Survey	Score	Result	Interpretation
Tobacco	0	Neg	Does not smoke/use tobacco
Alcohol	2	Neg	Low probability of problematic drinking
Drug	2	Neg	Low level of drug use (brief counseling, outpatient treatment)
BPD	3	Neg	Low likelihood of borderline personality disorder

*Additional clinical assessment needed for DSM–IV diagnosis and treatment planning

© 2018, *Practice-Based Research: A Guide for Clinicians*, R. Trent Codd, III, Routledge.

APPENDIX B

Sample De-Identified Discharge Report

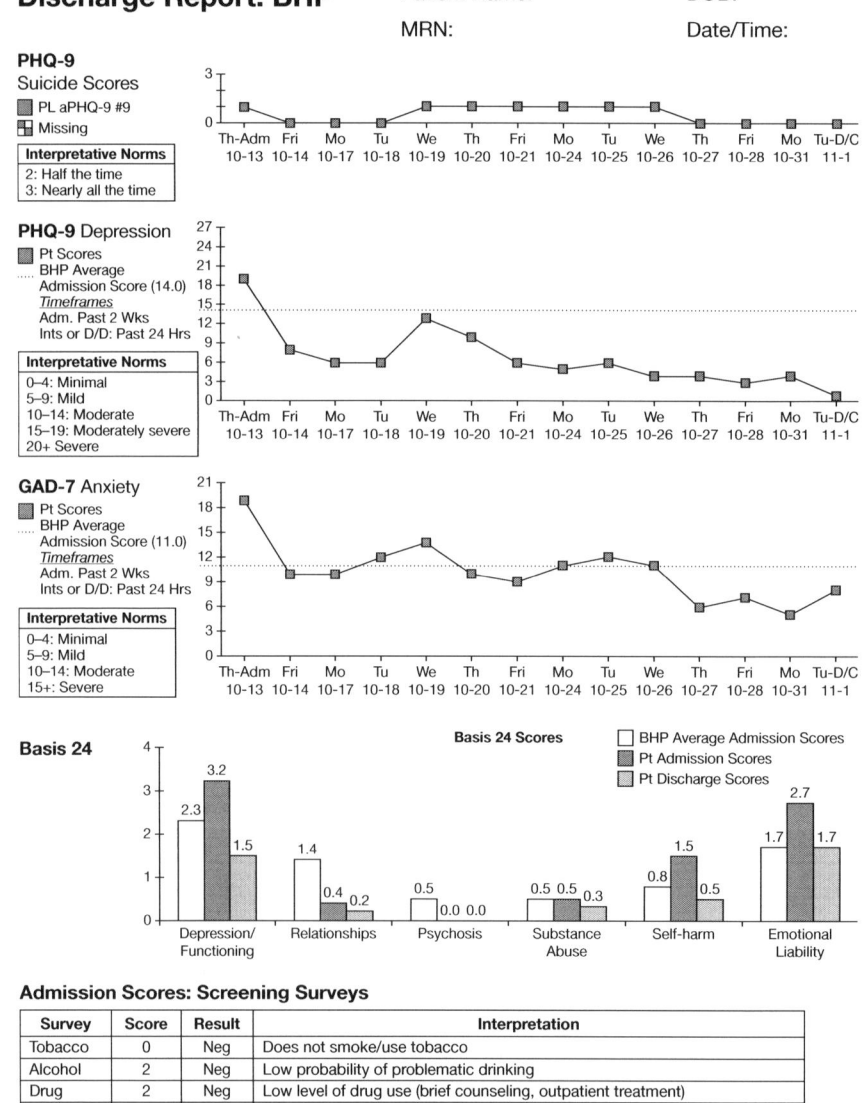

Discharge Report: BHP Patient Name: DOB:
MRN: Date/Time:

PHQ-9
Suicide Scores
- PL aPHQ-9 #9
- Missing

Interpretative Norms
2: Half the time
3: Nearly all the time

PHQ-9 Depression
- Pt Scores
- BHP Average
Admission Score (14.0)
Timeframes
Adm. Past 2 Wks
Ints or D/D: Past 24 Hrs

Interpretative Norms
0–4: Minimal
5–9: Mild
10–14: Moderate
15–19: Moderately severe
20+ Severe

GAD-7 Anxiety
- Pt Scores
- BHP Average
Admission Score (11.0)
Timeframes
Adm. Past 2 Wks
Ints or D/D: Past 24 Hrs

Interpretative Norms
0–4: Minimal
5–9: Mild
10–14: Moderate
15+: Severe

Basis 24

Basis 24 Scores — BHP Average Admission Scores, Pt Admission Scores, Pt Discharge Scores

Admission Scores: Screening Surveys

Survey	Score	Result	Interpretation
Tobacco	0	Neg	Does not smoke/use tobacco
Alcohol	2	Neg	Low probability of problematic drinking
Drug	2	Neg	Low level of drug use (brief counseling, outpatient treatment)
BPD	3	Neg	Low likelihood of borderline personality disorder

*Additional clinical assessment needed for DSM–IV diagnosis and treatment planning

© 2018, *Practice-Based Research: A Guide for Clinicians*, R. Trent Codd, III, Routledge.

APPENDIX C

Summary Checklist
Research in Partial Hospital Settings

The Research Team

- Identify staff interested in actively participating in the design/implementation of research:
    - Any staff members, regardless of training or role, can make valuable contributions to research provided that they are able to find the time and are committed to a project. Constituting a research team that is diverse in levels of training and interests will ensure that different roles can be filled and that different perspectives are represented. *Example: Core members of our research staff include the program director, assistant director of research, research coordinator, one of our postdoctoral fellows, and undergraduate volunteer research students (recruited by word-of-mouth or by email announcements). Every year, several psychology interns, practicum students, and program counselors also volunteer to take on active roles in our research program.*
- Organize clear structure for supervision, mentorship, and delegation of tasks:
    - Designate research supervisors for all members in training; provide regular supervision times during which nuts-and-bolts issues can be discussed
    - Encourage validation and discussion of challenges related to conducting research while performing clinical duties, and the integration of research and clinical care in general
    - Provide opportunities for students to conduct their own independent research (e.g., undergraduate poster presentation, doctoral dissertation, etc.) *Example: All of our undergraduate research students have regular supervision meeting times with the associate director of research and/or the postdoctoral fellow; during these meetings, progress on individual tasks, specific skills to be learned/applied, problems to be solved, as well as professional development issues are discussed.*
- Organize a research meeting:
    - Meet regularly (we suggest once a week) to discuss overall progress on projects and provide a forum that creates a community for all involved in research. In addition to a typical meeting agenda, we encourage teams

© 2018, *Practice-Based Research: A Guide for Clinicians*, R. Trent Codd, III, Routledge.

to create a project list to periodically review all projects, their progress, and make decisions. We have found that the project list becomes imperative when collaborators from outside are involved, to help keep track of projects and maintain accountability. *Example: In our program, the research team meets every Wednesday from 3–4pm in the program director's office. We review the project list once a month: this project list includes all manuscripts in preparation or under review/revision, active data collection projects, and potential future projects currently in design. The names of individuals leading manuscripts/projects are included for references. We find that "less is more" when preparing the project list: keeping all descriptions very concise (1–2 sentences) is generally enough and helps discussions move along efficiently.*

Planning Research

- Inform clinical care by research:
    - Conduct structured interviews to be able to research how diagnoses (or areas of concerns) relate to other variables. *Example: Most of our patients complete the Miniature International Neuropsychiatric Interview with their individual therapist on the second day of treatment. The postdoctoral fellow provides training and regular supervision to all clinicians administering the MINI, as well as to the research coordinator and undergraduate research students entering MINI data in our research database. In addition, students double-enter the MINI to ensure data accuracy.*
    - To be able to research treatment outcomes, operationalize treatment clearly: What kind(s) of treatment is delivered? What evidence-based principles are implemented, and where are they described? What content is covered in groups? The use of group protocols provides clarity regarding interventions delivered. *Example: Individual and group therapy in our program focuses on skills described in manuals of Cognitive-Behavioral Therapy, Dialectical Behavior Therapy, and Acceptance and Commitment Therapy. For each group, a group protocol describes the content covered in group and what skill is practiced (using handouts). Group protocols are designed to be flexible and helpful, and feedback from group leaders on their improvement is encouraged and appreciated.*
- Collect and manage data:
    - Identify when, where, and by whom data will be collected. Plan out what equipment is needed for secure data collection, and how records will be de-identified. *Example: All of our patients complete daily assessments in the morning before the program begins (8:30–9am). Assessments are*

administered by our research coordinator on encrypted computers which stay in a designated research room. This room is locked and is only accessible by the research coordinator, program director, associate director of research, and postdoctoral fellow. All assessments are administered on REDCap, a secure HIPAA-compliant data collection platform. All patients are assigned a unique deidentified ID number.
- o Identify which measures will be administered, and when. When selecting measures, take care to balance clinical usefulness with practical feasibility. You may need to prioritize short questionnaires. *Example: All of our patients complete brief measures of depression and anxiety symptoms (the PHQ-9 and GAD-7) every day of the program. We have selected additional measures to administer based on clinical and research relevance. We limit our daily surveys to five minutes in total. We limit our admission and discharge surveys to 30 minutes in total.*
- o Decide if other clinical data will be recorded for program evaluation and research purposes, and create secure database for this purpose. *Example: We record groups attended by each patient, as well as medication changes, in research databases that are updated regularly.*
- o Merge data from different sources on a regular basis following a systematic procedure to ensure data integrity. *Example: We merge data from our surveys, structured interviews, and clinical databases at least every six months. We have created syntax for this purpose, which is frequently updated.*
- Obtain input from all clinical staff:
  - o Ask clinical staff for feedback about current research projects and/or projects in design. Speak openly and transparently about the different considerations the research team attempts to balance and possible dilemmas requiring compromise. Explicitly state that all members of the clinical team are welcome to meet with research team members to discuss ideas or concerns.
  - o Organize forum for research-related concerns, ideas, and findings to be discussed in a large group. *Example: All of the staff at our partial program participates in a monthly research seminar during which research-related concerns, ideas, and findings are discussed. This meeting is a great opportunity to address ongoing issues and thank the clinical staff for their role in the research program. In addition, clinical staff generally express interest and enthusiasm for completed projects.*

© 2018, *Practice-Based Research: A Guide for Clinicians*, R. Trent Codd, III, Routledge.

PART V

Conclusion and Future Directions

CHAPTER 13

Future Directions for Practice-Based Research

Shannon Wiltsey Stirman

The exciting promise of Practice Based Research is that it allows clinicians, or networks of clinicians, to address the questions that are most pressing and clinically relevant for their practice. As LeJeune and Luoma point out in this volume, the ability to do so becomes even more essential when funding agendas diverge from the types of "on the ground" challenges that clinicians face. Furthermore, questions that are highly relevant to clinicians, for example, questions about the optimal strategies to increase session attendance or completion of CBT homework, or about whether the use of mobile apps can enhance clinical outcomes, may be best addressed through practice-based research. Many of the practical and methodological challenges and potential solutions have been outlined in this book (Waltman, Persons, this volume). Two other developments may have an impact on the future of practice-based research: the increasing interest in forming academic partnerships for implementation research, and the availability of technology to facilitate practice-based research.

As others have noted, academic partnerships can facilitate PBR (Persons, this volume; Koerner & Castonguay, 2015). While recent years have seen prioritization of research on underlying biological and psychological processes that underlie mental health problems, the importance of research on the implementation of evidence-based interventions and practices has also been highlighted, and this development represents an opportunity for PBR partnerships with researchers. Clinicians are essential partners in this endeavor, as clinically representative, "real world" settings are necessary for this type of research. Much attention has been devoted to the importance of true partnership in implementation research, with recognition that clinicians need a seat at the table through all phases of research—from the formulation of research questions all the way through to interpreting and understanding results. At times, challenges can arise in finding funding to support research ideas that are generated through these partnerships, but often small grants can be found, or ideas will align with major funding announcements. Funding can reduce the burden of PBR on the clinician by supporting personnel to assist with data collection and recruitment, IRB submission, and other tasks.

Even in the absence of funding, partnerships can make the conduct of practice-based research feasible. Students and interns who are looking for dissertation topics or research experience can assist with data collection and analysis, and, as Persons (this volume) indicated, access to some university resources can facilitate research. These relationships are often synergistic, as students seek opportunities to conduct research for their theses or dissertations, faculty seek partnerships with practitioners, and therapists wish to use their practice data to advance knowledge. However, it can take time for such partnerships to develop. Offering to contribute to academic researchers' stakeholder panels and working with students who are developing a program of research are ways to explore partnerships with academic researchers who focus on implementation. Often, the best approach is to start small, to be sure that the goals, needs, and constraints placed on each organization are aligned in such a way that the partnership is mutually beneficial.

One area of interest to implementation researchers and clinicians alike is the study of the impact of fidelity, adaptations and selection of therapeutic strategies on clinical change. Many therapists practice from a transdiagnostic or conceptualization-based treatment approach rather than delivering treatment manuals exactly as specified, particularly when there are multiple presenting problems. Information about which treatment elements are more commonly delivered or removed, combined with patient diagnostic, demographic, and symptom or functioning data, can provide essential information about both the antecedents and consequences of decisions to deliver or not deliver certain treatment elements. If a transdiagnostic approach is being used, a fidelity checklist that includes elements from transdiagnostic protocols, modular approaches, or multiple therapies could be completed (Barlow et al., 2011; Chorpita, Daleiden, & Weisz, 2005; Fairburn et al., 2009) to identify common practice patterns with different case profiles, as well as outcomes of these practice patterns.

Balancing rigor and feasibility is a challenge to research of this nature, and partnerships with academics can help. Student trainees can make formal diagnostic assessment for research more feasible. They can also conduct observer ratings of fidelity, although advances in assessing fidelity suggest that session observation may not always be necessary to produce reliable estimates of fidelity when a particular intervention is being studied (Ward et al., 2013; Wiltsey Stirman et al., 2016). Reports during case consultation may be used to assess fidelity (Ward et al., 2013). Early research also suggests that cognitive behavioral therapy worksheets that are completed in session might be used as indicators of whether key aspects of the treatment model are being adequately covered in session (Wiltsey Stirman et al., 2016). There is also some emerging research suggesting that adherence checklists may adequately capture session elements (Hogue, Ozechowski, Robbins, & Waldron, 2013). Concerns about the validity of the data may be lessened if therapists complete self-reported fidelity measures in the context of trusting partnerships that are intended to learn how treatments work as delivered in routine care contexts. While some of the analyses to examine these questions may be somewhat complex, partnership with academic researchers may make them possible. Furthermore, simpler analyses may provide some basic information about important patterns and relationship between patient factors, the use or removal of certain treatment elements, and clinical change.

Another related question in implementation research that is very relevant to clinical care, is the impact of modifying and adapting treatment protocols. Recent clinical findings coincide with therapists' own experiences, that modifications and adaptations are sometimes, or even frequently, made to evidence-based treatments when delivered in everyday practice (Aarons, Miller, Green, Perrott, & Bradway, 2012; Cook, Dinnen, Thompson, Simiola, & Schnurr, 2014; Stirman et al., 2013a). However, short of component analyses and dismantling studies, which can shed light on the impact of adding or removing treatment elements (Bell, Marcus, & Goodlad, 2013), there is very little information about the antecedents or impact of other forms of adaptation, such as tailoring language or treatment materials, lengthening or shortening treatment protocols, repeating or re-sequencing session elements, or integrating aspects of other therapeutic approaches. Given the variety of adaptations that can be made to a given treatment, carefully controlled research to examine the impact of each one, for each intervention, is not feasible, although some studies have examined the impact of clinician latitude in making certain adaptations (Galovski, Blain, Mott, Elwood, & Houle, 2012; Levitt, Malta, Martin, Davis, & Cloitre, 2007). Collaborative practice-based research involving patient data and a checklist of session elements and possible adaptations (Stirman, Miller, Toder, & Calloway, 2013b) could eventually produce a sufficiently large database to begin to investigate these questions. Findings could ultimately inform practice and training endeavors by providing guidance about when and for whom certain types of adaptation may be necessary or advantageous, and when, for whom, and which types adaptations could be expected to have a negative impact on treatment outcome (Chambers & Norton, 2016). This is an area in which academic partnerships may be valuable, and may produce information that is very clinically relevant, but may be difficult to study in the absence of a partnership between a group of clinicians and researchers.

Particularly when paired with technologies to facilitate research and involvement in PBR networks, there is significant potential to answer highly clinically relevant research questions and advance PBR. As authors in this volume (e.g., Persons) have described, the use of electronic resources to collect data on symptom, functioning, and other factors of interest can minimize the burden of data collection. There are a number of web-based platforms, available free or for a licensing fee, that can collect this information, including the OQ analyst platform (www.oqmeasures.com/products/), Willow (www.willow.technology/), PROMIS (www.healthmeasures.net/explore-measurement-systems/promis/obtain-administer-measures), and Outcome Tracker (www.outcometracker.org/index Provider.php). Developers of these platforms typically comply with United States laws requiring privacy and confidentiality (e.g., HIPAA laws). Systems of this nature eliminate the need for data entry and many automate transmission to patients at the appropriate time, reducing disruption to therapists' workflow and allowing them to use session time for clinical work rather than data collection. They also minimize the likelihood of response errors through forced-choice entry and reminders when items are left blank. Use of these systems can yield practice-based data with minimum burden to the provider or practice. Data from some of these systems can be exported and merged with local data, such as whether patients were randomized into a particular condition, dates of service, or other information that providers collect for their research or evaluation. For example, if therapists within a given practice were interested in learning whether different ways of presenting treatment options were more effective in terms of engaging patients, they could standardize their procedures for presenting treatment options, operationalize outcomes (e.g., decision outcome, dropout rates, session frequency, and symptom change), and use a combination of local (e.g., appointment and scheduling data) and web-based data to examine those outcomes. If a therapist or practice group could not support a randomized trial, a time series design or an ABA design could be used, with the electronic data used for program evaluation that is collected at each time period easily being categorized according to the strategy that is being evaluated.

Utilization of electronic outcomes monitoring software can also facilitate pooling of data through research networks. Research networks can allow practitioners to work together to answer questions that are of mutual interest and can yield sufficient samples for research more quickly. Some of the pragmatic burdens associated with data collection, such as personnel to administer and enter measures are eliminated when this approach is used. Merging of local databases generated from the same online platform can minimize the time investment and potential errors and inconsistencies that may occur when multiple datasets are combined. Thus, some of the potential barriers to collaboration across practices can be addressed through the use of the monitoring software. Creation of electronic data repositories, as suggested by Persons (this volume), with a common set of measures allows therapists the opportunity to work with a large pool of archival data from more diverse settings to answer questions that can be addressed using previously collected data. Combined with other approaches, research networks that use electronic data capture can also facilitate randomized trials and other prospective study designs.

Infrastructure for practice-based research can also support processes of continuous quality improvement (CQI) and learning collaboratives dedicated to addressing practice-level challenges to a common goal (e.g., increasing treatment engagement or effectiveness, implementing new treatments). While CQI principles have been investigated and used in medical settings for decades, only recently have they been applied in mental health settings (Haine-Schlagel, 2013; Nadeem, Olin, Hill, Hoagwood, & Horwitz, 2014). Practice-based networks with shared electronic data would be well-positioned to participate in learning collaboratives or test the application of CQI approaches in addressing common challenges.

When a formal study is planned that would require informed consent, technology can be used to facilitate the process and reduce the amount of time that clinical or administrative staff spend on this important aspect of research. Electronic informed consent (eIC) procedures can reduce burdens associated with conducting research. The United States Department of Health and Human Services recently released guidelines for the use of eIC (United States Department of Health and Human Services, 2016). Electronic platforms can be used in place of, or to supplement the use of paper consent forms. A video describing the study goals and activities, planned steps to ensure confidentiality, alternatives to participation, potential benefits and risks, and other elements of informed consent could be used. This would standardize the information that is provided to potential participants, and they could also have the option of viewing it and considering participation in advance of their appointment. Viewing a video presentation might be easier than reading through a form and might better prepare potential participants to ask questions in person, potentially increasing efficiency and ensuring that more of the appointment can be used for clinical work. Full eIC is also an option that could further reduce the time that therapists or administrative staff spend conducting the informed consent process. However, it is important to be sure that potential participants have a way to have their questions answered and that the process results in true informed consent by making someone available by telephone or in person to respond to questions as needed in a timely manner.

The development of eIC procedures may also facilitate "rolling" informed consent and facilitate transparency in the use of clinical data. While some healthcare organizations include notification that de-identified medical records may be used for research purposes and that patients may be contacted about research opportunities in the initial paperwork that new patients sign, this approach can lead to confusion, as people often do not read paperwork carefully, or they may not remember providing permission with their signature. A process of rolling informed consent could allow patients to opt in or out of specific projects that involve their records. For example, a therapist, group practice, or network could initially inform their patients about how symptom data collected over the course of their care would be used, including for evaluation and research projects, and receive consent. As project ideas developed, a practice could contact past and current patients to request that they opt in (by providing consent), or opt out (by notifying the therapist or administrator by a certain date if they do not wish for their data to be used) for specific projects. Potential pooling and later use of electronic data in particular can raise concerns about privacy and this added step ensures that they are aware of how their information is being used. Although this approach is not required by IRBs in the United States, as de-identified data collected for clinical purposes or program evaluation can, under certain circumstances, subsequently be used for research or to promote generalizable knowledge if the primary intent of data collection was for clinical or evaluation purposes (U.S. Department of Health and Human Services, 2008), adding the extra step of notifying patients about the planned uses of the data increases transparency and can result in greater trust between provider and patient. Furthermore, it helps patients understand how allowing the use of their clinical information can contribute to broader knowledge. Following up with a newsletter or information about the findings is a way to continue to engage patients and show them what their willingness to participate has helped the practice or research network accomplish.

Practice-based research networks founded decades ago struggled with time constraints and resource demands that technology has now reduced (Koerner &

Castonguay, 2015), although some challenges remain. Ultimately, the endeavor of practice-based research is to contribute to providers' knowledge about what works and about how to optimize care and clinical outcomes. The opportunity to address real-world clinical challenges through research, particularly through partnerships and with more recently available tools, has never been greater.

References

Aarons, G. A., Miller, E. A., Green, A. E., Perrott, J. A., & Bradway, R. (2012). Adaptation happens: A qualitative case study of implementation of the incredible years evidence-based parent training program in a residential substance abuse treatment program. *Journal of Children's Services*, 7(4), 233–245.

Barlow, D. H., Farchione, T. J., Fairholme, C. P., Ellard, K. K., Boisseau, C. L., Allen, L. B., & Ehrenreich-May, J. (2011). *The Unified Protocol for Transdiagnostic Treatment of Emotional Disorders: Therapist Guide*. New York: Oxford University Press.

Bell, E. C., Marcus, D. K., & Goodlad, J. K. (2013). Are the parts as good as the whole? A meta-analysis of component treatment studies. *Journal of Consulting and Clinical Psychology*, 81(4), 722–736.

Chambers, D. A. & Norton, W. E. (2016). The adaptome: advancing the science of intervention adaptation. *American Journal of Preventive Medicine*, 51(4), S124–S131.

Chorpita, B. F., Daleiden, E. L., & Weisz, J. R. (2005). Identifying and Selecting the Common Elements of Evidence Based Interventions: A Distillation and Matching Model. *Mental Health Services Research*, 7(1), 5.

Cook, J. M., Dinnen, S., Thompson, R., Simiola, V., & Schnurr, P. P. (2014). Changes in implementation of two evidence-based psychotherapies for PTSD in VA residential treatment programs: A national investigation. *Journal of Traumatic Stress*, 27(2), 137–143.

Fairburn, C. G., Cooper, Z., Doll, H. A., O'Connor, M. E., Bohn, K., Hawker, D. M., ... Palmer, R. L. (2009). Transdiagnostic cognitive-behavioral therapy for patients with eating disorders: A two-site trial with 60-week follow-up. *American Journal of Psychiatry*, 166(3), 311–319.

Galovski, T. E., Blain, L. M., Mott, J. M., Elwood, L., & Houle, T. (2012). Manualized therapy for PTSD: Flexing the structure of cognitive processing therapy. *Journal of Consulting & Clinical Psychology*, 80(6), 968–981.

Haine-Schlagel, R. (2013). *Evaluating a Learning Collaborative Approach to Enhance Caregiver Engagement in Early Childhood Services*. Paper presented at the Society for Social Work and Research 17th Annual Conference: Social Work for a Just Society: Making Visible the Stakes and Stakeholders.

Hogue, A., Ozechowski, T. J., Robbins, M. S., & Waldron, H. B. (2013). Making Fidelity an Intramural Game: Localizing Quality Assurance Procedures to Promote Sustainability of Evidence-Based Practices in Usual Care. *Clinical Psychology: Science and Practice*, 20(1), 60–77.

Koerner, K. & Castonguay, L. G. (2015). Practice-oriented research: What it takes to do collaborative research in private practice. *Psychotherapy Research*, 25(1), 67–83.

Levitt, J. T., Malta, L. S., Martin, A., Davis, L., & Cloitre, M. (2007). The flexible application of a manualized treatment for PTSD symptoms and functional impairment related to the 9/11 World Trade Center attack. *Behaviour Research and Therapy*, 45(7), 1419.

Nadeem, E., Olin, S. S., Hill, L. C., Hoagwood, K. E., & Horwitz, S. M. (2014). A literature review of learning collaboratives in mental health care: used but untested. *Psychiatric Services*, 65(9), 1088–1099.

Stirman, S. W., Calloway, A., Toder, K., Miller, C. J., DeVito, A. K., Meisel, S. N., . . . Crits-Christoph, P. (2013a). Community mental health provider modifications to cognitive therapy: Implications for sustainability. *Psychiatric Services, 64*(10), 1056–1059.

Stirman, S. W., Miller, C. J., Toder, K., & Calloway, A. (2013b). Development of a framework and coding system for modifications and adaptations of evidence-based interventions. *Implementation Science, 8*(65).

U.S. Department of Health and Human Services, Office for Human Reseach Protection (2008). Engagement of Human Subjects in Research. Retrieved from: www.hhs.gov/ohrp/regulations-and-policy/guidance/guidance-on-engagement-of-institutions/index.html

U.S. Department of Health and Human Services, Office for Human Reseach Protection (2016). Use of Electronic Informed Consent in Clinical Investigations (Guidance). Retrieved from: www.hhs.gov/ohrp/news/announcements-and-news-releases/2016/use-electronic-informed-consent-clinical-trials/index.html

Ward, A. M., Regan, J., Chorpita, B. F., Starace, N., Rodriguez, A., Okamura, K., . . . Health, R. N. o. Y. M. (2013). Tracking evidence based practice with youth: Validity of the MATCH and Standard Manual Consultation Records. *Journal of Clinical Child & Adolescent Psychology, 42*(1), 44–55.

Wiltsey Stirman, S., Gutner, C., Gamarra, J., Vogt, D., Suvak, M., Wachen, J., . . . Resick, P. (2016). Leveraging Routine Clinical Materials to Assess Fidelity to CPT. In Proceedings of the 3rd Biennial Conference of the Society for Implementation Research Collaboration (SIRC) 2015: advancing efficient methodologies through community partnerships and team science. *Implementation Science, 11*(1), 1.

APPENDIX

Research Consultant Directory

Name: Courtney Beard, PhD
Affiliation: McLean Hospital/Harvard Medical School
Contact information: *617–855–3557*; *cbeard@mclean.harvard.edu*
Website: www.mcleanhospital.org/biography/courtney-beard
Areas of consultation: implementing quality assurance and program evaluation in clinical settings, implementing technology-based treatments in clinical settings
Type of consultation offered: individual, group

Name: Thröstur Björgvinsson, PhD, ABPP
Affiliation: McLean Hospital/Harvard Medical School
Contact information: 617 855 4180; tbjorgvinsson@mclean.harvard.edu
Website: www.mcleanhospital.org/biography/throstur-bjorgvinsson
Areas of consultation: Integrating state-of-the-art systematic data collection into existing evidence-based treatments to enhance clinical care, research and training; this includes implementing quality assurance and program evaluation in clinical settings, as well as ecological momentary assessment (EMA)
Type of consultation offered: Individual, groups

Name: Guy Bruce, EdD, BCBA-D
Affiliation: Appealing Solutions, LLC
Contact information: 309–303–1527; guybruce@appealingsolutions.com
Website: appealingsolutions.com
Areas of consultation: Organizational Performance Engineering: Pragmatic Supervision: System, Process, Individual Evaluation, Analysis, Recommendations and Change.
Type of consultation offered: Organizational

© 2018, *Practice-Based Research: A Guide for Clinicians*, R. Trent Codd, III, Routledge.

Name: Louis G. Castonguay, PhD
Affiliation: Penn State University
Contact information: lgc3@psu.edu
Website: http://psych.la.psu.edu/directory/lgc3
Areas of consultation: Practice-oriented research; Practice-research network; Process-outcome research;
Type of consultation offered: individual, group

Name: Daniel B. Fishman, PhD
Affiliation: Graduate School of Applied and Professional Psychology, Rutgers-New Brunswick
Contact information: 152 Frelinghuysen Road, Piscataway, NJ 08854
Website: http://pcsp.libraries.rutgers.edu/
Areas of consultation: Systematic case studies
Type of consultation offered: Individual or group

Name: Jason Luoma, PhD
Affiliation: Portland Psychotherapy Clinic, Research, and Training Center
Contact information: 503–281–4852 x213; jbluoma@portlandpsychotherapyclinic.com
Website: www.drluoma.com
Areas of consultation: Development of a successful independent mental health practice that integrates practice-based research into its core functions, high shame prone and self-critical clients using Acceptance and Commitment Therapy.
Type of consultation offered: Individual

Name: Travis L. Osborne, PhD, ABPP
Affiliation: Evidence Based Treatment Centers of Seattle (EBTCS) and Behavioral Health Research Collective (BHRC) IRB
Contact information: 206–374–0109; tosborne@ebtseattle.com
Website: www.ebtseattle.com
Areas of consultation: Provide consultation on practice-based research, including consultation about research program set-up and infrastructure, study design, and troubleshooting barriers to successful implementation. Provide consultation about set-up and management of IRBs to support practice-based research.
Type of consultation offered: Individual

© 2018, *Practice-Based Research: A Guide for Clinicians*, R. Trent Codd, III, Routledge.

Name: Jacqueline B. Persons, PhD
Affiliation: Oakland Cognitive Behavior Therapy Center
Contact information: persons@oaklandcbt.com
Consultation areas: Consultation to psychologists who work in a private practice setting who would like help conducting research in that setting. Also provides half-day or day-long workshop on this topic. Issues related to institutional review board requirements, informed consent, study design for projects that can be conducted in private practice, clinical and ethical issues involved in doing research in a clinical setting, library access, recruiting collaborators, submitting work for publication, finding time for research in the context of clinical practice, and related issues.
Type of consultation offered: Individual or group; Video conferencing options available

Name: Scott Waltman, PsyD, ABPP
Affiliation: Warrior Resiliency Program, Brooke Army Medical Center
Contact information: walt2155@pacificu.edu
Website: www.researchgate.net/profile/Scott_Waltman
Areas of consultation: Practice-Based Research design, single-case studies, qualitative analyses, and cognitive-behavior therapy or evidence-based psychotherapy training and implementation.
Other: For lines of practice-based research that I'm especially interested in, I will also partner as a co-investigator who can be involved in research design, data analyses, and manuscript preparation.
Type of consultation offered: individual or project-specific

Name: Amy Wenzel, PhD, ABPP
Affiliation: Wenzel Consulting, LLC; University of Pennsylvania School of Medicine
Contact information: 267.746.0566; awenzel@dramywenzel.com
Website: http://dramywenzel.com
Areas of consultation: scholarship on cognitive behavioral therapy, perinatal distress, suicide prevention; proposing and authoring/editing books
Type of consultation offered: Individual or group

Name: Soo Jeong Youn, PhD
Affiliation: Massachusetts General Hospital
Contact information: sooj.youn@gmail.com
Areas of consultation: Practice-oriented research; Practice-research networks; Process-outcome research; Implementation and dissemination of evidence based treatment; Psychotherapy Training; Measurement based care/outcome monitoring
Type of consultation offered: individual, group

© 2018, *Practice-Based Research: A Guide for Clinicians*, R. Trent Codd, III, Routledge.

Index

Page numbers in *italic* refer to figures, those in **bold** to tables. A lower-case 'n' after a page number signifies a note; pages followed by 'App.' refer to appendices.

A-B designs 51–52
A/A+B design 55
ABA designs 47–48, 246
academic settings, as research locus 3–4
acceptability 197, **198**, 200
Acceptance and Commitment Therapy (ACT) 52, 142–143, 147, 215
accountability 184
Accountable Care Organizations (ACOs) 204, 208
actuarial methods 44–45
acuity 224; of patient symptoms 228–229
adaptation 245
adherence checklists 244
administrative support staff 136
admission measures 217–218
admission report, sample de-identified 235 App.
adoption **198**, 200–201
Affordable Care Act (ACA; 2010) 193
Agency for Healthcare Research and Quality (AHRQ) 207–208
alternating treatments designs (ATDs) 52–53
ambiguous temporal precedence 48
American Psychological Association (APA): books 180; clinical journals of 178; Division 12 165; ethical principle of 163
analysis: of archival data 70–72; of results 40–41; of variance (ANOVA) 38
ancillary studies 219
anxiety: disorders 142–143, 146, 156, 171–172; and routine changes 15
Anxiety and Depression Association of America (ADAA) 165
Apgar and Associates 101 App.

arbitrary matching 68
articles, reviews of 177–179
assessments: at intake 155–157; follow-up 35; mid-point 35
Association of Behavioral and Cognitive Therapies (ABCT) 133, 164–165, 179; Clinical Research Methods and Statistics Special Interest Group 162
association study 33, 35
attrition 49
autism spectrum disorder 55

barriers, to research 3, 6, 26–30, 130, 132–141
baseline 68; rates 70; stable 50–51
Beck, Aaron "Tim" 159, 173, 175
Beck Depression Inventory (BDI) 160
Beckner, Victoria Lemle 158
behavior change 62–63; of individuals 67; sensitive measures of 67–69
Behavior and Symptom Identification Scale (BASIS-24) 217
Behavioral Health Partial Hospital Program (BHP) 213–214; ancillary studies 219; clinical research in 222–226; data collection 204–205, 216–219; managing research team and projects in 215–216; program evaluation and development in 221–222; progress monitoring 217–218, 220–221; treatment philosophy 215; treatment planning 220–221; uses of data 220–226
Behavioral Health Research Collective (BHRC) 82–83; IRB founding organizations 99n1; IRB liability insurance 99n2; IRB Member (and

Consultant) Conflict of Interest Agreement 106–107 App.; IRB Member Appointment Agreement 102–104 App.; IRB Member Confidentiality Agreement 105 App.
Belmont Report 99n6, 163
benchmarking 144–145
between-group differences 33, 36
bias 26–28, 30
blogging 181–182, 186–187
books: authoring and editing of 179–181; reviews of 177–179
bottom line 113, 119–122
Boulder model 170–171, 188
Boyle, Robert 3
Brain and Behavior Research Association 173
burnout: in IRB members 96; syndrome 27
Burns, David 159
business models 113

case series 142–143
case studies: compared to SCEDs 46–47; practice-based research 141–142
causation studies 33
celeration 67; efficiency 68, 70–73, 76
Center for Collegiate Mental Health (CCMH) 11
Centers for Disease Control (CDC) 87
change, assessment of 11–13
chi-square (X^2) 39
child maltreatment 10–11
Childhood Trauma Questionnaire (CTQ) 221, 229
Clark, Roseanne 172
clients: characteristics of 13; lack of response in 12; outcomes 197
clinical care, routine 46
clinical chart information 219
clinical practice: fee-for-service 108–109; implementing research findings in 8; PRNs in 11; as research locus 3–4
clinical research, in BHP 222–226
clinical science, products and methods of 154–155
clinical settings, lack of research culture in 133–134
clinical tasks, and research 17
clinical work, case formulation-driven approach to 154–158
clinical-research social business model 113–119; autonomy 126; isolation 126;

money 125; personal values 127; preparedness 127; profit margin 127; research 127; social impact required 126; steps to implementing research funding 125–127; strategic planning 126
clinician-scientists 208
clinicians 159, 243; gaps in research-related skills 137–138; innovative research by 147–148; lack of researcher identity among 132–133; payment of 111–112; progress monitoring by 147–148; supervision of 175–177
Codd, Trent 187
cognitive bias 172–173
Cognitive Therapy Rating Scale 175
cognitive-behavior therapy (CBT) 54–55, 141, 175–176, 215; for depression (CBT-D) 175
collaboration 183; with investigators at research institutions 173–174; in primary health care 193; problems with 15–16
Collaborative Institutional Training Initiative (CITI) 164; Research Ethics Trainings 101 App.
collaborators 161
collegial support 164–165
communication 18; problems with 15–16
comorbidity 224; in PHPs 213
comparison sets, and sample 70
compliance 158
concept, proof of 40
conditional discrimination 68–69
conferences 207
confidentiality 18; breaches in 15
confounding variables 34
consequences, type and timing of 71
continuing education (CE) programs 131
continuous quality improvement (CQI) 246
control groups, and PHPs 227
Coping Cat 201
correlations 38
cost **199**, 202
cost effectiveness, of SCEDs 46
counterbalancing 70
curiosity 154–155

data: analysis of 35, 56, 70–72; anxieties about 15; archival 70–72; cleaning of 40–41; de-identified 162, 164, 206, 247; group design 44–45; missing 228; plan

creation 38–39; uses in BHP 220–226; visual analysis of 50
data collection 204–205, 216–219; electronic 245–246; extensive 155
data entry methods 41
day treatment 212
de Oliveira, Irismar Reis 174
Deepdyve 160–161
demonstration studies 197
dependent variable (DV) 34–35; behavior change as 62; in SCED implementation 55–56
depression 144–145; perinatal 172, 176
Depression Anxiety Stress Scales (DASS) 156–157
descriptive studies 33–34
design: A-B 51–52; A/A+B 55; ABA 47–48; alternating treatments (ATDs) 52–53; determination in SCEDs 56; of low-impact methodology 206–207; multiple-baseline 53–55
Diagnostic Screening Tool 156
Diagnostic and Statistical Manual (DSM) 219; DSM-5 diagnostic criteria 14
dialectical behavior therapy (DBT) 131, 141, 146, 215, 222
Dialectical Behavior Therapy Ways of Coping Checklist 223
Difficulties in Emotion Regulation Scale (DERS) 146, 156
discharge measures 217–218
discharge report, sample de-identified 236 App.
disorders, and PRNs 11
disruptive behavioral problems (DBP) 10
dissemination 207–208; research 195
Dissemination and Implementation Science (D&I Science) 196–197
distress, expression of 13
double entry 41
double-blind studies 28
drinking 148
drop-out 27

ecological momentary assessments (EMA) 223
effect sizes 37
effectiveness 8, 143–145, 194–195
efficacy 194–195
Eidelman, Polina 157–158
Einstein, Albert 3
electronic health records (EHR) 202–206

electronic informed consent (eIC) 246–247
empirical imperialism 8
empirically supported treatments (ESTs) 4; protocol 154
environmental benefit, from social enterprise 121
ethical issues 93–94, 100–101 App., 162–164
evaluation 40; of low-impact methodology 206–207
evidence, reliance on multiple types 155
Evidence Based Treatment Centers of Seattle (EBTCS) 130, 148–149; and access to IRB review 138–139; administrative support staff 136–137; contingencies undermining research 134–135; Director of Research 135; gaps in research-related skills in 137–138; non-clinical sample studies 148; postdoctoral training 131, 137; practice-based research at 131; psychometric studies 145–147; research costs 140–141; research program development strategies 133; research staffing 135–137; research-supporting culture 134; student volunteers in 136; therapist-related variable studies 147–148
evidence-based treatments (EBTs) 195, 197, 201
Excel software 40, 162
expectancy 28
experience, sharing of 18
experimental conditions, sequence of 72
experimental control 63, 69–72
experts, consultation with 31–33
external validity: low 26; threats to 29–30
extraneous variables 34

fading procedure 71
feasibility, of protocols 15
Federal Drug Administration (FDA) 87
Federalwide Assurance (FWA) 87–88
fee-for-service setting 108–109; embedding research in 110; financial barriers to research in 111–112; reason for researching in 109–111
feedback 18; alerts 12; from IRBs 94–95; seeking consultation 39–40
fidelity **198**, 201–202, 244
filing, web-based 95
finance 5

Index

findings, dissemination of 41
follow-up assessments 35
forms, drafting for IRBs 88–89
full disclosure 31–32
Functional Analytic Psychotherapy (FAP) 53, 55
fundability, low 26
funding: grants 166; research 109–110

G*Power 3 37
generalizability: low 26; in PHPs 227; of SCEDs 47
Generalized Anxiety Disorder 7-item (GAD-7) scale 157, 217, 220, 223
generalized anxiety disorder (GAD) 223
goal setting 31
Google Forms 157
Google Scholar 32, 160
Grameen Bank 113
grant funding 166
group mean differences 38
group therapy 226–227
guilt 148

Hamilton Rating Scales for Depression (HAM-D) 176
Harvey, John 172, 180
health care system, impact of PRNs and POR on 17
Health Insurance Portability and Accountability Act (HIPAA; 1996) 193, 204; authorization forms 91; compliance 157, 239; Privacy Rule 206, 245; regulations 98, 164; survey administration 217
helpers 161
history 27–28, 48
Holt, Craig 172
homework 158
Hong, Janie 157–158
hrp Consulting Group 101 App.
hypochondriasis 160
hypothetical deductive method 63

identity matching 70
immunization 195
impact 194
implementation: RE-AIM model of 203; research 195; strategy 204
implementation outcomes 197–203; applied to primary care **198–199**
Implementation Science (IS) 193
imposter syndrome 15

incentive procedure 71
independent variables 34, 62
individual behavioral studies 44
inductive approach 63; to PBR 66–67
informed consent 162, 205, 229, 246–247
institutional review boards (IRBs) 81–82, 98, 133, 163–164; burnout in 96; business structure of 85–87; compliance resources 100–101 App.; conducting reviews 92–96; consultation 97–98; continuing staff education in 92; costs 86; credentialing 97; documentation 92, 96–97; drafting SOPs and forms 88–89, 96–97; ethical concerns 82–83, 93–94, 100–101 App.; exemption from 37; experiences useful in 84; feedback 94–95; financial structure 85–86; Forum 100 App.; founding organizations (BHRC) 99n1; goals 82–84; host organizations 85; lack of access to 5, 81, 138–139; liability insurance (BHRC) 86–87, 99n2; meeting schedules 92–93; Member (and Consultant) Conflict of Interest Agreement (BHRC) 106–107 App.; Member Appointment Agreement (BHRC) 102–104 App.; Member Confidentiality Agreement (BHRC) 105 App.; members 90–91; mission 82–84; and primary care research 205–206; recruitment 97; registration with OHRP 87–88, 90–91; resources 97; review types 95–96, 163; reviewer system 93; role of chair 90; and SCEDs 47; selecting colleagues for 84–85; in social enterprise 118; staffing of 89–92; step-by-step guide to formation of 82–98; sustainable 96–97; training 91–92, 97–98; values 82–84; volunteers in 86; voting on protocols by 94
instructions: differences in effectiveness of 74; timing of 66
instrument selection 37
instrumentation 49
insurance companies, and fees 116
intake: assessment at 155–157; reducing appointment no-shows at 25–26
Intake Questionnaire 156
interaction time, of subjects 75
interactive effects 49
internal validity: low 26; in PHPs 227; in SCEDs 47–49; specific SCED threats 48–49; threats to 26–29, 47–49

interpersonal psychotherapy (IPT) 172
interval scales 29
interventions 196; cost of 202; efficacy and effectiveness of 194–195; novel 225–226; real-world settings for 195; technology-based 226
inventories, administration of 176
IRB Forum 100 App.

Jensen, Alexandra 158
Joule, James 3
journals 207; open-access 185; review articles in 178

Kleiman, Karen 180–181, 187

liability insurance 86–87; BHRC IRB 99n2
libraries, access to 160–161, 185
life, demands of 182
Likert scales 29
Lindsley, Ogden 67
Linehan, Marsha 159
literature: consultation of 31–33; in result comparisons 41
logic, implementation of 56

McLean Hospital, Behavioral Health Partial Hospital Program (BHP) 213–214; ancillary studies 219; clinical research in 222–226; data collection 204–205, 216–219; managing research team and projects in 215–216; program evaluation and development in 221–222; progress monitoring in 217–218, 220–221; treatment philosophy 215; treatment planning 220–221; uses of data 220–226
McLean Screening Instrument for Borderline Personality Disorder (MSI-BPD) 217–218
major depressive disorder (MDD) 223
Malott, Krista 183
management: of research teams and projects 215–216; skills 128
mania 229
market economy 112
marketing 125; skills 128
maturation 28, 49
Meaningful Use 204
measurement, continuous 56
measures: of behavior change 67–69; reliability of 29

Medical Outcomes Study Social Support Survey 156
mental health: measures of change 12; provision of 193–194
Mental Health Continuum–Short Form (MHC-SF) 217
mental health practitioners 193–194; question selection by 194–197; research rate of 5
mental illness, stigma of 225
Mental Measurements Yearbook 29
meta-analysis, conducting of 177
method development 195
Mikami, Amori 159
mindfulness 30
Mini International Neuropsychiatric Interview (MINI) 219, 221
Minnesota Multiphasic Personality Inventory-2 (MMPI-II) 176
money: contingencies in fee-for-service setting 111–112; problems of 165–166
motivation 31, 166
multi-element designs *see* alternating treatments designs (ATDs)
multiple-baseline design 53–55

National Institutes of Health (NIH) 87, 115, 196; Office of Extramural Research, Protecting Human Research Participants Training 100 App.; success rates of R01 grants *115*
National Institutes of Mental Health (NIMH) 108, 172, 224; clinical trials 175
naturalistic treatment 226–228
needs assessments 33, 35
negative findings 15
negative impact 18
NEO (Neuroticism, Extraversion, Openness) Personality Inventory Revised (NEO-PI-R) 176
network analysis 223–224
networking 183–184
neuropsychology 176
Newman, Cory 173
Newman, Tim 173
no-shows, reduction of 25–26
nominal scales 29
non-clinical samples, studies on 148
novel intervention approaches 225–226

observer bias 28
Obsessive Beliefs Questionnaire-44 (OBQ-44) 156

258 Index

obstacles, overcoming of 184–185
Office for Human Research Protections (OHRP) 82, 100 App., 164; registering IRBs with 87–88
O'Hara, Michael 172, 174
opportunities 187; acceptance of 186; identification of 183–184
OQ analyst platform 245
ordinal scales 29
organizational support 4
outcome: data 18; monitoring *see* standardized outcome monitoring; tracking 26; variable 35–36
Outcome Tracker 245
outpatient treatment 212
Overall Anxiety Severity and Impairment Scale (OASIS) 146
Owen, Daniela 158

paranoia 229
partial hospital programs (PHPs) 212; barriers to research in 226–231; naturalistic treatment in 226–228; program culture 229–231; research checklist 237–239 App.; research in 213, 231; staff attitudes 229–231
participants, number examined 50
partnerships 243–244
Patient Health Questionnaire-9 (PHQ-9) 29, 156–157, 203, 217, 220, 223
patient-focused approach *see* standardized outcome monitoring
patients: acuity of symptoms 228–229; BHP presentations of 214–215; high-risk 230; informed consent by 162; lack of response in 12; LGBTQ 222; stepped up and down 214
Pavlov, Ivan 63, 69, 75
paywalls 32–33
penetration **199**, 203
Pennsylvania State University Psychological Clinic, as a PRN 11
perinatal depression (distress) 172, 176, 180
Perloff, Jeffrey M. 159
Perseverative Thinking Questionnaire (PTQ) 156–157
Persons, Jaqueline 133, 144–145
pilot studies 40
planning research, in PHPs 238–239 App.
Portland Psychotherapy 115–116, 118–120, 122

post-traumatic stress disorder (PTSD) 54, 146
practice, simultaneous with research *see* simultaneous-practice-and-research model
Practice Institute 184
Practice Integration Profile (PIP) 202
practice research networks (PRNs) 19; benefits of 16–17; challenges in establishing 14–16; common-setting-based 11; definition of 9–10; disorder-specific 10–11; establishment of 17–19; professional organization 10
practice settings 6; mental health 4
practice-based research 130, 148–149; administrative support staff 136; advantages of 4–5, 243; at EBCTS 131; barriers to 3, 6, 26–30, 132–141; and Boulder model 170; case series 142–143; case studies 65–66, 141–142; contingencies undermining 134–135; costs 140–141; effectiveness studies 8, 143–145; examples of 25–26; future directions 243–248; lack of access to IRB review 138–139; lack of researcher identity among clinicians 132–133; models for conducting research 141–148; non-clinical sample studies 148; pragmatic approach to 61, 66–77; psychometric studies 145–147; and research questions 33; research staffing 135–137; teamwork in 133–134; therapist-related variable studies 147–148
practice-based research network (PBRN), primary care 208
practice-based scholarship 170–171, 185–188; initiation and execution of 182–185; types of 173–182
practice-oriented research (POR) 8–9; benefits of 16–17; challenges conducting 14–16; client and therapists characteristics in 13; conducting of 17–19
pragmatism 61, 64–67, 77
prediction studies 33, 36
primary care, implementation outcomes in **198–199**
Primary Care Behavioral Health Model (PCBHM) 200, 202, 204
primary health care 193; research opportunities in 193–194; Triple Aim 194, 196

Index   259

Primary Health Care Research and Information Service (PHCRIS) 207
procedural integrity 75
process studies 13–14
processes, definition of 61
professional development, and PRNs 16–17
program culture 230–231
program development and evaluation, in BHP 221–222
progress monitoring 147–148, 157–158, 217–218; in BHP 220–221
PROMIS 245
Protected Health Information (PHI) 206
PsycCRITIQUES 179
PsychINFO 185
psychologists: career choices of 108; payment of 111–112
Psychology Today blogs 181
psychometrics 145–147, 222–223
psychopathology 214; understanding of 222–224
psychosis 225, 228–229
psychosocial research, funding of 108
psychotherapy: effectiveness of 14; process of change in 159
Public Responsibility in Medicine and Research (PRIM&R) 100 App.
publication, modal rate of 4
publishability 32, 41; low 26
publishers and publishing 180–181
PubMed 185

qualitative research 39
quality improvement projects 205–206
questions *see* research questions

R software 162
randomization 27, 207
randomized controlled trials (RCTs) 5, 8, 14, 143–145, 147; feasibility of 38; and PHPs 227
Rappaport, Lance 157
rater bias 28
ratio scales 29
RE-AIM model of implementation 203
reach 194, 196, 203
recruitment 46; in IRBs 97; targets 37
REDCap software 41, 217, 220
referral ratios 200–201
refinement 40
regression 39, 49; studies 36; to the mean 28

reinforcement 62, 65
reliability, of measures 29
replication 62; emphasis of 50; within- and across-subject 75–76
research: abilities 128; barriers to 3, 6, 26–30, 130, 132–141, 226–231; basic 195; and clinical tasks 17; culture lack in clinical settings 133–134; design 226–227; different way to do 61–65; directory of consultants 250–252 App.; embedded in settings 110; ethics 36; exempt from IRB review 95–96; five phases of *195*; funding 109–110; locus of 3–4; management of projects 215–216; in partial hospitals 213; patient informed consent in 162; in PHPs 213, 226–231, 237–239 App.; planning 238–239 App.; practice-based *see* practice-based research; prime opportunity for 193–194; private practice models 141–148; qualitative 39; repertoires 5; setting up infrastructure 214–216; simultaneous with practice *see* simultaneous-practice-and-research model; skills 137–138, 158–160; and social enterprise 121; strategy 204; types of 11–14
research assistants (RAs), students as 161
Research Domain Criteria (RDoC) 224
research institutions, collaborations with 173–174
research methods: poor training 5; practice-based 25, 30–31, 41–42; triggering 229
research questions 31; choice of 159; definition of 33
research studies, supervision within 175–177
research teams: management of 215–216; in PHPs 237–238 App.
research-related skills, clinician gaps in 137–138
ResearchGate 32–33, 40–41, 160
resources 18–19, 244; for IRBs 97
response rate, individual vs. group 64
results: analysis of 40–41; interpretation of 41
reviews: access to mechanisms 162–164; of book proposals 187; writing of 177–179
rolling informed consent 247
romantic relationships 172
RSS feeds 32
Rubin, David 172

rumination 196

sample, and comparison sets 73–74
sampling bias 30
Sanchez, Amy 158
SAS software 162
scaling-up 197
scholarship 171; pursuit of 186, *see also* practice-based scholarship
scientific thinking 154–155
scientist-practitioner model 170
selection 26–27, 48
self-funding 166
self-practice 25
self-report 229
self-selection bias 30
sensitivity 65
Session Assignment and Feedback Form (SAFF) 158
shame 54, 148
shareholder benefit, from social enterprise 122
significance, standard chart use 76
simple outcomes study 33, 35
simultaneous-practice-and-research model 153–167; access to a review mechanism 162–164; case formulation-driven approach 154–158; collaborators and helpers 161; collegial support 164–165; ethical issues 162–164; library access 160–161; research skills and training 158–160; solutions to time and money problems 165–166; statistical assistance and software 162; synergy of elements of 167; treatment agreement 162
single-case experimental designs (SCEDs) 45, 57; compared to case studies 46–47; competence in 56; design myths 46–49; generalizability of 47; and internal validity threat control 47–49; key features 49–51; procedural implementation steps 55–56; reasons for use 45–46; specific internal validity threats 48–49; types of 51–55
skills, therapeutic 225
Skinner, Burrhus Frederic 61–65, 67–69, 75
small business skills 128
social benefit, from social enterprise 120–121
social enterprise 128; autonomy maximization 124; behavior guidance 123–124; business skill development in 118; community and connectedness 121; community membership of 117; environmental benefit 121; example of 113–119; generating profit margin in 116–117; generosity across multiple levels 124–125; guiding considerations in *114*; hiring for synergy 122–123; infrastructure development in 118; internal cooperation 122–123; introduction to 112–113; IRBs in 118; key success strategies 122–125; marketing program development 125; model 112; motivation 123–124; outcomes 119; perceived value of treatment in 117; resources/skills needed 127–128; and scientific research 121; shareholder benefit 122; sliding scale services in 117–118; social benefit 120–121; spectrum of possible business *113*; support for staff 123–124; training program 123; value guided 117–118, 120, 123–124
Society of Clinical Psychology 165
Society for Psychotherapy Research (SPR) 165
Society for a Science of Clinical Psychology (SSCP) 165
software: EHR 203; free 152; meta-analysis 177; outcomes monitoring 246; SSPS 40–41, 140, 162; statistical 41, 137–138, 140, 154, 162, 166; tracking 158
spirituality 226
Sprecher, Susan 180
staff attitudes 230–231
standard charts, use in significance 76
standard operating procedures (SOPs) 84–85; drafting for IRBs 88–89
standard progress note 157
standardized outcome monitoring 157; and change assessment 11–13; software 246
statistical analysis software 41, 137–138, 140, 154, 162, 166
statistical assistance 162
statistical regression 49
statistical skills 138
statistical tutorials 38
stepped wedge designs 207
stickK 184
storage system, web-based 90
strategic planning 128
strategy 204; low-impact design 204–207

students: as research assistants 161; volunteering by 136
studies: conduction to scale 40; design of 34–39; process 13–14; types of 11–14
subject interaction time 75
suicide 214, 225
supervision: of clinicians 175–177; skills 128
sustainability 197, **199**, 203
symptom exacerbation 229
symptomatology, tracking changes in 12

t-tests 38
TAU vs. TAU + innovation studies 36–37
technology, and routinization 19
technology-based interventions 226
temporal precedence, ambiguous 48
testing 49
thematic analysis 39
therapeutic alliance 225
therapeutic skills 225
therapist-related variables 147–148
therapists: characteristics of 13; progress monitoring by 147–148
Thomas, Cannon 160
Thought Records 159
time 18–19, 37; problems of 165–166
training 158–160; postdoctoral 131, 137; programs 123; protocols 16

transdiagnostic processes 224, 244
transparency 18, 247
treatment: agreement 162; in BHP 214, 220–221; duration in PHPs 228; naturalistic 226–228; in PHPs 227–228; planning 220–221; process 157; as usual (TAU) 36–37
treatment outcomes 157, 224–226; predictors of 224–225
treatment protocols, modification and adaptation of 245
triple bottom-line 113, 116, 119–122

University of California, San Francisco (UCSF) 207

values clarification 182–183
variables: continuous measurement of 50; types of 34
Veteran's Affairs (VA) 175

Wenzel, Amy, career story of 171–173
Willow 245
Work and Social Adjustment Scale 156
writing, reviews 177–179

Yale-Brown Obsessive-Compulsive Scale 157
yoga 226